BARBECUE NATION

Fred Thompson

350 Hot-Off-the-Grill, Tried-and-True Recipes from **America's Backyard**

The Taunton Press

The Taunton Press, Inc.,
63 South Main Street, PO Box 5506
Newtown, CT 06470-5506
e-mail: tp@taunton.com

Jacket/Cover design: Chika Azuma
Front cover photographers: Scott Phillips (grill),
    Fred Thompson (people)
Front cover photo composite (grill): Richard Booth, Bill Godfrey
Back cover photographers: Brian Hagiwara, B. Ellis (author photo)
Interior design: Laura Palese/Silverfish Design
Layout: David Giammattei
Photographers: Brian Hagiwara (food); Fred Thompson (people);
    photograph on p. 255 by Bruce Newman
Food Stylist: Fred Thompson
Prop Stylists: Bret Baughman, Francine Matalon-Degni
Illustrator: Archie Mortera

Library of Congress Cataloging-in-Publication Data
Thompson, Fred, 1953-
    Barbecue nation : 350 hot-off-the-grill, tried-and-true
recipes from America's backyard / Fred Thompson.
        p. cm.
    Includes bibliographical references and index.
    ISBN-13: 978-1-56158-814-5 (alk. paper)
    ISBN-10: 1-56158-814-8 (alk. paper)
    1. Barbecue cookery. 2. Side dishes (Cookery) I. Title.

TX840.B3T53 2007
641.5'784--dc22

                                                                2006032140

Printed in the United States of America
10 9 8 7 6 5 4 3 2 1

To Mom, what a year

acknowledgments

My food-writer friend Pableux Johnson told me once that writing a book is like being a farmer, and in many ways he's right. You have to scratch some ground, plant a seed, nurture and watch it grow, weed it out occasionally, and, when it comes together, hope that it tastes as good as it looks and that the elements don't get you before you get to market. Like a farmer, it takes the help of other professionals, neighbors, and friends to cultivate a book.

My editor and friend, Pam Hoenig, scratched that dirt with me to make a place for the seed to flourish. Pam's patience and understanding was outstanding, and she weeded gently and with care. *Barbecue Nation* is better for her efforts. Many others at The Taunton Press played large roles in this creation, including assistant editor Katie Benoit; editorial production manager, Kathleen Williams; design manager, Carol Singer; art director, Chris Thompson; marketing director, Melissa Possick; and sales director, Kevin Hamric. Of course, my agent, Lisa Ekus, crossed the Ts and dotted the Is.

Brian Hagiwara did an exceptional job with the food photos. His creativity makes the book bloom, and he did yeoman's work.

Of course, the real thanks go to the folks found in the pages of this book. I've been fortunate, and I now have a whole new coterie of friends from all over the country. Folks opened their homes to me and gave up more than a few family secret recipes for you to enjoy. You'll meet these people in the pages that follow, and they have earned my thanks and respect.

A group of people I love and feel honored to be a part of, the Southern Foodways Alliance, had many members point the way to people I should meet. There's one thing about real food people—they are as open as any bunch I've ever been around and are always willing to help. My friends and colleagues with the International Association of Culinary Professionals also filled in many voids. Special thanks to Belinda Ellis, who helped plow some fields in the right direction, as well as Susan Nash and Martha Johnston for some exceptional leads.

Once again, my neighbors endured a cookbook project. I know I fouled up many a dinner plan when I showed up with ribs and insisted they be tasted. Thanks to Barry and Linda Johnson, Henry and Nancy Wood, and Robin and Rachel Thomas. Many of my cooking-school classes became recipe guinea pigs as I used their reactions to gauge the taste and difficulty of a recipe I had collected. Many of those students were also great sources for people I needed to know. Nikki Parrish was always quick to solve a word-processing problem for me. As always, thanks to Toni Allegra for knowing that I could be a food writer.

contents

welcome to the
Barbecue Nation

Since our humble backyard grilling beginnings in the 1950s with the advent of the brazier grill, we as a nation have explored every conceivable way that we can cook with fire.

We lug our grills to stadium parking lots to soothe our hunger pains before the best team—our team—takes the field. In the South, a politician would have a tough time getting elected without hosting a barbecue feed or two. The sense of neighborhood is heightened with a grilling get-together. The thrill of cooking the day's catch beside a mountain stream or just grilling some hot dogs at a campsite gives us great pleasure.

Forty years ago, most of us would pack away our little 16-inch aluminum-foil-lined round grills on the Tuesday after Labor Day. Not anymore. And grilling is no longer a once-a-week phenomenon but rather a godsend, cooking up fast, delicious meals all week long.

Like so many things that make our country great, the influx of cultures from around the globe has had a profound influence on how and what we cook in our backyards. The beginnings of true barbecue appear to have come over from Africa with the slaves, then was adopted and taken in a variety of directions by America's other ethnic populations. As we expanded west, Mexican flavors and methods were adopted. Native Americans were already versed in smoking fish, long before the first bagel arrived on these shores. The Germans brought their own special methods as they settled into the Midwest and eventually Texas, heavily influencing the foodways of the region. The Cuban migration has changed the way South Florida cooks, and the Jamaicans have gifted us with their fiery jerked pork and chicken. The contributions of America's immigrants to our grill cooking have been deliciously innovative and continue to occur as new populations reach our shores.

I travel a lot to teach cooking classes and to do research for my cookbooks. Everywhere I go, someone is always telling me about a friend or relative who is a great cook. E-mails in response to my newspaper columns have added to the culinary wealth, and then I got to thinking about the friends I've had for years whose invitation to a meal is something special. So when I decided I wanted to do a grilling book because of my great love for cooking outdoors, I thought, why not bring all these recipes together, why not a national community cookbook of sorts for grilling and barbecue?

The search for these recipes has been a joy *and* a frustration. In the beginnings of my travels, I seemed to be the harbinger of bad weather. Schedule a meal and interview with me and inevitably a hurricane would get there first. Katrina sadly chased me from the Gulf Coast and kept me from untold stories and recipes. Many of the people I had wanted to meet and eat with are still displaced; some I have yet to find and worry for their well-being. Rita slowed me down in Texas, and I was driven from Florida on four different occasions by hurricanes and tropical storms. A weekend of grilling was washed out in New York City with eight inches of rain over two days.

But as much as the bad weather dogged me, the 20 pounds I've gained during the writing of this book attest to the fact that good food was abundant and waiting to be found. I've had dinner with the mayor and fire chief of Byhalia, Mississippi, a sign maker in Houston, an oyster shucker in New Orleans, a country ham man in East Tennessee, a fish broker in Northern California, and many more generous people who have opened their homes and pantries and fired up a grill to share their best with me and now you. But what has elevated this adventure beyond my imagination is the number of people all over this country that I can now call friends. There is something about an outdoor fire that binds us and gives us pleasure. I was actually kind of sad when it came time to compile the recipes because I wanted to keep searching and expanding this new circle of friends.

For the most part, the folks I have met on this journey are not professional barbecue or grill people. Most have regular jobs that don't involve food. There are some food writers and a few chefs hanging around in these pages, but they cook out for the same reason you do—to have fun and enjoy the unique flavor that an outdoor flame imparts to food. I have also included recipes of my own that family and friends have embraced and adopted as their own.

Put these recipes work. They are tried and true, backyard tested, and damn good. And you don't need a thousand-dollar grill to reproduce them. You do need one with a lid, though. All have been tested over gas and charcoal, and they have performed equally well. Each recipe carries an icon, either 🔥, which means you'll be grilling over a direct fire, or 🔥, which indicates you'll be cooking over an indirect fire, either smoking or grill roasting.

I hope that this book becomes one of the most stained and splattered books at your house, I also anticipate that you will use these recipes as springboards to your own fabulous creations, your own house specialties. When it comes time to write the next chapter in *Barbecue Nation*, I hope that your backyard is the next place I'll be headed for great grilling.

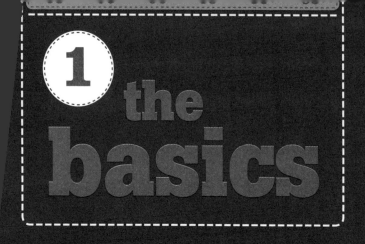

1 the basics

The number-one rule in outdoor cooking is that there are no absolutes. When cooking over a fire out of doors, everything is variable. But then, that's part of the fun. What you want to do over time is to get in touch with your own inner Grill Meister or Mistress. There is a little bit of art to this magic called grilling, but it ain't rocket science, so don't let anything get in the way of having fun at the fire.

It Starts with the Grill

There are more grill choices on the market today than ever before. Any good-quality covered charcoal grill (22 inches in diameter is best) or a three-burner gas grill will get you through the vast majority of the recipes in this book. That is not to say that your rectangle- or square-shaped grill or offset smoker or two-burner gas grill or egg-shaped grill won't work. You may have to adjust the recipes to those particular grills.

Most of us have made the switch to gas (about 70 percent at last count), but many gas grill owners also have a charcoal grill for special recipes. I used to be a diehard when it came to charcoal, yet in the last five years, I've found myself using my gas grill more often just because it's so incredibly convenient. I've discovered that today's well-built gas grills can take charcoal head on, even when doing low and slow smoking.

> You may read in other places about building duel-height charcoal fires for semi-indirect cooking. It's more work than results.

When buying a grill, one of the key factors to check out is the number of factory-assembled parts, meaning less for you to put together. The more a grill has, the better the product. It's the same for gas or charcoal.

Everybody asks me what grills I own. I have a 22.5-inch Weber® kettle charcoal grill that's more than 25 years old. My gas grill is a three-burner Weber that is on its last legs but has lasted for 18 years. My Chargriller with a side fire box is a new addition, and I bought a Weber Baby Q for tailgating and camping.

GAS VS. CHARCOAL VS. BRIQUETTES

If you own a gas grill, the biggest decision you have to make is the size of the propane container or whether to have a direct line hookup. Charcoal is another matter. It used to be all about briquettes, but hardwood lump charcoal has made a big dent in that market. Although more expensive than briquettes, hardwood charcoal burns hotter and cleaner. If you're a beginner at the grill, though, lump hardwood charcoal is not necessarily the best way to go because the lumps burn at different rates. Regular briquettes contain fillers and tend not to burn as hot or as long, but they do burn consistently, making it easy to judge how much charcoal you will need. Solid hardwood charcoal briquettes are the best. They burn clean, hot, and for a long time. Many restaurants use this type for live-fire grills. If you have access to food-service distributors, they are the best source for them; otherwise they can be hard to find. Make certain that the label clearly states "solid hardwood charcoal briquettes"; if it doesn't, you are buying briquettes with fillers.

What about the Weather?

In cold weather, you are going to have to increase cooking times slightly and pay closer attention to the fire to maintain the proper temperature. In windy conditions, cooking on a charcoal grill may not be the smartest thing to do. You probably will need more charcoal and need to keep a closer watch on the fire's temperature even in a moderate wind. Most gas grills will work better if placed perpendicular to the wind flow. Check the match-light hole to make sure your fire has not blown out. If it has, turn off the gas and open the lid. Wait 5 to 10 minutes before relighting.

LIGHTING THE FIRE

If you have a gas grill, follow your manufacturer's instructions and preheat all the burners on high with the lid down, usually for about 15 to 20 minutes. If cooking with charcoal, open all the vents. I highly recommend that you get yourself a chimney starter. Fill it with charcoal, place some crumbled paper or nontoxic fire starter underneath it, then light it with a long match or a long butane fireplace lighter and wait until the coals are ash gray. At this point, the coals are ready to use. If you haven't purchased a chimney starter yet, then form a pyramid with the charcoal and place nontoxic fire starters around the edge and light. Notice I haven't said anything about lighter fluid? Use lighter fluid only as a last resort. It tends to leave a flavor residue in your food.

Cooking Direct vs. Indirect

When you cook with direct heat, you are placing your food directly over the fire. This is what you want to do for quick-cooking items, like burgers, steaks, fish, some pork cuts, chicken wings, and boneless chicken. A good rule of thumb is if an item is going to take less than 20 minutes to cook, direct heat is the way to go. For a direct charcoal fire, after the coals have become ash gray, spread them out evenly. With a gas grill, just keep all your burners fired up on high, unless the recipe directs you to turn them down some.

When cooking indirect, the food is placed away from the fire. With charcoal, you would divide your ash gray coals and pull equal amounts to each side of the grill, leaving a gap in the middle with no coals. This setup works well with a round or square grill. If you've got a rectangular grill, it seems to work better to push all of the coals to one side. When you're going to be smoking for a time, it is helpful to place a drip pan (a disposable aluminum pan, typically 9x13 inches) in the space where there are no coals. Filling the pan with water, beer, or juice (usually apple juice) will add moisture to the air in the closed grill, resulting in greater succulence, which is a plus since long smoking tends to dry out food.

For a gas grill, preheat the grill with all the burners on. Then shut one of the burners off, usually the middle burner in a three-burner setup. Whether cooking with gas or charcoal, the food is placed on the grate over the area with no active heat source below it and the lid of the grill is closed. Cooking indirect is the preferred method for bone-in chicken, super-thick pork chops, large roasts, a whole chicken, as well as anything you want to smoke over a period of hours—a whole turkey, pork shoulder, brisket.

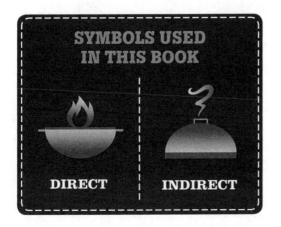

SYMBOLS USED
IN THIS BOOK

DIRECT   INDIRECT

In an indirect setup, you are actually grill roasting or grill baking, the grill functioning more like the oven in your home. The temperature, if you are cooking for a shorter amount of time, say, less than an hour, should be maintained at about 350°F to 400°F. For slow cooking over a number of hours, the temperature should be lower—I like a temperature of about 275°F to 300°F, even up to 325°F is okay. The pros are cooking around 200°F to 210°F, but their equipment is built to more easily maintain these lower temperatures. On a gas grill, you can maintain your temperature by adjusting your controls. For charcoal, it's a bit trickier. Charcoal demands a little more attention and a little zen. First, you have a fuel source that is literally burning itself away. Some experts say that 20 charcoal briquettes will give you an hour of cooking, but your temperature will be falling the entire time. When the coals are almost white and look like they are puff balls, your fire is almost gone. You want to add more charcoal before the fire reaches this stage, so if you are planning to cook for longer than 45 minutes, just to be covered, add fresh charcoal. To do this, place a few pieces around the outside edge of the existing fire. I sometimes start another fire in a small tabletop brazier that I bought for that purpose and carefully transfer over the burning coal. Never pour unlighted charcoal over an existing fire—you will extinguish it. Hardwood charcoal and hardwood lump charcoal burn hotter and a little longer than briquettes, but the procedure for adding them is the same.

When cooking with charcoal, you control the temperature of your fire with the grill's vents. The wider open the vents are, the hotter and faster burning the fire; close vents some and you slow the fire and bring down its temperature. Your grill's instruction manual will go into more detail as it pertains

What's That Wood You're Smoking?

- **Hickory:** The most popular of smoking woods, hickory has a cured pork essence like bacon and is great for pork, chicken, beef, game, and trout.

- **Mesquite:** The Sons of Texas favorite. This wood is more delicate than hickory but has a pronounced spiciness. Mesquite burns hotter than other woods, so take note. I would rather use mesquite charcoal than the wood. Use with beef, pork, and vegetables.

- **Oak:** The workhorse of woods. Oak gives a balanced smoke and is used from the Hill Country of Texas to the pits of Lexington, North Carolina. Works with most anything.

- **Apple:** The new darling. Apple wood is the new thing—having been used to win several major barbecue contests, everybody's cooking with it. Easy to find, with a delicate sweet taste, it's great with pork and most poultry, and is outstanding for smoking salmon.

- **Cherry:** One of the new kids. Cherry has a mild sweetness, with an interesting afternote that can be quite tart. I love this wood with game of all kinds and lamb.

- **Alder:** The wood of the Northwest. Alder is used to smoke and grill salmon. It is mild and matches with fish very well. Also use with vegetables.

- **Pecan:** Pecan leaves an interesting nutty flavor that is perfect with pork.

to your particular grill. Some grills still have adjustable cooking grills or charcoal grates, which you can raise and lower to adjust how close your food is to the heat source.

But cooking doesn't have to be indirect *or* direct. I often use a combination. Take bone-in chicken. I will sear the chicken, getting some nice grill marks on all sides and tasty caramelization, directly over the coals or burners in an indirect setup, then move them to the area with no direct heat to finish out the cooking.

Where There's Smoke, There's Flavor

To enhance the grilling experience, you can add smoke. The primary choices for doing this are wood chips or wood chunks. Sawdust is also good. The wood needs to be hardwood, like oak, hickory, apple, alder wood, and cherry, for example. According to Alton Brown, Food Network's food geek, it takes six hours for the distinctive flavor of a particular wood to transfer over to the protein of your choice, so the exact wood you use doesn't really matter in most circumstances. And be wary of too much smoke—if you expose food to smoke too long, it can end up imparting a bitter taste.

The good news is that food picks up a great deal of smoke flavor in just a couple of hours. Start slowly to develop your smoke flavor palate.

Smoking on a charcoal grill is simple. Take a handful or two of wood chips, or a couple of chunks, and soak them in water. Thirty minutes is okay, but an hour is much better. When the charcoal is

How Hot Is My Fire?

Part of being a Grill Master is knowing when your fire is the right heat for what you're cooking. Again, with a gas grill, you can adjust the heat with the controls. With a charcoal fire, it's a matter of letting the fire burn down to the level you want and using your vents to help you achieve that. But how hot is hot? You don't want to be incinerating food. I like the Mississippi Method: If you can count, while holding your hand a few inches above the cooking grate, one Mississippi, two Mississippi, before the heat is too intense for you to keep your hand there, then you have a hot fire. Throw on the burgers and steaks. The temperature will be at 500°F or above. For a medium-hot heat, you need to get to three Mississippi. The temperature now should be around 400°F. Four Mississippi will get you to medium heat, about 350°F. Five and six Mississippi and you are in the medium-low to low range, perfect for cooking barbecue, around 250°F to 300°F.

ash gray, drain a handful, or pull out one of the chunks, and place them over the coals. A handful of chips will usually smoke for 15 to 20 minutes, as will a single chunk. Add more as you desire, again being mindful that too much smoke can cause a bitterness in the food. I tend to add chips about every hour. Remember to include a pan of liquid when smoking. It will help counteract any drying out that smoking can cause.

Smoking is a bit more difficult on a gas grill but not enough to break a sweat over. Chips, not chunks, are the way to go with gas. If your grill has a smoke-box attachment, then just follow the directions the manufacturer has provided. You can also buy gas grill smoke boxes, but using a small disposable foil pan (or making a packet with heavy-duty aluminum foil with a few holes punched in the bottom) works just fine. Again, start by soaking your chips. Remove the grill's cooking grate. Fill the pan with chips, and place it right on the flavor bars, lava rock, or ceramic briquettes. I find that the upper left-hand corner is the best location; this is usually the hottest spot on most gas grills. Replace the grate and preheat your grill on high, as normal. Once you see smoke, adjust the burners to indirect and to the temperature necessary for the item you are cooking. Put the food on and close the lid. You should get enough smoke flavor from one full pan of chips.

Handy Tools for Effortless Grilling

Here's a list of tools that I and most of the people I visited with think are handy:

Tongs. Forget those monstrosities sold as grilling tongs. They are usually way too long and difficult to work with. Buy a couple of 12-inch cooking tongs. The locking ones make for easier storage. Most cooking stores carry them. If you are a charcoal person, you'll also want a longer pair on hand to push the coals with.

Spatulas. You want a good, wide metal spatula to use with burgers and two fish spatulas, one small for fillets and one large if you plan on grilling whole fish.

Grill-cleaning brush. Use one with brass bristles for porcelain-enameled grates and steel for cast-iron grates.

Heat-resistant silicone basting brush. For a griller, this is the best thing since sliced bread. It won't leave bristles all over your food and cleans up like a charm.

Barbecue mitts. When you're wielding hot skewers, you need something serious to protect your hands. I also like the new heat-resistant gloves sold as oven gloves.

Skewers. Wooden or metal are fine; I use the 8-inch or 12-inch size. If you're buying metal, look for the flat-bladed skewers—they'll prevent your food from spinning around as you try to rotate the skewers on the grill. If you're using wooden skewers, be sure to soak them in water for at least 30 minutes before using them to keep from singeing.

Small aluminum drip pans. When smoking, you'll need these to fill with the liquid of your choice to add needed moisture to the air.

High-capacity charcoal chimney starter. This is the most efficient way to start charcoal—use it once and you'll wonder what took you so long. They're sold in hardware stores and home centers.

Extra tank of propane. Believe me, nothing is worse than running out of gas halfway through your cooking. It will happen when you have company or your mother-in-law is visiting. Be prepared.

Nice to have but not necessary

Rib racks, which hold ribs vertically and effectively double the amount of ribs you can cook on most grills; a V-shaped roasting rack for larger items like a whole turkey—and some smart folks will fill this rack upside down and use it for ribs or chicken pieces;

Why You Need to Buy a Grill Thermometer

✧ Many grills come with a built-in thermometer, which I have found, through sad experience, foolish to trust. I now use a probe thermometer, which has a long wire attached to a digital readout. You can set this unit to the temperature you want and an alarm will go off when it is reached. You also can use this thermometer as you would an instant-read meat thermometer—you can even stick it in your meat, walk away from it, and the alarm will go off when the meat reaches the internal temperature you've set it for. They run from $25 to $40 and are well worth the money if you plan to cook more than just steaks.

cast-iron cooking grates because they last forever and, when seasoned, become nonstick; charcoal storage bins; and a vertical chicken rack, which is useful for beer-can chicken recipes because it stabilizes both the chicken and the beer can. There are also vertical racks for turkeys.

The Barbecue Pantry

I thought it would be helpful for you to know what I keep in my pantry and what I used in testing and developing the recipes in this book.

Salt. I always use kosher salt because I like the way it dissolves and flavors food. Some rub recipes and injection solutions suggest that you finely grind kosher salt. I don't. I like sea salt for the final seasoning of meat and especially fish, but that's my taste.

Pepper. Please use freshly ground black pepper. An investment in a pepper mill will pay off volumes in how your food tastes.

Sugar. Light brown sugar shows up in a lot of rub recipes, even though some barbecue pros think that white sugar is better because it doesn't have the moisture that brown sugar does, which inhibits caramelization. I like sugar in the raw, or turbinado sugar. It has a flavor somewhere between white and brown sugar and is dry. You may want to run it through a spice grinder to make the granules smaller.

Chili powder. You will get a better bang for your buck with pure chili powder or what's sold as New Mexican-style chili powder, which also contains oregano and a bit of cumin—it has a brighter, fresher taste than regular chili powder.

Hot sauce. Tabasco®, Louisiana hot sauce, Frank's, and Texas Pete® are the best, although each has a slightly different taste. If a recipe calls for a specific one, use it if you've got it; otherwise choose the one you like. I tend to use Texas Pete and Frank's Original.

Mayonnaise. I like Dukes® and JFG® mayonnaise the best. They have very little sugar, and both have a bright, lemony taste that reminds me of homemade. If these brands are not available in your area, find one with the least amount of sugar in the ingredients. If a recipe specifies Hellmann's®, use it; the flavor profile of Hellmann's is important to the final result.

Ketchup. If you are adding a lot of ingredients to ketchup to make a sauce, then it really doesn't matter which brand you use.

Soy sauce. It costs more, but I prefer to use tamari over regular soy sauce. It is lower in sodium and has a richer flavor.

Cider vinegar. If you plan to make your own sauces and injection solutions, keep jugs of this on hand.

Granulated garlic. Granulated has a much fresher and cleaner taste than garlic powder (same holds true for granulated onion over onion powder). Use granulated garlic for all your dry garlic needs.

Spices. Pick up some herbes de Provence, cinnamon, rosemary, ground cumin, dry mustard, and ground coriander, and you are ready for about any grilling moment. Also keep some dry rubs on hand, either homemade (this book is full of them) or a reliable store-bought brand, one for emergencies. Be sure to get a good prepared rub, preferably from your favorite barbecue joint. Remember that dried spices have a maximum shelf life of six months. Replace your spices frequently.

Beer. Always have beer on hand. Does that need an explanation?

It's All in the Fingertips: Determining Doneness by Feel

There is a simple way to check the doneness of most meat without cutting into it. Open your mouth in an O shape. Press on your cheek with a finger. Fairly loose, right? That's a rare steak or a piece of chicken that has a ways to go. Now push on the tip of your nose. That's the way a medium steak will feel. Finally, press your forehead between your eyebrows. That's a well-done feeling. Use this method along with your instant-read thermometer to gauge your doneness. With a little practice, you'll be amazed at how accurate you will be.

Now it's time for you to start cooking. Please read the recipes that you have chosen from beginning to end, even before you go to the grocery store or butcher shop. That way all surprises will be pleasant. There are some great recipes in this book for every level of Grill Master. Start with foods and methods that are familiar to you and then venture forward. My best wishes for your success. Now jump in and become part of the Barbecue Nation.

2 teasers from the grill

and a couple that aren't

There is no reason not to use your grill for party finger foods, hors d'oeuvres, or a stunning first course. ∽◦◦∽◦◦∽◦◦∽◦◦∽◦◦∽

I routinely **grill** oysters, satays, shrimp, pizza, and chicken wings for premeal tidbits. Using the grill early on at a **party or family gathering** gets folks clustered around and talking with each other.

This chapter has something for everyone. Grilled figs stuffed with cheese, quail, oysters Rockefeller—all guaranteed to please the palate. There are even a couple of nongrilled **classics** here, like deviled eggs.

Sounds like a good reason to have a party. Fire up the grill and let's get going.

1 pound natural almonds

About 1½ tablespoons hot sauce

2 teaspoons of your favorite barbecue rub, or to taste (optional)

1. Set up the grill for indirect grilling (see pp. 6–9). Oil your grill's cooking surface.

2. Toss together all the ingredients until the nuts are well coated with the hot sauce and rub, then pour into a disposable aluminum pan (at least 9 inches square) in an even layer, and set on the top rack of the smoker. (You can also place a piece of heavy-duty aluminum foil on the rack and spread the almonds on top.) Cover and smoke until the nuts are crisp, about 3 hours.

3. Let cool completely, then store in an airtight container.

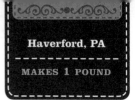

Jennifer's Spicy
smoked almonds

Jennifer Linder McGlinn is a pastry chef, food historian, and food writer who lives in Haverford, Pennsylvania. I knew when I asked her about grilling that she would have something unique, and she didn't let me down. Smoked almonds, now how many cans of those have you bought? If you follow this recipe, I doubt you will ever buy another can. Jennifer offers, "I particularly like to make them after smoking a more main event item, such as chicken or pork, when the smoker is still hot but the smoke is a bit less pungent, though you can throw them on from the beginning if you like."

One 14–ounce can artichoke hearts, drained and chopped

1½ cups light mayonnaise

Two 4½-ounce cans green chiles, drained and diced

1 cup shredded Monterey Jack cheese

½ cup freshly grated Parmesan cheese, plus more for sprinkling over the top

1 to 2 dashes hot sauce, to your taste

⅛ teaspoon cayenne pepper

Sharon Benton's Awesome
artichoke dip

SERVES 10 TO 12

For something to serve your guests before the steaks come off the grill, look no further than this awesome concoction. To guild the lily, stir in 8 ounces of crabmeat.

1. Preheat the oven to 325°F degrees.

2. Combine the artichokes, mayonnaise, chiles, Monterey Jack, and ⅓ cup of the Parmesan. Stir in the hot sauce and cayenne. For a little more kick, add more of both.

3. Spread the mixture in a shallow 1½-quart baking dish. Sprinkle the remaining Parmesan evenly over the top, adding more if you want. (You can prepare up to this point a day ahead. Cover with plastic and refrigerate.) Bake, uncovered, for 30 minutes, then serve hot with crackers, toast points, or raw vegetables.

½ cup (1 stick) unsalted butter

½ cup chopped scallions (white and green parts)

2 pounds frozen peeled and cooked crawfish tails, thawed and well drained

Three 8-ounce packages cream cheese, at room temperature

2 teaspoons garlic powder

1½ teaspoons crushed red pepper

1½ teaspoons freshly ground black pepper

¼ cup low-sodium chicken broth

Fritos and assorted crackers for serving

1. In a large skillet, melt the butter over medium heat and add the scallions. Cook, stirring, until just softened, then add the crawfish tails and cook for 10 minutes, stirring a few times.

2. Stir in the cream cheese, garlic powder, red and black pepper and stir until combined. Pour in the broth and stir until combined. Cook until thick enough for a dip, 3 to 4 minutes. Add more broth if the mixture becomes too thick.

3. Transfer to a serving dish and serve hot with Fritos and crackers.

Becky's
hot crawfish dip

Becky Hollingsworth and her husband, Don, are part of the Byhalia, Mississippi, crowd that entertained me so well at Bobby and Susan Bonds' home (see their goat cheese-topped filet mignon on page 43). We had Becky's great crawfish dip while sipping mango martinis and waiting for Bobby's steaks to cook up perfect. It's a fabulous starter for any barbecue gathering. Be sure to get all the water out of the tails or your dip will be soupy. Becky served Fritos® Scoops® with this dip, which made it easy to get a goodly amount in your mouth. You'll want it that way.

When Becky brings her crawfish dip, folks gather for good eating, in this case her friends Billy and Linda Sproles, Alice Ray, and Phil Malone.

6 large eggs

¼ cup sweet pickle juice, or more to taste

¼ cup Miracle Whip® salad dressing, or more to taste

½ teaspoon prepared yellow mustard

Rachel's

bewitching deviled eggs

Deviled eggs are a key side to any classic barbecue feed. Even at Blue Smoke in New York City, Manhattan's high-end interpretation of a barbecue joint, deviled eggs are offered as a first course. Rachel Thomas's deviled eggs may be the finest on earth and are simple to make. She also shares her secret for getting a more tender hard-boiled egg. Rachel says that you can double or triple the amount of eggs as long as you cover them with an inch of water and they are in a single layer in the pan.

– ꙮ –

1. Place the eggs in a medium saucepan, cover with 1 inch of water, and bring to a boil. Remove the pan from the heat, cover, and let sit for 12 to 15 minutes. Meanwhile, fill a bowl with cold water and ice cubes. Drain the eggs, place in the ice water, let sit 5 minutes, then drain and peel.

2. While the eggs are still warm, cut them in half lengthwise and drop the yolks into a medium bowl. (Warm egg yolks will absorb more flavor.) Set the whites on a plate. Add the pickle juice (Rachel uses the juice from her homemade three-day sweet pickles), Miracle Whip, and mustard, and beat with a hand mixer until smooth. Rachel's advice is that "you may have to add more ingredients to get a smooth consistency. I always taste to see what I need. Usually I need more pickle juice. If the sweetness is to your liking but the consistency is not smooth enough, add a couple more tablespoons of Miracle Whip and a bit more mustard. Remember, it is better to add too little than to get too much of something. Tasting is the key."

3. Pipe or spoon the filling into the whites and serve or cover with plastic wrap and refrigerate for up to 4 hours.

Fred's Two Cents on Deviled Eggs

I love deviled eggs, and Rachel's are especially good. Sometimes I will start with her base and add a small amount of horseradish for a sweet and hot taste. Many folks will add a drop or two of hot sauce or Worcestershire sauce. You can also gussy up deviled eggs by adding fresh herbs. Tarragon is especially good.

9 ounces soft goat cheese

6 teaspoons grated orange zest

Kosher salt and freshly ground black pepper

9 tablespoons olive oil

6 tablespoons orange juice

2 small red onions, sliced into ¼-inch-thick rounds

Twelve ⅓-inch-thick diagonal slices sourdough baguette

4 cups arugula leaves

¾ cup Kalamata olives, drained, pitted, and cut in half

Grilled Bread Topped with

arugula and goat cheese

Katrina Moore, my conscience on all things that have a vegetarian bend and an absolute cheese freak, enjoys serving this dish as a first course or finger food for a party. All the flavors and textures blend so well that even the Buffalo-wing set will enjoy this nibble.

– 🙐 –

1. Combine the cheese and 4 teaspoons of the orange zest in a small bowl, mashing it together until well mixed. Season with salt and pepper. (This can be prepared up to a day ahead. Cover with plastic wrap and refrigerate until needed.)

2. Light a charcoal fire or preheat your gas grill on high. Oil the grill's cooking surface. Let the coals burn down to a medium-hot fire or adjust the gas grill burners to medium-high.

3. Whisk 6 tablespoons of the olive oil, the orange juice, and the remaining 2 teaspoons orange zest together in a 9x13-inch glass baking dish. Season with salt and pepper. Add the onion slices and turn to coat. Using a metal spatula, transfer the onions to the grill and cook until tender and golden, turning occasionally and keeping the slices intact, about 10 minutes. Return the onions to the dressing in the dish and turn to coat again. Set aside.

4. Brush the remaining 3 tablespoons oil over both sides of the baguette. Grill until the baguette is golden, about 2 minutes per side. Spread the cheese mixture over the warm baguette.

5. Add the arugula to the dressing and toss to coat. Top the cheese baguette evenly with the arugula, onions, and olives and serve.

2 tablespoons extra-virgin olive oil

1 teaspoon minced garlic

1/2 cup tightly packed fresh basil leaves, torn into small pieces

1 tablespoon chopped fresh oregano

1/2 teaspoon kosher salt

1/4 teaspoon freshly ground black pepper

1 recipe Corn Bread Crust (recipe at right), rolled out into four 10-inch rounds

1 cup tomato sauce, or 8 to 10 ripe plum tomatoes, cored and thinly sliced

8 ounces mozzarella cheese, shredded (about 2 cups)

1. In a large bowl, combine the olive oil, garlic, basil, oregano, salt, and pepper and stir to blend.

2. Light a charcoal fire or preheat your gas grill on high. Oil the grill's cooking surface. Let the coals burn down to a medium fire or adjust the gas grill burners to medium.

3. Place the pizza dough on the grill, and cook until toasted on the bottom, 1 to 3 minutes. Remove with a pizza peel or large spatulas, and distribute about ¼ cup of the tomato sauce on the toasted side of each crust, leaving any liquid in the bowl. Sprinkle the top of the sauce with the garlic herb mixture. Top each pizza with about ½ cup of the cheese, leaving a ½-inch border around the edges.

4. Return the pizzas to the grill, and cook until the crusts are crisp and the cheese has melted, 4 to 6 minutes. Remove from the grill, let cool just a bit to let the cheese settle, and cut into wedges. Serve warm.

Grilled
pizza margherita

Grilled pizza is an exceptional treat. If you are a fan of the restaurants with wood- or coal-fired pizza ovens, the same smoky, crackling crust occurs when you throw a pizza over the grill. You can make your dough from scratch using the recipe below, or feel free to use store-bought frozen or refrigerated dough instead. Pizza makes for a great patio party appetizer—just cut it into small wedges or squares when it comes off the grill and pass it around.

corn bread pizza crust
MAKES FOUR 10-INCH OR TWO 12-INCH PIZZA CRUSTS

This pizza dough is a little different from the norm, but the cornmeal adds a nice touch. Belinda Ellis developed this recipe.

1½ cups warm water (105°F to 115°F)	2 cups self-rising cornmeal mix
1 package (2¼ teaspoons) active yeast	2 teaspoons sugar
1 tablespoon olive oil	1 teaspoon kosher salt
	2 cups bread flour

1. Pour the water into a large bowl and sprinkle the yeast over it. Stir gently. Add the oil, cornmeal mix, sugar, and salt and mix well. Gradually add the flour until the dough pulls away from the side of the bowl and is soft. Flour your hands and turn the dough onto a lightly floured work surface. To knead, press with the heel of your hand and fold the dough over. Turn the dough and continue working it in this way (press, fold over, turn) until the dough is no longer sticky and feels springy, about 10 minutes.

2. Grease a medium bowl with olive oil. Place the dough in the bowl and turn once to coat it with oil. Cover with plastic wrap, and allow to rise in a warm place until doubled in size, about 1 hour.

3. Punch the air bubbles out of the dough. The dough may be used immediately or wrapped in plastic wrap and refrigerated for up to 24 hours. If using refrigerated dough, allow it to sit at room temperature to warm for 30 minutes before rolling it out.

4 large romaine leaves, hard rib trimmed

Two 2-ounce bocconcini (small balls of fresh mozzarella), drained

Sea salt and freshly ground black pepper

2 very thin slices prosciutto, each sliced in half crosswise

Two-Tomato Relish (recipe at right)

1. Gently press flat the romaine leaves (the rib needs to be somewhat flexible so it won't break open). Blanch the leaves by dipping them one at a time in a large pot of boiling water, just long enough to take the starch out of them. Drain, then pat dry with paper towels.

2. Cut each bocconcini half. Salt and pepper each piece to taste. Wrap each half in a piece of prosciutto. Place a prosciutto-cheese bundle in the middle of each romaine leaf; fold the sides in, and roll up snugly. This can be done up to an hour ahead of time. Refrigerate until ready to grill.

3. Light a charcoal fire or preheat your gas grill on high. Oil the grill's cooking surface. Let the coals burn down to a medium-hot fire or adjust the gas grill burners to medium-high.

4. Grill the romaine bundles until nicely browned, about 2 minutes per side. Serve immediately topped with a generous spoon of relish. Pass additional relish at the table.

Robin's Grilled Romaine and
mozzarella with two-tomato relish

Cocktail time at Robin Kline's home in Des Moines, Iowa, might well include these little nibbles. At first read this recipe may sound like a little work, but it's really not and the simplicity of what goes into this recipe belies the thunderous taste impact. It's easily doubled, tripled, heck, just make a party. These little packets will make a great side to almost any grilled meat, just serve two per person.

two-tomato relish — MAKES 1½ TO 1¾ CUPS

3 ripe tomatoes, seeded and diced

8 oil-packed sun-dried tomato halves, diced

¼ cup chopped fresh basil

2 garlic cloves, minced

2 tablespoons olive oil

2 teaspoons balsamic vinegar

¼ teaspoon cayenne pepper

Sea salt to taste

1. In a medium bowl, combine the tomatoes, basil, garlic, olive oil, vinegar, and cayenne and toss to mix well. Salt to taste.

2. Cover with plastic wrap and let stand at room temperature for 1 hour to let flavors blend. Refrigerate if keeping longer than an hour, but bring back to room temperature before serving. This is best made the day it's to be enjoyed.

16 fresh Mission or Brown Turkey figs

¾ cup balsamic vinegar

4 ounces Point Reyes blue cheese,
at room temperature

4 ounces mascarpone, at room
temperature

Freshly ground black pepper

6 ounces thinly sliced country ham
or prosciutto

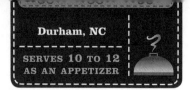

Grilled Fresh
figs with country ham

When figs are in season, I find myself throwing together this little nibble two or three times a week. The idea came from Ben Barker, chef-proprietor of the Magnolia Grill in Durham, North Carolina. I also swiped a thing or two from Frank Stitt, chef-proprietor of Highlands Restaurant in Birmingham, Alabama. Most figs done this way use prosciutto, but I find I prefer a thinly sliced country ham, especially one from Benton's Ham Shop in Madisonville, Tennessee. The Point Reyes blue cheese has character without being overly bold. If you're a true blue cheese freak, you might prefer a Maytag. In other words, put these figs together to your taste. I tend to use them as finger foods but you could certainly serve three halves over a bed of dressed lettuces as a first course.

1. Slice the figs in half lengthwise. Using a grapefruit spoon, remove a bit of the inside flesh from each and place in a bowl.

2. In a small saucepan over medium heat, cook the vinegar until it is reduced to about 6 tablespoons and syrupy. Let cool and keep at room temperature.

3. Add the blue cheese and mascarpone to the bowl with the fig flesh and mix well. Season generously with pepper and stir to combine.

4. Take each fig and stuff with about 1 tablespoon of the cheese mixture. Wrap a piece of ham around the fig and cheese. Place on a baking sheet, cover with plastic wrap, and refrigerate for about 1 hour or up to 4 hours.

5. Light a charcoal fire or preheat your gas grill on high. Oil the grill's cooking surface. Let the coals burn down to a medium-hot fire or adjust the gas grill burners to medium-high.

6. Place the figs on the grill cut side up. Cook until the ham is a bit crispy and the figs are warm, about 5 minutes. Remove to a platter and drizzle with the balsamic syrup. Serve immediately.

4 medium eggplant, trimmed and sliced ¼ inch thick

3 tablespoons plus ¼ cup olive oil

8 ounces feta cheese, crumbled (2 cups)

1 jalapeño, seeded and minced

1 tablespoon fresh lemon juice

3 tablespoons chopped fresh mint

Grilled Eggplant Roll-ups
with feta, mint, and jalapeño

It seems as if every day I meet somebody new or an old friend who's gone the vegetarian route, which has forced me to experiment with vegetarian dishes. Here's a great vegetarian cocktail nibble, a little eggplant roll-up that you'll find committed carnivores snapping up with equal relish.

– ⌘ –

1. Light a charcoal fire or preheat your gas grill on high. Oil the grill's cooking surface. Let the coals burn down to a medium-hot fire or adjust the gas grill burners to medium-high.

2. Brush the eggplant slices liberally with the 3 tablespoons oil just before placing on the grill to keep them from going soggy. Baste them again once on the grill and cook 4 to 5 minutes, until tender and you have nice grill marks, turning once. Carefully remove from the grill so the slices don't rip.

3. In a medium bowl, mash together the feta, the remaining ¼ cup oil, the jalapeño, lemon juice, and 1 tablespoon of the mint.

4. Evenly divide the feta mixture over the eggplant slices and roll up. Place on a serving platter and sprinkle with the remaining 2 tablespoons of mint.

One 4-pound London broil (top round steak)

¼ cup soy sauce

¼ cup sugar

¼ teaspoon garlic powder

¼ teaspoon ground ginger

2 tablespoons dry white wine

16 to 20 bamboo skewers, soaked in water for at least 1 hour

1 tablespoon sesame seeds, toasted in a dry skillet over medium heat until light brown

Amanda, Julie, and Katrina Pierzchala's

steeplechase beef satays

These three sisters decided that they would class up their next tailgate party at the University of Georgia, so they promptly swiped this recipe from their mom, who only prepares it for the Atlanta Steeplechase. "You know steeplechases are much fancier than a football game. Heck, they probably wouldn't let us in," the girls say, laughing.

These satays are fun for a tailgate or backyard party and make cocktail party food that your guests will remember. I like to serve them with some rice noodles and pickled vegetables for a Southeast Asia taste. By the way, the girls insist that you include the sesame seeds.

– ୧ଙ୍ଗ –

1. Slice the London broil across the grain about ¼ inch thick. You should be able to get 16 to 20 slices. You might find it easier to slice the beef if you stick it in the freezer for 20 minutes.

2. Combine the soy sauce, sugar, garlic powder, ginger, and wine in a small bowl, then pour it into a large zip-top plastic bag. Add the beef slices, seal the bag, and squish it to distribute the marinade and coat all the pieces. Place in the refrigerator and let marinate overnight.

3. Light a charcoal fire or preheat your gas grill on high. Oil the grill's cooking surface. Let the coals burn down to a low fire or adjust your gas grill burners to low.

4. Remove the beef from marinade, discarding the marinade. Weave each slice onto a single skewer. Place the skewers on the grill and cook for about 4 minutes per side.

5. Transfer the skewers to a platter, sprinkle with the sesame seeds, and hand around.

12 large jalapeños

2 boneless, skinless chicken breast halves

Two 8-ounce packages cream cheese

8 cloves garlic, minced

½ pound sliced bacon, cut in half lengthwise

Mark's Outrageously Good
chicken jalapeño poppers

It seems that if you belong to the National Barbecue Association, you've got to have your own version of jalapeño poppers. This is Mark Cheeseman's excellent take on them—he includes chicken in his, which makes for a hearty appetizer.

– ᘓᓂᗢᘖ –

1. Remove the stems from the jalapeños, cut them in half lengthwise, and remove the seeds. Cut the chicken breasts crosswise into ¼- to ½-inch-thick strips.

2. Sprinkle the top of each block of cream cheese with 4 cloves of the minced garlic. Cut each block in half lengthwise, then cut each half into 6 equal pieces for a total of 12 pieces per block. Stuff each pepper half with a piece of the cream cheese, then press a chicken strip on top of the cream cheese. Wrap each stuffed pepper with a piece of bacon, using a toothpick to hold it in place.

3. Set up the grill for indirect grilling (see pp. 6–9). Oil your grill's cooking surface.

4. Set the wrapped peppers on the grill away from the heat and cook, turning several times, until the bacon is cooked. Serve immediately.

JAPANESE YAKITORI MARINADE

¾ cup soy sauce

½ cup mirin (sweet rice wine)

¼ cup ketchup

2 tablespoons rice vinegar

2 teaspoons minced garlic

1 teaspoon toasted Asian sesame oil

2 pounds boneless, skinless chicken breasts

Wooden skewers, soaked in water for 1 hour and drained

Vegetable oil

Tokyo, Japan

SERVES 8 TO 10 AS AN APPETIZER

Eiji's
yakitori chicken

Yakitori is basically the Japanese equivalent of satay, served on special skewers. There are certain areas in Tokyo where the streets are lined with small, hole-in-the-wall restaurants that only offer yakitori. Friend and client Eiji Takano, head of the largest fruit purveyor in Japan, gave me this recipe for chicken yakitori. They make wonderful appetizers, or you can enjoy them as a full meal. Shrimp and pork also work with this marinade.

– ᘓᘓᘓᘓ –

1. Combine the marinade ingredients in a medium bowl until well mixed.

2. Rinse the chicken under cold water and pat dry with paper towels. Cut into 1½-inch chunks. Place the chicken in a large zip-top plastic bag and pour in the marinade. Seal the bag and squish the chicken around to coat it evenly. Let marinate in the refrigerator for at least 30 minutes and up to 2 hours, turning the bag a few times.

3. Remove the chicken to a plate, and pour the marinade into a small saucepan. Bring to a boil and let boil for 1 minute. Remove from the heat and set aside. Thread the chicken onto the skewers. Lightly brush with vegetable oil.

4. Light a charcoal fire or preheat your gas grill on high. Oil the grill's cooking surface. Let the coals burn down to a medium fire or adjust the gas grill burners to medium.

5. Place the skewers on the grill and cook until the meat is firm to the touch and cooked through, 8 to 10 minutes total, turning to cook the meat evenly and basting once with the marinade after all the sides have been seared. Remove to a platter and serve immediately.

2 pounds chicken drummettes

1 to 2 tablespoons of your favorite rib rub

½ cup (1 stick) unsalted butter

4 large garlic cloves, finely chopped

½ cup hot sauce of your choice, more if
you like your wings spicy

I'm always cooking something up on the grill.

Fred's Second Avenue
grilled buffalo wings

On Second Avenue in the East 30s in New York City there's a little place called Rocky's. While they have more than adequate pizza, their Buffalo wings are truly outstanding. What separates them from the pack is the presence of copious amounts of garlic in their Buffalo sauce. Now, I love chicken wings, but I'm not always in New York, so I decided that I needed to come up with a recipe as close as possible to Rocky's. I also didn't want to have to fry them. You do need to start these the day before because sprinkling them with rib rub and letting them sit overnight is a crucial part of the process.

– ∽◦∽ –

1. At least 8 hours before you intend to cook the wings, sprinkle them liberally with the rib rub. Toss them in a large zip-top plastic bag and refrigerate.

2. Light a charcoal fire or preheat your gas grill on high. Oil the grill's cooking surface.

3. Meanwhile, in a large skillet, melt the butter over medium heat. Add the garlic and cook for about 2 minutes, just long enough for the garlic flavor to infuse the butter. Pour in the hot sauce, stir to combine, and remove from the heat.

4. Place the chicken wings on the grill. Cook for about 15 minutes, turning frequently so that all the sides brown and have grill marks.

5. Remove from the grill and place in the skillet with the sauce. Set the pan over low heat and toss to completely coat the wings. Let heat for about 5 minutes, until the sauce and the wings are nice and warm.

6. Remove the wings to a platter, pour any additional sauce over them, and serve with plenty of napkins.

24 chicken wings

JERK MARINADE

1 large onion, chopped

^{2}/$_3$ cup chopped green onions (white and green parts)

6 tablespoons dried onion flakes

2 tablespoons ground allspice

2 tablespoons freshly ground black pepper

1 tablespoon cayenne pepper

2 tablespoons sugar

1½ tablespoons dried thyme

1 tablespoon ground cinnamon

1 teaspoon ground nutmeg

1 tablespoon soy sauce

¼ cup vegetable oil

Bottled ranch or blue cheese dressing

Brooklyn Jerked
chicken wings

Brooklyn, New York, has a diverse population. Jamaican jerked chicken wings are everywhere, at street vendors and being grilled by picnicking families watching Sunday soccer matches. Most Jamaican cooks are secretive about their special jerk seasoning, but I was given enough clues to come up with this authentic-tasting recipe. I make these for Super Bowl parties—I mean, football is football, right?

– ✍✍✍ –

1. Place the chicken wings in a large zip-top plastic bag.

2. Place the marinade ingredients in a food processor and pulse to combine, then process until smooth. Pour over the chicken wings, seal the bag, squish everything together to coat the wings, and refrigerate overnight (2 days is even better), turning the bag occasionally.

3. Light a charcoal fire or preheat your gas grill on high. Oil the grill's cooking surface.

4. Remove the chicken from the marinade, discarding the marinade. Place the wings on the hot grill and cook for about 15 minutes, turning them frequently so they don't char. They should be golden brown and cooked through when finished.

5. Transfer to a platter and serve with the dressing in a small bowl for dipping.

LA DI DA MARINADE

3/4 cup canola oil

1/3 cup cider vinegar

1/3 cup soy sauce

1/4 cup Worcestershire sauce

3 tablespoons fresh lemon juice

1 teaspoon dry mustard

3/4 teaspoon dried parsley flakes

1 teaspoon white pepper

1 teaspoon garlic powder

1 garlic clove, crushed

1/4 cup bourbon (optional)

---

2 pounds boneless venison loin

2 green bell peppers, seeded and sliced into thick strips

2 large portobello mushrooms, sliced

1 pound sliced bacon, cut in half

La Di Da
venison kebobs

Deer hunting is still a manly pursuit in the South. It's almost a rite of passage from boyhood to manhood. Down around Pritchards Island off South Carolina, you'll find these kebobs showing up at well-to-do parties. They're marinated in a hearty liquid designed to take the wild game flavor from the venison loin. If you don't have a hunter close by, you can use farm-raised, but then don't marinate it more than 6 hours.

– ᥒᥱᥣᥱᥒ –

1. Combine the marinade ingredients in a blender or food processor. Blend on high for 1 minute.

2. Cut the venison into 1/2-inch-wide strips and place in a large zip-top plastic bag. Pour over the marinade, seal the bag, squish everything around to coat, and let marinate overnight in the refrigerator.

3. Remove the venison from the marinade, keeping the marinade. Take a piece of venison, a piece of bell pepper, and a slice of mushroom and wrap it with a bacon strip. Secure with a toothpick. Place these "kebobs" back in the marinade for another 30 minutes at room temperature.

4. Meanwhile, light a charcoal fire or preheat your gas grill on high. Oil the grill's cooking surface.

5. Remove the kebobs from the marinade, discarding the marinade. Place them on the grill and cook, turning just once, for a total of 5 to 8 minutes. Let cool for a minute, then pass for hors d'ouevres.

¼ cup (½ stick) unsalted butter

¼ cup chopped garlic

4 dozen medium Pacific oysters

Nellie's Special Sauce (recipe below)

1. Light a charcoal fire or preheat your gas grill on high. Oil the grill's cooking surface.

2. Meanwhile, in a small saucepan over low heat, melt the butter. Add the garlic and keep warm.

3. Place the oysters on the grill flat side down. Grill for 3 to 4 minutes but not until they open. Remove from the grill.

4. Open the oysters, removing the top shell, then place back on the grill, round side down, and spoon some of the garlic butter mixture on each. Cook 2 to 3 minutes longer, to your desired degree of doneness. Serve immediately with Nellie's Special Sauce.

Nellie Gamez and her fabulous smile.

Nellie Gamez's Grilled
oysters and special sauce

Nellie Gamez is a treat. Her face is always happy, with a sparkle in her eyes that say, "Life is good." She runs the retail sales shack of Lunny Oyster Ranch out near Point Reyes, California. Nellie has worked at the place for more than 20 years. And if you want to sample the oysters, she'll be glad to shuck a few for you or, in my case, two dozen sweet Pacific Japanese oysters. I asked her how she would grill them. "I do it different than most people and I know my way keeps more oyster liquor with the oyster." She partially cooks them over the coals, round side up (most folks grill them round side down), takes them off, removes the top shell, puts the oyster back over the fire, and spoons on some garlic and butter. When they're done, she serves them with her special (and up to now secret) sauce—part cocktail sauce, part marinara, and darn good. These oysters are first rate, and the sauce works with most seafood.

nellie's special sauce

MAKES A LITTLE MORE THAN 6 CUPS

This sauce will keep in an airtight container in the fridge for up to 2 weeks. Thin it a bit and you have a cioppino base.

4 cups ketchup

¾ cup distilled white vinegar

2 tablespoons chopped garlic

2 tablespoons prepared horseradish

2 tablespoons Italian seasoning blend

¼ cup fresh lemon juice

¼ teaspoon prepared yellow mustard

Mix all the ingredients together in a large bowl until well combined.

1 pound 24-count shrimp, peeled, with the tail left, and deveined

Kosher salt and freshly ground black pepper

24 large fresh basil leaves, or 40 if small

12 thin slices prosciutto, cut in half lengthwise

4 bamboo skewers, soaked in water for 1 hour

Your favorite Asian-style dipping sauce or cocktail sauce (or try my recipe at right)

1. Season the shrimp with salt and pepper. Take each shrimp and wrap a basil leaf around it, then a piece of prosciutto. Thread 6 shrimp onto a skewer. Repeat until all the shrimp are skewered.

2. Preheat your gas grill on high or light a charcoal fire. Oil your grill's cooking grate. Let the coals burn down to a medium-hot fire or adjust the gas grill burners to medium-high heat.

3. Place the shrimp on the grill and cook 3 to 4 minutes per side, until just cooked through. Take care not to overcook. The shrimp are ready when they form a gentle C.

4. Remove the shrimp to a platter and serve with your sauce for dipping.

Sharon's shrimp, ready for the grill.

Sharon Benton's Simply Wonderful
grilled shrimp wrapped in basil and prosciutto

Sharon and Allan Benton, from Madisonville, Tennessee, are the most delightful folks you'd ever want to meet. Sharon, who is a school administrator, thrilled me with an artichoke dip (p. 16), but her impressive shrimp were the high point of the meal.

These grilled shrimp have a slight hint of Southeast Asia, which comes from pairing the basil and the prosciutto. Allan, a producer of artisanal country hams, also produces an American prosciutto. You can assemble the shrimp early in the day, keeping them covered in the refrigerator until ready to cook. The shrimp can serve double duty as a finger food at a party.

spicy green tomato dipping sauce
MAKES ½ TO ⅔ CUP

I played around with a sauce for these shrimp and found this to be a good mate. It's also great with grilled or chicken and pork.

¼ cup Thomas's Gourmet Green Tomato Chutney or other green tomato chutney

3 tablespoons Capsicana Zing Sauce® or a hot chili sauce

1 tablespoon Joe Bud's Everything Sauce or a mustard-based barbecue sauce

1 tablespoon tamari or low-sodium soy sauce

1 tablespoon rice vinegar

2 tablespoons creamy peanut butter

1 teaspoon toasted sesame oil

1 green onion (white and green parts), finely chopped

Place all the ingredients except the green onion in a small saucepan over medium heat. Cook, stirring until the peanut butter has melted and the ingredients are well combined. Sprinkle the green onion over the top and remove from the heat. Serve warm.

America's love affair with beef has returned with a vengeance.

More choices of beef cuts are now available to a wider audience, giving all of us the **chance to experiment** and indulge in what were once regional delights. Skirt and hanger steaks that were only available in butcher shops can now be found in local supermarkets, as can tri-tip, once a Santa Barbara, California, phenomenon. The same is the case with veal.

You will find all sorts of fun things to do with beef. From low and slow briskets and chuck, to sizzling fajitas. The marinades and seasonings range from the simple to the exotic and transverse a world of flavors.

We're Talking Steak

Steaks, after hamburgers (check out chapter 8 for more on that subject), have long been the choice of many for outdoor cooking. The **loin** is the source of the very best steaks—the strip steak (also referred to as New York strip), T-bone, porterhouse, and filet mignon all come from this region. From the rib area, you've got the **rib-eye,** also called a Delmonico steak. This is the same cut used for prime rib and standing rib roast. When choosing steaks, thicker is better.

From the **flank** and upper body of the cow come tougher cuts, which, quite frankly, provide more flavor and better value. The flank steak is fairly tender when you don't overcook it (medium or less) and slice the meat thinly against the grain. This was the steak originally used to make London broil (London broil is really a recipe from the 1930s, not a cut of meat). Top round, which now seems to be always labeled as London broil, loves to be marinated and should be treated like flank steak. Hanger steaks and skirt steaks are the new kids on the block to most folks. The skirt steak comes from the region close to the **brisket and short ribs.** It is well marbled and is commonly used in fajitas but is

excellent on its own. The hanger steak comes from just below the last rib and the loin and, frankly, after a New York strip or porterhouse, it is my favorite steak. It's also known as the "butcher's tenderloin," a piece of beef that was typically ground but more than likely taken home for the butcher's family's enjoyment. It makes an awesome steak—just make sure that the central vein has been removed.

From the **chuck** comes the chuck roast, which makes darn good hamburgers when ground. From the top of the chuck is the blade steak or the flat iron, so named because the shape is similar to the bottom of an iron. Full of flavor with some tough gristly parts, blade steaks are cheap and take well to marinating.

King Brisket and Beef Ribs

The brisket is the king of low and slow barbecue. You want some fat, but you'll find a lot of briskets carry a heavy coat of fat that you'll want to trim. What's called "first cut" brisket is leaner, which is a great choice when ordering a pastrami sandwich, not for smoking.

As for beef ribs, there are two types on the market. One will be the long bones cut from the rib-eye roasts. They have a fair amount of meat and are fun to grill. The short ribs tend to be sold as "flanken" ribs, three ribs in one piece. They are perfect for a quick grill, then a long braise to make them tender.

Veal on the Grill

Veal comes in just about the same cuts as beef, of course, since it is young beef. The more common cuts for grilling are the loin and rib chops, sirloin chops, and breast of veal makes for nice kebobs. Look for a nice pinkness or a slightly rosy color. Avoid meat that looks even a little gray. Marbling is not an issue with veal.

4 well-marbled 1½-inch-thick New York strip steaks, bone on if possible

Kosher salt to taste, about 1 teaspoon per steak

Freshly ground black pepper, about 1 teaspoon per steak

Olive oil (not extra virgin), as needed

¼ cup (½ stick) unsalted or seasoned butter

1. Remove the steaks from the refrigerator at least 30 minutes before cooking.

2. Light a charcoal fire or preheat your gas grill on high. Oil the grill's cooking surface.

3. Pat the steaks dry with a paper towel and sprinkle each on both sides with the salt and pepper, then drizzle with a light coating of olive oil. Put the grill grates in place and wait a few minutes to heat. Place the steaks on the grill. Cook for a couple of minutes, until you can lift them up from the grill without sticking, then give each steak a quarter turn. Continue cooking for another couple of minutes, then flip the steaks over. So far they've cooked for 5 to 6 minutes. Grill for another 5 to 6 minutes on the second side.

4. Touch the meat to gauge its doneness and remove or continue cooking. When done, remove the steaks to a platter, top each one with a pat of butter, then wait 5 minutes, giving the butter time to melt and the internal juices time to settle. Serve, pouring any melted butter and accumulated juices over the steaks.

The Perfect
grilled steak

Grilling a steak seems simple, but a few home truths need to be observed. Start with the best-quality meat. If you can find American-raised, grass-fed beef that's prime or aged, I urge you to purchase it. Look for good marbling: That's the little white lines of fat running through the solid muscle of the meat. Remember that fat transfers flavor, so check your cholesterol fears at the door. My recommendation is eat good red meat, just less often. When it comes to fuel, both charcoal briquettes and gas are fine, although you might want to give true hardwood charcoal a try. It burns hotter, which is what you want (most steakhouses are cooking at 800°F plus). Also, the flavor from hardwood charcoal is clean, natural, and unadulterated. Season your steak very simply. Make sure the surface is dry except for a little oil. Wet beef won't sear as well. I drizzle oil on my steaks to help the heat transfer begin—I get a better sear and more caramelizing, a 10-cent word for lots of flavor. Guild the lily at the end with butter, either a purchased seasoned butter or mix up your own. Plain unsalted butter is just fine as well.

Checking for Doneness without Cutting

Touch your cheek. When you push on a steak and it feels like that, it's rare. The tip of your nose is medium, and your forehead is well done. Timing helps, but feeling it in your fingertips is foolproof.

One 8- to 10-ounce sirloin steak, 1 inch thick

½ cup Dale's Seasoning Sauce® or Moore's® Seasoning Sauce

½ cup Sprite®

Callahan's
marinated steak

College student Callahan Parrish and an ever-changing number of friends gather every Sunday night at Callahan's parents' house in Cullman, Alabama. Callahan is actually a bit of a cattle rancher and probable heir to a livestock market owned by his father and grandfather.

If it's meat in the Parrish household, it's beef. Callahan and his friends each take a steak, drop it in a zip-top bag, and marinate it to their liking. Then they all gather at the grill, joke, tell stories, and cook their steaks. Occasionally, Callahan's mom will fix some potatoes, but for the most part this is a protein-only party.

Don't let the ingredients in this recipe put you off. Try it. You'll be pleasantly surprised.

– ෴ –

1. Place the steak in a large zip-top plastic bag. Add the seasoning sauce and Sprite, seal the bag, and squish the ingredients around to combine. Let sit at room temperature while you start the fire.

2. Light a charcoal fire or preheat your gas grill on high. Oil the grill's cooking surface.

3. Remove the steak from the marinade, discarding the marinade. Pat dry with paper towels. Place it on the grill and cook for about 8 minutes per side for medium to medium rare, or to your desired degree of doneness.

4. Remove to a plate, let rest a few minutes, and dig in.

2 sirloin steaks, 1 ½ pounds each

Kosher salt and freshly ground black pepper

⅓ cup olive oil

2 to 3 tablespoons fresh lemon juice

8 cups arugula, stemmed

3 cups chopped radicchio

½ pound Parmesan cheese, shaved with a vegetable peeler

Sliced Steak
with radicchio and parmesan on arugula

One of my best discoveries upon moving to New York City a decade and a half ago was steak and bitter greens. Creamed spinach has always been a "must" side dish in the steakhouses of New York, but as more bistro restaurants began to open, the spinach became less creamed and more sautéed, and arugula, kale, and watercress joined the mix. At first glance this may look like a salad to you, but the heat from the steak actually wilts the arugula and radicchio, giving you a warm and comforting experience. If you have the time, serve this with some Tuscan white beans (p. 323) for a real European experience.

– ୧ଚ୭ଚ୬ –

1. Season both sides of the steaks with salt and pepper.

2. Light a charcoal fire or preheat your gas grill on high. Oil the grill's cooking surface.

3. Place the steaks on the grill and cook 5 to 6 minutes per side for medium-rare or to your desired degree of doneness. Remove from the grill and let stand as long as 30 minutes before slicing.

4. Meanwhile, whisk the oil, lemon juice, and salt and pepper to taste together in a large bowl. Add the arugula and toss until well coated. Place on a platter, arrange the sliced steak on top, then top with the radicchio and Parmesan. Serve immediately.

1 porterhouse steak, cut 2 inches thick
(about 2¾ pounds)

½ cup Goode's BBQ Beef Rub (p. 298)

Jim Goode's
barbecued steak

Jim Goode is a master of barbecue in the Houston area, and this simple steak preparation takes flight because of his BBQ Beef Rub, which gives it a definite Texas flair.

– ᘓᗢᘐᗡᘓ –

1. Work the steak well all over with the rub. Wrap it tightly in plastic wrap and let rest in the refrigerator overnight.

2. Light a charcoal fire or preheat your gas grill on high. Oil the grill's cooking surface. Let the coals burn down to a medium-hot fire or adjust your gas grill burner to medium-high.

3. Grill the steak for 10 to 12 minutes per side for medium-rare meat, or more or less to your taste.

4. Let the steak rest for 5 to 10 minutes before slicing it thin. Serve immediately.

Fat Can Be a Good Thing

When purchasing beef, look for grade and color. Marbling, those little white lines of fat running through beef, is a great indicator of quality. The better the marbling, the better the steak. Very little beef is prime—most of that is reserved for restaurants. Certified Angus Beef (CAB) is not a grade but it does denote quality—only about 7 percent of beef gets this label. Most of what you see is choice, which actually is excellent for grilling because the marbling is not as intense, resulting in less fat drips on the fire and less flare-up. Select is not a choice I would use for grilling—it's too lean and almost always needs something added to it to boost its flavor. In fresh beef, look for cream-colored marbling and fat and bright red meat. Aged beef, if you are lucky enough to find it, will be marked as aged and have a duller color.

4 rib-eye steaks, cut about ¾ inch thick

2 teaspoons kosher salt

2 teaspoons lemon pepper seasoning

Juice of 1 lemon

1. Remove the steaks from the refrigerator at least 1 hour before cooking.

2. Light a charcoal fire or preheat your gas grill on high. Oil the grill's cooking surface.

3. Just before cooking, sprinkle each steak on both sides with about ½ teaspoon of salt and ½ teaspoon of lemon pepper. Drizzle the lemon juice equally over the steaks on both sides.

4. Cook the steaks no more than 4 minutes per side for medium-rare. Carolina believes that is the proper doneness for steak. Serve immediately.

Steaks on the grill.

Michael and Carolina's
steak "sal ta argentina"

An international tobacco buyer, Michael Spissu traveled the world—Europe, the west coast of Africa, China, Southeast Asia. But it was in Guatemala City where Carolina (pronounced Car-o-LEE-nah), who worked for a tobacco company, captured his heart. They soon were married, and Michael took a long-term assignment that found them living in a remote part of Argentina, near the Bolivian border, at the base of the Andes. This part of Argentina is where the last of the true gauchos still reign. And where you have gauchos, you have some of the world's finest beef.

I caught up with Michael and Carolina at their beach cottage on Bogues Banks, North Carolina. Carolina quickly laid down the law about what makes for a great steak. "You must let the steak come to room temperature. Let it sit out for at least an hour, two is better. Americans are afraid about leaving food out, but the rest of the world has known this trick forever," says Carolina. "It opens the pores in the meat, making the meat more tender, ready to be cooked. And the seasoning must be applied at the last minute, but since the meat's pores are open, the seasoning is absorbed quickly."

This is a great way to do a steak, especially a thin cut. While in New York City, I was able to buy some true Argentinean steaks. All Argentinean beef is grass fed, which increases the earthiness and depth of flavor. If it's available in your area, by all means try it. Dry aged beef also works well with this technique.

Michael pays close attention to the "sal ta Argentina."

RUSTIC HERB MARINADE

⅓ cup extra-virgin olive oil

2 tablespoons minced fresh thyme

2 tablespoons minced fresh savory

2 anchovy fillets, mashed into a paste

Four 16-ounce rib-eye steaks, cut about 1½ inches thick

Kosher salt and freshly ground black pepper

2 tablespoons minced fresh parsley

Greensboro, NC

SERVES 8

Rustic Herb-Marinated
rib-eye steaks

I grew up believing that the only true steak was a rib-eye. Even though I lean more toward strip loins and porterhouses today, there's something really special about the way a rib-eye steak absorbs an herb marinade. And don't leave out the anchovies—they add a critical flavor point to the marinade. Serve these up with the French potato salad on p. 331 for a true taste of the good life.

– ᘓᘓᘓᘓ –

1. In a small bowl, whisk together the oil, thyme, savory, and anchovies. Place the steaks in a glass baking dish large enough to hold. Pour the marinade over the steaks, turning to coat them evenly. Let stand at room temperature for 1 hour or cover with plastic wrap and refrigerate overnight.

2. Light a charcoal fire or preheat your gas grill on high. Oil the grill's cooking surface.

3. Remove the steaks from the marinade and pat dry. Sprinkle with salt and pepper, then grill 6 to 7 minutes per side for medium-rare or to your desired degree of doneness.

4. Transfer to a cutting board and let stand for 5 minutes, then slice the steak on the diagonal and divide between 8 plates. Sprinkle the parsley evenly over the top, pour over any juices that accumulated on the cutting board over the meat, and serve immediately.

Getting with the Grill Grid

Getting grill cross-hatching on a steak like the restaurants do is simple. Start with a hot grill grate and toss on the steak. Let it set for 2 to 3 minutes, then give it a quarter turn. Finish cooking on that side, then turn the steak over. You can do the same on the other side, but when was the last time you looked at the bottom of a steak on your plate? The cross-hatch is all about looks.

CHIPOTLE-GARLIC SPICE PASTE

4 cloves garlic, peeled

1 cup loosely packed fresh cilantro sprigs including stems

3 tablespoons chopped canned chipotle chiles in adobo sauce

2 tablespoons kosher salt

2 tablespoons freshly ground black pepper

2 tablespoons ground cumin

2 tablespoons ground coriander

1 tablespoon dry mustard

¼ cup fresh lime juice

¼ cup olive oil

4 bone-in rib-eye steaks, cut at least 1 inch thick

CILANTRO-LIME BUTTER

¼ cup (½ stick) unsalted butter, at room temperature

2 tablespoons finely chopped fresh cilantro

1 clove garlic, minced

2 tablespoons fresh lime juice

1 teaspoon freshly ground black pepper

Maria Martin's Cowboy Rib-Eye
steaks with cilantro-lime butter

I met Maria Martin, who works for the Northern California Innocence Project, a nonprofit organization that works to get people out of prison who were wrongly convicted, at the Mendocino, California, Crab and Wine Festival. She and I had the good fortune of dining together at the anniversary dinner for the Mendo Bistro, one of the finest restaurants in Fort Bragg, California. She started telling me about this wonderful steak recipe that her brother had given her, and I cajoled her into sending me the recipe. When I received the e-mail the following week, I rushed to the store to get the ingredients. She hadn't steered me wrong. This is an awesome way with a rib-eye steak. She tells me that the rub is also good on shrimp, but I haven't gotten my fill of this recipe with beef yet.

– ༦ঞৣ৽ –

1. Combine the spice paste ingredients in a food processor and pulse to combine, then let the machine run until you have a nice puree.

2. Remove from the processor and rub the paste thoroughly over the steaks. Set aside.

3. For the cilantro-lime butter, mash the butter in a small bowl with a fork or spoon. Add the cilantro, garlic, lime juice, and pepper, and cream together until well mixed. Cover with plastic wrap and refrigerate until the steaks are done.

4. Light a charcoal fire or preheat your gas grill on high. Oil the grill's cooking surface. Let the coals burn down to a medium-hot fire or adjust the gas grill burners to medium-high.

5. Place the steaks on the grill and cook until nicely seared, about 7 minutes. Turn and cook another 7 minutes for medium-rare or to your desired degree of doneness.

6. Remove the steaks to a platter and spoon a couple of tablespoons of the butter over each. Serve immediately.

Four 1½-inch-thick rib-eye steaks
(about 12 ounces each)

FRENCH DRESSING MARINADE

¼ cup soy sauce

¼ cup canola oil

3 tablespoons bottled French dressing
(yes, the orange kind)

1 tablespoon Worcestershire sauce

½ teaspoon garlic powder

1. Place the steaks in a baking pan large enough to hold them in a single layer. Combine the marinade ingredients in a medium bowl, then pour the marinade over the steaks. Cover with plastic wrap and leave at room temperature for 3 to 4 hours or in a refrigerator overnight.

2. Light a charcoal fire or preheat your gas grill on high. Oil the grill's cooking surface. Let the coals burn down to a low fire or adjust your gas grill burners to low.

3. Remove the steaks from the pan and discard the marinade. Pat the steaks dry. Place the steaks on the grill and cook 4 to 5 minutes per side for medium-rare. Add a minute or two to each side for medium; subtract a minute or two from each side for rare.

4. Remove the steaks to a platter. Tent with aluminum foil and let rest for 5 to 10 minutes to settle the juices before serving.

Allan Benton's
fabulous rib-eyes

Allan Benton, in my opinion and that of others, cures the finest country hams in his Madisonville, Tennessee, "ham house." He once told me, "You know, I can do more than hams. Come visit and I'll cook you one of the best steaks you ever ate." Now Allan is modest about the reputation of his hams, so his enthusiasm for his steak made me curious.

"I'm not going to tell you what's in the marinade until you taste the steak," he told me as we sat on his deck overlooking the Smoky Mountains. After one bite, I couldn't have cared less what he had marinated them in as long as he gave me the recipe. "The secret ingredient is just old plain orange French dressing—isn't that weird?"

I usually don't like steak marinades; in most cases, they cover the taste of the beef. This one does not. If anything, it doubles the impact of the beef while adding an interesting flavor note or two. Like everything Allan does, this marinade is first-rate.

Four 8- to 12-ounce filets mignons, cut 2 inches thick

½ cup soy sauce

½ cup Bristol cream sherry

1 tablespoon fresh lemon juice

1 teaspoon granulated garlic (not garlic powder)

3 tablespoons vegetable oil

Michelle Conley's
marinated filet mignon

I know this marinade sounds odd, but don't judge it until you taste it. Michelle is the sister-in-law of Allan Benton, a superb country ham maker from east Tennessee.

- ᴄᵒᵍᵒᵥ -

1. Place the filets in a large zip-top plastic bag. In a small bowl, combine the soy sauce, sherry, lemon juice, and garlic, then whisk in the oil. Pour over the meat, seal the bag, squish everything around to coat the steaks, and refrigerate overnight, turning the bag once or twice.

2. Light a charcoal fire or preheat your gas grill on high. Oil the grill's cooking surface.

3. Remove the filets from the bag and discard the marinade. Pat the filets dry, place them on the hot grill, and cook about 4 minutes per side for rare to medium-rare. Please don't cook filets past medium—they become shoe leather.

4. Remove to a platter, tent with aluminum foil, and let rest for 5 to 10 minutes so the juices can settle, then serve.

Eight 12-ounce filets mignons, cut about 1½ inches thick

Meat tenderizer of your choice

1 bottle Dale's Seasoning (Moore's is an acceptable substitute)

Lemon pepper seasoning

Honey

8 ounces soft goat cheese, more if you like, cut evenly into 8 slices

Freshly ground black pepper

1. Sprinkle the steaks on all sides with the meat tenderizer. Pour the Dale's seasoning in a large glass baking dish. Place the steaks in the dish and sprinkle both sides with the lemon pepper. Let them sit in this marinade for 3 to 4 hours, covered with plastic wrap, in the refrigerator. Turn them over every hour or so.

2. Remove the steaks from the refrigerator and drizzle on both sides lightly with honey. Return to the refrigerator for about another hour.

3. Remove the steaks from the refrigerator and let come back to room temperature, which will take about 1 hour. Drizzle with honey one more time before placing on the grill.

4. Meanwhile, light a charcoal fire or preheat your gas grill on high. Oil the grill's cooking surface.

5. Place the steaks on the grill and cook for about 8 minutes, turn, and top each with a slice of goat cheese. Cook for another 6 minutes for medium-rare to medium or to your desired degree of doneness. Transfer to a platter, season with black pepper, and serve.

Bobby and Susan Bonds'
goat cheese-topped filet mignon

Sometimes hecklers can be a good thing. One night I was teaching a grilled seafood class at the Viking Culinary Center in Greenwood, Mississippi. There were three couples in the back row that I decided might be trouble and I was right. It didn't take too long into the class or many glasses of wine before I was being challenged on just about my every word. After class I decided to find out just how good at cooking these folks really were.

Bobby and Susan Bonds of Byhalia, Mississippi, had taken the hour trek down to Greenwood with their two best-friend couples for a weekend of cooking classes and luxury at the Alluvian Hotel. I'm really glad they were vocal during my class because when I challenged them to tell me what their favorite and most outstanding grilling recipe was, I got invited to their house for a feast. What I thought was going to be a quiet evening cooking a few filets mignons turned into a great party with all of Bobby's golfing buddies, Susan's girlfriends, and even the mayor of Byhalia himself. I came away with enough recipes from everyone there to start a whole other cookbook. A couple of the recipes that you'll find in these pages are Mayor Dempsey's Chocolate Pie (p. 341) and Becky Hollingsworth's Hot Crawfish Dip (p. 17). But the main event was Bobby's marinated filets. The most important thing is to let the steaks marinate at each step along the way.

1/4 cup (1/2 stick) unsalted butter

1 cup chopped leek (white and pale green parts)

4 teaspoons minced garlic

4 cups sliced mixed fresh wild mushrooms

2/3 cup dry Marsala

2/3 cup low-sodium beef broth

Four 8-ounce beef tenderloin steaks, cut about 1 1/2 inches thick

Olive oil

Kosher salt and freshly ground black pepper

Grilled Beef Tenderloin Steaks
with marsala mushroom sauce

Washington and Oregon have become huge mushroom-growing states, with Oregon even producing some very acceptable domestic truffles. It's no wonder, then, that folks in the Northwest are crazy about their mushrooms. On a recent trip I took to Seattle, it seemed that mushroom and Marsala sauces were everywhere. So when I got back I decided to pair it with one of the most elegant meals that can come off of a grill—steaks cut from a whole beef tenderloin.

– ∾∾ –

1. Melt 2 tablespoons of the butter in a large, heavy skillet over medium-low heat. Add the leeks and garlic and cook, stirring, until almost tender, about 5 minutes. Increase the heat to medium-high, add the mushrooms, and cook, stirring a few times, until golden brown, about 6 minutes. Add the Marsala and broth, and boil until the liquid is reduced by half, about 4 minutes. Strain the sauce, reserving the mushrooms. You can prepare this up to a day in advance. Cover the strained sauce and mushrooms separately and refrigerate until ready to use.

2. Light a charcoal fire or preheat your gas grill on high. Oil the grill's cooking surface. Let the coals burn down to a medium-hot fire or adjust the gas grill burners to medium-high.

3. Brush the steaks with olive oil and sprinkle with salt and pepper. Place on the grill and cook to your desired degree of doneness, about 4 minutes per side for medium-rare. Transfer to a platter and tent with aluminum foil.

4. Bring the sauce to a simmer in a large, heavy skillet, then remove from the heat. Gradually whisk in the remaining 2 tablespoons butter. Add the reserved mushrooms and stir over low heat until heated through, about 2 minutes. Season to taste with salt and pepper.

5. Place the steaks on plates, spoon over the sauce and mushrooms, and serve immediately.

²/₃ cup bottled balsamic vinaigrette

¼ cup fig preserves or chopped dried figs

Four 6- to 8-ounce flat-iron steaks or beef chuck-eye steaks, cut 1 inch thick

One 5.2-ounce package semisoft boursin cheese with garlic and herbs

Salt and freshly ground black pepper to taste

Grilled
steaks balsamico

In Rome I had this wonderful steak that was sweet and tart and covered with an herb-infused cheese. My Italian stinks, but I got the basics on the marinade: balsamic vinegar, olive oil, and figs. I fiddled around with some combinations and discovered that using a few convenience items gave me the closest result. Do yourself a favor and give this one a try.

– ⊱⊙⊙⊙⊰ –

1. In a blender or food processor, combine the vinaigrette and fig preserves and process until smooth. Place the steaks in a large zip-top plastic bag and add the marinade. Seal the bag, squish everything around to coat the steaks, and let marinate in the refrigerator for at least 2 hours—overnight is better.

2. Light a charcoal fire or preheat your gas grill on high. Oil the grill's cooking surface.

3. Drain the steaks, discarding the marinade. Place the steaks on the grill, cook for 5 to 7 minutes, then turn and cook 5 to 7 minutes longer for medium-rare.

4. Remove the steaks to a platter and let rest for 5 minutes to settle the juices.

5. Meanwhile, in a small saucepan, heat the cheese over medium-low heat, stirring, until melted, 2 to 4 minutes. (You can also do this in a microwave.)

6. Season the steaks with salt and pepper, and serve each with a spoonful of the melted cheese.

¼ cup soy sauce

2 tablespoons ketchup

2 tablespoons vegetable oil

1 teaspoon freshly ground black pepper

1 teaspoon dried oregano

2 medium garlic cloves, finely minced

One 1½-pound flank steak

1. Combine the soy sauce, ketchup, oil, pepper, oregano, and garlic in a large zip-top plastic bag.

2. Cut shallow diagonal slashes into both sides of the steak. Place the steak in the bag along with the marinade, seal the bag, and massage the marinade so that it coats the steak. Let marinate in the refrigerator for at least 4 hours or overnight.

3. Light a charcoal fire or preheat your gas grill on high. Oil your grill's cooking surface.

4. Remove the steak from the marinade, discarding the marinade. Place on the grill and cook for 5 to 6 minutes per side for medium-rare.

5. Remove to a platter and let rest for 5 minutes to settle the juices, then slice very thinly against the grain. Serve at once or at room temperature.

Bruce Wightman's
cedar crest inn teriyaki flank steak

"Rita, I love you, but I'm not having fun anymore," remarked Bruce Wightman to his wife one evening. No, he wasn't easing her into a divorce but into a career change, a dramatic one. After years as a computer executive, Bruce needed a different direction. He and Rita sat down and wrote out all the things they loved to do and that list pointed them in the direction of being innkeepers. They spent the next eight years studying the business and visiting inns. Then seven years ago they bought the Cedar Crest Inn and moved from the urbanization of Michigan to the eclectic city of Asheville, North Carolina, at the base of the Great Smoky Mountains.

I've stayed with the Wightmans many times over the years. Bruce is commander of the kitchen and Rita runs the front. One day I asked him what he really likes to cook and eat when it's just the family. "My teriyaki flank steak, and it's one of Rita's favorites." The steak is a perfect blend of flavors, the marinade not overpowering but joining with the beef to tickle your taste buds. You will be doing yourself a favor by trying this simple, uncomplicated grilled steak. Then plan a trip to Asheville and the Cedar Crest. I know Bruce and Rita will show you a great time.

Sometimes Simple Is Best
When Bruce served me this flank steak, it was accompanied by grilled veggies that were just bursting with flavor. When I asked for the recipe, he just smiled. "It's nothing but vegetables sprayed with PAM® and cooked quickly over high heat. If you are going to cook vegetables, you should be able to taste the vegetables." So, if you, like me, have been oiling and herbing your grilled vegetables, give Bruce's method a try. You will be pleasantly surprised and delighted.

One 3½-pound flank steak

Kosher salt and freshly ground black pepper

Grilled or sautéed mushrooms

SHALLOT-BALSAMIC MARINADE

4 large shallots, chopped

⅓ cup balsamic vinegar

¼ cup sugar

¼ cup soy sauce

Larry's Simple Sunday
marinated flank steak

Back when I used to play golf, I would throw a flank steak into this marinade on a Friday night, knowing that it would be ready to get kissed by the fire when I finished my golf match Sunday evening. Larry Harrington, the head chef at Raleigh Country Club, gave me the recipe years back. He said it was something he kept around so he would have something quick and easy after a dog-tired day in his kitchen.

– ৵৵৵ৎ –

1. Pat the steak dry and cut crosswise at a 45-degree angle into four equal pieces. Season steaks with salt and pepper and transfer to a large zip-top plastic bag.

2. Combine the shallots, vinegar, sugar, and soy sauce in a medium bowl and mix well. Pour the marinade into the bag, seal, and squish everything around to coat the steak. Let marinate in the refrigerator, turning the bag over at least once, for at least 2 hours and up to 2 days.

3. Light a charcoal fire or preheat your gas grill on high. Oil the grill's cooking surface. Let the coals burn down to a medium-hot fire or adjust the gas grill burners to medium-high.

4. Remove the steaks from the bag and discard the marinade. Pat the steaks dry, place them on the grill, and cook for 7 to 9 minutes per side for medium-rare or to your desired degree of doneness.

5. Transfer to a cutting board and let rest for 10 minutes before thinly slicing at a 45-degree angle across the grain. Serve the steak with grilled or sautéed mushrooms.

Fort Walton Beach, FL

SERVES 6 TO 8

Linda's
secret ingredient flank steak

Linda Scovill of the Fort Walton Beach area in Florida shares this tasty flank steak with its secret marinade ingredient, mango chutney.

MANGO MARINADE

2/3 cup soy sauce
2/3 cup salad oil
2 tablespoons instant minced onions
6 tablespoons red wine vinegar
1/4 cup mango chutney, chopped
1/4 teaspoon garlic powder

Three 1- to 1 1/2-pound flank steaks

1. Combine the soy sauce, oil, onions, vinegar, chutney, and garlic powder in a medium bowl.

2. Place the steaks in a large glass baking dish, pour over the marinade to coat evenly, cover with plastic wrap, and let marinate in the refrigerator for 6 hours, turning the steaks occasionally.

3. Light a charcoal fire or preheat your gas grill on high. Oil the grill's cooking surface.

4. Remove the steaks from the marinade and discard the marinade. Put the steaks on the grill and cook 5 minutes per side for rare or to your desired degree of doneness.

5. Remove to a cutting board, let rest for 10 minutes, then thinly slice the steak on the diagonal, and serve.

¼ cup store-bought olive oil and vinegar vinaigrette, such as Ken's™

1 tablespoon fresh lime juice

1 teaspoon ground cumin

1 teaspoon ground chipotle chile

½ teaspoon kosher salt

1 teaspoon minced garlic

¼ teaspoon freshly ground black pepper

One 1-pound flank steak

Helena Perez's
marinated flank steak

Helena and her family first came to this country as migrant workers. She and her husband soon found jobs as farm managers in the Mississippi Delta. When they have a big gathering of friends, she always makes this recipe.

– ⲉⲟⲟⲟⲟ –

1. Combine the vinaigrette, lime juice, cumin, chipotle, salt, garlic, and black pepper in a small bowl.

2. Make shallow crisscross slashes on both sides of the steak. Place it in a large zip-top plastic bag and pour in the marinade. Seal the bag, then squish the ingredients around to coat the steak. Let marinate in the refrigerator overnight.

3. Light a charcoal fire or preheat your gas grill on high. Oil the grill's cooking surface.

4. About 30 minutes before you plan to cook, remove the steak from the refrigerator. Take the steak from the bag and discard the marinade. Place the steak on the grill and cook for 8 to 10 minutes. Turn and cook 8 minutes longer for medium-rare to medium or to your desired degree of doneness.

5. Remove to a cutting board and let rest for about 5 minutes. Slice the steak thinly across the grain and serve.

One 1½-pound flank steak

CHILI-ORANGE MARINADE

¼ cup fresh orange juice

2 tablespoons prepared chili sauce

2 tablespoons soy sauce

2 tablespoons vegetable oil

1 teaspoon honey

2 cloves garlic, minced

1½ teaspoons grated orange zest

2 tablespoons chili powder

½ teaspoon kosher salt

¼ teaspoon cayenne pepper

1 medium orange, thinly sliced

Fred's Spicy Fruit Salsa (p. 316) or the salsa of your choice

Orange wedges for garnish

Fresh cilantro sprigs for garnish

Joyce's
southwestern flank steak

Flank steak is one of those beautiful meats that just loves to absorb flavor but still keeps its beefy character. Joyce Hildebrand of Scottsdale, Arizona, passed this recipe on to me, and it's full of the taste of the Southwest. Be sure to slice the flank steak across the grain into thin slices, otherwise it will be extremely tough.

– ୧୦୭ଓ –

1. Shallowly score the steak diagonally across the grain at 1-inch intervals on both sides, then place in a large baking dish.

2. Combine the marinade ingredients in a small bowl and pour over the steak. Arrange the orange slices over the steak. Cover with plastic wrap and let marinate in the refrigerator for 8 hours, turning occasionally.

3. Light a charcoal fire or preheat your gas grill on high. Oil the grill's cooking surface. Let the coals burn down to a medium-hot fire or adjust the gas grill burners to medium-high.

4. Remove the steaks from the marinade and discard the marinade. Place the steaks on the grill and cook, with the lid down, for 7 to 8 minutes per side for medium-rare or to your desired degree of doneness.

5. Transfer to a cutting board and let rest for 5 minutes, then thinly slice the steak diagonally across the grain. Serve with salsa, garnished with orange wedges and cilantro, if desired.

One 2-pound flank steak

HONEY-SOY MARINADE

¾ cup vegetable oil

1 small onion, finely chopped

¼ cup soy sauce

¼ cup honey

2 tablespoons cider vinegar

1½ teaspoons garlic salt

1½ teaspoons ground ginger

½ teaspoon freshly ground black pepper

The Searing Truth

The food scientists tell us that searing a steak does little to hold in the juices. What it does do to perfection is caramelize the surface proteins, which adds a bagload of flavor to your steak. But remember, too much of most anything is a bad thing, so don't overcook your steaks.

Wake County, NC

SERVES 8

North Carolina Beekeepers'
honey-grilled flank steak

I have to have a very good reason to eat honey. Just by itself it has never been one of those flavors that thrills me. Each year at the North Carolina State Fair, I stop by the North Carolina Beekeepers Association booth in hopes that they will change my mind. One year they gave me a recipe for a flank steak marinade with oil, honey, vinegar, and some garlic salt. I was pretty skeptical, especially about honey and beef, but it wasn't bad. So I kept playing with the recipe until it evolved into what you see below. The honey is quite good in the marinade and brings a bright, sweet tone to the flank steak.

- ᴇᴏᴏ -

1. Shallowly score the steak diagonally across the grain at ¾-inch intervals on both sides, then place in a large zip-top plastic bag. In a medium bowl, combine the marinade ingredients and pour over the steak. Seal the bag, squish it around to coat the steak, and let marinate in the refrigerator for 8 hours, turning the bag occasionally.

2. Remove the steak from the marinade. Pour the marinade into a small saucepan and bring to a boil. Remove from the heat and set aside.

3. Light a charcoal fire or preheat your gas grill on high. Oil the grill's cooking surface. Let the coals burn down to a medium-hot fire or adjust the gas grill burners to medium-high.

4. Place the steak on the grill and cook 8 to 10 minutes on each side for medium-rare or to your desired degree of doneness, basting with reserved marinade for the last 5 minutes.

5. Remove the steak to a cutting board and let rest for 10 minutes before slicing thinly across the grain.

NORTH AFRICAN MARINADE

1 cup finely chopped onions

1½ tablespoons peeled and finely chopped fresh ginger

1 tablespoon minced garlic

½ cup olive oil

6 tablespoons fresh lemon juice

2 tablespoons soy sauce

1 tablespoon dry sherry

¼ cup chopped fresh cilantro

1 tablespoon chili powder

1 tablespoon ground cumin

2 teaspoons harissa or Asian chili-garlic sauce

2 teaspoons kosher salt

1 teaspoon freshly ground black pepper

1 teaspoon turmeric

1 teaspoon dried marjoram

¼ teaspoon saffron threads (optional)

Two 1- to 1¼-pound flank steaks

Mohammad's Flank Steak

with north african marinade

Mohammad, who lives across the hall from me in New York City, runs an import clothing business that keeps him in his homeland of Morocco about half the year. When we both are in New York, we get together to cook. I want North African foodways and he wants Southern American. The man loves grits. This marinated flank steak delivers the brightness of the Moroccan palate, with its American twist on beef.

– ୧ଠ⑥ଡ଼ –

1. In a small bowl, combine the marinade ingredients and mix well.

2. Pierce the steaks all over on both sides with a sharp fork. Place in a large zip-top plastic bag. Pour the marinade over, seal the bag, and squish everything to coat the meat well. Let marinate in the refrigerator overnight, turning the bag occasionally. Let it come to room temperature before cooking.

3. Light a charcoal fire or preheat your gas grill on high. Oil the grill's cooking surface. Let the coals burn down to a medium-hot fire or adjust the gas grill burners to medium-high.

4. Pat the steaks dry, place it on the grill, and cook 5 to 6 minutes per side for medium-rare or to your desired degree of doneness.

5. Remove to a platter, cover loosely with aluminum foil, and let rest for 5 minutes, then cut across the grain into ¼-inch-thick slices. Serve immediately.

MISO DRESSING

¼ cup mirin

¼ cup water

2 tablespoons yellow miso

2 tablespoons rice vinegar

2 teaspoons toasted sesame oil

One 1-pound flank steak

2 heads romaine lettuce, bottoms trimmed and cut in half lengthwise

2 tablespoons olive oil

Kosher salt to taste

2 scallions (white and green parts), thinly sliced

2 teaspoons sesame seeds, toasted in a dry skillet over medium heat until golden brown

Stella's
grilled romaine and flank steak with miso dressing

After sharing a wonderful dinner in Seattle with fellow foodie Stella Fong, I asked her what she grilled in her home state of Montana. "I've got a great recipe that my husband, Joe, and I will grill once a week during the summer. We also like to add grilled asparagus or broccoli or both to the mix," Stella told me. The Asian influences that abound in her dressing really lift the humble flank steak to a serious eating level. I found the dressing to be good with simply prepared fish as well. Most of the dressing ingredients you can find in any large grocery store. The yellow miso is sold in health-food stores and Japanese markets. Plate this up for friends and family and sit back for the accolades.

– ༒ଊ༒ –

1. Whisk together the dressing ingredients in a small bowl. Pour half the dressing in a large zip-top bag and add the flank steak. Seal the bag, squish everything around to coat the steak, and let marinate in the refrigerator at least 2 hours; overnight is better.

2. Light a charcoal fire or preheat your gas grill on high. Oil the grill's cooking surface. Let the coals burn down to a medium-hot fire or turn the gas grill burners to medium-high.

3. Remove the steak from the dressing and discard the dressing. Place the steak over the fire and grill for about 8 minutes total, turning once, for medium-rare. Transfer the steak to a platter and let rest for 5 minutes before slicing thinly across the grain.

4. Meanwhile, brush the romaine with the olive oil and season lightly with salt. Grill until slightly wilted and the leaves have some color, about 1 minute per side. Cut into quarters.

5. Place 2 quarters of the romaine on each plate. Divide the meat slices between the plates. Drizzle with the remaining dressing, sprinkle each plate with the scallions and sesame seeds, and serve.

ITALIAN MARINADE

6 tablespoons red wine vinegar

2 tablespoons olive oil

2 teaspoons dried oregano

1 1/2 teaspoons kosher salt

1 teaspoon freshly ground black pepper

2 cloves garlic, chopped

2 bay leaves

1/4 teaspoon whole cloves

Two 1 1/2-pound flank steaks

FILLING

3 tablespoons unsalted butter

3/4 cup chopped onions

3/4 cup shredded zucchini

2 cloves garlic, minced

3 tablespoons chopped fresh cilantro

1 teaspoon chili powder

1 teaspoon ground cumin

1/2 teaspoon kosher salt

1/2 teaspoon freshly ground black pepper

1 cup plain dry breadcrumbs

Eight 1/4-inch-thick slices Monterey Jack cheese

Monterey
stuffed flank steak

Flank steaks are routinely stuffed and rolled with spinach and cheese, then usually sliced into steaks that need to be panbroiled. This recipe takes some very Mid–California influences, couples them with an Italian-style marinade, keeps the steak whole, and allows you to grill the concoction. The result is an awesome meal in itself. Add a starch and you have a dinner party. Gary Spratt of Rutherford, California, provided the inspiration for this recipe.

– ୧୭ଈ୬ –

1. Combine the marinade ingredients in a small bowl until well mixed.

2. Place each steak in a separate large zip-top plastic bag. Divide the marinade evenly between the bags. Seal the bags and squish them around to coat the meat evenly. Let marinate in the refrigerator for 8 to 12 hours, turning the bags occasionally.

3. Melt the butter in a medium skillet over medium heat. Add the onions, zucchini, and garlic and cook, stirring, until softened, about 4 minutes. Add the cilantro, chili powder, cumin, salt, and pepper, then stir in the breadcrumbs and cook, stirring, until golden. Remove from the heat and allow to cool.

4. Remove the steaks from the marinade and pat dry. Divide the filling between the steaks, spreading it evenly over the top of each. Place 4 cheese slices on the upper third of each steak. Roll up each steak and tie with cotton string, at 1-inch intervals. You can prepare the steak up to this point 1 hour ahead.

5. Light a charcoal fire or preheat your gas grill on high. Oil the grill's cooking surface.

6. Grill the stuffed steaks 10 to 15 minutes total, turning frequently for even cooking. Remove to a platter and let stand for 5 minutes before slicing into spirals. You don't want to cut this too thin, no less than 1 inch thick—1 1/2 inches is a good size for bigger eaters.

Two 1-pound skirt or flank steaks

PEPPERED LIME-GARLIC MARINADE

⅓ cup fresh lime juice

⅓ cup olive oil

4 large cloves garlic, minced

1½ teaspoons ground cumin

2 teaspoons cracked black peppercorns

Eight 8-inch flour tortillas

1 medium onion, sliced and separated into rings

1 tablespoon unsalted butter

Kosher salt and freshly ground black pepper

Guacamole, chopped tomatoes, sour cream, and shredded lettuce for toppings

My Beef Fajitas with
peppered lime-garlic marinade

Fajitas have become standard fare in every Mexican cantina. There's good stuff and bad, but it's a dish that I always thought I could do better at home. The trouble has been finding skirt steak. When I was in New York, it was relatively easy to find, but it was harder to locate in North Carolina. Fortunately, grocery stores throughout the country have realized that they can sell skirt steak. It's a wonderful cut of beef that's extremely flavorful and, when cut thinly against the grain, it's succulent and tender.

– ᥫᩚᩚ –

1. Place the steaks between two sheets of heavy-duty plastic wrap or waxed paper and gently pound to an even thickness. Transfer to a large zip-top plastic bag.

2. Combine the marinade ingredients in a small bowl, then pour over the steaks. Seal the bag, squish everything to coat the meat well, and let marinate in the refrigerator for 8 hours, turning the bag occasionally.

3. Remove the steaks from the marinade. Pour the marinade into a small saucepan and bring to a boil. Remove from the heat and set aside.

4. Light a charcoal fire or preheat your gas grill on high. Oil the grill's cooking surface.

5. Place the steaks on the grill and cook 6 to 8 minutes per side for medium or to your desired doneness, basting often with marinade once you've seared both sides. Remove to a platter and let rest for 5 minutes.

6. Meanwhile, wrap the tortillas in aluminum foil and place on the grill until thoroughly heated, about 10 minutes.

7. When the meat comes off the grill, place the onion rings and butter on a piece of heavy-duty foil; sprinkle with salt and pepper to taste. Wrap tightly and grill until tender, about 5 minutes.

8. Thinly slice the steaks diagonally across the grain. Divide the meat and onion rings evenly among the tortillas. Top each serving with guacamole and other toppings. Roll up the tortillas and serve immediately.

Kosher salt and freshly ground black pepper

2½ to 3 pounds skirt steak

½ cup soy sauce

½ cup distilled white vinegar

½ cup vegetable oil

4 bell peppers, different colors preferred, seeded and cut into eighths

2 large onions, cut into ¼-inch-thick slices

Fajita makings: tortillas, sour cream, shredded cheese, guacamole

Ralf's Way with
fajitas

German-born Ralf Brehm does more than just smoke sausage at his Houston, Texas, home. He started cooking when he was in college and shared a house with a bunch of guys. He knew that if *he* didn't cook, he wasn't going to eat. His first house had a brick barbecue in the backyard, where he honed his skills cooking over charcoal and wood. While he loves to smoke sausages, he also enjoys whipping up fajitas.

– ᕦᕤᕦᕤ –

1. Light a charcoal fire or preheat your gas grill on high. Oil the grill's cooking surface.

2. Lightly salt and pepper the skirt steaks. Combine the soy sauce, vinegar, and oil in a small bowl.

3. When ready to cook, brush the soy sauce mixture over both sides of the skirt steak as well as the bell peppers and onions. Place the steak and vegetables on the grill. Cook the beef for about 5 minutes, basting with the soy sauce mixture. Turn and cook another 5 minutes, basting with the soy sauce mixture. Do the same with the onions and peppers, cooking until they're soft but still hold their shape and basting each time you turn them.

4. Remove the beef and vegetables to a cutting board and let the meat rest for 5 minutes before slicing thinly across the grain. Cut the peppers into thin slices. Toss the onions so that the rings separate. Arrange it all on a large platter in mounds, and serve with the tortillas and remaining makings for your diners to construct their tortillas as they wish.

SOUTH TEXAS MARINADE

1 teaspoon cumin seeds

¼ cup fresh lime juice

2 tablespoons canola oil

2 tablespoons finely chopped fresh cilantro

1 tablespoon ketchup

2 teaspoons light brown sugar

1 teaspoon minced garlic

1 teaspoon minced jalapeño (with the seeds)

½ teaspoon kosher salt

2 skirt steaks, about 1 pound each, or substitute 2 pounds flank or top round steak

FRESH TOMATO SALSA

1½ cups coarsely chopped ripe tomatoes

¼ cup chopped red onions

4 green onions (white part only), finely chopped

2 tablespoons finely chopped fresh cilantro

2 teaspoons minced jalapeño (with the seeds)

2 teaspoons fresh lime juice

Kosher salt and freshly ground black pepper

Eight 10-inch flour tortillas

South Texas
skirt steak fajitas with fresh tomato salsa

Much the way blackened anything spread the word of New Orleans cooking, fajitas have become the vehicle for Tex-Mex. This represents the best of a few different versions, but the main inspiration comes from "Cotton" Morgan in Richmond, Texas. Also try the marinade on chicken.

– ౿౭ఁౕౚ –

1. For the marinade, toast the cumin seeds in a small dry skillet over low heat until fragrant, 2 to 3 minutes, shaking the pan. Place the seeds in a small bowl and combine with the remaining marinade ingredients.

2. Trim the steaks of any excess fat, place them in a large zip-top plastic bag, and pour in the marinade. Seal the bag, squish everything around to coat the meat, and let marinate in the refrigerator for 8 to 12 hours, turning occasionally.

3. Combine the salsa ingredients in a medium bowl. For the best flavor, don't do this more than 1 hour before you plan to serve it.

4. Remove the steaks from the bag and discard the marinade. Allow the steaks to stand at room temperature for 30 minutes before grilling.

5. Light a charcoal fire or preheat your gas grill on high. Oil the grill's cooking surface.

6. Place the steaks on the grill and cook for 3 to 5 minutes total for medium-rare or to your desired degree of doneness, turning once. Remove to a cutting board and let rest for 2 to 3 minutes.

7. Meanwhile, divide the tortillas and wrap in two aluminum foil packets. Throw them on the grill until warmed through, about 2 minutes, turning once.

8. Cut the steaks into thin slices on the diagonal. Serve immediately on a platter with the warm tortillas and salsa in separate dishes and let your guests/family make their own.

One 3-pound London broil

Two 16-ounce bottles Italian dressing
(Laura uses Wishbone®)

2 tablespoons Worcestershire sauce

1 tablespoon dry sherry

1. Cut a diamond-cross pattern on the London broil on one side about ⅛ inch thick. Pour the dressing, Worcestershire, and sherry in a large zip-top plastic bag. Add the meat, seal the bag, and squish it to coat the London broil. Let marinate in the refrigerator overnight and up to 3 days, turning it occasionally.

2. Light a charcoal fire or preheat your gas grill on high. Oil the grill's cooking surface.

3. Remove the meat from the marinade, discarding the marinade. Place on the grill and cook for about 10 minutes per side for medium-rare to medium or to your desired degree of doneness.

4. Remove from the grill and let rest for 10 minutes. Slice the meat thinly across the grain and serve.

Laura's So Easy
london broil

My daughter, Laura Thompson, is now a graduate of Western Carolina University in Cullowhee, located in the mountains of southwest North Carolina. Once a year she hosts a tailgate party for all her friends. When she was a freshman, she served this London broil along with her usual fried chicken. Her friends loved the beef and now insist on having it every year. It's simple and the longer it marinates, the better it gets.

Laura enjoys her London broil and fried chicken.

MUSHROOM-BOURBON MARINADE

1/2 cup bourbon (Jack Daniel's® preferred)

1/4 cup red wine vinegar

3 cloves garlic, peeled

1/4 cup roughly chopped shallots

1 ounce dried mushrooms (don't soak them)

2 to 3 gratings of whole nutmeg or 1/8 teaspoon ground nutmeg

1/4 teaspoon kosher salt

1/8 teaspoon cayenne pepper

Freshly ground black pepper to taste

1/4 cup peanut oil

One 2-pound London broil or flank steak

Pete's
mushroom-bourbon grilled london broil

Pete Singleton has spent most of his life in the low country of South Carolina. Here's his twist on London broil. This recipe has at its core the soul of Southern beverages—bourbon.

- ᢌᢙᢍᢑᢍᢓ -

1. Several days ahead of your meal, combine the marinade ingredients, except the oil, in a food processor or blender and process, pulsing, until the shallots and mushrooms are chopped very fine. With the motor running, slowly pour in the oil and process until well incorporated. Transfer to a tightly covered jar and let the flavors develop in the refrigerator for at least 2 days.

2. The day before your meal, take out the meat and make shallow criss-cross slashes about 1 inch apart on both sides of it. Place it in a large zip-top bag, pour the marinade over it, and seal the bag. Squish everything around to coat the meat and let marinate in the refrigerator overnight.

3. Light a charcoal fire or preheat your gas grill on high. Oil the grill's cooking surface.

4. Remove the steak from the marinade, letting any excess drain back into the container. Discard the marinade. Place the steak on the grill and cook for 4 to 5 minutes. Be careful: This marinade may cause your fire to flare. Turn and cook another 4 minutes for medium-rare, 6 minutes for medium, or to your desired degree of doneness. Don't overcook this cut of meat or it will become extremely tough.

5. Remove the steak to a platter and let rest for 5 minutes. Slice thinly across the grain at a 45-degree angle and serve at once.

SESAME-GINGER MARINADE

½ cup soy sauce

4 cloves garlic, minced

2 tablespoons toasted sesame oil

2 teaspoons peeled and minced fresh ginger

3 tablespoons sugar

4 teaspoons red wine vinegar

4 teaspoons sesame seeds

2 teaspoons freshly ground black pepper

One 2-pound top round London broil, at least 1 inch thick, cut into 1-inch cubes

Ten 7-inch-long bamboo skewers, soaked in water for 1 hour

16 scallions, roots and greens trimmed so they're about 3 inches long

Sesame Beef and
scallion kebobs

Anything with sesame seeds delights me. Maybe it's that Southern thing—you know, we even make cookies out of them down here. This is a straightforward kebob—a few Asian ingredients, some scallions, and those wonderful sesame seeds combine to give a humble dish loftier ambitions.

– ᘓᗝᗝᘔ –

1. In a small bowl, whisk together the marinade ingredients.

2. Thread the steak cubes loosely onto 8 of the skewers and thread the remaining skewers crosswise through the middle of each green onion so that the scallions stand parallel to one another. Put the beef and green onion kebobs in a shallow dish just large enough to hold them. Pour the marinade over them, coating them well, and let the kebobs marinate in the refrigerator, turning them frequently, for 25 minutes and up to 2 hours.

3. Light a charcoal fire or preheat your gas grill on high. Oil the grill's cooking surface.

4. Place the kebobs and onions on the grill and cook, turning once, for about 10 minutes total.

5. Remove the beef and the scallions from the skewers and divide between 4 plates. Serve immediately.

SHERRY MARINADE

½ cup dry sherry

½ cup soy sauce

3 tablespoons sugar

3 tablespoons distilled white vinegar

½ teaspoon garlic powder

½ teaspoon kosher salt

½ teaspoon freshly ground black pepper

---

2 pounds sirloin steak, cut into 1-inch cubes

2 small red onions, cut into 8 wedges each

½ pound white mushrooms, stems removed

2 medium green bell peppers, seeded and cut into 1-inch pieces

1 small pineapple, peeled, cored, and cut into 1-inch chunks

2 cups cherry tomatoes

Fred's Backyard, NC

SERVES 6

Sherried Sirloin
vegetable kebobs

This is a pretty slick way of getting folks to eat their vegetables. The zesty marinade for the beef leaches out to the peppers, mushrooms, and onions as they cook together joined by a skewer, or literally burned on a stake. The sweet touch of pineapple and the acidity from the cherry tomatoes complete the picture for a wonderful all-in-one meal.

– ༄ఌౚ –

1. Combine the sherry, soy sauce, sugar, vinegar, garlic powder, salt, and pepper in a large zip-top plastic bag. Add the beef cubes, seal the bag, squish everything around to coat the cubes, and let marinate in the refrigerator for 2 hours or up to overnight, turning the bag occasionally.

2. Light a charcoal fire or preheat your gas grill on high. Oil the grill's cooking surface. Let the coals burn down to a medium-hot fire or adjust the gas grill burners to medium-high.

3. Meanwhile, remove the beef cubes from the marinade. Pour the marinade into a small saucepan and bring to a boil. Remove from the heat and set aside.

4. Alternately thread the beef cubes, onions, mushroom caps, bell peppers, and pineapple onto metal skewers. Place the kebobs on the grill and cook, with the lid down, for 10 to 12 minutes total or to the desired degree of doneness, turning and basting occasionally with the marinade once all the sides have been seared. Add the tomatoes to the end of the skewers during the last minute of grilling.

5. Remove from the grill and serve immediately.

1 pound top round beef steak

¼ cup distilled white vinegar

1 large onion, thinly sliced

1 medium green bell pepper, seeded and cut into rings

1 medium red bell pepper, seeded and cut into rings

⅛ teaspoon cayenne pepper

1 tablespoon minced garlic

2 tablespoons chopped fresh cilantro

½ teaspoon kosher salt

2 slices Farmer pimento sausage or Italian hot sausage

½ teaspoon extra-virgin olive oil

¼ cup tomato sauce

Norma's
bistec a la salsa

Norma Castro moved from the warm, slow pace of Puerto Rico to the wild and woolly state of Connecticut, but she brought the flavors and cooking methods of her home country with her. This recipe is somewhat like a Cuban *ropa vieja*, but the grilling of the meat adds another level of flavor. The braising intensifies everything, and the result is a dish with loads of character. Farmer's sausage is found in some specialty food stores, but any spicy sausage will do. Serve with hot rice or some smashed and sautéed plantains.

– ⁓◌◔◑⁓ –

1. Place the beef in a baking dish along with the vinegar, onion, bell peppers, cayenne, garlic, cilantro, and salt. Let marinate at room temperature for 20 minutes.

2. Meanwhile, light a charcoal fire or preheat your gas grill on high. Oil the grill's cooking surface.

3. Brush the sausage slices with the oil, place on the grill, and cook until browned, about 4 minutes per side.

4. Remove the steak and peppers from the bowl and place on the grill. Cook for about 5 minutes total, turning once.

5. Transfer the steak to a cutting board, let rest for 5 minutes, then slice thinly. Place the sliced steak, any meat juices, the peppers, and sausage in a large saucepan over medium-high heat. Pour the remainder of the ingredients from the bowl into the saucepan and add the tomato sauce. Stir to combine, then cover, bring to a boil, reduce the heat to low, and simmer gently for 30 minutes.

6. Remove from the heat, pour into a serving bowl, and serve immediately over rice.

SUGAR, SPICE, AND A TOUCH OF THE GOOD STUFF MARINADE

¼ cup Worcestershire sauce

2 teaspoons sugar

2 ounces whiskey

Pinch of ground ginger

1 clove garlic, minced

½ teaspoon freshly ground black pepper

One 6-pound eye of round or tenderloin beef roast

¼ cup kosher salt

¼ cup confectioners' sugar

Florida
sugar seared beef

I had heard about roast beef being rolled in sugar and cooked on a grill up and down the Atlantic coast of Florida. Back in the test kitchen, this is what I came up with, piecing together the various descriptions I had heard, and it's surprisingly good.

– ౭ఎఁౚ –

1. Combine the marinade ingredients in a small bowl.

2. Place the beef in a large glass baking dish, pour the marinade over it to coat completely, cover with plastic wrap, and let marinate for 2 hours in the refrigerator or at room temperature, turning it occasionally.

3. Light a charcoal fire or preheat your gas grill on high. Oil the grill's cooking surface. Let the coals burn down to a medium fire or adjust the gas grill burners to medium.

4. Meanwhile, combine the salt and confectioners' sugar on a large plate.

5. Remove the roast from the marinade and roll it in the sugar mixture, coating it evenly.

6. Grill the roast, with the lid down, turning it every 10 minutes, for 45 minutes total. The outside will be charred but the inside will remain juicy and cooked to about medium.

7. Let rest on a cutting board for 10 minutes before thinly slicing. Serve immediately.

One 3-pound tri-tip roast

Kosher salt

Freshly ground black pepper

Garlic salt

Santa Maria Salsa (recipe below)

Santa Maria-Style Beans (p. 324)

1. At least 1 hour before cooking, remove the meat from the refrigerator. Generously season all sides of the roast with salt, pepper, and garlic salt and let come to room temperature.

2. Set up the grill for indirect grilling (see pp. 6–9). Oil your grill's cooking surface.

3. Place the meat directly over the coals and sear each side of the roast, but take care not to char it. Once the meat is browned, move it away from the fire, close the grill, and cook to medium or medium-rare, whichever you prefer, about another 45 minutes.

4. Remove the roast from the grill to a cutting board and let rest, covered with aluminum foil, for 15 minutes. Slice very thin against the grain, and serve with any accumulated meat juices, the salsa, and the beans.

Skip Skipworth's
santa maria barbecue

My Santa Barbara buddy, Skip Skipworth, coached me on the proper way to make Santa Maria barbecue. A little heads up here. This is not barbecue in the sense that we know it in the South. The meat is browned over direct heat, then cooked indirectly but only to medium-rare or medium. It is always made with tri-tip, a cut of the cow, that, for many years you could only find in California. Fortunately, tri-tip, which is an upper part of the sirloin, is now available throughout much of the country. If you can't find it, though, substitute a thick piece of sirloin. Instead of a sauce, the meat is served with a salsa and is always accompanied by pinquito beans, a tossed green salad, and, most of the time, macaroni and cheese. When you put all of the elements together, you have some fine, fine eating.

santa maria salsa   MAKES 3½ CUPS

This salsa is also pretty good as a dip and very tasty mixed in with scrambled eggs.

3 medium ripe tomatoes, seeded and chopped

½ cup finely chopped celery

½ cup finely chopped scallions (white and green parts)

½ cup seeded and chopped Anaheim chiles

3 tablespoons chopped fresh cilantro

1 tablespoon white wine vinegar

1 teaspoon Worcestershire sauce

½ teaspoon garlic salt

½ teaspoon dried oregano

Hot sauce to taste

In a medium bowl, combine the tomatoes, celery, scallions, chiles, cilantro, vinegar, Worcestershire, garlic salt, and oregano, mixing well. Taste for heat and add hot sauce to taste. Cover with plastic wrap and let stand at room temperature for 1 hour to allow the flavors to marry.

Kosher salt and freshly ground black
pepper

6 pounds boneless beef ribs

⅓ cup soy sauce

⅓ cup balsamic vinegar

Juice of 1 lemon

6 cloves garlic, crushed

2 medium onions, chopped

½ cup olive oil

1. Salt and pepper the beef ribs. Set aside
on a platter at room temperature for about
30 minutes.

2. Meanwhile, light a charcoal fire or preheat your gas grill on high. Oil the grill's
cooking surface. Let the coals burn down to a
low fire or adjust the gas grill burners to low.

3. Combine the soy sauce, vinegar, lemon
juice, garlic, and onions in a medium saucepan and bring to a boil. Remove from the
heat and whisk in the oil. Set aside.

4. Place the beef ribs on the grill and cook
until tender, about a total of 30 minutes,
turning them every 5 to 10 minutes and
brushing with the sauce once both sides
are seared.

5. Serve immediately, discarding any
remaining sauce.

Brett Unzicker and Steve Hobson's
barbecue beef ribs

I think these two guys are nuts, cooking for a hundred or so Georgia
Bulldog fans before every home game, but you can tell they enjoy it. The
day I met them, Brett and Steve were cooking boneless beef ribs, a relatively new offering at the meat counter. Their marinade is first-rate and
really penetrates the meat. These ribs will not be as tender as they would
be if you braised them, so a knife and fork are in order, but for sheer beef
goodness, they're hard to beat.

These guys love grillin' and Bulldog football!

6 large cloves garlic, peeled

2 tablespoons kosher salt

2 tablespoons cracked black peppercorns

1 tablespoon paprika

1 teaspoon red pepper flakes

2 tablespoons olive oil

2 racks (7 ribs each) beef ribs, cut from a standing rib roast (2½ to 3 pounds) each, excess fat trimmed

Mock Ridgewood Barbecue Sauce (p. 307)

1. On a cutting board, coarsely chop the garlic. Sprinkle with the salt and chop through a few times. With the flat side of a chef's knife, mash the mixture to a paste. Scrape the garlic paste into a small bowl and stir in the cracked black pepper, paprika, red pepper, and oil.

2. Place the ribs in a large roasting pan. Rub all over with the garlic mixture, then cover with plastic wrap and let stand at room temperature for 1 hour.

3. Set up the grill for indirect cooking (see pp. 6–9). Oil your grill's cooking surface.

4. Place a disposable aluminum foil drip pan away from the heat. Place the ribs on the grill over the drip pan and cook for about 2 hours, with the lid down, turning them every 30 minutes, until browned and tender. If cooking with charcoal, replenish the coals as necessary.

5. When the ribs are done, brush with some of the sauce and grill a few minutes more, just until glazed.

6. Remove to a platter and let rest for 5 minutes, then cut into half racks or individual ribs and serve immediately with the remaining sauce on the side.

Barbecued Black
pepper beef ribs

I really don't know who to give credit to for this recipe. I got it from Marcie Cohen Ferris and she got it from Miriam Rubin, a Detroit native, who is a former New York chef and now lives on a farm in New Freeport, Pennsylvania, with her husband, David. Both of these two fine women write about food and are very involved in the Southern Foodways Alliance. Marcie is the author of the award-winning *Matzoh Ball Gumbo,* which is a wonderful book filled with memories and recipes of growing up Jewish in the South. I've known Miriam for 10 years. Both of these women have advanced the cause of cultural foodways through their work and are passionate about keeping memories alive.

I like this recipe because it's like eating steak au poivre on the bone. Sure, beef ribs are tougher than steak, but there is something fun about this dish.

KOREAN SOY SWEET MARINADE

½ cup Japanese or Korean soy sauce

¼ cup firmly packed light brown sugar

1 tablespoon ketchup

2 tablespoons minced garlic

1 tablespoon peeled and minced fresh ginger

2 tablespoons rice or cider vinegar

2 tablespoons toasted sesame oil

½ teaspoon red pepper flakes (optional)

Six 2- to 3-inch-thick short ribs (3 to 3½ pounds total)

3 tablespoons finely chopped scallions (white and green parts)

32nd Street

korean marinated and barbecued short ribs

The folks in the Korean market I go to on 32nd Street in Manhattan tell me there's really no need to engage in all the fancy knife work that the Korean restaurants do when making barbecued short ribs boneless. The rib, I heard over and over again, actually adds flavor, which makes perfect sense.

This marinade comes from at least seven Koreans, who stood around me at the meat counter, all wanting to explain how to prepare traditional Korean ribs. I think my efforts are pretty doggone close.

– ᴄᴏᴏᴏ –

1. In a small bowl, combine the marinade ingredients and whisk together.

2. Place the ribs in a large zip-top plastic bag and add the marinade, covering them on all sides. Seal the bag and let marinate for up to 2 hours at room temperature or overnight in the refrigerator, turning the bag occasionally.

3. Light a charcoal fire or preheat your gas grill on high. Oil the grill's cooking surface. Let the coals burn down to a medium-hot fire or adjust the gas grill burners to medium-high.

4. Remove the meat from the marinade; discard the marinade and pat the ribs dry. Place on the grill and cook until the surface is brown, about 10 minutes per side. Do not overcook. Short ribs are best cooked medium to medium-well.

5. Remove the ribs to a serving platter and serve at once, garnished with the scallions.

Kosher salt and freshly ground black pepper

3 pounds short ribs

2 onions, quartered

2 carrots, cut into 1-inch pieces

1 large head garlic, separated into cloves (12 to 15) and left unpeeled

4 bay leaves

1 teaspoon dried thyme

1 teaspoon dried oregano

3 tablespoons red wine vinegar

¼ cup balsamic vinegar

2 tablespoons dark soy sauce

1 tablespoon black peppercorns, coarsely crushed

3 cups dry red wine (preferably a cabernet sauvignon or a deep, fruity red)

1 tablespoon cornstarch or potato starch dissolved in 2 tablespoons water

1 tablespoon chopped fresh parsley

Ben and Jacques's

grilled and braised short ribs

Most recipes are really bits and pieces of somebody else's recipes, reworked to satisfy one's own needs. That being said, I admit to totally ripping off two chefs to give you this incredibly yummy dish.

Grilling the ribs instead of browning them in a pan adds immense flavor. For that technique, I thank Ben Barker of Magnolia Grill. The braising liquid is from a Jacques Pepin recipe for braised beef stew.

The braise pulls out a lot of fat, and the least messy way of getting rid of it is to refrigerate it overnight. The next day you can just pull the solidified fat off the top. I like using a slow cooker to braise these ribs, but the oven works fine. You have got to serve these with mashed potatoes.

– ✿✿✿ –

1. Light a charcoal fire or preheat your gas grill on high. Oil the grill's cooking surface.

2. Salt and pepper the ribs. When the grill is ready, cook the ribs on each side until nicely seared and brown, 3 to 5 minutes. Let cool. They will keep in the refrigerator up to 4 days or the freezer for 3 months.

3. Preheat the oven to 325°F or get out your slow cooker. Place the onions, carrots, garlic, bay leaves, herbs, vinegars, soy sauce, peppercorns, ½ teaspoon salt, and the wine in a Dutch oven or the slow cooker. Add the ribs, cover, and cook in the oven for 2 to 3 hours, or in the slow cooker on high for 5 to 6 hours or on low for 8 to 10 hours, until the meat is super tender.

4. Remove the ribs to a plate, cover, and refrigerate. Strain the braising liquid into a container, cover, and refrigerate. The next day, carefully remove all the fat from the top of the liquid and scrape any solidified fat from the ribs. Reheat the ribs in the liquid over medium heat for 10 to 15 minutes. Remove the ribs to a platter and tent with foil.

5. Bring the braising liquid to a boil and add the starch slurry, whisking until thickened. Divide the ribs between 4 dinner plates or large-rimmed soup bowls and pour some sauce over each. Garnish with the parsley and serve.

Two 5- to 6-pound beef briskets

8 cloves garlic, thinly sliced

2 tablespoons Creole seasoning

6 cups pecan wood chips

1. Using a knife, cut small slits throughout both briskets and slide a slice of garlic into each slit. Sprinkle each brisket with 1 tablespoon of the seasoning. Let sit at room temperature until your grill is ready to smoke.

2. Set up your grill for indirect cooking (see pp. 6–9). Oil your grill's cooking surface. Place the wood chips in a bucket of water to soak.

3. When the fire is ready, sprinkle a cup of the wood chips directly over the charcoal. If you're using a gas grill, place them in a smoke box or wrap in aluminum foil. Place the box or the foil packet next to one of the heat sources. Place both briskets on the grill away from the heat and cover. Smoke the briskets for 6 to 8 hours, adding more wood chips and charcoal as necessary to keep the smoke going. Try to keep the temperature around 275°F to 300°F. After 6 hours, check the meat with an instant-read thermometer; 180°F is where you want to be.

4. Remove the briskets from the smoke and wrap them each in aluminum foil. Let one brisket cool completely, then wrap it again in foil and freeze it for later use. (To reheat it, let thaw overnight in the refrigerator, then put it in a preheated 350°F oven until warm, about 30 minutes. This way you've set up your grill only once, but you get to eat twice.) Let the other brisket rest for 15 to 20 minutes, then slice thinly across the grain and serve.

Sugarland, TX

SERVES 12
TWICE

Cotton's
sugarland, texas, brisket

Laurence "Cotton" Morgan came by his nickname as a child when his hair was the shade of a cotton ball. While he earned his living rice farming, it was hunting and cooking that he really loved. Cotton taught my best friend, Hugh Lynn (see Hugh's Awesome Smoked Ribs, p. 106), a great deal about both.

Cotton's cooking reputation is legendary around the area, as he used to cook 400 pounds of brisket for the Little League opening every year and once served 1,200 folks at a brisket dinner to benefit the Katey, Texas, police department. "The secret," he told me many times, "is to cook it slow."

Smoking a brisket is a real commitment of time, so this recipe has you smoke two at once, one to eat now, one to freeze and eat later. Order your briskets from your butcher in advance. Sometimes the price clubs carry this size brisket.

"Cotton" Morgan has cooked "tons" of brisket, mainly for fundraisers around the area.

6 tablespoons liquid smoke

6 tablespoons Worcestershire sauce

One 5-pound beef brisket, trimmed of excess fat

Onion salt

Celery salt

Garlic salt

One 16-ounce bottle of your favorite barbecue sauce

The Texas Crutch

Don't let your ego stop you from using what's called on the championship barbecue circuit a "Texas Crutch," or wrapping a piece of meat in aluminum foil. It's a foolproof way of ensuring juicy results. Heck, the pros do it, why not you?

Mark's Mother's
marinated brisket cooked his way

Mark Cheeseman from Corpus Christi, Texas, just loves to cook on his grill and has an exceptional group of grilling recipes scattered throughout this book. This recipe for brisket originated with his mother, but she totally cooked it in the oven. Mark has tweaked it to suit the grill. The result is a super-moist brisket with plenty of flavor. Mark uses a gas grill, which is much easier when it comes to controlling the temperature, but a charcoal fire works as well. If you need to, finish the brisket in a 300°F oven. Saddle the beef with your favorite barbecue sauce—Virginia Pruitt's Perfect Barbecue Sauce with Fred's Tasty Mistake (p. 313) would be a good choice.

- ᘒᘓᘒᘓ -

1. Line a 9x13-inch disposable aluminum pan with enough foil to fold over the brisket. Pour 3 tablespoons each of the liquid smoke and Worcestershire in the pan. Sprinkle both sides of the brisket with onion salt, celery salt, and garlic salt to taste and place in the pan, moving it around to coat it with the smoke and Worcestershire. Pour the remaining 3 tablespoons liquid smoke and Worcestershire over the brisket. Fold the foil over the brisket and seal. Refrigerate overnight.

2. Remove the brisket from the foil.

3. Set up the grill for indirect grilling (see pp. 6–9). Oil your grill's cooking surface.

4. Grill the brisket over direct heat until seared, about 10 minutes on each side. Return to the foil, placing it fat side up, and seal. Reposition away from the fire, put the lid down, and cook at 250°F to 300°F for 5 to 6 hours, replenishing the coals as needed to maintain the temperature.

5. Open up the foil and pour the barbecue sauce over the brisket. Seal up again, close the lid, and continue to cook until an instant-read meat thermometer inserted in the thickest part registers 180°F, about another hour.

6. Transfer to a cutting board and let stand for 10 minutes, still wrapped up. Slice against the grain and serve immediately.

Goode's BBQ Beef Rub (p. 298)

One 5-pound brisket, trimmed of excess fat

8 carrots, cut in half lengthwise

Goode's Garlicky Bacon Fat BBQ Mop (p. 301)

Perfect brisket.

Jim Goode's
barbecue brisket

Jim Goode is synonymous with good barbecue in Houston, Texas. He has never been afraid of sharing his recipes with anyone who asks. This is a shortcut method that Jim devised for making brisket easier to prepare at home.

– ᴄᴏᴑᴑᴕ –

1. Set aside 2 tablespoons of the dry rub to add to the mop, then rub the remaining mixture all over the brisket. Wrap tightly in plastic wrap and refrigerate overnight.

2. Light a charcoal fire or preheat your gas grill on high. Oil the grill's cooking surface. Let the coals burn down to a medium-hot fire or adjust the gas grill burners to medium-high.

3. Preheat the oven to 350°F.

4. Remove the brisket from the plastic wrap and place it on the grill. Sear both sides for 3 to 5 minutes.

5. Transfer the brisket to a large ovenproof enameled cast-iron or other heavy pot with a tight-fitting lid. Add the carrots, pour in the mop, cover, and cook in the oven until tender when pierced with the tip of a sharp-pointed knife, about 1½ hours.

6. Transfer the brisket to a cutting board and thinly slice across the grain. Then return the brisket to the pot, trying to maintain its original shape. Cover and cook in the oven, basting occasionally, until very tender, about another hour.

7. Let rest for about 10 minutes, then serve as is or pile it on hamburger buns or white bread for sandwiches if desired.

BRISKET

One 4- to 5-pound beef brisket

1 tablespoon kosher salt

1½ teaspoons freshly ground black pepper

1 teaspoon garlic powder

Hickory or mesquite wood chips, soaked in water for at least 1 hour

JEAN'S BRISKET BARBECUE SAUCE

2 tablespoons margarine (not butter)

¼ cup finely chopped onions

1 clove garlic, pressed

1 cup ketchup

¼ cup firmly packed light brown sugar

¼ cup fresh lemon juice

1 tablespoon Worcestershire sauce

1 tablespoon prepared yellow mustard

1. Prepare your grill for indirect cooking (see pp. 6–9). Oil grill's cooking surface.

2. Sprinkle the brisket evenly and on both sides with the salt, pepper, and garlic powder. Place the brisket away from the direct heat, add the wood chips, and cover. Smoke at 250°F to 300°F for 1 to 1½ hours. If using charcoal, replenish your fire as needed.

3. Preheat the oven to 250°F. Wrap the brisket tightly in aluminum foil. Place on a baking sheet and put in the oven. Roast until the brisket is fork tender, 5 hours or longer.

4. Make the sauce. Melt the margarine in a small saucepan over medium heat. Add the onions and garlic and cook, stirring, until softened but not colored. Stir in the remaining ingredients and bring to a boil, then reduce the heat to a simmer and cook, uncovered, until thickened, 15 to 20 minutes.

5. Let the brisket sit for 10 minutes, then slice across the grain. Serve with the sauce.

Jean Lynn's
beef brisket, by way of kansas city

Jean hails from Bonner Springs, Kansas, worked in Kansas City, and lived in North Carolina, all before settling in Cordova, Tennessee, a suburb of Memphis. Her husband, Hugh, and I were golfing partners during their time in North Carolina, and we have been fast friends for more than two decades, watching our kids grow into adults and weathering life's storms. Food and the privilege of sharing a meal (and some libations) have always been a hallmark of our friendship.

This is a busy cook's brisket. You get the smoke flavor, but by using the oven you are free to do other things. In my travels through the beef brisket regions of the United States, I saw many outdoor barbecue units that were being used more like ovens than smokers.

I wouldn't dream of serving this brisket without the sauce. Jean tells me the base recipe came from a 30-year-old Real Lemon® cookbook, and she and Hugh have tweaked it into the sauce it is today. Its sweetness and acidity marry with the boldness of the beef and its gentle, smoky afternotes.

If you have never dealt with a brisket before, this recipe is a great place to start. I guarantee superb results.

Jean gets her brisket ready for smoke.

6 veal chops, about 1½ inches thick

Kosher salt and freshly ground black pepper

½ pound Italian fontina cheese, thinly sliced

12 fresh sage leaves

1 tablespoon fresh rosemary leaves, finely chopped

Olive oil

Cheese-Stuffed
veal chops with rosemary and sage

I experienced this dish in a small restaurant in San Francisco's Italian section, North Beach. It's such a simple concept but the taste will just knock your socks off. You could as easily do this recipe with a thick chicken breast or boneless pork chop. Be sure to serve it over creamy polenta.

– ꙮ –

1. With a small, sharp boning knife, on the meaty side of the veal chops, start to make a horizontal cut back toward the bone. Cut almost to the bone and open the chop up. If one side or the other is a little thicker, take a piece of waxed paper and pound the thicker side down a bit.

2. Light a charcoal fire or preheat your gas grill on high. Oil the grill's cooking surface.

3. With the veal chops opened, sprinkle each with salt and pepper. Place a slice or two of cheese on each side of the chop. Make sure, however, that no cheese extends past the meat. Lay two sage leaves on top of the cheese, and equally sprinkle the rosemary over the chops. Fold the two sides back together and skewer with toothpicks. Brush both sides of the chops with olive oil.

4. Place the chops on the grill and cook for about 4 minutes, then carefully turn and cook another 4 minutes, until the chop is lightly browned and the cheese is oozing a bit from the slit. Remove from the grill and let rest for about 5 minutes before serving.

4 veal chops, rib or loin, about 1 inch thick

Kosher salt and freshly ground black pepper

3 or 4 gratings from a whole nutmeg or ⅛ teaspoon ground nutmeg

Grated zest of 1 lemon

1 tablespoon chopped fresh Italian parsley

¼ cup all-purpose flour

1 large egg, lightly beaten

1 cup plain dry breadcrumbs

¼ cup (½ stick) unsalted butter, melted

Grilled Breaded
veal chops

This dish is a variation on a recipe from the first cookbook to chronicle Southern food, *The Virginia House-wife*. I've had a lot of fun with this recipe, and if you're looking for something totally off the wall to do on your grill, try this recipe. The breading is unexpected and becomes toastier than when you pan-fry. It also works with boneless pork chops.

– ⌇⊙⊙⌇ –

1. Season the chops on both sides with the salt, pepper, nutmeg, lemon zest, and parsley. Gently rub the seasonings into the meat.

2. Using 3 pie plates, place the flour in one, the egg in another, and the breadcrumbs in the remaining one. Coat each chop on both sides with the flour, dip into the egg, then toss in the breadcrumbs. Place the chops on a wire rack and let set for 30 minutes (this wait will help the coating to adhere).

3. Meanwhile, light a charcoal fire or preheat your gas grill on high. Oil the grill's cooking surface. Let the coals burn down to a medium-hot fire or adjust the gas grill burners to medium-high.

4. Lightly drizzle the chops with about half the melted butter on one side. Place on the grill, buttered side down, and cook until the bread-crumbs are toasted golden brown, about 3 minutes. Then drizzle the other side with the remaining butter, turn the chops, and cook for another 3 to 4 minutes for medium-rare. If you prefer your meat a little more done, then move the chops to the edges of the grill or a cooler spot on the grill and continue cooking for another 1 or 2 minutes. Remove to a platter and serve immediately.

3 tablespoons olive oil

1 ½ cups chopped carrots

1 ½ cups chopped celery

1 ½ cups chopped onions

3 tablespoons tomato paste

3 tablespoons black peppercorns

1 ½ tablespoons chopped fresh rosemary or 1 ½ teaspoons dried

1 tablespoon grated lemon zest

2 bay leaves

One 750-ml bottle merlot or other dry red wine

1 ½ cups low-sodium beef broth

1 ½ cups low-sodium chicken broth

Kosher salt and freshly ground black pepper

Four 10-ounce veal chops, cut about 1 ½ inches thick

Grilled
veal chops with merlot sauce

When you open a bottle of merlot instead of a bottle of Chianti by mistake, you wind up with a merlot sauce, no matter where you were initially headed. But then I've always contended that some of the best recipes come about by pure accident. This sauce marries well with grilled veal. Rich to begin with, veal becomes earthier and a little more rustic when treated to a session on the grill. The merlot sauce is also pretty snazzy with a grilled steak and perfect atop a simply seasoned grilled salmon.

– ෙൟൟ –

1. Heat the oil in a large, heavy skillet over high heat. Add the carrots, celery, and onions, and cook, stirring, until browned, about 10 minutes. Stir in the tomato paste. Add the peppercorns, rosemary, lemon zest, and bay leaves, and stir for 1 minute. Pour in the wine, bring to a boil, then continue to boil until the mixture is thick, about 15 minutes. Pour in both broths and bring back to a boil. Reduce the heat to a simmer and cook until the liquid is reduced to about ¾ cup and thickly coats the back of a spoon, about 20 minutes. Strain the sauce and season with salt and pepper if necessary. This can be made up to a day ahead. Cover with plastic wrap and refrigerate until ready to use; bring to a simmer before using.

2. Light a charcoal fire or preheat your gas grill on high. Oil the grill's cooking surface. Let the coals burn down to a medium-hot fire or adjust the gas grill burners to medium-high.

3. Season the veal with salt and pepper. Place on the grill and cook for about 5 minutes per side for medium-rare or to your desired degree of doneness.

4. Remove the chops to individual plates and spoon a little sauce over each. Pass the remaining sauce at the table. Serve immediately.

4 everything on the hog is good:

pork

Pork is tailor-made for the grill.

Whether it's pork chops or a tenderloin, rubbed and sauced ribs, sausages, or the pulled pork barbecue from the shoulder, you can't go wrong with pork. Even if you screw it up somehow, a good sauce will cover up a multitude of sins. Pork is a succulent, neutral canvas for us to paint with any number of seasonings.

For most of the country, **pork is the gold standard of barbecue**. Pulled and chopped pork and pork ribs, whether wet or dry, spare or baby back, remain our favorite low and slow 'que. Pork tenderloin has become the fast and friendly cut of harried folks who still want a taste of the flame.

The biggest key to great pork is not to overcook it. Yes, some things you want cooked until it's falling-off-the bone tender, but that comes from low heat over a long period of time. Too high a heat can toughen pork quickly, especially these days with pork being raised to be so lean. Use medium to medium-high heat with pork cooked over direct heat. But even more important, know that trichinosis has been all but gone since the late 1960s and that there's no need to cook pork much over an internal temperature of 150°F. And at 150°F you're guaranteed pork that's moist and juicy.

In your butcher's case, you will find many choices. From the **loin**, you will find the leanest, most tender, and, of course, most expensive cuts of pig. Rib chops (my personal favorite), loin or T-bone chops, and the tenderloin all come from this area, as well as the ribs referred to as baby backs. The side of the animal gives us the belly, which becomes bacon (what Southerners call side meat), but if you can find a fresh one, it smokes up on the grill to a surreal treat. Also in this area are the spare ribs. If the **brisket or flank** has been removed from the ribs, then it is called a "St. Louis cut." If I am buying spareribs and want the extra meat, I will cut it off to create a St. Louis rib because it makes the ribs cook more evenly but that piece of meat is going to be seasoned and put on the grill as well. Spareribs are a little longer than baby backs, with less meat, but some consider them much more flavorful. Baby back ribs have a large meat to bone ratio—they are considered the "prime rib" to many, but they are usually costly. I buy what's on sale, both spareribs and baby backs.

From the hindquarter comes the **ham**, and I hope that you will give this cut a turn on the grill—it's fabulous. The **shoulder**, whole or half, and pork butt come from the front quarter of a hog. This is excellent barbecue material, the higher fat content perfect for the long, low heat of smoking.

Brines and Injection Solutions

With pork as lean as it has become, brining chops and **tenderloins** and injecting larger pieces of pork that are going to be smoked have become popular. Sometimes I brine, sometimes not, depending on how much time I've got. What's most important is not to overcook the pork. Injection solutions act a bit like brines but get the liquid deeper into the meat and usually have a flavor added. Particularly for beginners at smoking, injecting a solution is a good idea because it increases the chances that you'll end up with a succulent final result.

MANGO SALSA

2 ripe mangos, cut in half lengthwise, peeled, flesh cut off the pit, and cut into ½-inch dice

¼ cup seeded red bell pepper cut into a tiny dice

2 tablespoons fresh lime juice

3 tablespoons chopped fresh cilantro

1 Serrano chile, seeded and minced

½ teaspoon salt

CUMIN CRUST

1 tablespoon cumin seeds

1 tablespoon coriander seeds

1 teaspoon dried herbes de Provence

1 teaspoon kosher salt

1 teaspoon crushed black peppercorns

2 pork tenderloins (2½ to 3 pounds total), silverskin removed

2 tablespoons olive oil

Certify They're Hot

Carla reminds us that Serrano chiles are usually hotter than jalapeños but you never really know until you taste them. Taste a small section of the chile to check for heat and add it to the salsa accordingly. If the chile is a dud, you can add some red pepper flakes or chopped pickled jalapeños to give it more kick.

Carla's Pork Tenderloin with

cumin crust and mango salsa

When I asked fellow food writer, cookbook author, and cooking school teacher Carla Snyder to share a recipe, I knew it would be packed with flavor and she didn't let me down. "Summers in northeast Ohio can be hot, so we take advantage of the opportunity to cook outside whenever possible. We've learned to keep the kitchen cool by doing the whole dinner on the grill by adding a few farmstand vegetables alongside this pork tenderloin," says Carla. "Eating on the patio and watching another summer evening slide by reminds me that living on the north coast isn't so bad at all." We all could take a lesson from Carla.

– ⌒⌒ –

1. In a medium bowl, combine the salsa ingredients and toss to mix well. Leave at room temperature for at least 30 minutes. You can make this up to 3 hours ahead, cover, and keep refrigerated; let come to room temperature before serving.

2. In a small dry skillet over medium heat, toast the cumin and coriander seeds until fragrant. Transfer to a mortar or spice mill and finely grind. Mix with the herbes de Provence, salt, and pepper.

3. Rub the pork tenderloins with 2 tablespoons of the spice mixture and let sit at room temperature for 1 hour. The remaining spice can be stored, tightly covered, up to a month. (It's also great on chicken or beef.)

4. Light a charcoal fire or preheat your gas grill on high. Oil the grill's cooking surface.

5. Drizzle the tenderloins with the oil and place on the grill. Cook for about 10 minutes, then turn and cook for another 7 minutes. They're done when an instant-read meat thermometer inserted into the thickest part registers 150°F.

6. Remove the tenderloins to a platter, loosely cover with aluminum foil, and let sit for about 5 minutes, then cut on the diagonal into ¾-inch-thick slices. Serve 3 slices per serving. Top with mango salsa and serve immediately.

One ¾-pound pork tenderloin

¼ cup mild-flavored (light) molasses

3 tablespoons cider vinegar

2 tablespoons Dijon mustard

2 tablespoons coarse-grain mustard

Kosher salt and freshly ground black pepper

Grilled Pork Tenderloin with

molasses and mustard

When pork tenderloins go on sale, I load up. It's a super cut of meat that cooks quickly and takes on flavorings with ease. As far as I'm concerned, pork, molasses, and mustard is one of the most holy of culinary trinities, especially when you add the char of an outdoor fire. This recipe is a no-brainer for weekday cooking but an equally good choice when company comes.

– ᴇᏕᏬᏬ –

1. With a sharp paring knife, remove the silverskin from the tenderloin.

2. Whisk together the molasses, 2 tablespoons of the vinegar, and both mustards in a small bowl. Place the pork in a zip-top plastic bag, pour the marinade over it, seal the bag, squish everything to coat the pork well, and refrigerate for 4 hours.

3. Light a charcoal fire or preheat your gas grill on high. Oil the grill's cooking surface. Let the coals burn down to a medium fire or adjust the gas grill burners to medium.

4. Remove the pork from the marinade. Pour the marinade into a small, heavy saucepan and set aside.

5. Sprinkle the pork with salt and pepper, then place on the grill and cook until an instant-read thermometer inserted into the center registers 150°F, turning occasionally with tongs, about 20 minutes total. Transfer the pork to a platter; let rest for 5 minutes.

6. Add the remaining 1 tablespoon vinegar to the saucepan and place over medium heat. Bring to a boil and cook until thickened to a saucy consistency, about 1 minute.

7. Cut the pork crosswise on a slight diagonal into ½-inch-thick slices. Arrange the slices on a platter, drizzle the sauce over, and serve.

ZYDEQUE
CAJUN BARBEQUE
It's Music To Your Mouth!

One 1½ -pound pork tenderloin

½ cup blood orange olive oil or orange-flavored olive oil (check specialty food stores for these)

¼ cup peach champagne vinegar

2 cloves garlic, finely minced

1. Using a sharp paring knife, remove the silverskin from the tenderloin. Place in a large zip-top plastic bag.

2. In a small bowl, whisk together the olive oil, vinegar, and garlic, then pour it over the pork, seal the bag, and squish everything to coat the pork. Let marinate overnight in the refrigerator, turning the bag a few times.

3. Light a charcoal fire or preheat your gas grill on high. Oil the grill's cooking surface. Let the coals burn down to a medium-hot fire or adjust the gas grill burners to medium-high.

4. Remove the tenderloin from the marinade and discard the marinade. Place it on the grill and cook, turning it every 5 minutes, until an instant-read thermometer inserted into the thickest part registers about 150°F, a total of 15 to 20 minutes.

5. Remove the pork to a platter and let rest, tented with aluminum foil, for 5 minutes before slicing.

Milan, TN

SERVES 4

Peggy Quartermont's
really interesting pork tenderloin

When I met Peggy Quartermont at her olive oil business, Sepay Groves, in the valley northeast of San Francisco, I immediately picked up on an accent that had nothing to do with California. "Oh, I grew up in Milan, Tennessee," she said. "Do you know Milan? It's north of Memphis. My mom and grandmother came out here when I was 12." I knew she couldn't have lived that close to the barbecue mecca of Memphis without knowing a thing or two about cooking outside. Isn't it genetic in that part of Tennessee? She didn't let me down with this wonderful pork dish. She also suggested using lemon oil and raspberry vinegar for chicken and garlic oil and herb vinegar for beef, and both are excellent, I can testify. If you can't find peach champagne vinegar, give Peggy a call and she'll gladly ship you some.

Two 12- to 16-ounce pork tenderloins

1 canned chipotle chile in adobo sauce

¼ cup fresh orange juice

2 tablespoons sugar

1 tablespoon vegetable oil, plus more for rubbing the pork

1 teaspoon ground cinnamon

1 teaspoon ground cumin

1 teaspoon unsweetened cocoa powder

1 teaspoon kosher salt

¼ teaspoon freshly ground black pepper

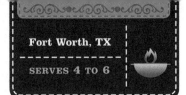

Chipotle Charred
pork tenders

To tailgate or not to tailgate, is that even a question? If you are a football fanatic, nothing is as sacred as the tailgate, and thanks to all the new portable grills available, grilling on the go is easy.

Pork tenderloins are very tailgate friendly. First, they're an elegant parking lot offering. Second, they cook in short-order time. Third, pork tenderloins don't have to be served up hot to taste great. The marinade for this can be made a day or two ahead and the tenderloins cooked the night before the game to be served up cold, leaving Saturday morning free for more relaxing pursuits. Otherwise, you can grill it up in 18 to 20 minutes at the stadium.

– ᔕᕆᕐᕋ –

1. Using a sharp paring knife, trim the silverskin membranes from each tenderloin. Place the pork in a large zip-top plastic bag.

2. Place the remaining ingredients in a food processor and pulse to combine, then run the machine to puree. Pour the marinade over the pork, turn the pork to coat it evenly, and let stand at room temperature for 45 minutes. You can also stick the pork in the refrigerator for up to 4 hours (if you do this, turn the pork after 2 hours).

3. Light a charcoal fire or preheat your gas grill on high. Oil the grill's cooking surface. Let the coals burn down to a medium-hot fire or adjust the gas grill burners to medium-high.

4. Remove the pork from the marinade and pat dry with paper towels. Drizzle each tenderloin with a little oil and rub over the surface. Place on the grill and cook for 18 to 20 minutes, turning every 5 minutes, until an instant-read thermometer inserted into the thickest part registers 150°F.

5. Remove to a platter and let rest 5 to 10 minutes before slicing crosswise on an angle into ¼-inch-thick slices.

Get Your Pork Straight Up

An almost surreal result of raising pork to be so lean is that a number of pork producers actually inject their pork cuts with a sodium-rich solution to help retain its juiciness when it cooks. Please avoid these products and seek out some of the new heirloom pork products in the market. I would also caution you about all the premarinated pork on the market today. These products are very salty and include a lot of chemicals I think you'd rather not be eating. If you are in a hurry, just use simple seasonings on a fresh piece of pork. I know you will be happier with the result.

Three 1-pound pork tenderloins

ROBIN'S PIGSKIN RUB

2 tablespoons paprika

2 teaspoons kosher salt

2 teaspoons light brown sugar

2 teaspoons granulated sugar

2 teaspoons chili powder

2 teaspoons ground cumin

2 teaspoons freshly ground black pepper

ROBIN'S PIGSKIN SAUCE

½ cup smoky tomato-based barbecue sauce of your choice

½ cup ranch salad dressing

½ cup hot pepper jelly, at room temperature, stirred to make spreadable

18 mini sandwich buns, sliced horizontally

½ cup fresh cilantro leaves

Robin Kline's
pigskin tailgating sandwiches

Robin Kline and her husband, Bill Summers, have become good friends through IACP (International Association of Cooking Professionals), Southern Foodways, and the Greenbrier Food Writers Symposium. Robin owns her own culinary business called Savor Food Communications, which does public relations for food companies and associations, marketing, and recipe development and feature food writing. When I talked to Robin about what she grilled, I knew that the answer would be pork, being that she lives in Iowa, one of our great pork-producing states. Robin tells me that these sandwiches are great any time of the year, but they are a special treat when tailgating before your favorite team's gridiron performance. Enjoy the tenderloin warm or cold.

– ᥰᥱᥰᥱᥰ –

1. Pat the tenderloins dry with paper towels. In a small bowl, combine the rub ingredients. Use about 2 tablespoons of this mixture on each tenderloin, rubbing it in all over.

2. In a small saucepan, stir together the barbecue sauce and salad dressing. Heat gently over low heat, stirring, until hot. Keep warm. (Put in a Thermos® bottle if you're tailgating.)

3. Light a charcoal fire or preheat your gas grill on high. Oil the grill's cooking surface. Let the coals burn down to a medium-hot fire or adjust the gas grill burners to medium-high.

4. Place the pork on the grill and cook, turning occasionally to brown evenly until an instant-read meat thermometer inserted into the thickest part registers 150°F, 15 to 20 minutes total. A few minutes before removing from the grill, glaze each tenderloin well by brushing on the jelly with a basting brush.

5. Transfer the pork to a cutting board and let stand 5 to 10 minutes before slicing thinly for sandwiches. Place 3 to 4 slices of pork on each sandwich bun, top with some cilantro leaves, and garnish with a dollop of sauce. Offer extra sauce on the side.

VANILLA RUB

1 teaspoon paprika

1 teaspoon vanilla sugar

1 teaspoon ground vanilla bean powder

1 teaspoon kosher salt

½ teaspoon freshly ground black pepper

½ teaspoon ground allspice

½ teaspoon ground cinnamon

2 pork tenderloins (2½ to 3 pounds total), silverskin removed

Olive oil

Vanilla Rubbed
pork tenderloin

Ground vanilla bean powder is a fantastic base in a rub used for pork, seafood, and even poultry. It can be hard to find but usually a gourmet food store or specialty baking shop will have it. Alternatively, you can grind any old vanilla beans in a spice grinder or food processor. If you're a vanilla freak, I think you'll find this recipe extremely interesting.

– ⌇⌇⌇ –

1. Combine the rub ingredients in a small bowl.

2. Remove the tenderloins from the refrigerator at least 30 minutes before grilling. Brush them with oil, then spread the rub over them, massaging it into the meat.

3. Light a charcoal fire or preheat your gas grill on high. Oil the grill's cooking surface. Let the coals burn down to a medium fire or adjust the gas grill burners to medium.

4. Place the pork on the grill and cook until an instant-read meat thermometer inserted into the thickest part registers 150°F, a total of about 20 minutes, turning the pork every 5 minutes.

5. Remove from the grill to a cutting board and let rest for 5 minutes. Slice on the diagonal about ¼ to ½ inch thick. Serve immediately.

2 pork tenderloins (about 1½ pounds total)

2 cups water

1½ tablespoons salt, plus more for seasoning

1½ tablespoons maple syrup

1 tablespoon chili powder

Robyn's Grilled Pork Tenderloin

cutlets with chili-maple glaze

Robyn McCall, who lives near the Ohio-Kentucky border, passed on this recipe to me. Slicing the tenderloins and pounding them into cutlets is a slightly different take. Doing it this way, they cook in literally a few minutes, and the sweet, hot glaze really makes them interesting. A light brine will ensure that they stay extremely moist. Serve them any time, but I like them for breakfast or brunch with a couple of sunny-side-up eggs on top and a mound of cheese grits to the side.

– ৶৶৶ –

1. In a bowl large enough to hold the pork covered with the water, stir together the salt and water until the salt is dissolved. Add the pork, making sure it is completely covered by the brine. Cover with plastic wrap and marinate in the refrigerator overnight.

2. Light a charcoal fire or preheat your gas grill on high. Oil the grill's cooking surface.

3. Meanwhile, in a small bowl, stir together the syrup and chili powder.

4. Take the tenderloins out of the refrigerator and discard the brine. Cut the pork on the diagonal into ¾-inch-thick slices. In a single layer, place the pork between sheets of plastic wrap or waxed paper and flatten with a rolling pin to make ¼-inch-thick cutlets. Pat the pork dry with paper towels and season with salt.

5. Place the cutlets on the grill and cook 2 to 3 minutes per side. Brush both sides with the glaze and grill 15 seconds more per side. Remove to a platter and serve immediately.

2 tablespoons chopped fresh cilantro

2 teaspoons ground cumin

1 teaspoon freshly ground black pepper

1 teaspoon garlic powder

2 pork tenderloins (2 to 2½ pounds), trimmed of silverskin

Black Bean Salsa (recipe at right)

1. Combine the cilantro, cumin, pepper, and garlic powder in a small bowl. Rub this mixture into the pork tenderloins and let sit at room temperature for 15 minutes. To keep the pork from sticking to the grill, spray the pork lightly with cooking spray.

2. Light a charcoal fire or preheat your gas grill on high. Oil the grill's cooking surface.

3. Place the pork tenderloins on the grill and cook for about 15 minutes per side, until an instant-read meat thermometer inserted into the thickest part registers 150°F.

4. Transfer the pork to a cutting board and let stand for 5 minutes, then cut into ½-inch-thick slices. Serve with the salsa spooned over the slices.

Nina's
southwestern pork tenderloin

Nina Swan-Kolher is from Robins, Iowa. She's a public relations person who loves food and is happiest when she is cooking. Of course, being from Iowa, pork lands on her table a bunch, and this is her favorite grilling recipe.

black bean salsa MAKES ABOUT 3 CUPS

This black bean salsa is made different by adding cucumber, which provides a cool freshness. Also try it with grilled chicken or mahimahi.

One 15-ounce can black beans, drained and rinsed

1 cup peeled, seeded, and chopped cucumber

1 medium ripe tomato, seeded and diced

½ cup sliced green onions (white and green parts)

¼ cup fresh lime juice

1 tablespoon chopped fresh cilantro

1 tablespoon olive oil

½ teaspoon kosher salt

½ teaspoon ground cumin

⅛ teaspoon cayenne pepper

Combine all the ingredients in a medium bowl. Cover with plastic wrap and refrigerate for several hours to blend the flavors.

MUSTARD-MINT SAUCE

¼ cup horseradish mustard

1 tablespoon mayonnaise

2 tablespoons finely chopped onions

2 tablespoons fresh lemon juice

2 tablespoons soy sauce

1 tablespoon dried or chopped fresh mint

1 tablespoon dry mustard

1 teaspoon freshly ground black pepper

2 cloves garlic (optional), finely chopped

Two ¾-pound pork tenderloins, trimmed of silverskin

Vincent and Jeanne's
pork tenderloin with mustard-mint sauce

My sister was ecstatic. "I've been working with this Italian couple in Woodbury, Connecticut, and they are great foodies!" she exclaimed. Educators in the local school system (my sister works with teachers on new teaching methods), Vincent and Jeanne Tomkalski had made quite the impression on my culinarily challenged sister. "Find out what they grill," I asked. "Get them to send me their favorite grilling recipe." This combination of mint, mustard, and horseradish-infused pork is heavenly and well worth a spot on your dinner table. You can also use the sauce as a baste or table sauce instead of a marinade, and it's very tasty served with boiled potatoes.

– ✐✐✐ –

1. Combine the sauce ingredients in a small bowl and mix well. This can be made up to a day ahead. Cover and refrigerate until needed.

2. Place the pork tenderloins on a large sheet of plastic wrap. Add the sauce, coating the tenderloins well. Close the wrap tightly around them and place in the refrigerator for at least 2 hours or, better, overnight. Using a zip-top plastic bag works OK, but the flavor seems less intense.

3. Light a charcoal fire or preheat your gas grill on high. Oil the grill's cooking surface. Let the coals burn down to a medium-hot fire or adjust the gas grill burners to medium-high.

4. Remove the tenderloins from the plastic, place on the grill, and cook 15 to 20 minutes, depending on the thickness of the tenderloins, turning as needed to cook evenly and keep the sauce from burning.

5. Remove to a cutting board and let rest 5 minutes before slicing.

GARLIC-LIME MARINADE

6 large cloves garlic, chopped

½ cup olive oil

⅓ cup fresh lime juice

2 tablespoons soy sauce

2 tablespoons peeled and grated fresh ginger

2 teaspoons Dijon mustard

Cayenne pepper to taste

Kosher salt and freshly ground black pepper

4 pork tenderloins (about ¾ pound each), silverskin removed

Jalapeño-Onion Marmalade (p. 316)

Grilled
garlic-lime pork tenderloin

Pork tenderloins are so quick cooking that they're a great choice for weekday meals. Mix up this marinade the night before and let its flavors infuse the pork while you're out doing your day's work. Light a grill and with 20 minutes of cooking time, you've put an above-average plate on your table.

- ᘓᓭᘙᕀ -

1. Combine the marinade ingredients in a blender or food processor and process until smooth.

2. Place the tenderloins in a large zip-top plastic bag and pour the marinade over them. Seal the bag and squish it around so that everything gets coated. Let marinate in the refrigerator, turning it a few times, overnight and up to 2 days.

3. Light a charcoal fire or preheat your gas grill on high. Oil the grill's cooking surface. Let the coals burn down to a medium fire or adjust the gas grill burners to medium.

4. Take the pork out of the refrigerator about 30 minutes before grilling. Remove it from the marinade, letting the excess drip off. Discard the marinade.

5. Place the pork on the grill and cook until an instant-read meat thermometer inserted into the thickest part registers 150°F, 15 to 20 minutes total, turning them every 5 minutes.

6. Transfer to a cutting board and let stand for 5 minutes before slicing and serving with the onion marmalade.

One 1-pound pork tenderloin, trimmed of silverskin

PINEAPPLE-SOY MARINADE

½ cup pineapple juice

¼ cup reduced-sodium soy sauce

2 tablespoons frozen orange juice concentrate

2 tablespoons firmly packed light brown sugar

½ teaspoon peeled and grated fresh ginger

PINEAPPLE GLAZE

⅓ cup pineapple or apricot preserves

2 teaspoons reduced-sodium soy sauce

¼ teaspoon peeled and grated fresh ginger

mango and papaya salsa
MAKES ABOUT 2 CUPS

1 papaya, peeled, seeded, and diced

1 mango, peeled and flesh cut off the seed into dice

¼ cup seeded and diced red bell pepper

2 tablespoons diced red onion

1 jalapeño, seeded and finely chopped

2 tablespoons fresh lime juice

2 tablespoons rum

1 teaspoon sugar

Sea salt and freshly ground black pepper to taste

1 tablespoon chopped fresh cilantro

In medium bowl, stir together the ingredients. Refrigerate until ready to serve.

Hayley's Hawaiian
tropical pork tenderloin

Hayley Matson-Mathes is a displaced mainlander living the good life in Honolulu. With husband, Mike, a lieutenant colonel in the U.S. Army, they are dedicated foodies and travelers. Hayley has her own culinary business and is involved in the Slow Food movement. There's nothing slow about this pork tenderloin, though. It's actually a quick trip to the tropics. Hayley warns not to overmarinate the pork. While the pineapple juice enhances the pork, too long of a bath in it causes the pork's texture to become mushy. She serves this with a wonderful salsa that's also great with grilled fish.

1. Place the pork in a zip-top plastic bag, then add the marinade ingredients. Seal the bag and squish everything around until well combined and coated. Let marinate in the refrigerator for at least 4 hours but no more than 6 hours, turning the bag a few times.

2. In small bowl, mix together the glaze ingredients, then set aside.

3. Remove the pork from the marinade and discard the marinade.

4. Light a charcoal fire or preheat your gas grill on high. Oil the grill's cooking surface. Let the coals burn down to a medium-hot fire or adjust the gas grill burners to medium-high.

5. Place the pork on the grill and cook for 7 minutes per side. Brush with a small amount of the glaze and grill for another 2 to 4 minutes per side, until an instant-read thermometer inserted into the thickest part registers 150°F.

6. Transfer to a platter, cover with aluminum foil, and let rest for 5 to 10 minutes, then slice and serve with the remaining glaze on the side.

One 2-pound boneless pork top loin roast

1 teaspoon coarse salt

1 teaspoon freshly ground black pepper

¾ cup fresh lime juice

¾ cup orange juice

10 cloves garlic, minced

LIME-JALAPEÑO SALSA

2 cloves garlic, coarsely chopped

½ small white onion, coarsely chopped

6 large jalapeños, seeded and coarsely chopped

1 teaspoon kosher salt

1 tablespoon fresh lime juice

3 cups mild-flavored wood chips like cherry or apple, soaked for 1 hour in water

Citrus-Garlic Marinated Pork Top Round

roast with lime-jalapeño salsa

When we think of pork, many of us only look to ribs, chops, shoulders, or tenderloins for the grill. Top round roast is another excellent cut and usually more economically priced. The method here is similar to the way Colombians prepare their top round beef for grilling. It allows a great deal of smoke flavor to invade the pork without requiring a long cooking time. The seasoning is part Cuban, with the salsa being all Southwest.

- ᘓᘓᘓ -

1. Trim any fat from the meat, then carefully start slicing the pork horizontally in the center to butterfly the roast, taking care not to cut all the way through. It should open like a book.

2. Season the meat all over with the salt and pepper. Place it in a large zip-top plastic bag. Add the citrus juices and garlic, then seal the bag and squish it to coat the meat well. Let marinate in the refrigerator for 2 to 3 hours, turning the bag a few times.

3. For the salsa, use a mini food processor to combine the garlic, onion, jalapeños, and salt, and process just until combined. Add the lime juice; process just until the mixture forms a coarse-textured sauce. This can be prepared up to 3 days ahead and kept, covered, in the refrigerator.

4. Set up the grill for indirect grilling (see pp. 6–9). Oil your grill's cooking surface. When ready to cook, add the wood chips, cover, and allow the smoke to build in the grill.

5. Remove the pork from the marinade, discarding the marinade. Place the meat on the grill away from the heat with a drip pan underneath it. Cover and grill until an instant-read meat thermometer inserted into the thickest part registers 150°F, about 25 minutes.

6. Remove the meat to a platter and let rest, tented with aluminum foil, for 5 minutes, then slice and serve with the salsa.

¼ cup allspice berries

One 1½-inch piece of cinnamon stick

1 teaspoon freshly grated nutmeg

6 scallions (white and green parts), sliced

1 Scotch Bonnet or habanero chile or to taste, stemmed and seeded if you want to tame the flame

Kosher salt and freshly ground black pepper

1 tablespoon dark Jamaica rum

One 4–pound boneless pork loin

1. Preheat the oven to 350°F. Roast the allspice berries on a baking sheet for 10 minutes. Pulverize them in a spice mill with the cinnamon and nutmeg. Place the spice mixture in a mortar with the scallions, chile, and salt and pepper to taste and grind into a paste. Stir in the rum. Rub the mixture all over the pork loin. Cover with plastic wrap and let marinate for at least 1 hour at room temperature. (If you put this in the refrigerator, you're going to mute the flavor of the paste.)

2. Set up the grill for indirect grilling (see pp. 6–9). Oil your grill's cooking surface.

3. Set the pork on the grill away from the heat, cover, and cook until an instant-read meat thermometer inserted into the thickest part reads 150°F, about 1 hour, replenishing your fire if necessary.

4. Transfer to a warm platter, let rest for 10 minutes, then slice and serve.

Jessica's
jerked pork

Brooklyn resident, food historian, and linguist Jessica B. Harris has always fascinated me with her knowledge of how African and Caribbean foodways have intertwined themselves in American cooking. When I asked her to share a favorite recipe with me that had some history, she immediately came up with jerked pork. According to Jessica, the maroons, escaped renegade slaves who lived in the Cockpit country of the Blue Mountains of Jamaica, developed this classic island dish. From Montego Bay to Ocho Rios, the highway is dotted with numerous pork pits offering up good-tasting Jamaican jerk. Jerked pork traveled through the islands and with the immigrants into the United States.

2 cups plain yogurt

3 tablespoons chopped garlic

2 tablespoons peeled and chopped fresh ginger

1 tablespoon chopped shallot

2 tablespoons olive oil

½ cup mild curry powder

Kosher salt and freshly ground black pepper

6 boneless pork loin chops, about 1 inch thick

"Curry Hill"
curried pork chops

"Curry Hill" is at the corner of Lexington Avenue and 28th Street in Manhattan and is where the best Indian spice shops in the city are located. I'm always playing with exotic flavors in the kitchen, and a friend asked me to do something simple with curry. Even if you're not a big curry fan, I think you'll enjoy the subtlety of these chops. The marinade is a combination of yogurt and curry powder, and it forms an interesting sort of crust around the pork, which insulates it from the heat and tends to make the chops juicier. I like to serve a little mint jelly alongside for a sweet note.

– ༼ꙮ༽ –

1. Combine the yogurt, garlic, ginger, shallot, and oil in a food processor or blender and pulse until smooth. Add the curry powder and process to combine. Taste for salt and pepper.

2. Place the pork chops in a large zip-top plastic bag. Pour the marinade over them, seal the bag, and squish around to coat the chops. Let marinate in the refrigerator overnight, turning the bag a few times.

3. Light a charcoal fire or preheat your gas grill on high. Oil the grill's cooking surface. Let the coals burn down to a medium-hot fire or adjust the gas grill burners to medium-high.

4. Remove the pork chops from the refrigerator at least 30 minutes before cooking. When your fire is ready, remove the chops from the marinade, letting the excess drain back into the bag. Discard the marinade.

5. Place the chops on the grill and cook for about 6 minutes. Turn and cook another 6 to 7 minutes, until they are somewhat firm to the touch, barely white at the center, and the juices are clear. Remove to plates and serve immediately.

YUCATAN CITRUS MARINADE

¼ cup orange juice

¼ cup pineapple juice

3 tablespoons fresh lime juice

2 tablespoons olive oil

1 tablespoon chopped fresh oregano or
1 teaspoon dried

2 teaspoons ground cumin

2 teaspoons chili powder

2 teaspoons minced garlic

2 teaspoons kosher salt

1 teaspoon freshly ground black pepper

½ teaspoon ground allspice

½ teaspoon hot sauce

----

6 pork loin chops, cut about 1½ inches
thick

Orange-Pineapple Salsa (recipe below)

orange-pineapple salsa

MAKES ABOUT 2½ CUPS

This salsa also works with fish and chicken. Combine all the ingredients and mix well. This will keep, tightly covered, up to 2 days in the refrigerator.

1 navel orange, peeled and cut into
½-inch dice

1 cup pineapple chunks, cut into
¼-inch dice

1 medium jalapeño, seeded and
finely chopped

1 cup roughly chopped fresh cilantro

2 tablespoons chopped fresh mint

½ teaspoon ground cumin

2 scallions (white and green parts),
finely chopped

Yucatan Grilled
pork chops

This Cal-Mex recipe has some interesting flavors in the marinade. The allspice, coupled with the oregano, and the spicy stuff combine for a unique and delicious experience. This is another of Tim and Salina Huckins' wonderful recipes that blend Mexico, Southern California, and Florida.

– ᏇᏋᏇ –

1. In a small bowl, combine the marinade ingredients and whisk together thoroughly.

2. Place the pork in a large zip-top plastic bag and pour in the marinade. Seal the bag and squish everything around to coat evenly. Let marinate overnight in the refrigerator, turning the bag occasionally.

3. Remove the pork from the refrigerator 30 minutes before grilling.

4. Light a charcoal fire or preheat your gas grill on high. Oil the grill's cooking surface. Let the coals burn down to a medium-hot fire or adjust the gas grill burners to medium-high.

5. Remove the pork from the marinade and discard the marinade. Pat dry with paper towels. Put the chops on the grill and cook for 5 to 6 minutes per side, until they are somewhat firm to the touch, barely white at the center, and the juices are clear, turning the meat 2 or 3 times.

6. Remove to a platter, let rest for 5 minutes, then slice the pork into ½-inch-thick strips, leaving some meat on the bones for those who like to gnaw. Serve with the salsa.

Four 1- to 1½-inch-thick boneless pork chops

Olive oil

Your favorite seasoned salt

Mark Cheeseman's

simple seasoned pork chops

Folks love to get invited to Mark Cheeseman's house in Corpus Christi, Texas. This recipe shows just how easy good taste can be.

– ∽৩৩৩৩৩ –

1. Brush both sides of the pork chops with olive oil. Sprinkle with seasoned salt to taste.

2. Set up the grill for indirect grilling (see pp. 6–9). Oil your grill's cooking surface.

3. Place the chops on the grill away from the heat, close the lid, and cook for 25 to 30 minutes, turning halfway through the cooking time, until they are somewhat firm to the touch, barely white at the center, and the juices are clear.

One 15.25-ounce can apricot halves, drained and chopped

1 cup plain dry breadcrumbs

⅓ cup coarsely chopped walnuts

One 1-ounce envelope onion soup mix

2 tablespoons unsalted butter, melted

Four 1 ½-inch-thick boneless pork loin chops (about 1¾ pounds), trimmed of fat ½ cup apricot preserves

1 tablespoon hot water

Apricot-Stuffed
pork chops

Fruit and pork are a heavenly marriage. Pork pairs up with the flavor of fruit like no other meat. The sweet glaze is a perfect finish to a delicious dish. The onion soup mix brings a heartiness to the stuffing, like it does in so many recipes, and becomes your base seasoning. I've enjoyed this recipe for some time, and I believe it came from a community cookbook, usually the best source for a tried-and-true recipe. Serve with some couscous for a little North African flair.

– ⚬⚬⚬ –

1. Combine the chopped apricots, breadcrumbs, walnuts, soup mix, and butter in a small bowl. Cut a slit into the side of each chop and cut a pocket, but take care not to butterfly the chop. Stuff about ⅓ cup of the mixture into each pocket of the pork chops. Secure the openings with wooden toothpicks.

2. In a small bowl, combine the preserves and hot water, stirring well. Set aside.

3. Light a charcoal fire or preheat your gas grill on high. Oil the grill's cooking surface. Let the coals burn down to a medium-hot fire or adjust the gas grill burners to medium-high.

4. Place the chops on the grill and cook, with the lid down, for 16 minutes total, turning once halfway through. Brush the chops with the preserve mixture, turn, and grill for 3 minutes. Brush on the preserve mixture, turn, and grill 3 more minutes, until they are somewhat firm to the touch, barely white at the center, and the juices are clear. Remove from the grill and serve immediately.

ITALIAN RELISH

¾ pound ripe plum tomatoes, seeded and chopped

¾ cup chopped red onion

¼ cup red wine vinegar

2 tablespoons olive oil

1 tablespoon chopped garlic

1 tablespoon chopped fresh basil or 1 teaspoon dried

1 tablespoon chopped fresh oregano or 1 teaspoon dried

Kosher salt and freshly ground black pepper to taste

Four 1- to 1½-inch-thick boneless pork chops

Grilled Pork Chops with
italian relish

The pork chop is just the vehicle here. It gives you a nice protein to eat along with this Italian relish. I learned this recipe in culinary school. It was sort of passed on from class to class. We always had leftover tomatoes, onions, basil, or garlic, so this Italian salsa-like mixture became our snack. We put it on everything—grilled portobello mushrooms and fish in particular. It's especially good with grilled tuna. With a good center-cut pork chop, it will send you right to the rustic hills of Umbria.

- ৩৩৩ৎ -

1. Combine the relish ingredients in a medium bowl and mix well. Let stand at room temperature for at least 15 minutes or up to 1 hour.

2. Light a charcoal fire or preheat your gas grill on high. Oil the grill's cooking surface. Let the coals burn down to a medium fire or adjust the gas grill burners to medium.

3. Meanwhile, arrange the pork chops in an 8-inch square baking dish. Drain the liquid from the relish and spoon it over the pork. Let the pork marinate in this for at least 15 minutes, turning a few times.

4. Place the pork on the grill and cook until they are somewhat firm to the touch, barely white at the center, and the juices are clear, about 6 minutes per side.

5. Remove the chops to plates, spoon the relish over, and serve immediately.

HERB BUTTER

1 pound (4 sticks) unsalted butter, softened

6 scallions (white and green parts), finely chopped

Juice of 1 lemon

1 tablespoon freshly ground black pepper

2 tablespoons Tiger® seasoning or seasoned salt

4 cloves garlic, peeled

Leaves from 4 to 5 fresh sprigs parsley

---

1 tablespoon Tiger seasoning or seasoned salt

1 tablespoon of your favorite rib rub (Kelly uses one from Memphis)

One 3-pound boneless pork loin, cut into six 8-ounce chops, about 1 inch thick

1 cup orange marmalade (she uses Dickerson's)

Knoxville, TN

SERVES 6

Kelly Litton's
pork loin chops with herb butter

If you live anywhere near Knoxville, Tennessee, you bleed University of Tennessee orange. Kelly Litton is no different. Kelly is a Knoxville native whose family has owned the local favorite Litton's Restaurant for decades. It is a place for great burgers with homemade buns and way too many decadent desserts. When Kelly cooks at home, she likes to be adventuresome and loves to create recipes. If UT women's basketball is on TV, she usually has a bunch of girlfriends over, and this is a dish they all love.

1. Place the herb butter ingredients in a food processor and pulse to combine, then process together for 2 to 3 minutes on medium speed. Remove from the processor, form into a log, wrap in plastic wrap, and refrigerate for up to a week or freeze for up to 3 months.

2. Mix together the seasoning and rub and sprinkle liberally over the pork chops.

3. Light a charcoal fire or preheat your gas grill on high. Oil the grill's cooking surface. Let the coals burn down to a medium-hot fire or adjust the gas grill burners to medium-high.

4. Place the chops on the grill and cook for 2 minutes, then turn. Brush with the marmalade. Repeat about every 2 minutes until they are somewhat firm to the touch, barely white at the center, and the juices are clear, about 15 minutes total.

5. Remove the chops to a platter and serve each with a pat of the herb butter.

MANGO MOJO

1 ripe mango, peeled, seeded, and coarsely chopped

¼ cup fresh lime juice

1 large clove garlic, minced

1 tablespoon chopped jalapeño (including seeds)

1 teaspoon kosher salt or to taste

2 tablespoons finely chopped fresh cilantro

ANISE SEED RUB

1 tablespoon anise seeds

¾ teaspoon black peppercorns

1½ teaspoons kosher salt

1½ teaspoons sugar

3 tablespoons olive oil

Four 1-inch-thick boneless pork chops, trimmed of fat

Grilled Pork Chops with
anise seed rub and mango mojo

Here, Mexican and Caribbean styles collide to form an impressive result. Peaches can be substituted for the mango, with little change in flavor. The mojo has a cooling heat that adds taste, not intense mouth burn. If you need more heat or want that traditional Caribbean burn, replace the jalapeño with a habanero chile (but take the seeds out) and watch the flames begin. You've been warned!

– ⌘ –

1. Light a charcoal fire or preheat your gas grill on high. Oil the grill's cooking surface. Let the coals burn down to a medium-hot fire or adjust the gas grill burners to medium-high.

2. Meanwhile, make the mojo. Place the mango, lime juice, garlic, jalapeño, and salt in a blender and process until smooth. Stir in the cilantro.

3. Make the rub by finely grinding together the anise seeds, peppercorns, salt, and sugar in an electric coffee/spice grinder. Transfer to a small bowl and stir in the oil. Brush the mixture over both sides of the pork.

4. Grill the pork chops about 6 minutes per side, until they are somewhat firm to the touch, barely white at the center, and the juices are clear. Move off to a cooler side of grill if they start to get too crispy.

5. Transfer to a platter and let stand, loosely covered with aluminum foil, for 5 minutes, then serve with the mojo.

Four 1¼-inch-thick boneless pork chops

CORIANDER-PEPPER MARINADE

¼ cup soy sauce

2 cloves garlic, crushed

1 tablespoon ground coriander

1 tablespoon coarsely ground black pepper

1 tablespoon light brown sugar

Robin Kline's

coriander-pepper pork chops

Robin Kline, who lives in Iowa, is a fellow writer and foodie. Robin says about these chops, "I've never served these to anyone who hasn't subsequently asked me for the recipe; this is a winner! The seemingly disparate ingredients in the marinade come together for an amazing taste sensation, marrying perfectly with lean pork on the grill. And the flavors are imparted with only a 30-minute marinating time."

- ᥫᎧᏬᏬᎧᥫ -

1. Place the chops in a large baking dish or zip-top plastic bag.

2. In a small bowl, combine the marinade ingredients until the sugar dissolves, then pour it over the chops and let marinate at room temperature for 30 minutes.

3. Light a charcoal fire or preheat your gas grill on high. Oil the grill's cooking surface. Let the coals burn down to a medium-hot fire or adjust the gas grill burners to medium-high.

4. Remove the pork from the marinade and discard the marinade. Grill the chops for 9 to 15 minutes total, until they are somewhat firm to the touch, barely white at the center, and the juices are clear, turning once.

ASIAN SPICE PASTE

1 teaspoon kosher salt

½ teaspoon freshly ground black pepper

½ teaspoon ground allspice

¼ teaspoon ground star anise

¼ teaspoon ground cinnamon

2 tablespoons canola oil

Four 1½-inch-thick boneless pork loin chops

¼ cup dried plums (prunes), chopped

2 tablespoons armagnac or other brandy or warm water

2 tablespoons canola oil

½ cup (1 stick) unsalted butter, cut into tablespoons

2 cups peeled, seeded, and diced pumpkin or acorn or butternut squash

12 fresh sage leaves, finely minced

SERVES 4

Boneless Pork Loin Chops with
sage, pumpkin, and dried plums

While traveling around Umbria in the fall a few years back, I fell in love with the Italian tradition of serving pumpkin as a side dish with pork. The key to the dish is infusing the butter with sage. I added a French touch with the dried plums (the new name for prunes) and gussied up the pork with a hint of Asian spice.

- ⌒⌒⌒ -

1. Combine the salt, pepper, allspice, star anise, and cinnamon in a bowl. Whisk in the oil to form a paste. Rub the mixture on all sides of the pork steaks. Cover and let sit at room temperature for about 30 minutes.

2. Place the dried plums in a bowl, pour the brandy over, and allow them to soak for about 15 minutes.

3. Light a charcoal fire or preheat your gas grill on high. Oil the grill's cooking surface.

4. Meanwhile, heat the oil and 2 tablespoons of the butter together in a large sauté pan set over medium-high heat. Add the pumpkin and cook, stirring and turning every few minutes, until all sides have lightly browned, 18 to 20 minutes. Add the plums and any remaining soaking liquid and cook another 2 minutes. Remove the pan from the heat and keep warm.

5. Place the chops on the grill and cook about 4 minutes, turn, and cook another 4 minutes. Turn again, cook for about 5 minutes. Turn once more and cook for about 4 minutes, until they are somewhat firm to the touch, barely white at the center, and the juices are clear. Remove the pork chops to a platter. Tent with aluminum foil and let rest.

6. Place a small saucepan over medium heat and add the remaining 6 tablespoons of butter. Cook the butter until it melts and just begins to take on a brown hue, about 3 minutes. Stir in the sage and remove from the heat.

7. To serve, divide the pumpkin and plums evenly among 4 plates and top each with a steak. Ladle the sage brown butter over each portion and serve immediately.

Six 10- to 12-ounce boneless pork chops, cut 1 ½ inches thick

Kosher salt and freshly ground black pepper

BANANA GLAZE

1 tablespoon unsalted butter

2 large shallots, minced

1 large clove garlic, minced

1 large ripe banana, peeled and mashed

½ cup low-sodium chicken broth

¼ cup fresh orange juice

2 teaspoons Worcestershire sauce

1 teaspoon light brown sugar

Vegetable oil spray

Banana-Glazed
butterflied pork chops

I first had bananas in a savory dish at a Puerto Rican food stand at the annual Ninth Avenue Street and Food Fair in Manhattan. Pork was a part of that dish, and the recipe was not forthcoming from the vendor. So I hunted around for a way to re-create some of those flavors.

Bill and Cheryl Jamison have made their life's work in developing recipes to cook on the grill. They had a butterflied pork chop with a banana glaze in one of their cookbooks, which became the basis for this recipe.

– ଏଓଚ –

1. If your butcher won't butterfly your pork chops, it's easy to do yourself. Take a sharp knife and make a horizontal cut halfway through the pork chop, almost all the way through. The chop should open like a book and lay relatively flat, even with the bone there. Sprinkle with salt and pepper and let sit at room temperature while you make the glaze.

2. To make the glaze, in a small, heavy saucepan, melt the butter over medium heat. Add the shallots and cook, stirring, until translucent. Toss in the garlic and cook until fragrant. Add the banana, broth, orange juice, Worcestershire, and brown sugar, reduce the heat to medium-low, and cook for about 10 minutes, stirring frequently. The finished glaze should be thick and coat the back of a spoon.

3. Light a charcoal fire or preheat your gas grill on high. Oil the grill's cooking surface. Let the coals burn down to a medium fire or adjust the gas grill burners to medium.

4. Spray the chops with oil and place them on the grill. Cook for 20 to 24 minutes total, turning them several times. Begin brushing the chops with the glaze during the last 5 minutes of cooking. The chops are done when they are somewhat firm to the touch, barely white at the center, and the juices are clear. Brush again with the glaze as the chops come off the grill. Serve immediately with any remaining glaze on the side.

Six 10-ounce boneless pork chops about 1³/₄ inches thick

MONGOLIAN MARINADE

1 cup hoisin sauce

1 tablespoon sugar

1¹/₂ tablespoons tamari or low-sodium soy sauce

1¹/₂ tablespoons sherry vinegar

1¹/₂ tablespoons rice vinegar

1 scallion (white part and two-thirds of the green part), minced

1 teaspoon hot sauce

1¹/₂ teaspoons Asian black bean chile sauce (I use Lee Kum Kee®)

1¹/₂ teaspoons peeled and grated fresh ginger

1¹/₂ tablespoons minced garlic

³/₄ teaspoon freshly ground black pepper

¹/₄ cup fresh cilantro leaves, chopped

1 tablespoon toasted sesame oil

Mongolian

double-cut pork chops

When I think of Mongolian food, I taste gutsy, hearty flavors, and that's exactly what you will get with this recipe. This dish developed from a cross-fertilization of culinary ideas I got from a New York City cab driver and the chef at my local Chinese restaurant. You could use thinner pork chops and serve a couple to each person, but the pounding of the thicker ones is a great stress reliever and makes for an awesome plate presentation.

– ᘓᘏᘓᘔ –

1. "French" the pork bones, which simply means trim the excess meat and fat away from the ends of the chop bones, leaving them exposed. You could also ask your butcher to do this for you. Put the pork chops one at a time in a large zip-top plastic bag and lightly sprinkle with water to prevent the meat from tearing when you pound it. Using the smooth side of a meat mallet, pound the meat down to an even 1-inch thickness, being careful not to hit the bones. When you're done, put all the chops in the bag or use a new bag if that one has been perforated at all in your pounding.

2. Combine the marinade ingredients in a medium bowl, then pour into the bag, seal, and squish everything to coat the pork chops. Let marinate for at least 3 hours and up to overnight in the refrigerator.

3. Light a charcoal fire or preheat your gas grill on high. Oil the grill's cooking surface.

4. Remove the chops from the marinade and discard the marinade. Place the chops on the grill and cook until they are somewhat firm to the touch, barely white at the center, and the juices are clear, about 5 minutes per side, rotating them a quarter turn after 2 to 3 minutes to produce nice crosshatch marks.

5. Remove the chops to a platter and garnish with the cilantro. Drizzle with the sesame oil and serve immediately.

BEER BRINE

2 cups water

2 cups dark lager beer

¼ cup coarse salt

3 tablespoons firmly packed dark brown sugar

3 tablespoons mild-flavored (light) molasses

1 cup ice cubes

Six 1- to 1¼-inch-thick center-cut bone-in pork chops

GARLIC-SAGE RUB

7 large cloves garlic, minced

1 tablespoon coarsely ground black pepper

2 teaspoons kosher salt

2 teaspoons dried sage

Beer-Brined
grilled pork chops

Let's face it—beer and hog meat just really like to be together. This recipe brings out the best in both in an outstanding way. The dark beer, coupled with molasses and brown sugar, penetrates the pork to add a layer of mouthwatering richness. Put this one on your must-try list.

– ꙮꙮꙮ –

1. Combine the water, beer, coarse salt, brown sugar, and molasses in a large bowl. Stir until the salt and sugar dissolve. Stir in the ice. Place the pork chops in a large zip-top plastic bag. Pour the beer brine over the chops and seal the bag. Refrigerate for 4 hours, turning the bag a few times.

2. Light a charcoal fire or preheat your gas grill on high. Oil the grill's cooking surface. Let the coals burn down to a medium-hot fire or adjust the gas grill burners to medium-high.

3. Remove the pork chops from the beer brine and pat dry. Combine the rub ingredients in small bowl, then work in to both sides of the chops.

4. Grill the chops until they are somewhat firm to the touch, barely white at the center, and the juices are clear, about 10 minutes per side, occasionally moving them to the cooler part of the grill if the rub starts to burn.

5. Transfer the chops to a platter; cover with aluminum foil and let stand 5 minutes before serving.

½ cup tamari or reduced-sodium
soy sauce

¼ cup ketchup

2 tablespoons firmly packed light
brown sugar

2 tablespoons mirin (sweet rice wine)
or dry sherry

2 teaspoons peeled and grated
fresh ginger

1 clove garlic, crushed

Four 1¼-inch-thick boneless pork chops

Huli Huli Pork

hayley's style

Huli huli, which literally means turn and turn, often is a Hawaiian favorite, and Hayley Matson-Mathes wanted to share her version. This marinade is sometimes used with larger cuts of pork, and you really do need to turn them often. Keep a close eye on these chops, and if they get a little too crisp before they are done, move them to a cooler part of the grill.

– ෴ –

1. Mix the tamari, ketchup, brown sugar, mirin, ginger, and garlic in a large zip-top plastic bag. Add the chops, seal the bag, squish everything around to coat well, and let marinate overnight in the refrigerator, turning the bag a couple of times.

2. Light a charcoal fire or preheat your gas grill on high. Oil the grill's cooking surface. Let the coals burn down to a medium-hot fire or adjust the gas grill burners to medium-high.

3. Place the chops on the grill and cook 8 to 10 minutes total, until somewhat firm to the touch, barely white at the center, and the juices are clear, turning them often. Remove from the grill and serve.

¾ cup plus 2 tablespoons olive oil

4 cloves garlic, put through a garlic press or smashed with the side of a knife

2 teaspoons dried sage

1 teaspoon dried oregano

½ teaspoon dried thyme

½ teaspoon dried rosemary, crushed between your fingers

2 tablespoons balsamic vinegar

Four ¾- to 1-inch-thick bone-in rib or loin pork chops (about ¾ pound each)

4 leeks (white and light green parts only)

Kosher salt and freshly ground black pepper

Italian Grilled Pork Chops
with grilled leeks

Anytime you add a member of the onion family to the grill, something special happens. Of course, in this recipe it doesn't hurt that the pork chops are marinated in a killer concoction. The sweet tone of the leeks accents the richness of the balsamic vinegar. It's a simple dish with over-the-top taste. You can prepare this with boneless chops. If you do, reduce your cooking time by a few minutes.

– ༄ଓ –

1. Pour the ¾ cup of the olive oil into a medium bowl. Add the garlic and herbs and stir to combine. Whisk in 1 tablespoon of the vinegar. Place the pork chops in a 1-gallon zip-top plastic bag and pour the marinade over them. Seal the bag and squish everything together to coat the chops. Let marinate in the refrigerator overnight, turning the bag a few times.

2. Light a charcoal fire or preheat your gas grill on high. Oil the grill's cooking surface. Let the coals burn down to a medium-hot fire or adjust the gas grill burners to medium-high.

3. Cut each leek in half lengthwise down almost to the root but *not* through it. Make a second cut in the same manner across the first in a crosshair pattern. Rinse the leeks well under cold running water and shake dry. Place in a shallow bowl and toss with the remaining 2 tablespoons oil. Lightly salt and pepper, then set aside.

4. Remove the pork chops from the marinade, shaking off any excess. Salt and pepper lightly.

5. Place the chops and the leeks on the grill and cook for about 3 minutes, then give each chop a quarter turn to get those nice crossed grill marks and continue to cook for another 6 minutes. Turn the leeks every 2 to 3 minutes. Turn the chops over and cook for another 6 to 8 minutes, until somewhat firm to the touch, barely white at the center, and the juices are clear.

6. Remove the chops to a platter and let rest for 5 minutes.

7. Return the leeks to the bowl and toss with the remaining 1 tablespoon vinegar. Cut the leeks through the root and divide them equally among the serving plates. Place one pork chop on top of the leeks on each plate and serve.

ORANGE GLAZE

½ cup orange marmalade

2 tablespoons peeled and minced fresh ginger

2 tablespoons fresh lime juice

4 teaspoons coarse-grained Dijon mustard

1 teaspoon grated lime zest

Four 6-ounce smoked bone-in pork chops

1 teaspoon coarsely ground black pepper

Grilled Smoked Pork Chops with
peppered orange glaze

Most folks think that the only thing Southerners smoke is ham. Not true. Loins of pork cut into smaller pieces were also routinely smoked. It was the best way to preserve the meat after you had just butchered a hog. Nowadays, the easiest way to find a smoked pork chop is to buy one at your grocery store. When tossed on the grill, their smoky flavor is enhanced. I like to glaze them with preserve-based sauces. This is one of my favorites, with orange marmalade, Dijon, and some citrus juice. It takes a simple, unassuming meat and turns it into something special.

– ༄ –

1. Light a charcoal fire or preheat your gas grill on high. Oil the grill's cooking surface. Let the coals burn down to a medium-hot fire or adjust the gas grill burners to medium-high.

2. In a small, heavy saucepan, combine the orange glaze ingredients and stir over low heat until the marmalade melts. Remove from the heat.

3. Sprinkle both sides of the pork chops with the pepper and press lightly so the pepper adheres. Brush the chops with some of the glaze.

4. Place the chops on the grill and cook until heated through, lightly browned, and beginning to crisp at the edges, brushing occasionally with more of the glaze, about 3 minutes per side.

5. Transfer the chops to plates, brush them with any remaining glaze, and serve immediately.

3 racks baby back ribs, 5 to 6 pounds total

3 to 4 tablespoons Dancing Pigs Original
Dry Seasoning or your favorite rib rub

1 bottle Allegro Original Marinade

1 bottle Carolina Treet Cooking Barbecue
Sauce®

Jean's Brisket Barbecue Sauce (p. 72) or
your favorite sauce

1. With a sharp paring knife, remove
the connective tissue and membrane from
the back of the ribs. Cut the racks in half.
Liberally sprinkle the dry seasoning over
both sides of the ribs and place in a 2-gallon
zip-top plastic bag. Pour in the marinade
and refrigerate for at least 6 hours or
overnight.

2. Set up the grill for indirect grilling
(see pp. 6–9). Oil your grill's cooking surface. Hugh will sometimes add a chunk of
hickory or pecan wood that he's soaked in
water for at least 1 hour. Set the ribs on the
grill away from the heat and cover. Cook
for about 2½ hours, adding more charcoal
as necessary. Baste with the Carolina Treet
every 15 minutes for the last hour. When
the racks easily bend, they are done. Cut
into individual ribs and serve with Jean's
Barbecue Sauce.

Hugh's Awesome
smoked ribs

Hugh Lynn is one of my best friends and probably the guy who had the
most to do with my love of cooking and especially grilling. A native Texan,
Hugh has lived in North Carolina, Kansas City, and now Memphis, all home
to world-renowned barbecue. He has borrowed from every region he's
lived in to develop this recipe. These ribs are so good that if I know he's
about to crank up his grill ribs, I'm liable to catch a plane to Memphis, roll
up my sleeves, and chow down.

Hugh's indirect smoking set-up.

KANSAS CITY SWEET RUB

¾ cup firmly packed light brown sugar

½ cup paprika

2½ tablespoons kosher salt

2½ tablespoons freshly ground black pepper

1 tablespoon onion powder

½ teaspoon cayenne pepper

---

3 large racks spareribs (about 9 pounds), membranes removed

4 cups oak or hickory chips, soaked in water for at least 30 minutes and drained

1½ cups Kansas City Sweet and Hot Barbecue Sauce (p. 306) or your favorite barbecue sauce

Tricks of the Rib Trade

Most folks in Kansas City don't want to give up their secrets and, if they do, they sure don't want to be identified. Here are a couple I learned.

*Mop the ribs with melted butter while they're smoking.

*Take the ribs off the fire after 2 hours and wrap them tightly in aluminum foil for up to 1 hour. This steams the ribs to make them even more tender.

Kansas City
spareribs

They may fight between "wet" or "dry" ribs in Memphis, Tennessee, but in Kansas City, there's only one way to make them—wet. Sticky, sweet, and a little heat are the hallmarks of Kansas City-style ribs. Folks around Kansas City also prefer spareribs to any other type of rib. Sauce is the thing here. Most of the commercial sauces available in your grocery store are based on Kansas City-style gooey sauces. One of the best-selling sauces in the country is KC Masterpiece®, developed by Dr. Rich Davis, from—where else?—Kansas City. Use his or your own favorite.

At the Big Apple Annual Barbeque Block Party a few years ago, Kansas City barbecue baron Paul Kirk, North Carolina pulled pork pitmaster Ed Mitchell, and I were sitting around chewing the fat after the first day of the event. Ribs was the subject, and while this recipe is nowhere near as complex as Paul's version, it keeps the spirit of Kansas City in tow.

-ᏨᏨᏨ-

1. Combine the dry rub ingredients in a small bowl until well mixed. Sprinkle ⅔ cup of the rub evenly over the ribs. Cover the ribs with plastic wrap and refrigerate overnight. Store the leftover rub in an airtight container at room temperature.

2. Unwrap the spareribs and sprinkle all over with half of the remaining rub. Let stand at room temperature for 30 minutes.

3. Meanwhile, set up the grill for indirect grilling (see pp. 6–9). Oil your grill's cooking surface.

4. Add the chips to the fire. Arrange the ribs on the grill away from the heat, close the lid, and cook for about 2 hours, maintaining a temperature in the grill of around 275°F. Add more wood chips every 30 minutes or so. After 2 hours, sprinkle the ribs evenly with the remaining rub. Continue cooking about 1 hour longer.

5. Start brushing with the sauce every 5 to 10 minutes, and don't be bashful with it—slather it on thick. Cook another 30 minutes. If you can, take tongs, hold the rack of ribs up, and, if it droops, the ribs should be done. Transfer the ribs to a large platter, cut into individual ribs, and serve.

3 pounds baby back pork ribs (spareribs also work)

¼ cup water

¼ cup Dijon mustard

1 tablespoon firmly packed light brown sugar

1 tablespoon paprika

1 teaspoon chili powder

¼ teaspoon cayenne pepper

¼ teaspoon kosher salt

Coarsely ground black pepper to taste

1 cup of your favorite barbecue sauce or East Tennessee-Style Barbecue Sauce (p. 305)

2 tablespoons clover honey, or as needed

tip: In the last few years I've added a wrinkle to these ribs that takes them to the next level; if you have the time, give this a try. Don't precook the ribs in the oven. Set up your grill for indirect heat or stoke a smoker. Add some wood chips or hunks of wood, using hickory or oak. Brush the mustard over the ribs, followed by the rub. When the grill is ready to go, place the ribs on the grill, bone side down, and adjust the vents on your grill to almost closed. You want the temperature to stay at about 200°F. Smoke for about 3 hours, replenishing the fuel source and the wood chips as needed. About every 45 minutes, spray the ribs with apple cider. The ribs are ready for the next step when you can grab them with a pair of tongs, lift them up, and they bend easily. Place them over direct heat and proceed with the application of the sauce and honey for total cooking time of about 15 minutes.

Fred's Finest
baby back ribs

This recipe took about 20 years to get right. There's a touch of all the barbecue capitals in it—Memphis, Kansas City, Texas, and North Carolina. This is the most requested recipe from my newspaper column, most of the time in sheer desperation because someone has misplaced the original. Try these paired with Martha and Fred's Fabulous Baked Beans (p. 322), my second most requested recipe, and Jean Lynn's Potato Salad (p. 330) and you will be in barbecue nirvana. The true secret is the honey glaze, applied right before the ribs come off the grill. No offense to Colonel Sanders, but these bones are true "finger-licking good," make-my-mouth-happy perfection.

– ⌒⌒⌒ –

1. Preheat the oven to 300°F. Rinse the ribs and pat them dry, place in an aluminum roasting bag, and add the water. Seal the bag tightly, place on a baking sheet, and place in the oven. Cook the ribs for 45 minutes to 1 hour.

2. Remove the ribs from the oven and let cool in the roasting bag for another 30 minutes. Carefully open the bag away from you in case there is still some steam in the bag. Place the ribs on the baking sheet and brush them generously with the mustard. Combine the brown sugar, paprika, chili powder, cayenne pepper, and salt, and sprinkle evenly over both sides of the ribs. Grind the black pepper to taste over the ribs.

3. Start a charcoal fire or preheat your gas grill on high. Oil your grill's cooking surface. Let the coals burn down to a medium fire or adjust the gas grill burners to medium.

4. Place the ribs, meaty side down, on the grill, cover the grill, and cook for about 15 minutes, then turn. Brush the seared side with the sauce, cover, and cook another 10 to 15 minutes. Turn, brush with the sauce, cover, and let them enjoy the heat for another 10 minutes. Brush the same side with sauce again, cover, and cook for no more than 5 minutes. Drizzle the meaty side of the ribs with the honey and let them stay on the heat a couple of minutes more to allow the honey to glaze.

5. Remove to a platter and serve to hoots and hollers.

4 pounds baby back ribs

4 cups apple cider or juice

BARRY'S APPLESAUCE BBQ SAUCE

1 cup ketchup

1 cup unsweetened applesauce

½ cup apple cider

½ cup cider vinegar

¼ cup Worcestershire sauce

1 tablespoon prepared yellow mustard

3 cloves garlic, chopped

½ teaspoon ground cinnamon

1. Preheat your oven to 300°F. Place the ribs in a roasting pan large enough to hold them in a single layer. Pour the cider over the ribs, cover with aluminum foil, and place in the oven for 1½ to 2 hours.

2. Meanwhile, combine the sauce ingredients in a 2-quart saucepan over medium heat. Slowly bring to a boil, reduce the heat to low, and simmer for about 20 minutes. Remove from the heat until needed. It will keep, tightly covered, in the refrigerator up to 2 weeks.

3. Light a charcoal fire or preheat your gas grill on high. Oil the grill's cooking surface.

4. Remove the ribs from the roasting pan and place them on the grill. Cook about 4 minutes per side, then start basting with the sauce and turning the ribs every 5 minutes. Cook the ribs a total of 20 to 25 minutes. If the sauce starts to burn too much, move the ribs to a cooler area of the grill.

5. Remove the ribs to a platter. Cut into 3-rib serving pieces and serve with extra sauce passed at the table.

Barry Johnson's
indiana-style ribs

Barry is a pharmaceutical marketing fellow from the Indianapolis area. He has some solid roots in the state of Virginia and Raleigh, NC, though, and that may be why he knows what to do with a slab of pork ribs. His ribs have a unique sweet twang of apples—not overbearing, mind you, just enough to make them interesting. The apple note is carried in his sauce as well, which also works nicely with grilled pork chops and chicken.

3½ pounds baby back ribs

Kosher salt and freshly ground black pepper

ORIENTAL GLAZE

⅔ cup ketchup

⅔ cup orange juice

3 tablespoons Asian black bean garlic sauce

2 tablespoons peeled and minced fresh ginger

2 tablespoons Asian chili-garlic sauce

2 tablespoons dry sherry

2 tablespoons firmly packed light brown sugar

1 tablespoon toasted sesame oil

1 tablespoon soy sauce

1 tablespoon sesame seeds

Baby Back Ribs with
oriental glaze

Here's a recipe that has all the yin and yang typical of Asian foods. The orange juice and ketchup add sweetness, there's saltiness from the black bean sauce, and sharpness and heat from the chili-garlic sauce and ginger. Put it all together and you've got a rib glaze you won't soon forget.

- ꙮ -

1. Preheat the oven to 400°F.

2. Sprinkle the ribs with salt and pepper. Wrap each rack in aluminum foil and place on a rimmed baking sheet.

3. Mix together the glaze ingredients in a medium bowl. Stir well to blend and set aside.

4. Place the ribs in the oven and bake for about 45 minutes.

5. Meanwhile, light a charcoal fire or preheat your gas grill on high. Oil the grill's cooking surface. Let the coals burn down to a medium fire or adjust the gas grill burners to medium.

6. Remove the ribs from the foil and place them meaty side down on the grill. Cook 3 to 4 minutes and turn. Cook another 3 to 4 minutes so that both sides are slightly seared, then start brushing the ribs with the glaze every 5 to 10 minutes, turning each time, and cook an additional 30 minutes total.

7. Sprinkle with the sesame seeds and cook about another 5 minutes. Remove from the grill and cut into individual ribs. Serve immediately or at room temperature.

2 slabs spareribs (about 6 pounds total)

Two 40-ounce bottles barbecue sauce of your choice

1½ cups cider vinegar

¼ cup Texas Pete or your favorite hot sauce

¼ cup Worcestershire sauce

3 tablespoons fresh lemon juice

1. Remove the membrane from the back of the ribs or have your butcher do it for you. Cut each slab in half and place in a large stockpot. Cover with water and place over medium-high heat. Bring to a fast boil, immediately lower the heat to a simmer, and cook for 45 minutes.

2. Light a charcoal fire or preheat your gas grill on high. Oil the grill's cooking surface. Let the coals burn down to a medium fire or adjust the gas grill burners to medium.

3. Using tongs, remove the ribs from the stockpot. When cool enough to handle, cut into three-rib pieces. Place each section on the grill and cook until nicely browned, about 5 minutes per side. Remove from the grill.

4. Preheat the oven to 300°F.

5. Place the browned rib pieces in a large roasting pan. Combine the barbecue sauce, vinegar, Texas Pete, Worcestershire, and lemon juice in a large bowl, then pour this evenly over the rib pieces. Cover with aluminum foil and place in the oven for 45 minutes. (You can also do this on a covered grill, especially a gas grill, where you have greater temperature control).

6. Remove the roasting pan from the oven and check the ribs. The meat should literally come right off the bone when you prod it with a fork. Using tongs, carefully remove the rib pieces to a platter. Spoon the extra sauce over the top and serve.

Tony Inscore's
three-way ribs

I'm thankful every day that Tony Inscore befriended my sister's family when they bought a place at Atlantic Beach, North Carolina. Tony, who lives in the Rocky Mount area, has been coming to this beach for more than 30 years and knows the South Outer Banks like the back of his hand. Fishing secrets, great picnic spots, boating, and day trips—Tony has passed his knowledge on to my sister. His cooking repertoire has impressed me, and many of his recipes, especially for seafood, I cook with regularity.

Tony's special ribs, however, are an event that brings his kids running. His daughters' eyes glaze over when they talk about them, and I could hardly wait for Labor Day weekend, when he had promised to cook them for me.

When Tony has plenty of time to attend to the grill, he will first cook the ribs for an hour over an indirect charcoal fire with nothing on them. When he's got grandchildren to play with, it's Tony's Three-Way Ribs: He parboils the ribs, then grills them a bit to add the outdoor flavor and caramelize the pork. He then braises them in the barbecue sauce (the third way) until they are falling-off-the-bone tender. Tony confesses to using the parboil method most often. And according to Tony, regular spareribs (called St. Louis cut) are better than baby backs.

Tony dishes up his falling-off-the-bone ribs.

Peter H. D. McKee's
seattle ribs

Barbecue can smite a person almost as quickly as love. But to look at Peter McKee, this educated, quirky, middle-aged man, you wouldn't think he could fall so hard for a food he didn't grow up with. Californian by birth, the smoked kissed 'cue of the South was not a part of his life. After law school at Brown University, he became a Vista legal volunteer. He was hoping for a posting in the Appalachian Mountains, where his love of folk music and banjo picking could flourish. Instead, it was to be central Georgia, where he would find a new obsession.

It started in 1974, when an afternoon ride brought him face to face with a shrine of central Georgia—Fresh Air Barbecue—just south of Jackson. Fresh Air, open since 1929, is one of the foundation blocks of Southern barbecue, and McKee fell under its spell with one taste of vinegar-laden, smoke-infused pork.

Deprived of this experience once he got back to the left coast, Peter had to do something. In 1981, he started the "Seventh Annual Jackson Fresh Air Barbecue Cook-off and Feed" or, as it is simply known, "The Jackson." His thinking was that "Seventh Annual" sounded more impressive than "First Annual." The contest is usually in July or August. He gives awards for best entrée, side dish, and dessert, as well as more questionable categories, like "best disguised vegetable."

Peter loves to smoke shoulders and ribs, and this recipe has been a Jackson award winner. The sauce looks involved but is really just a dump-and-stir kind of recipe. Peter says you can cheat and just stop with the Stubbs prepared sauce, but I encourage you to make it his way. The sauce, which is enough for 9 pounds of ribs, will keep for several weeks in the refrigerator, but I doubt it will last that long. This recipe also works for a water-smoker grill.

Peter gets his coals just right.

SEATTLE RIB SAUCE

¼ cup (½ stick) margarine

1 large yellow onion, diced

1 small clove garlic, minced

Two 18-ounce bottles Stubb's®
regular barbecue sauce

One 15-ounce can tomato sauce

¼ cup cider vinegar

2 cups water

¼ cup ketchup

¼ cup prepared chili sauce or chili ketchup

¼ cup beer

1 tablespoon soy sauce

3 tablespoons Worcestershire sauce

2 tablespoons dark molasses

¼ cup fresh lemon juice

2 fresh bay leaves

2 tablespoons Bac-Os® imitation
bacon bits

3 tablespoons Wright's® Liquid Smoke

1 tablespoon Kitchen Bouquet®

3 tablespoons dried parsley flakes

7 dashes Tabasco sauce

1 teaspoon dry mustard

1 teaspoon baking soda

Peter has been known to add one or more
of the following:

2 tablespoons instant coffee crystals

2 tablespoons Hershey's® chocolate syrup

1 large dollop chunky peanut butter

1 tablespoon sauerkraut, pureed

Three 3-pound racks of spareribs (ask the
butcher to "crack" the ribs but not to cut
them apart)

2 to 4 cups hickory chips (not chunks)

Garlic powder

Freshly ground black pepper

1. Melt the margarine in a large pot over medium heat, then add the onions and garlic and cook, stirring, until limp and translucent. Add the barbecue sauce, tomato sauce, vinegar, water, ketchup, chili sauce, beer, soy sauce, Worcestershire, molasses, lemon juice, bay leaves, Bac-Os, liquid smoke, Kitchen Bouquet, parsley, Tabasco, and mustard and stir until simmering. Add the baking soda and stir until the soda stops bubbling. Let the sauce simmer slowly for at least 30 minutes but preferably for the entire time the ribs are cooking. Periodically taste, adding water to keep it fairly thin and more of any of the ingredients or others that strike your fancy until the sauce suits your taste.

2. Bring the ribs to room temperature. Prepare the grill for indirect cooking (see pp. 6–9). Soak the hickory chips in cold water. Drain.

3. Sprinkle the ribs with a light dusting of garlic powder and coarsely ground pepper. Slap it into the ribs with your hand. Lay the racks, bone side down, in the center of the grill, which is not yet on the barbecue.

4. Add a handful of wet hickory chips to each side of the barbecue on top of the white-hot coals.

5. Lift the top grill onto the barbecue, centering the meat above a drip pan and the spaces on each side of the grill to allow adding further coals and hickory chips. Close down the top vent of the barbecue about halfway. Cook the ribs for 1 hour, adding a few more hickory chips every 30 minutes.

6. After 1 hour of cooking, add 7 or 8 more briquettes to each side of the barbecue. Flip the rack of ribs over to meat side down.

7. After a total of 1 hour and 50 minutes, open the barbecue, lift off the top grill, remove the drip pan using long tongs, and move the separated pile of coals into the center.

8. Thoroughly coat the rack of ribs in hot barbecue sauce. Replace the top grill and place the ribs directly above the coals, meat side down. After 5 minutes, brush with the sauce and flip the ribs to bone side down and cook another 5 minutes.

9. Pull the ribs off the grill. With a large cleaver, cut the ribs apart. Place on a platter and pour some of the remaining sauce over the pile of ribs.

6 country-style pork ribs (3 pounds)

TENNESSEE BOURBON-
MARMALADE MARINADE

⅓ cup Tennessee sipping whiskey, like
Jack Daniel's® Black

⅓ cup orange marmalade, gently heated
until liquid

2 cloves garlic, finely minced

2 tablespoons orange juice

2 tablespoons firmly packed dark
brown sugar

4 cloves

Freshly ground black pepper to taste

Gentleman Jack
country pork ribs

My dad used to say, "The nearer the bone, the sweeter the meat." And he was so right. Any meat with some bone attached tastes better. Country-style pork ribs are a cross between a bone-in pork chop, which is hard to find, and a true rib. They have much more meat than a sparerib, less fat, and are usually more economical than spareribs and baby back ribs. This recipe includes my dad's favorite libation.

– ເອົ◌ອ◌ –

1. Place the pork ribs in a large zip-top plastic bag.

2. In a small bowl, combine the marinade ingredients, then pour over the ribs. Seal the bag, squish everything to coat evenly, and let marinate in the refrigerator for 6 to 8 hours or overnight. Bring to room temperature before cooking.

3. Preheat the oven to 350°F. Light a charcoal fire or preheat your gas grill on high. Oil the grill's cooking surface. Let the coals burn down to a medium-hot fire or adjust the gas grill burners to medium-high.

4. Remove the ribs from the marinade and place in a 9x13-inch baking dish, reserving the marinade. Bake for 35 minutes, basting occasionally with the marinade.

5. Place the remaining marinade in a small saucepan. Bring it to a boil, reduce the heat to a simmer, and cook until slightly thickened, about 10 minutes.

6. To finish the ribs, place them on the grill 3 to 4 inches from the heat source. Grill, brushing them well with the thickened marinade and turning them once or twice, until browned, glazed, and fork-tender, 8 to 10 minutes. Remove from the grill and enjoy.

8 meaty country-style pork ribs

JIM AND MARTHA'S
VERY FINE RIB SAUCE

¼ cup vegetable oil

1 medium onion, finely chopped

1 rib celery, finely chopped

1 clove garlic, minced

1½ cups water

1 cup ketchup

½ cup cider vinegar

3 tablespoons Worcestershire sauce

1 tablespoon chili powder

1 tablespoon firmly packed dark
brown sugar

1 teaspoon dry mustard

1 teaspoon kosher salt

1 teaspoon freshly ground black pepper

East Hampton, NY

SERVES 8

Jim Villas's
barbecued country-style pork ribs

This is another of Jim and Martha Pearl Villas's wonderful Southern kitchen recipes. This recipe was originally concocted to be prepared completely in the oven, but it takes well to the outdoor grill. Mrs. Villas's key concern is that you slowly simmer the pork ribs, never boil them for very long, as they will get tough. I think you'll find the homemade barbecue sauce that goes along with this to be far superior to anything you'll buy at the grocery store. Just in case you're not familiar with country-style ribs, they are cut from the shoulder end of the loin and have little fat and the highest meat to bone ratio of any rib. It's almost like eating a small pork chop.

– ເຊຣ໐໐໑ –

1. Arrange the ribs in a large pot, add enough water to cover, and bring to a boil, skimming the top if there's any froth. Reduce the heat to low, cover, and simmer the ribs until fork-tender, about 2 hours.

2. Meanwhile, heat the oil in a large, heavy saucepan over medium heat. Add the onion, celery, and garlic and cook, stirring, for about 5 minutes. Add the remaining sauce ingredients and stir until well blended. Bring the sauce to a simmer and cook, uncovered, for 20 minutes, stirring from time to time to prevent sticking.

3. When your ribs are ready, light a charcoal fire or preheat your gas grill on high. Oil the grill's cooking surface. Let the coals burn down to a medium-hot fire or adjust the gas grill burners to medium-high.

4. Remove the ribs from the water, pat them dry, and place on the grill. Cook until slightly browned, 2 to 4 minutes per side. Brush with the sauce, turn the ribs sauce side down, and cook for a few minutes and turn. Brush again. Continue doing this, turning and basting every few minutes, for about 20 minutes to no more than 30 minutes.

5. Remove the ribs to a platter and serve immediately.

Island-Style
roasted pig
with nut stuffing

Sam Schegel has always loved the ocean and boats but also felt a huge calling to the ministry. He followed the ministry first, going to seminary. He also saw a need that filled his other love: Folks who lived on their boats in marinas needed spiritual guidance. Thus, the Water Folk Ministry was founded, and Sam, with his wife, B. A., went about God's work. They were pulled in many directions, but a decade or so ago they were posted to Hawaii.

Sam tells me this recipe is the real deal. You will need some metal skewers and heavy kitchen string, or a lardering kit (check out a kitchen store or restaurant-supply house for this), to hold in the stuffing.

– ᏣᎾᎾᏏᎾ –

1. Wash the pig under cold running water; pat dry, inside and outside. Combine the soy sauce, oil, sherry, sugar, salt, pepper, and garlic, stirring until the sugar dissolves. Let stand for 20 to 30 minutes, then brush the entire cavity of the pig with the marinade; save the remaining marinade. Refrigerate the pig until it's time to stuff and roast it.

2. Set up the grill for indirect grilling (see pp. 6–9). Oil your grill's cooking surface thoroughly.

3. Meanwhile, combine the bread cubes and corn bread in a large bowl. Place a saucepan over medium-high heat and melt the butter. Stir in the onions and celery and cook until softened, about 5 minutes. Add to the bread mixture and toss lightly. Stir in the pineapple, nuts, eggs, salt, and pepper until well mixed.

4. Before stuffing the pig, brush its cavity again with the marinade, then fill it loosely with the stuffing. Any excess may be spooned into the pan, covered, and cooked along with the pig during the last 45 minutes. Close the cavity by skewering it shut and lacing the skewers together with heavy white cord. Stuff a lime, cube of wood, or hard ball of aluminum foil into the pig's mouth to hold it open during roasting. Cover its ears, tail, nose, and front feet with small pieces of foil to prevent burning. Skewer the back feet forward under the pig. Place the pig in a kneeling position, front feet forward, on the grill away from the heat over a drip pan filled with the water. Brush the pig with the marinade. To keep the skin from splitting, prick it with a large needle or knife in several places behind the head. Insert a meat thermometer in the thickest part of the thigh, away from bone and fat, or check with an instant-read thermometer later in the cooking.

5. Cover the grill and cook until tender, basting frequently with the remaining marinade until 30 minutes before the end of the cooking time. Remove the foil from the tail, ears, nose, and feet 1 hour

One 12- to 15-pound oven-ready suckling pig (order from your meat man several days in advance)

½ cup soy sauce

⅓ cup vegetable oil

¼ cup dry sherry

¼ cup firmly packed light brown sugar

Kosher salt to taste

½ teaspoon freshly ground black pepper

1 clove garlic, crushed

MACADAMIA NUT STUFFING

4 cups ¼-inch cubes soft white bread (about 8 slices)

3 cups crumbled corn bread

½ cup (1 stick) unsalted butter

½ cup coarsely chopped onions

½ cup finely diced celery

1 cup well-drained canned crushed pineapple

¾ cup chopped macadamia nuts or pecans

2 large eggs, beaten

1 teaspoon kosher salt

¼ teaspoon freshly ground black pepper

2 cups water

Limes and in-season fruit for garnish

2 maraschino cherries for garnish

Watercress or fresh mint leaves for garnish

before the end. Allow 25 minutes per pound to cook a 12- to 15-pound pig to 170°F. Be sure the meat is fully cooked! If there is a trace of pink in the juices, continue roasting. The juices from a well-done pig will be light yellow.

6. Remove the pig to a large wooden platter or cutting board using large spatulas and two people. Remove the brace from the pig's mouth and replace with a fresh lime. Remove all the skewers and string. Push a small maraschino cherry in each eye and secure with wooden picks. Garnish the platter and pig with an assortment of your favorite fresh fruits, watercress, and maraschinos. Let the pig rest 20 to 30 minutes before carving.

Teaching an Old Dog New Tricks

✤ Since I was born and raised in North Carolina, it is considered blasphemous to even let the thought cross your mind that another state's pulled pork barbecue might be better. Even worse is to consider that a method for doing barbecue might be superior. Chad Ballenger, of Morristown, Tennessee, has made me a sinner. I met Chad at one of Morristown's First Baptist Church's socials. The barn was decked out for eating and square dancing and, just outside, was Chad, with one of those pig cookers shaped like an oil drum and set on an axle. Now, in North Carolina, this would be the scene for a "pig picking," where a whole hog is slowly cooked for up to 12 hours, mopped occasionally with a vinegar-based sauce. The pig is turned halfway through the process. For folks east of Raleigh, this is the only way to cook barbecue. From a distance, it looked like Chad was doing the North Carolina method. Wrong. He had taken a 90-pound dressed hog, which will feed about 80 to 100 people, and had it quartered. The four pieces are much easier to turn and manipulate, and you don't need such a huge grill. Plus you get more "outside brown," i.e., meat that has some char, which adds volumes of flavor to the final chopped pork. Chad starts the cooking with a base of about 40 pounds of Kingsford® charcoal, and adds split hickory wood to keep the fire going at 200°F. His mopping sauce was straight Kraft Original BBQ Sauce. Instead of the 12-hour cooking time (or more), Chad smokes this pig for about 9 hours. Some of the best pulled pork I've eaten and it kicked a little North Carolina butt.

One 14-pound pork leg (fresh ham)

4 to 6 cups wood chips, soaked in water
for 1 hour and drained

Your favorite barbecue sauce with a
kick, or try Mock Ridgewood Barbecue
Sauce (p. 307) or Kansas City Spicy
Barbecue Sauce (p. 306).

Barbecued
leg of pork

A leg of pork is basically a fresh ham. Many barbecue restaurants will add
a fresh ham to their pit for their customers who like sliced 'que instead of
pulled or chopped. If you want something new for your holiday table but
still keeping in tradition, try this for Christmas or Easter.

1. Set up the grill for indirect grilling (see pp. 6-9). Oil your grill's
cooking surface. Try to get the temperature about 275°F by closing the
grill's vents.

2. Place the pork on the grill away from the heat and cook, with the lid
down, for 4½ hours, turning the pork occasionally and replenishing the
fire as needed. Add a handful of the smoking chips, about every 20 minutes until they are gone. The meat will pick up its smoke flavor early in
the cooking process.

3. Start basting with the barbecue sauce and continue to baste about every
20 minutes for another hour or until an instant-read thermometer inserted
into the thickest part registers 160°F.

4. Remove from the grill and let rest 10 to 15 minutes before slicing.

5. Meanwhile, place the remaining barbecue sauce in a small saucepan
and bring to a boil. Serve on the side with the pork.

One 6-pound pork butt

2 to 3 tablespoons prepared yellow mustard

Cam Campbell's Georgia Dry Rub (p. 298)

Wood chips, soaked in water for 1 hour and drained

Steve Marcember's 100-Year-Old Family-Secret BBQ Sauce (p. 308)

White hamburger buns

Eastern North Carolina-Style Slaw (p. 333)

1. Coat the pork with the mustard and liberally sprinkle on the rub.

2. Meanwhile, set up the grill for indirect grilling (see pp. 6-9). Oil your grill's cooking surface.

3. When the fire is ready, add the wood chips. Place the butt on the grill away from the heat, close the lid, and smoke at 200°F to 250°F for 4 to 6 hours, until an instant-read meat thermometer inserted into the thickest part away from the bone registers

4. Transfer the butt to a cutting board and let cool slightly, enough to where you can handle the pork. Pull apart and then roughly chop the pork. Sprinkle with a bit more rub and moisten with the sauce. Serve piled on buns with slaw and extra sauce on the side.

Dawgville
pork barbecue

Dawgville is this ruckus scene that sets up camp on football weekends in Athens, Georgia, home to the University of Georgia and their bulldog mascot. Like all SEC schools, football is serious business and families have long-standing traditions for tailgating before the games. Steve Lyons, his wife, kids, parents (Richard and Judy), brother-in-law Cam Campbell and his kids, all gather for every Bulldog home game. Steve and his parents are from Brunswick, Georgia, a coastal community close to the Florida-Georgia border. Cam drives in from Atlanta with his red truck (the only color for a Georgia fan) laden with coolers and his prized Big Green Egg® smoker grill. Green Eggs are fashionable now, and their owners swear by them. I was amazed at how the temperature stayed constant in it with little work. The protein of choice the day I spent with them was pork butt, smoked and pulled into barbecue.

The Lyons family swears by the Green Egg.

One 5- to 7-pound Boston butt pork roast

1 tablespoon paprika

1 tablespoon light brown sugar

1 tablespoon kosher salt

1 tablespoon freshly ground black pepper

1 teaspoon white pepper

1 teaspoon garlic powder

1 teaspoon dry mustard

6 cups hickory wood chips, soaked in water for at least 1 hour

Eastern North Carolina-Style Barbecue Sauce (p. 304) or Lexington-Style North Carolina Barbecue Sauce (p. 302)

1. Remove the pork from the refrigerator 1 hour before cooking. Set up the grill for indirect grilling (pp. 6-9). Oil the cooking surface.

2. Mix the paprika, brown sugar, salt, the peppers, garlic powder, and mustard together. Rub all over the pork butt.

3. Put 1 cup of the wood chips it in your gas grill's smoker box, or sprinkle over the charcoal. Cover the grill until smoke appears from the vents. Put the pork on the grill away from the heat, cover, and turn the gas burners to low or, for charcoal, close the vents almost completely. Every hour, add more chips and, for charcoal, about 10 briquettes. Your grill's temperature should be 275° to 300°F. Cook until the pork registers 175° to 180°F on an instant-read meat thermometer. This will take 4 to 7 hours. The longer it takes, the better the smoke flavor, so don't hurry it up.

4. Let the pork rest 20 minutes. Remove any skin and excess fat. Pull off the meat in chunks (a pair of latex gloves is helpful). The browned outside meat is considered a prize. Chop or shred the meat, then add 1 cup of the sauce, tossing with your hands to coat the pork evenly with it. Serve with the remaining sauce on the side.

Fred's Backyard, NC

SERVES 12 TO 15

Fred's
north carolina-style barbecue

What you've got to understand is that in some parts of this country, barbecue is a noun. Where that is the case, it refers to meat (either pork or beef brisket) that's been slow cooked by fire until it shreds into mouthwatering succulence, served up with sauce. Whether it's beef or pork and exactly what kind of sauce you'll be served is a function of where you are. North Carolina lays claim to two styles of barbecue.

In eastern North Carolina, the whole hog is slowly smoke-roasted, then served with a vinegar-based sauce. Around Lexington, in the Piedmont, only the shoulders of the hog are cooked and a little ketchup slips into the sauce, which they call a "dip."

In this recipe, we will get low and slow with a Boston butt, which is more practical for the home cook. A half shoulder will also work and is frequently on sale during the summer. Try both sauces and decide for yourself which is better. The rub for the pork is more Memphis or northwestern North Carolina than you might find in Goldsboro or Lexington, but I find that it helps produce better "outside" meat, those prized bits of char, when smoking a butt at home.

This barbecue is a great choice for a neighborhood party, family reunion, or a holiday gathering, served up with Lexington-Style Red Slaw (p. 334) and Eastern North Caroline-Style Mustard Slaw (p. 333). It will also freeze for up to 3 months, so you might want to double the recipe. If you're going to be cooking with charcoal, you'll want to have 20 pounds of it on hand. And remember that great barbecue is great barbecue wherever it comes from. Also know that in North Carolina, barbecue is a noun.

8 large baking potatoes

One 8-ounce container whipped cream cheese

½ cup mayonnaise

1 tablespoon white wine vinegar

1 teaspoon seasoned pepper

2 teaspoons fresh lemon juice

¾ teaspoon kosher salt

3 cups leftover chopped barbecued pork, warmed

4 ounces medium-sharp Cheddar cheese, shredded (1 cup)

¼ cup chopped fresh chives

Would You Like Your Barbecue in a Cone or a Cup?

While Oxford, Mississippi, may not be one of the major capitals of barbecue in the South, it certainly has gained a reputation for some unique presentations. Along with barbecue stuffed potatoes, you'll find a barbecue sundae, where you get baked beans on the bottom, slaw in the middle, and barbecue on top, served just like you would an ice cream sundae. I laughed at this arrangement when I first saw it, but guess what—it's pure enjoyment.

Double-Stuffed
barbecue potatoes

Buddy's Barbecue in eastern Tennessee has always been a favorite among those who enjoy eating smoked pork. A few years back they put a stuffed barbecue potato on their menu and it's now one of their hottest-selling items. This recipe from Carolyn Walthall of Oxford, Mississippi, I think gilds that basic lily with cream cheese, Cheddar cheese, and fresh chives, elevating the humble potato and equally humble barbecue to a fun and sort of semi-elegant eating experience. This is a great way to deal with leftovers after you've smoked a pork shoulder.

– ᘓᕲᖆᕲᖇ –

1. Preheat the oven to 425°F.

2. Wrap each potato in a piece of aluminum foil, place them in the oven, and bake until tender, about 45 minutes. Reduce the oven temperature to 375°F.

3. Cut a 4x2-inch strip from the top of each baked potato. Carefully scoop out the potato pulp into a large bowl, leaving 8 intact potato skin shells. Set aside about 2 cups of the pulp for another use.

4. Add to the remaining potato pulp the cream cheese, mayonnaise, vinegar, pepper, lemon juice, and salt, and mash together until well blended. Stir in the pork. Spoon the mixture evenly back into the shells. Top the potatoes equally with the Cheddar and chives. Place on a lightly greased baking sheet. Bake until thoroughly heated, 20 to 25 minutes, and serve.

One 7- to 8-pound smoked, fully cooked ham half, regular or spiral cut

½ cup dry mustard

½ cup firmly packed light brown sugar

½ cup water

4 to 6 cups wood chips (hickory is the best), soaked in water for 1 hour and drained

It's a Classic!

If you want to do a grilled version of the classic clove-embellished ham with pineapple rings, remove the ham from the grill about 30 minutes before it's ready. Stud with cloves and add the pineapple rings. Return to the grill and cook until the internal temperature is 140°F.

Hickory
grilled ham

Most of us will encounter a fully cooked ham at some point. Once you have reheated a ham on the grill, I doubt you'll ever put it in the oven again. Smoking it on the grill reinforces the smoke flavor that makes this type of ham so good. This ham is particularly good sliced and served up on biscuits with a little green pepper or hot pepper jelly on the side. Make it your new party tradition.

1. Cut the ham bone loose from the meat (or ask your butcher to do this), but do not remove the bone. If using a spiral-cut ham, skip this step.

2. Combine the mustard and brown sugar in a small bowl and add the water, stirring until smooth. Brush the mixture evenly over the ham.

3. Set up the grill for indirect grilling (see pp. 6–9). Oil your grill's cooking surface.

4. Place the wood chunks on the coals, set the ham on the grill away from the heat, and close the lid. Cook the ham, turning and brushing it often with the mustard mixture until an instant-read meat thermometer inserted into the thickest part registers 140°F, about 1½ hours, replenishing the fire as needed.

5. Remove the ham to a cutting board and let set for at least 20 minutes or until room temperature, then slice thinly, if desired. Remove from the bone to slice if desired.

Six ¼-inch-thick center-cut country ham slices

1 cup orange juice

¼ cup firmly packed light brown sugar

3 tablespoons vegetable oil

3 tablespoons Jack Daniel's Tennessee Whiskey

1. Cut slashes in the rim of fat to prevent the ham slices from curling. Place them in a shallow glass baking dish.

2. Combine the orange juice, brown sugar, oil, and whiskey. Pour it over the ham and let marinate for 1 hour at room temperature.

3. Light a charcoal fire or preheat your gas grill on high. Oil the grill's cooking surface. Let the coals burn down to a low fire or adjust the gas grill burners to low.

4. Grill the ham over low heat 2 to 3 minutes per side, basting each side as you turn it. Be careful not to overcook. Serve hot or at room temperature.

Jack Daniel's
grilled country ham

Lynn Tolley is Jack Daniel's great-grandniece and keeper of the traditions at the Jack Daniel's® Distillery in Lynchburg, Tennessee. She also runs a bed and breakfast in town.

In this neck of the woods, country ham is a food group all to itself. Country hams are cured and smoked. You should be able to buy center-cut country ham slices at most stores. Ham steaks don't make a very good substitute. Lynn does what any close kin of America's favorite sour mash would do: Marinate the ham in the spirits, then grill it for a balanced taste that is just wonderful. Lynn says that cheese grits on the side are a must.

5 on the lamb with some wild things:

lamb, goat, and game

If you have some genetic material that places your ancestry in Northern Europe, you may have an aversion to lamb.

That part of the world ate mutton in the early centuries, which is older sheep and has a much stronger smell and taste than lamb. My dad, who was stationed in England for part of World War II, would not allow lamb in our house because of his experiences with mutton in England. If you were raised in the South or Midwest, lamb was probably not a meat on your table. However, if you have roots in Southern Europe, North Africa, or the Middle East, lamb has always been part of your **mealtime pleasure**. That same dad was also posted in Morocco and loved the stews (called tagines) he was served in local restaurants. He was always trying to describe them to my mother—what he didn't realize is that more than likely they were made with lamb.

Some of us with early memories of lamb probably remember it as overcooked and in dire need of mint jelly. Lamb is best when cooked to medium or less. For many, medium-rare (around 140°F) is perfect.

Lamb loves interesting seasonings, and an outdoor fire truly brings out the **exceptional flavor** that lamb has to offer. Take a look at what these pages have to offer and give lamb a try, if you haven't already.

Venison was once only available to those who hunted. I remember my mother trying to get the "gaminess" out of deer meat my dad would bring home. Now venison is also being raised domestically. Lean and heart healthy, with a mild taste, venison has become the darling of many chefs.

Lamb and venison both have cuts much like beef. The secret to success with both is not to overcook it. For **chops and tenderloins**, direct heat is best. If the lamb chops, especially the rib chops, get into triple cuts (three ribs thick), you probably want to go with the indirect method, giving it a good sear over direct heat first. The **leg of lamb** can be bone in, boned, rolled and tied, or butterflied. I like butterflied the best for the grill because there's more surface area that can be seasoned and caramelized over the fire.

With growing immigrant populations from Africa and the Caribbean, goat is becoming increasingly available in this country. Goat likes the strong flavor of curry. Look for goat in specialty ethnic or halal markets.

Know Your Chops

The most tender lamb comes from the chops. The rib chop, which in a group becomes the rack of lamb, can be cut into single, double, or triple chops. Singles cook fast and are wonderful appetizers. Double-cut chops to me are perfect for a meal, while triple cuts are kind of overkill and you're better off cooking them over an indirect fire. The loin chop or T-bone chop is a great treat. Like the beef porterhouse steak, it contains both tenderloin and the strip loin. Don't forget shoulder chops, which are cheaper and fattier but taste great. Just have a spray bottle of water around for the inevitable flare-ups.

CHILI-HONEY MARINADE

3 tablespoons light soy sauce

3 tablespoons clover honey

2 tablespoons Asian chili-garlic sauce

1 tablespoon peeled and minced fresh ginger

1 tablespoon minced garlic

Juice and finely grated zest of 1 lime

6 loin lamb chops, cut 1½ inches thick

Chinatown
lamb chops

For years I stayed away from lamb in Chinese restaurants. For some reason I just didn't think Asian seasonings and lamb would work. One night at Joe's Shanghai Café in New York's Chinatown, lamb chops were on their specials menu. I didn't order them, but one of my dining companions did, and as is our custom, every dish was passed around so that we all could sample. I was blown away with these chops and quickly inquired of the waiter what the ingredients were. I'm sure I missed a few, but the ones I remembered yielded this wonderful marinade that takes lamb to a whole other continent.

– ৩৩৩ –

1. Combine the marinade ingredients in a small bowl.

2. Place the lamb chops in a large zip-top plastic bag and add the marinade. Seal the bag and squish everything together to coat the chops evenly. Let marinate in the refrigerator for 2 to 3 hours, turning the bag a few times.

3. Light a charcoal fire or preheat your gas grill on high. Oil the grill's cooking surface. Let the coals burn down to a medium-hot fire or adjust the gas grill burners to medium-high.

4. Remove the chops from the marinade and discard the marinade. Grill the lamb 3 inches from the heat source for 4 to 5 minutes per side for medium-rare or to your desired degree of doneness.

2 tablespoons finely chopped fresh rosemary

4 cloves garlic, finely chopped

Kosher salt and freshly ground black pepper to taste

8 lamb loin chops, cut about 1 inch thick

2 tablespoons olive oil

Mustapha's
lamb chops

Mustapha Debbabi of Louisville, Kentucky, is originally from Tunisia, in North Africa. He, his wife, Wided, and their two children, Bassem and Sarri, love to grill, cooking outside at least two times a week unless it snows or they have a hard rain. Most days Mustapha uses a gas grill, but in the summer months he pulls out his charcoal grill. He truly loves the taste of charcoal smoke, reminding him of open-flame cooking in Tunisia. It's no surprise to see Mediterranean flavors in this recipe, and using fresh ingredients is very important to Mustapha.

– ⌘ –

1. On a cutting board using the back of a knife, work the rosemary, garlic, salt, and pepper together, almost to a paste. Rub this mixture evenly over the chops, then brush them with the olive oil. Cover with plastic wrap and refrigerate for 30 minutes.

2. Light a charcoal fire or preheat your gas grill on high. Oil the grill's cooking surface.

3. Place the ribs on the grill and cook about 4 minutes per side for medium-rare or to your desired degree of doneness, though Mustapha pleads with you not to overcook them. Serve immediately, two chops for each person.

CHILI RUB

3 tablespoons medium-hot chili powder

1 tablespoon ground cumin

2 teaspoons dried thyme, crumbled

2 teaspoons sugar

1 1/2 teaspoons kosher salt

1 teaspoon freshly ground black pepper

3/4 teaspoon ground allspice

16 rib lamb chops, cut about 1 1/2 inches thick, trimmed of excess fat

About 2 cups hot pepper jelly

Grilled Chili-Rubbed
lamb chops

Normally we think of lamb rib chops as an exquisite protein that has to be handled with kid gloves. Lamb holds up to so many different flavors, and individual rib chops can make a great hors d'oeuvre. These chops take on chili powder and other Southwestern spices. The hot pepper jelly is a wonderful side note, and I have on occasion brushed the jelly on each chop right before I take them up from the grill for another shot of flavor.

– ༐ဖြစ –

1. In a small bowl, combine the rub ingredients. Sprinkle over the chops, rubbing it evenly all over the meat. Cover the chops with plastic wrap and refrigerate for at least 4 hours or overnight.

2. Light a charcoal fire or preheat your gas grill on high. Oil the grill's cooking surface. Let the coals burn down to a medium-hot fire or adjust the gas grill burners to medium-high.

3. Place the chops on the grill and cook for 5 to 7 minutes per side for medium-rare. Remove to a platter and serve immediately with the pepper jelly on the side.

4 racks lamb spareribs

Lawry's® seasoned salt

Freshly ground black pepper

Paprika

1 ½ cups of your favorite bottled barbecue sauce, or I like East Tennessee-Style Barbecue Sauce (p. 305)

½ cup water

The Walker Family's
favorite lamb ribs

A longtime barbecue buddy of mine, Charla Draper, told me about her aunt and uncle in Chicago and their awesome lamb ribs. The Walkers, it seems, have a longstanding reputation for making lamb on the grill. This recipe is fairly simple and uses a cut of lamb you may not have tried—lamb spareribs. Lately these have become the darling of high-end chefs around the country, who are always looking for a new food twist. These ribs are falling-off-the-bone good. Charla says the sauce is a key flavor component, so make sure to use your favorite, not just any sauce on sale.

– ༒ –

1. Sprinkle the lamb ribs evenly on both sides with salt, pepper, and paprika. Place them in a shallow pan, cover with plastic wrap, and let marinate in the refrigerator overnight.

2. Remove the ribs from the refrigerator and let stand at room temperature for 30 minutes.

3. Set up your grill for indirect grilling (see pp. 6–9). Oil your grill's cooking surface. Add a drip pan opposite the coals if you're cooking with charcoal.

4. Place the ribs meaty side down on the cooking grate away from the fire. Cover and cook for 2 to 3 hours, turning the ribs every 30 minutes.

5. Remove the ribs from the grill, cut into 3- to 4-rib portions, and place in a disposable aluminum pan. Pour the barbecue sauce and water over the ribs. Cover tightly and return to the grill until extremely tender, about another 20 minutes. You can also put them in a preheated 350°F oven.

6. Remove the ribs from the grill and place on a platter. Pour the sauce into a separate bowl and pass at the table.

1½ cups plain yogurt

2 cloves garlic, pressed

1 tablespoon fresh lemon juice

Kosher salt

2 teaspoons ground cumin

1 teaspoon ground coriander

2¼ pounds boneless lamb sirloin, trimmed of fat and cut into 1-inch cubes

1 cup water

⅔ cup couscous

½ cucumber, seeded and chopped

1 medium ripe tomato, chopped

½ small onion, cut in half and sliced into thin half moons

2 tablespoons olive oil

2 tablespoons chopped fresh dill

Freshly ground black pepper

Six 6-inch-diameter pita breads

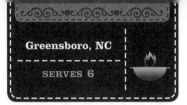

Grilled Cumin Lamb Shish Kebobs with
pitas and couscous

In the late 1950s and early 1960s, an exotic dish started showing up on the grills of suburbia. It was called shish kebob. My parents even bought a special shish kebob grill. This version is simple to do and is updated from some of the recipes of that decade. To me, grilled lamb with yogurt and cucumber wrapped in a pita is one of this world's greatest delights. I've thrown in some couscous to make this a full meal. This dish is fast enough for a weeknight—just let the yogurt drain the night before.

- ເຂົ້າ -

1. Set a strainer over a large bowl and line it with two layers of cheese-cloth. Don't let the strainer touch the bottom of the bowl. Spoon the yogurt into the strainer. Let stand at room temperature for 1 hour. The liquid will drain out and the yogurt will thicken. Discard the liquid. This can be done the night before.

2. Mix the thickened yogurt, garlic, and lemon juice together in a small bowl. Season to taste with salt.

3. Rub the cumin and coriander over the lamb pieces in a medium bowl. Thread the lamb onto 6 metal skewers. Set aside.

4. Combine the water and ¼ teaspoon salt in a medium saucepan. Bring to a boil, then add the couscous. Remove from the heat. Cover and let stand until the liquid is absorbed, about 5 minutes. Transfer the couscous to a large bowl and fluff with a fork. Let cool to room temperature, then stir in the cucumber, tomato, onion, oil, and dill. Season with salt and pepper.

5. Light a charcoal fire or preheat your gas grill on high. Oil the grill's cooking surface. Let the coals burn down to a medium-hot fire or adjust the gas grill burners to medium-high.

6. Place the lamb on the grill and cook to your desired degree of done-ness, turning frequently, about 10 minutes total for medium-rare. Transfer to a platter. Sprinkle with salt.

7. Grill the pitas until heated through and lightly toasted, about 1 minute per side. Place 1 pita on each of 6 plates. Spread the yogurt mixture evenly over the pitas. Spoon couscous down the center of the pitas. Slide the lamb off the skewers onto the couscous. Serve immediately.

LEMON-MINT MARINADE

1 cup olive oil

2 tablespoons fresh lemon juice

2 tablespoons chopped fresh mint or parsley

2 teaspoons dried oregano

1½ teaspoons kosher salt

1 teaspoon freshly ground black pepper

4 cloves garlic, minced

One 3-pound boneless leg of lamb, trimmed of fat and silverskin and cut into 2-inch cubes

3 small purple onions, quartered

2 green or red bell peppers, seeded and quartered

2 large ripe tomatoes, cored and quartered, or 8 cherry tomatoes

8 white mushrooms

3 tablespoons fresh lemon juice

3 tablespoons olive oil

New York, NY

SERVES 8

Mohammad's North African
shish kebobs

According to my Moroccan friend Mohammad, who has traveled all over the Middle East, this is as close to real North African kebobs as most of us will be able to make at home. As far as I'm concerned, who cares whether it's authentic if it tastes this good. Serve these kebobs up on a bed of saffron rice or couscous.

– ✐✐✐ –

1. Combine the marinade ingredients in a small bowl and stir well.

2. Place the lamb in a large zip-top plastic bag. Pour the marinade over the lamb and seal the bag. Squish everything around to coat the meat and let marinate in the refrigerator for at least 8 hours or overnight, turning the bag occasionally.

3. Remove the lamb from the marinade, discarding the marinade. Alternate the lamb cubes, onions, peppers, tomatoes, and mushrooms on eight 12-inch skewers.

4. Combine the lemon juice and olive oil in a small bowl. Brush on the kebobs.

5. Light a charcoal fire or preheat your gas grill on high. Oil the grill's cooking surface. Let the coals burn down to a medium-hot fire or adjust the gas grill burners to medium-high.

6. Place the kebobs on the grill and cook for 20 minutes total for medium doneness, turning them 4 times. Remove to a platter and serve.

Eight 8- to 10-inch-long sturdy fresh rosemary branches or 2-inch-long wooden skewers

FRESH HERB MARINADE

½ cup olive oil

3 tablespoons fresh lemon juice

1 tablespoon chopped fresh rosemary

1 tablespoon chopped fresh oregano or 1 teaspoon dried

1 tablespoon chopped fresh thyme or 1 teaspoon dried

½ teaspoon kosher salt

¼ teaspoon freshly ground black pepper

2 pounds boneless lean lamb, from the leg or sirloin, trimmed of fat and cut into 1½-inch cubes

Rosemary
skewered lamb

Ride through the Greek section of Astoria, Queens, in New York around dinnertime and your nostrils will fill with the smell of rosemary and lamb. Restaurants have taken to using rosemary branches as skewers, and now many supermarkets are selling foot-long branches for just this use.

– ⚬⚬⚬ –

1. Soak the rosemary branches or skewers in water for 2 hours.

2. Combine the marinade ingredients in a small bowl. Stir well.

3. Place the lamb in a large zip-top plastic bag. Pour the marinade over the lamb and seal. Squish everything around to coat the meat and let marinate in the refrigerator for 2 hours, turning the bag a few times.

4. Remove the lamb from the marinade, discarding the marinade. Thread the lamb onto the skewers.

5. Light a charcoal fire or preheat your gas grill on high. Oil the grill's cooking surface. Let the coals burn down to a medium-hot fire or adjust the gas grill burners to medium-high.

6. Place the skewers on the grill and cook for 8 minutes total for medium or to your desired doneness, turning a few times. Remove from the grill and serve immediately.

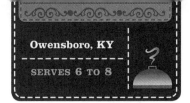
BARBECUE RUB

¼ cup freshly ground black pepper

2 tablespoons light brown sugar

1 tablespoon kosher salt

1 tablespoon garlic powder

¼ teaspoon ground allspice

One 7- to 8-pound lamb shoulder roast

½ cup Worcestershire sauce or as needed

BARBECUE MOP

½ cup distilled white vinegar

½ cup water

½ cup beer or low-sodium beef broth

2 tablespoons Worcestershire sauce

1 tablespoon coarsely ground black pepper

1 tablespoon firmly packed dark brown sugar

2 teaspoons kosher salt or to taste

2 teaspoons garlic powder

½ teaspoon cayenne pepper or to taste

BARBECUE DIP

1 cup Worcestershire sauce

1 cup distilled white vinegar

½ cup firmly packed dark brown sugar

2 tablespoons fresh lemon juice

2 teaspoons kosher salt

1 teaspoon garlic powder

1 teaspoon onion powder

½ teaspoon ground allspice

Owensboro-Style
barbecued lamb shoulder

This recipe is based loosely on one from the Moonlite BBQ Inn in Owensboro, Kentucky, where the barbecue tradition includes mutton. If you enjoy lamb, give this a try.

- ⌇ -

1. Combine the rub ingredients in a small bowl.

2. Rinse and pat dry the lamb shoulder with paper towels. Brush the meat with the Worcestershire. Sprinkle the rub evenly over the lamb, patting to help it adhere. Place the meat in a 2-gallon zip-top plastic bag, seal, and refrigerate several hours or overnight.

3. One hour before cooking, remove the meat from the refrigerator and let come to room temperature.

4. Meanwhile, combine the mop ingredients in a small saucepan over low heat and cook, stirring, just until the mixture boils. Remove from the heat and let cool before using.

5. Set up the grill for indirect grilling (see pp. 6–9). Oil your grill's cooking surface.

6. Place the lamb, fat side up, on the grate away from the heat and cover the cooker. After the first hour of cooking, baste with the mop about once an hour until the meat is done. Allow 1 to 1½ hours per pound, or 7 to 10 hours. Keep the temperature inside the cooker between 225°F and 250°F, replenishing the fire as needed. The meat should be well done and tender, with an internal temperature that registers 180°F to 190°F on an instant-read thermometer.

7. While the lamb is cooking, make the dip. Combine the dip ingredients in a small saucepan over medium heat. When the liquid boils, reduce the heat to low and simmer for 10 minutes, until slightly thickened.

8. Slice the meat or shred and chop it. Serve on a plate with the warm or room temperature dip on the side or in a sandwich.

RED WINE VINAIGRETTE

2 tablespoons red wine vinegar

1 teaspoon Dijon mustard

1 teaspoon honey

Kosher salt and freshly ground
black pepper

½ cup extra-virgin olive oil

CAPERED THYME TAPENADE

1 cup Kalamata olives, pitted and drained

2 anchovy fillets

1 tablespoon capers, drained

1 clove garlic, peeled

1 tablespoon chopped fresh thyme

⅛ teaspoon cayenne pepper

2 teaspoons fresh lemon juice

1 teaspoon grated lemon zest

2 tablespoons olive oil

GARLICKY HERB RUB

8 cloves garlic, finely chopped

¼ cup dried herbes de Provence

½ teaspoon freshly ground black pepper

1 tablespoon kosher salt

⅓ cup olive oil

One 7- to 8-pound leg of lamb, trimmed
of all fat, boned, and butterflied by the
butcher (4 to 4¾ pounds boneless)

12 cups mixed baby salad greens

Plano, TX

SERVES 8

Meredith and David's
provencal herb-crusted butterflied leg of lamb

This is one of Meredith and David Deed's ways of grilling lamb. The rich lamb is a great contrast to the earthy tapenade vinaigrette. Even though it has a few steps, they are all easy and the final dish comes together quickly.

– ເົຣ໑ນ –

1. Whisk together the vinegar, mustard, honey, salt, and pepper. Whisking constantly, add the oil in a slow, steady stream and continue whisking until thickened. Set aside. Whisk again just before using.

2. Place the olives, anchovies, capers, garlic, thyme, cayenne, and lemon juice and zest in a food processor and pulse to blend. Add the oil and pulse a few more times to form a coarse paste. Set aside. (This recipe makes more than you need; it will keep, refrigerated—enjoy it on crackers and toast.)

3. Combine the rub ingredients, then place the lamb in a large baking dish and cut ½-inch-deep slits all over the lamb. Work the rub mixture into the slits and all over the surface. Cover with plastic and marinate at room temperature for at least 1 hour and up to 4 hours.

4. Light a charcoal fire or preheat your gas grill on high. Oil the grill's cooking surface.

5. Lightly pat the lamb dry. Run two long metal skewers lengthwise and two skewers crosswise through the lamb, bunching the meat. Securing the lamb this way will help it to cook more evenly. Place it on the grill and cook for 10 minutes. Turn and cook until an instant-read meat thermometer horizontally inserted into the thickest part of the meat registers 125°F for medium-rare, another 10 minutes, or cook to desired degree of doneness. Remove to a cutting board and let rest for 15 minutes.

6. Meanwhile, toss the salad greens with half the vinaigrette. Divide equally among 8 plates. Mix the remaining vinaigrette with 3 tablespoons of the tapenade. Slice the lamb thinly against the grain. Arrange the warm slices on the salad. Drizzle with the tapenade vinaigrette. Serve immediately.

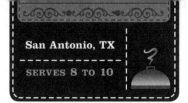

4 to 5 pounds bone-in goat meat

1 tablespoon unseasoned meat tenderizer

1 to 2 tablespoons seasoned salt

2 tablespoons peanut oil

3 rounded tablespoons prepared Jamaican jerk sauce

1 large onion, minced

Akeem's
slow-cooked jerk goat

Akeem Babatunde is originally from Nigeria. He came to this country to study engineering and specialized in manufacturing. Now living in Texas, he oversees a large group of flour and baking plants. When I asked him what he cooked that reminded him the most of home, it was this goat recipe. If you've never tried goat, this is an excellent way to add it to your repertoire.

– ᘓᕫᕬ –

1. Without removing any of the bones, cut the goat meat into small pieces. Thoroughly wash the meat and drain excess water. Pat dry with paper towels. Sprinkle the meat tenderizer and seasoned salt completely over all the pieces. Place the oil and jerk sauce in a 2-gallon zip-top plastic bag, then add the meat and onion. Seal the bag and squish all the ingredients together until the meat is well coated. Refrigerate overnight.

2. Set up the grill for indirect grilling (see pp. 6–9). Oil your grill's cooking surface.

3. Remove the meat from the bag and tightly wrap it in aluminum foil. Place the packet on the grill away from the fire. Close the lid and cook until very tender, about 3 hours, replenishing the fire as needed. Akeem says that goat is best eaten right off the grill with your friends and a dark stout.

HERBED MADEIRA MARINADE

2 tablespoons chopped fresh parsley

2 tablespoons chopped fresh chives

1 tablespoon chopped fresh chervil

3 tablespoons chopped shallots

1 tablespoon brandy

½ cup Madeira

½ cup extra-virgin olive oil

Kosher salt and freshly ground black pepper to taste

3 rabbits, defrosted if necessary and cut into 6 pieces each

1. Combine the marinade ingredients in a large bowl. Add the rabbit pieces to the marinade, turning them over to coat well, cover with plastic wrap, and let marinate in the refrigerator for at least 8 hours and up to 24 hours.

2. Light a charcoal fire or preheat your gas grill on high. Oil the grill's cooking surface. Let the coals burn down to a medium fire or adjust the gas grill burners to medium.

3. Remove the rabbit from the marinade and discard the marinade. Place the back legs on the grill (they will take the longest to cook). After about 3 minutes, place the front legs on the grill. After 1 minute more, place the loin portions on the grill. The back legs will take about 8 minutes total, turning once, the front legs about 6 minutes total, turning once, the loins about 4 minutes, turning once. Your rabbit should still be slightly pink inside. Transfer to a platter and serve immediately.

Dan's
grilled rabbit napa style

Dan Winston is an artist in the Napa Valley, and outside his studio is one of the most beautiful and productive gardens I've seen. While I was on a trip out there, he shared this rabbit recipe with me, plucking the fresh herbs for it right out of his garden. Rabbit is available most everywhere now, although it's most likely to be found in the frozen meat section. It's lean and tasty and really shines in this marinade.

How to Deal with a Swamp Rabbit

Fred Pirkle is the owner and designer of the Caldera smoker who once lived in Carlos Corner, Texas. Late one night, Fred was driving home after attending a friend's wedding and was starting to nod off when he hit something. Wide awake, he jumped out of the car and said, "I saw a swamp rabbit, kickin' his last. It was big as a dog. I stomped his head, and had a beer case in the car, so I stuck him in it so I didn't get blood on the floor of the car." He didn't get home until 3 A.M. but he said to himself, being a good Texas boy, "If you kill it, you eat it." So he got out his 30-gallon oil-drum pit, set to work, and, at 12:30 the next day, set out the fruit of his smoking labors on the table for coworkers. One said, "!@#$, you ain't feedin' me nobody's dog." He had to dig the rabbit's ears out of the trash to get them to eat it. But 20 minutes later, there wasn't anything left but the bones. "It was the best thing they ever ate."

2 pounds buffalo tenderloin

Juice from 1 lemon

½ cup olive oil

Kosher salt and freshly ground
black pepper

1 each red, yellow, and green bell pepper,
seeded and cut into pieces

1 large sweet onion, cut into eighths

Skewers (if using wooden, soak them in
water for 1 hour)

South Texas
buffalo shish kebob

Bison rancher Hugh Fitzsimmons makes his home is South Texas. Hugh takes his calling to bring back our native animal quite seriously and raises the bison in an all-natural way. He shared this recipe with me, but he credits Holly Hindt with developing it. This simple mixture of lemon, oil, and salt and pepper is also nice on buffalo steaks. Buffalo is a bit stronger than beef in its depth of flavor—there's no gaminess about it. Some supermarkets are now stocking buffalo, and natural-food stores usually carry it.

– ଔଊଡ଼ –

1. Cut the tenderloin into 1-inch cubes and place them in a large zip-top plastic bag. Drizzle with the lemon juice and olive oil, then sprinkle with salt and pepper. Seal the bag, squish everything around to coat evenly, and let marinate in the refrigerator for at least 1 hour but no more than 3.

2. Light a charcoal fire or preheat your gas grill on high. Oil the grill's cooking surface.

3. Alternate the meat and vegetables on the skewers. Place on the grill and cook for a total of 20 minutes, turning frequently for a medium doneness or to your taste. Remove to a platter and serve.

½ cup garlic-infused olive oil

½ cup soy sauce

½ teaspoon crushed celery seeds

2 pounds venison tenderloins

5 to 7 ounces ripe mangos, peeled and pitted, or one 1-pound 8-ounce jar mangos in light syrup (look in the refrigerated section of your grocery store)

¼ cup canola oil

½ cup rice vinegar

2 fresh mint leaves

Kosher salt and freshly ground black pepper

Fresh mint sprigs for garnish

Venison That Even
the wife and kids will eat

I was bequeathed some venison tenderloins from a group of friends who regularly go deer hunting near Kinston, North Carolina. They told me they wanted me to come up with something different and unusual so that their wives and kids would quit griping about eating venison all the time. I took their request to heart and developed this recipe. The mango and mint sauce is a nice foil to the lean richness of the venison tenderloin. It got rave reviews from my hunting buddies, and if you come into possession of some venison, I think you'll enjoy this, too.

– ༄༅ –

1. Combine the olive oil, soy sauce, and ¼ teaspoon of the celery seeds in a small bowl, mixing well. Place the tenderloins in a large zip-top plastic bag, pour over the marinade, and seal the bag. Squish everything around to coat and let marinate in the refrigerator for 2 hours.

2. Meanwhile, combine the mangos, canola oil, and vinegar in a blender or food processor and process until smooth. Add the mint leaves and the remaining ¼ teaspoon celery seeds, and season with salt and pepper. Pulse until the mint is finely chopped and set aside.

3. Light a charcoal fire or preheat your gas grill on high. Oil the grill's cooking surface.

4. Remove the venison from the marinade; discard the marinade. Grill the tenderloins until charred but rare. Transfer to a platter and cover with aluminum foil. Slice the tenderloins about ¼ inch thick and place on a platter. Spoon some of the sauce over the venison, garnish with the mint, and pass the rest of the sauce at the table.

5. Sauce 4 plates to the rim with the mango sauce, and arrange the sliced venison in the center. Garnish with the mint sprigs and serve.

4 gator tail steaks (about 3 pounds total)

1 quart buttermilk

1 teaspoon cayenne pepper

1 tablespoon dried rosemary, crushed

Kosher salt and freshly ground
black pepper

Peanut oil

Carla's Tallahassee
gator steaks

If you're a Florida Gator fan, you've enjoyed gator steaks more than once outside the football stadium. Carla Batchelor shared this recipe with me, which really belongs to her grandmother, who lives near Tallahassee, Florida. It's simple but adds punch to the gator. Soaking the meat first in the buttermilk does wonders to tenderize what can be a tough experience. I imagine there are a few boys around the catfish ponds in the Mississippi Delta who have put gator to a grill in similar fashion.

– ᥫᥣᥱᥬᥬ –

1. Place the gator steaks in a large zip-top plastic bag. Pour in the buttermilk, then add the cayenne and rosemary. Seal the bag and squish everything together to mix and coat. Let marinate in the refrigerator for 4 hours.

2. Light a charcoal fire or preheat your gas grill on high. Oil the grill's cooking surface. Let the coals burn down to a medium-hot fire or adjust the gas grill burners to medium-high.

3. Remove the gator steaks from the buttermilk, allowing any excess to drip off. Season with salt and pepper and drizzle with a little peanut oil. Place the gator on the grill and cook for about 10 minutes, turning frequently. You need to be careful here and not overcook it; gator will become shoe leather in a hurry. If you cut into one of the gator steaks, it should be opaque all the way through. Serve immediately.

6 ruffling feathers:
chicken and other fowl

In the 1950s when folks cooked over that brazier grill in the backyard, barbecued chicken was as much the rage as hamburgers, hot dogs, and steaks.

Today, chicken is one of the most cooked items on the grill, and we are clamoring for **new adventures with chicken** and its cousins. I've smoked-roasted my turkey many times for Thanksgiving to oohs and aahs. It also makes darn good lower-fat chopped barbecue. The darker meat poultry seem to be perfectly suited for the grill. The richness of **duck, quail, and squab** increases when maneuvered over an outdoor fire.

Poultry can be a troublemaker. After grilled shrimp, I hear more disaster stories about chicken in my grilling classes than anything. Yes, chicken needs to be fully cooked but dried out? No way. One of the most common problems I hear is chicken that's charred on the outside, raw on the inside. Bone-in chicken does take a bit of patience and some attention, especially on charcoal. Indirect cooking is the best way to cook bone-in or whole chicken so that it gets done but stays moist inside. Chicken pieces will take from 30 to 45 minutes, with **legs and wings** being done first. Chicken quarters and halves will need 45 to 60 minutes and a whole chicken probably 1 to 1½ hours, again depending on size and how you control your temperature.

Please buy an instant-read meat thermometer. It's the best grilling investment you'll make. Cook those thighs to 180°F and the breasts to 160°F. Don't go just by recipe times—they're guidelines, not absolutes. Start checking for doneness at least 10 minutes before a recipe indicates that it will be done. Other clues of impending doneness are juices that run clear when the meat is pierced and there is no pink around the bone when you cut into the chicken. It's okay to make a small slit to check out the insides. Another way is by feel. If the meat is beginning to feel firm to the touch, it's time to take its temperature. And you should always let the poultry rest before slicing.

Cleanliness Is Next to Godliness

While this saying is true in all parts of our lives, it is especially necessary when dealing with poultry. Cross-contamination has been a national concern lately, with many consumer-brand giants placing products on the shelves to combat cross-contamination. With 25 percent of our poultry testing positive for salmonella, we do need to be careful. The first thing you need to know is that salmonella dies with proper and complete cooking—that's why we don't order our chicken rare. The biggest culprit in this battle is the mixing of rare juices with cooked food. Hot water and soap are our best weapons. Wash the platter that took the raw poultry out to the grill before placing cooked foods back on it. Keep your hands and utensils clean. Any marinade that you want to use as a basting sauce needs to be brought to a vigorous boil and cooked for a minute or two. Also, don't apply it to the chicken on the grill until it's been seared on both sides. These are simple steps that will make your poultry experience a safe one.

¹/₃ cup honey

¹/₃ cup soy sauce

¹/₃ cup Dijon mustard

2 cloves garlic, finely minced

Six 4- to 6-ounce boneless, skinless
chicken breast halves

Kim and Peter's
soy sauce and dijon marinated chicken breasts

Kim and Peter Reid, specialty-food brokers who live in Toronto, believe it's never too cold to grill. I asked them if they had a recipe that made their neighbors weep. "Well, we do have one that all of our friends and family are always asking us to make, but it's so simple that we have never told anybody our secret," Kim explains. It is simple but an awesome show with chicken.

– ⁓ᘓᗯ⁓ –

1. In a medium bowl, combine the honey, soy sauce, mustard, and garlic. Add the chicken breasts and toss to coat. Pour all the ingredients into a large zip-top plastic bag and let marinate in the refrigerator for at least 30 minutes; 4 hours is better.

2. Light a charcoal fire or preheat your gas grill on high. Oil the grill's cooking surface.

3. Remove the chicken from the marinade, allowing the excess to drain off each breast. Place over the fire and cook until firm to the touch or just cooked through all the way, about 5 minutes per side. Serve immediately.

¼ cup achiote paste (available in larger supermarkets in the Hispanic section, sometimes frozen, and always available in Latin markets)

1 tablespoon Asian chili paste

¼ cup fresh orange juice

1 teaspoon grated orange zest

¼ cup red wine vinegar

¼ cup olive oil

6 boneless, skinless chicken breasts

½ cup sour cream

Fresh cilantro sprigs for garnish

1. Combine the achiote paste, chili paste, orange juice and zest, vinegar, and oil in a medium bowl. Pour half the marinade into a large zip-top plastic bag and add the chicken. Seal the bag, squish everything to coat the chicken well, and let marinate in the refrigerator for at least 2 hours and up to overnight. Cover the remaining marinade with plastic wrap and refrigerate.

2. Light a charcoal fire or preheat your gas grill on high. Oil the grill's cooking surface. Let the coals burn down to a medium fire or adjust the gas grill burners to medium.

3. Remove the chicken from the marinade, discarding the marinade. Place on the grill and cook 7 to 8 minutes per side, until firm to the touch and just cooked all the way through.

4. Remove the chicken to a platter. Pour the remaining marinade over the chicken. Dollop the sour cream equally over the chicken breasts and garnish with the cilantro. Serve immediately.

Juan Gomez's
grilled chicken breasts adobo

Just outside of San Diego, Juan Gomez treated me to these grilled chicken breasts that he swore wouldn't be nearly as good without the Asian chili paste. When I got back to North Carolina, I tested his theory and he was right. The chili paste makes all the difference in the world. Juan told me that an old friend, Harry Lee, suggested adding it years ago and, even though Harry is gone, "I think of him every time I cook this chicken."

Achiote is the musky flavored seed of the annatto tree and a key ingredient in many dishes from Spanish-speaking countries. You've had this spice before and probably not even known it—it's used to add color to butter, cheese, and smoked fish. Buying the paste is easier than grinding the seeds, and quite frankly the paste is more widely available than the seeds.

CHEESY GRITS

2 2/3 cups stone-ground grits

5 1/3 cups water

1/2 cup shredded medium-sharp Cheddar cheese

2 tablespoons unsalted butter or margarine

1/2 teaspoon kosher salt

1/4 teaspoon freshly ground black pepper

CARAMELIZED ONIONS

2 tablespoons unsalted butter or margarine

2 large onions, cut into 1/2-inch-thick slices

1/2 teaspoon kosher salt

1/2 teaspoon freshly ground black pepper

2 tablespoons bourbon or apple juice

BBQ CHICKEN

4 skinless, boneless chicken breast halves

1/2 cup barbecue sauce of your choice

6 ounces medium-sharp Cheddar cheese, shredded (1 1/2 cups)

Cheesy Grits with
bbq chicken and caramelized onions

Grits are a Southern staple but seemingly unknown elsewhere in the country. If you're one of those gritless souls, think of grits this way—if you grind them a bit finer they become polenta. So if you would rather call this "Chicken with Polenta," that's fine with me. My friend Belinda Ellis, of Jefferson City, Tennessee, developed this recipe.

– ✦✦✦ –

1. Rinse the grits according to the package directions. Bring the water to a boil in a Dutch oven; gradually stir in the grits. Reduce the heat to medium and simmer, stirring occasionally, for 25 minutes.

2. Stir in the cheese, butter, salt, and pepper until the cheese is well blended. Keep warm.

3. For the onions, melt the butter in a large skillet over medium heat; add the onions, salt, and pepper, and cook, stirring often, until the onions are caramel colored, about 30 minutes. Add the bourbon and stir constantly for 1 minute. Keep warm.

4. Light a charcoal fire or preheat your gas grill on high. Oil the grill's cooking surface. Let the coals burn down to a medium fire or adjust the gas grill burners to medium.

5. Place the chicken on the grill and cook until firm to the touch and just cooked all the way through, about 6 minutes per side.

6. Remove from the grill and let cool slightly, then shred. While the chicken cools, quickly warm up the barbecue sauce (a microwave is perfect for this). Then stir together the chicken and sauce. Top the grits with the chicken mixture, onion mixture, and cheese and serve immediately.

Grilled Chicken and Caramelized Onions over Grilled Polenta: Instead of keeping the polenta warm, spread it in a greased 11x7-inch baking dish, cover with plastic wrap, chill at least 1 hour, and cut into 2-inch-square cakes. When you throw your chicken on the grill, pop the polenta squares on as well, cooking them about 3 minutes per side. Then top with a generous spoonful each of the chicken and onions and serve.

CURRY-PEANUT MARINADE

1 cup salted dry-roasted peanuts, finely chopped

1 cup orange marmalade

½ cup extra-virgin olive oil

½ cup fresh orange juice

¼ cup Dijon-style mustard

¼ cup fresh tarragon leaves, chopped

2 teaspoons curry powder

1 teaspoon kosher salt

8 bone-in, skin-on chicken breasts

New York, NY

SERVES 8

Cooked-Twice

curried chicken breasts

Here's a variation on an old *Silver Palate Cookbook* recipe that's good, fun, and different. While curry is a dominant flavor, the fresh tarragon adds mystery to the dish.

The chicken is cooked in the oven *and* the grill, which allows it to absorb all the flavors of the marinade without burning. The final step on the grill gives just a little caramelization to finish the flavor profile. This is good for company or a weekend night. Do most of the heavy lifting the night before, even the baking step. Then it's only a quick 20-minute pass on the grill.

– ✐✐ –

1. Combine the marinade ingredients in a large bowl. Add the chicken breasts and coat thoroughly. Transfer the chicken to a roasting pan, pour over the marinade, and cover with plastic wrap. Let marinate in the refrigerator for 4 to 6 hours.

2. When ready to cook, preheat the oven to 350°F.

3. Place the roasting pan in the oven and bake for 35 minutes. (At this point, you can proceed with the recipe or let cool, cover, and refrigerate up to 3 days.)

4. Light a charcoal fire or preheat your gas grill on high. Oil the grill's cooking surface.

5. Remove the chicken from the marinade and place on the grill. Cook about 10 minutes per side to heat through, basting with the marinade. When done, remove the chicken to a platter and serve immediately.

2 small heads garlic, separated into cloves and peeled

¼ cup minced fresh Italian parsley

Kosher salt and freshly ground black pepper

4 bone-in skin-on chicken breast halves

2 tablespoons unsalted butter

2 tablespoons fresh lemon juice

Grilled Chicken Breasts with Lemon and Garlic

and a tip of the hat to james beard

Garlic lovers will rejoice with this recipe. Many years ago it became quite fashionable for chefs to stuff things under the skin of chickens and turkeys and other fowl. It really was a wonderful way of adding flavor to what sometimes can be a bland dish. I guess we all were inspired a bit by James Beard's 40 cloves of garlic chicken. This is a simple way to express that concept on the grill. Blanching the garlic makes it a little sweeter as well as easier to work with.

- ᘓᕬᕬᘔ -

1. Light a charcoal fire or preheat your gas grill on high. Oil the grill's cooking surface. Let the coals burn down to a medium-hot fire or adjust the gas grill burners to medium-high.

2. Meanwhile, blanch the garlic in a large pot of boiling water for 1 minute and drain. Thinly slice the cloves and place in a small bowl. Add the parsley and season well with salt and pepper. Gently run your fingers under the skin of each chicken breast to loosen the skin from the meat, creating a pocket. Set aside 2 tablespoons of the garlic mixture for use in the sauce. Fill the pockets equally with the remaining garlic mixture. Season the chicken with salt and pepper.

3. Place the chicken on the grill, skin side down, and cook about 6 minutes. Turn, cook for 6 minutes, and turn again. Continue cooking the chicken, turning about every 5 to 6 minutes. If the chicken starts to burn, adjust your fire or move the chicken to a cooler part of the grill. Cook for a total of 20 to 30 minutes, until the breasts are firm to the touch and just cooked through all the way. Transfer to a platter and tent with aluminum foil.

4. Meanwhile, to make the sauce, melt the butter in a small saucepan over medium heat. Add the reserved garlic mixture and cook, stirring, until the garlic is tender and soft, about 5 minutes. Remove from the heat and stir in the lemon juice. Season to taste with salt and pepper. Spoon the sauce over the chicken breasts and serve immediately.

GARLIC AND GINGER RUB

12 cloves garlic, finely minced or run through a garlic press

2 tablespoons peeled and finely minced fresh ginger

2 tablespoons freshly ground black pepper

2 tablespoons ground coriander

1/2 cup chopped fresh cilantro leaves

1/4 cup fresh lime juice (2 to 3 limes)

2 tablespoons canola oil

4 whole boneless, skinless chicken breasts (8 halves)

SPICY SWEET AND SOUR DIPPING SAUCE

1/4 cup distilled white vinegar

1/3 cup sugar

3 cloves garlic, finely minced or run through a garlic press

1 teaspoon red pepper flakes

1/4 cup fresh lime juice (2 to 3 limes)

1 to 2 teaspoons Asian fish sauce, to your taste

Nanci's
thai-style grilled chicken breasts in spicy sweet and sour sauce

Real Thai **author and friend Nanci McDermott shared this recipe with me, an adaptation of food research she did as a Peace Corps volunteer in Thailand. It's bold and brassy with subtle undernotes of flavor. I know this will become a favorite with your family.**

– ⌘ –

1. Combine the rub ingredients in a medium bowl. Use your fingers to mix everything together well. Rub the mixture over each chicken breast. Place on a platter, cover with plastic wrap, and refrigerate for at least 2 hours; 4 hours is better.

2. Meanwhile, make the dipping sauce. Combine the vinegar and sugar in a small saucepan over medium heat and stir until the sugar is dissolved. Add the garlic and red pepper flakes and cook for 2 minutes. Pour into a heatproof container. Add the lime juice and fish sauce and let cool to room temperature. (This can be made a day ahead and kept refrigerated.)

3. Light a charcoal fire or preheat your gas grill on high. Oil the grill's cooking surface. Let the coals burn down to a medium-hot fire or adjust the gas grill burners to medium-high.

4. Remove the chicken from the refrigerator and place on the grill. Cook until firm to the touch and just cooked through all the way, about 10 minutes per side.

5. Transfer to a platter and let rest for 5 to 10 minutes. Serve with the dipping sauce.

½ cup plus 2 tablespoons olive oil

½ cup balsamic vinegar

2 tablespoons olive paste or tapenade

1 large clove garlic, minced

Kosher salt and freshly ground black pepper

4 boneless skin-on chicken breast halves

4 teaspoons minced fresh thyme

One 4.5- to 5-ounce bag mixed baby greens

1 small fennel bulb, cored and thinly sliced

½ large head radicchio, thinly sliced

½ cup thinly sliced red onions

12 fresh figs, quartered (optional)

Pine nuts for garnish, toasted in a dry skillet over medium heat until lightly browned

Verla's
grilled chicken salad with radicchio and figs

Verla Gabriel is my neighbor down the hall in New York City and quite the gourmet, so of course her recipe for chicken salad wouldn't be the regular stuff with mayonnaise and such. The chicken is marinated in a tapenade-balsamic dressing, then grilled and set over a salad of greens, sweet fennel, and bitter radicchio. I tell Verla it's her version of a $15 restaurant salad. Verla tells me she knows all about that illegal grill setting out on my fire escape, so I'd do well to keep my comments to myself.

– ᏻᏫᏬᎶᏫ –

1. Whisk together ½ cup of the oil, the vinegar, olive paste, and garlic in a small bowl to blend. Season with salt and pepper.

2. Place the chicken in an 8-inch square baking dish and sprinkle with the thyme. Pour ½ cup of the dressing over the chicken, turning to coat. Whisk the remaining 2 tablespoons oil into the remaining dressing in a small bowl. Cover the chicken and dressing separately and refrigerate for at least 4 hours and up to 6 hours, turning the chicken a few times.

3. Light a charcoal fire or preheat your gas grill on high. Oil the grill's cooking surface. Let the coals burn down to a medium-hot fire or adjust the gas grill burners to medium-high.

4. Bring the dressing to room temperature. Remove the chicken from the marinade and discard the marinade. Sprinkle the chicken with salt and pepper, place on the grill, and cook until cooked through, about 5 minutes per side. Transfer to a platter.

5. Combine the greens, fennel, radicchio, and onions in a large bowl. Toss with the remaining dressing. Mound evenly on 4 plates. Slice the chicken breasts lengthwise into ¼-inch-thick slices. Arrange on top of the greens and garnish each with 3 figs, if using, and pine nuts.

2 whole boneless skin-on chicken breasts (about 2 pounds), each cut in half

4 pieces blue cheese cut ½ inch thick, ½ inch wide, and 2 inches long (try Point Reyes Blue)

4 thin slices cooked ham, each 4 inches square

Kosher salt and freshly ground black pepper

2 tablespoons Worcestershire sauce

2 tablespoons fresh lemon juice

¼ cup (½ stick) unsalted butter, cut into pieces

1. Insert a sharp paring knife into the thicker end of each chicken breast half and carefully cut a lengthwise pocket into it, making it as wide as possible without puncturing the sides.

2. Wrap each stick of the blue cheese in a ham slice, enclosing it. Insert a package into each pocket and close the opening securely with a toothpick. Season with salt and pepper on both sides.

3. In a small saucepan, whisk together the Worcestershire and lemon juice and bring just to a simmer. Remove the pan from the heat and swirl in the butter until melted.

4. Light a charcoal fire or preheat your gas grill on high. Oil the grill's cooking surface. Let the coals burn down to a medium-hot fire or adjust the gas grill burners to medium-high.

5. Place the chicken on the grill and cook, basting frequently with the sauce, for 12 minutes per side. Do not baste the chicken during the last 2 minutes of grilling. Remove to a platter and discard any remaining sauce. Serve immediately.

Boris's

grilled chicken breasts stuffed with ham and blue cheese

Boris was my first doorman in Manhattan. His last name was unpronounceable to me and he always told me not to worry about it. He had emigrated to New York from the Russian sector of Georgia. When he found out that I cooked for a living, almost daily he would bring me a little bowl or plastic container of some kind of food from his homeland that he continued to make here in the United States. One day he showed up with this dish. "American Chicken Kiev" he called it. "Everybody in U.S. grill and everybody love blue cheese, so I stuff chicken breast with ham and blue cheese and grill to make American-Russian food." Boris should have been a chef instead of an electrical engineer. This is showy food and absolutely delicious.

6 bone-in chicken breasts, skin on

½ cup kosher salt

4 to 6 cups water

Rachel's Barbecue Sauce (p. 310)

1. Place the chicken in a large zip-top plastic bag. In a large bowl, whisk the salt into the water to dissolve. Pour into the bag and seal. Place in the refrigerator overnight.

2. Set up the grill for indirect grilling (see pp. 6–9). Oil your grill's cooking surface.

3. Remove the chicken from the brine and pat dry. Place the chicken over the direct heat and cook for about 10 minutes per side, then move it away from the fire. Start basting (frequently) with the barbecue sauce, turning the chicken each time you baste. Cook with the lid down until the chicken is no longer pink at the bone, about 45 minutes. Remove to a platter and serve.

Robin and Rachel's
grilled barbecue chicken breasts

Robin and Rachel Thomas, my neighbors across the street in North Carolina, make great barbecued chicken. Rachel, a trained home economist, would smile whenever I asked what she did to make it taste so good and change the subject. It took this book to finally get at the truth. The chicken is brined overnight, then grilled slowly. They use a three-burner gas grill, but a charcoal grill will work fine. Her sauce is wonderful on anything. Robin also takes soaked hickory chips and lays them right on the grill's cooking surface.

Robin at work at his grill.

HOT CHILE MARINADE

1 tablespoon pure ground chile, like chipotle or ancho

1 tablespoon finely minced shallot

1 tablespoon finely minced garlic

2 tablespoons chopped fresh oregano

¼ cup chopped fresh cilantro

1 teaspoon ground cumin

⅓ cup fresh lemon juice

⅓ cup olive oil

Kosher salt and freshly ground black pepper

---

4 boneless, skinless chicken breast halves (about 6 ounces each)

Sweet and Sour Dipping Sauce (p. 313; optional)

South of the Border-Pacific Rim
chile-marinated chicken breasts

This recipe seems a bit like a culture clash. The marinade has a lot of Texan and Southwestern flavor notes, but I really like dipping the chicken in an Asian-flavored dipping sauce. The end result will bring heat to your mouth and a smile to your face. This recipe started as leftover chile chicken, which I was looking for a way to goose up. I had some Chinese duck sauce and tried glazing the chicken with it as I reheated the chicken. It turned out fairly good, so I started experimenting with the flavors to get this result. This marinade is also awesome with turkey or pork and more substantial cuts of fish like swordfish and shark.

- ཚོ฿฿ผ -

1. Whisk together the ground chile, shallot, garlic, oregano, cilantro, cumin, lemon juice, and oil in a medium bowl, then taste and season with salt and black pepper. Set aside at room temperature for about 30 minutes to allow the flavors to meld.

2. Put the chicken breasts in a large zip-top plastic bag. Pour the marinade over them and seal the bag. Squish the marinade around to coat the chicken well. Let marinate in the refrigerator overnight.

3. Light a charcoal fire or preheat your gas grill on high. Oil the grill's cooking surface.

4. Remove the breasts from the marinade and discard the marinade. Place on the grill and cook until the breasts feel firm to the touch and are just cooked through all the way, about 5 minutes per side.

5. Remove to a platter and let rest for 5 minutes. Slice each breast if desired and serve with the dipping sauce.

8 boneless, skinless chicken breast halves (about 6 ounces each)

Three 16-ounce bottles Wishbone red wine vinaigrette (do not substitute)

1. Place the chicken breasts in a large zip-top plastic bag. Pour in the vinaigrette, seal the bag, and squish everything around until well coated. Let marinate in the refrigerator for at least 8 hours or overnight.

2. Set up the grill for indirect grilling (see pp. 6–9). Oil your grill's cooking surface.

3. About 1 hour before cooking, remove the chicken from the marinade and discard the marinade. When the fire is ready, place the chicken away from the fire, close the lid, and smoke until firm to the touch and just cooked all the way through, about 1 hour. Transfer to a platter and serve immediately or at room temperature.

If It's Good with Chicken, It's Good with Shrimp

Kell's dad, Joe, has an even simpler recipe that he calls Hull Shrimp. Throw a pound of shrimp still in their shells in a plastic bag with a bottle of Italian dressing. Let them sit in the fridge for about an hour. Throw them on the grill for about 3 minutes per side, then peel, eat, and enjoy.

Douglas, GA

SERVES 8

Chicken
at kell's

Down in Douglas, Georgia, you'll find a father-and-son team that loves to collect—but not stamps or vintage cars. This duo collects smokers and grills. Kell Phelps and his father, Joe, live on the same street and have 18 cookers between them. Joe has a six-car garage with seven cookers stored in it. Kell's dad founded the *National Barbecue News*, a monthly paper with a circulation of about 6,000 worldwide. He and a friend, Dr. Don Gilling, started the paper because they had a barbecue team but couldn't find any information on where to go.

Kell says that since he was 10 years old, "I've been toting wood and stoking fires and tasting beer bottles that have been left around when my daddy and his friends have been cooking. I grew up thinking the only way to cook meat was outside. But nothing that Daddy did was overly complicated." Here's a perfect example of how simple and how good something can be on the grill.

Kell and Joe Phelps

LIME-CILANTRO MARINADE

5 cloves garlic, coarsely chopped

1 tablespoon grated lime zest

¼ cup fresh lime juice

¼ cup roughly chopped fresh cilantro

1 teaspoon kosher salt

½ teaspoon freshly ground black pepper

6 tablespoons olive oil

8 boneless, skinless chicken breast halves

Lime wedges

Grilled
lime-cilantro chicken breasts

I call this refrigerator chicken. By that I mean one night I opened up the refrigerator and found I had chicken breasts that needed to be eaten, cilantro that was on its last legs, and a couple of limes. What could I do? How could I make this work? It seemed simple enough. Let's make a lime-cilantro marinade with lots of garlic, then throw the marinated chicken on the grill. I've tinkered with it a little bit since that first night, and I like to marinate it a lot longer than the 1 hour when I first worked on this recipe. This is a great-tasting dish.

– ⋅⋅⋅⋅⋅ –

1. In a blender or food processor, combine the garlic, lime zest and juice, cilantro, salt, and pepper and blend until smooth. With the machine running, slowly add the oil through the top or feed tube and process until blended.

2. Place the chicken in a large zip-top plastic bag, add the marinade, seal, and squish around to coat everything. Let marinate in the refrigerator for at least 3 hours or overnight.

3. Light a charcoal fire or preheat your gas grill on high. Oil the grill's cooking surface. Let the coals burn down to a medium-hot fire or adjust the gas grill burners to medium-high.

4. Remove the chicken from the marinade and discard the marinade. Place the chicken on the grill and cook until firm to the touch and just cooked through all the way, 8 to 10 minutes total, turning once.

5. Serve immediately with lime wedges for squeezing.

6 bone-in, skin-on chicken breast halves

½ cup bourbon

½ cup soy sauce

1 cup apricot preserves, slightly melted

⅛ teaspoon cayenne pepper

1. Set up the grill for indirect grilling (see pp. 6–9). Oil your grill's cooking surface.

2. Place the chicken, skin side down, over the portion of the grill that has direct heat. Cook for about 15 minutes, turn, and cook another 15 minutes. Now move the chicken breasts away from the heat.

3. While the chicken is doing its initial cooking, stir together the bourbon, soy sauce, preserves, and cayenne. Baste the chicken after the first 30 minutes liberally with the sauce every 10 minutes or so and continue cooking the chicken for a total of 45 minutes to 1 hour, until firm to the touch and just cooked through all the way. Elizabeth says it is critical that all the sauce be used. Running out of it is also an indication that the chicken should be done.

4. Remove to a platter and serve immediately.

The glaze creates delightful-tasting crunchy bits of skin.

Elizabeth Sims's
grilled southern chicken breasts biltmore style

Elizabeth fussed on me about these breasts. "You have to use all the marinade, Fred. And get them charred some, that's when they're good," she explained. She had sent me out to cook the chicken while she finished the rest of the meal, and, foodie or not, I was going to do it right.

I think a lot of Elizabeth Sims. She's worked her way through the landmines of the advertising profession to be vice president of marketing for the Biltmore Company, the parent company behind Asheville's Biltmore House. She also was president of the Southern Foodways Alliance Board of Directors during a difficult year. She's a bunch of fun, can cut a rug with anybody, and loves good food and people. I think you'll find this recipe classy, with a touch of the South.

4 boneless skinless chicken breast halves

Grated zest of 2 lemons

Kosher salt and freshly ground
black pepper

Juice of 2 lemons

2 tablespoons extra-virgin olive oil, plus
more for brushing the chicken

1 cup chopped yellow onions

½ cup seeded and chopped green
bell peppers

¼ cup chopped carrots

2 cloves garlic, minced

1 jalapeño, seeded and chopped

2 bay leaves

1 tablespoon fresh thyme leaves

1 tablespoon chopped fresh Italian parsley

2 ounces salt pork

½ cup dry sherry

2 cups diced canned tomatoes with
their juice

4 scallions (white and green parts),
thinly sliced

Grilled
chicken breast
with creole sauce

The word *creole* simply put means "a mix of". In this case, the Creole sauce is a combination of African, Caribbean, and French cultures. The inspiration for this was a dish I enjoyed at Leah Chase's wonderful restaurant, Dookey Chase. Her blend of Creole and Southern foods has made her a legend among chefs in New Orleans. If you have a notion, grill some sliced eggplant to go alongside.

- ᘐᘐᘐ -

1. Place the chicken breasts in a large baking dish. Sprinkle them with the lemon zest, salt, and pepper. Pour the lemon juice over them, turning to coat. Cover and let marinate in the refrigerator at least 30 minutes—8 hours is better and overnight works, too. Turn the breasts over a couple of times.

2. Meanwhile, make the Creole sauce. Heat the oil in a medium saucepan over medium-high heat, then add the onions, bell peppers, and carrots and cook, stirring, until softened, about 4 minutes. Add the garlic and cook 1 minute longer, then stir in the jalapeño, bay leaves, thyme, parsley, salt pork, sherry, and tomatoes. Bring to a boil, then reduce the heat to a simmer and, stirring occasionally, cook until thick, about 1 hour.

3. Taste the sauce and adjust the seasonings, if necessary. Pull out the salt pork and bay leaves and discard. At this point, the sauce can be cooled and refrigerated for up to 3 days. Gently reheat before using.

4. Light a charcoal fire or preheat your gas grill on high. Oil the grill's cooking surface.

5. Remove the chicken from the marinade and brush with olive oil. Place on the grill and cook for 4 to 5 minutes. Turn and cook until firm to the touch and just cooked through all the way, another 3 to 4 minutes.

6. Stir the scallions into the warm sauce, then ladle a little over each breast and serve immediately.

2 tablespoons canola oil

1 teaspoon peeled and grated fresh ginger

1 teaspoon crushed garlic

1 teaspoon onion powder

1 teaspoon cayenne pepper

¼ teaspoon turmeric

1 teaspoon kosher salt

¼ teaspoon ground cumin

¼ teaspoon ground coriander

1 tablespoon tomato paste

¾ cup plain yogurt or buttermilk

1 pound boneless, skinless chicken breasts, cut into 1-inch cubes

1. In a medium bowl, whisk together the oil, ginger, garlic, onion powder, cayenne, turmeric, salt, cumin, coriander, tomato paste, and yogurt.

2. Place the chicken cubes in a large zip-top plastic bag and pour the marinade over it. Seal the bag, squish everything to coat the chicken evenly, and let marinate in the refrigerator overnight.

3. Light a charcoal fire or preheat your gas grill on high. Oil your grill's cooking grate.

4. Remove the chicken from the marinade, discarding the marinade. Thread the chicken cubes onto oiled skewers. Place on the grill and cook for 2 to 3 minutes on each of the four sides.

5. Remove from the heat and slide the chicken pieces off the skewers onto a platter. Serve over rice.

Indira Reddy's
grilled chicken tikka

Indira Reddy is a long way from her roots in Hyderabad, India. This San Antonio food scientist with a master's in food nutrition and a Ph.D. in cereal chemistry has been in this country for more than 20 years. Coming to Kansas State for graduate work, she fell in love with Michael, who would become her husband, and moved to Texas eight years ago to work for a flour company in research and development. She still holds on to much of her Indian background. "I give an Indian touch to all our food. There is always cumin seed, mustard seed, and garlic and onions. My mother used to keep her own spice blends and I do, too. The difference is she would get her spices ground fresh almost daily, which is hard to do here. Even with tomato sauce for pasta, I go through the ritual of toasting my spices. It makes such a difference."

This dish, which is normally not grilled, is a nod to Texas culture and her husband's Kansas background. The method and spices are authentic, while the grilling adds another level of flavor, making this a complex and wonderful meal.

Indira and her children.

Fred's Backyard, NC

SERVES 4

1/3 cup peach preserves

2 tablespoons white wine vinegar

2 to 3 teaspoons chopped canned chipotle peppers in adobo sauce

1/4 teaspoon ground nutmeg

1/2 teaspoon kosher salt

1/4 teaspoon freshly ground black pepper

8 skinless chicken thighs

Chipotle peach-glazed chicken thighs

This recipe had another life. Once I had this standard peach glaze that I used for pork and sometimes chicken. One night, in an effort to clean out my refrigerator, I found an opened jar of peach preserves and an open can of chipotle chiles in adobo. The meat for the evening was chicken thighs. I never made the basic peach glaze again. Understand?

1. In a small saucepan, combine the peach preserves, vinegar, chipotles, and half the nutmeg. Place over medium-high heat, stirring, just until melted. Set aside.

2. Combine the salt, black pepper, and remaining nutmeg in a small bowl. Sprinkle evenly over the chicken thighs.

3. Set up the grill for indirect grilling (see pp. 6–9). Oil your grill's cooking surface.

4. Place the chicken thighs bone side down on the grill away from the heat over a drip pan. Cover and grill until no longer pink at the bone, 50 to 60 minutes. Brush the chicken liberally on both sides with the peach glaze during the last 10 minutes of cooking and right as they come off the grill. Serve immediately.

Chipotle Peach-Glazed Chicken Breasts: If you prefer white meat, you can use 4 skinless, boneless chicken breast halves (about 1¼ pounds total) instead of the thighs. Prepare as directed through step 2. Place the breast halves on the grill and grill until firm to the touch and just cooked through all the way, 12 to 15 minutes, turning once halfway through grilling and brushing often with glaze during the last 2 minutes of grilling.

1½ cups Mr. Yoshida's Original Gourmet Sweet Teriyaki Marinade & Cooking Sauce®

1 cup Bull's Eye® Original BBQ Sauce

½ cup fresh orange juice (about 1 navel orange)

¼ cup firmly packed light brown sugar

1 tablespoon crushed garlic (the kind packed in water)

1 teaspoon ground ginger

⅛ teaspoon garlic salt

⅛ teaspoon freshly ground black pepper

3 to 4 pounds boneless, skinless chicken thighs

1. Combine the sauces, orange juice, brown sugar, crushed garlic, ginger, garlic salt, and pepper in a large bowl.

2. Place the chicken thighs in a large zip-top plastic bag. Pour the marinade over the chicken, seal the bag, and squish everything to coat the chicken. Let marinate in the refrigerator for at least 8 hours; overnight is better. Turn the bag occasionally.

3. Light a charcoal fire or preheat a gas grill at high heat. Oil the grill's cooking surface.

4. Remove the chicken from the marinade to a platter and discard the marinade. Using paper towels, pat the chicken dry. Place on the grill and cook for about 15 minutes, turning the pieces frequently. The chicken is done when no longer pink at the bone.

5. Remove to a clean platter and serve. Any leftovers make for awesome chicken sandwiches.

Tim Huckins's
florida grilled chicken thighs

Following your nose can lead to great discoveries. Chilling out from writing one Sunday afternoon at Carlson Beach on Florida's east coast, I got caught in a downpour of an outer band of then Tropical Storm Rita. I headed for one of the pavilions near the beach. Gathered there was a huge group of folks eating, drinking, and having a grand time. Then it hit me—the harmonious aroma of charcoal, flame, and meat. I walked up to the lady at the grill, introduced myself, and asked about the dish and its recipe. "It's not mine to give," the woman answered with the air of a National Security adviser. "Talk with my daughter." Well, daughter was just as suspicious and introduced me to her husband, saying, "I doubt he'll give you the recipe." That was my introduction to Tim and Salina Huckins.

It seems I had walked into a birthday celebration for Tim's mom and Tim and Salina's son, Christopher. Tim, who works in security, gave me a brief interrogation and decided that I really was a writer interested in how they did their chicken.

This chicken floored me with its exciting aroma and tang. When I retested this recipe at home and shared the results with my neighbors, it quickly became a favorite. As is the case with many marinades, the ingredients sound outrageous but together create a concert of flavor.

TANDOORI MARINADE

2 cups plain whole-milk yogurt

2 tablespoons fresh lemon juice

2 tablespoons peeled and minced fresh ginger

4 cloves garlic, minced

1 teaspoon kosher salt

1 teaspoon ground coriander

1 teaspoon turmeric

1/2 teaspoon saffron threads, crumbled

1/2 teaspoon ground cumin

1/2 teaspoon freshly ground black pepper

1/2 teaspoon cayenne pepper

---

8 skinless leg-thigh chicken pieces

3 tablespoons unsalted butter, melted

1 small red onion, thinly sliced crosswise and separated into rings

1/4 cup chopped fresh cilantro

San Antonio, TX

SERVES 8

Tandoori-Style
grilled chicken

After meeting Indira Reddy in San Antonio, I got to thinking about how much I love tandoori chicken and wondered how to do it on the grill. I called "Indie" and we talked through the spices. After a couple of attempts, I came up with a grilled chicken dish that was better than anything I had eaten in "Curry Hill," the Indian section of Manhattan. If you love South Asian flavors, then give this a try.

- ⌘ -

1. Process 1 cup of the yogurt and the remaining marinade ingredients together in a food processor until smooth. Transfer to a large bowl. Whisk in the remaining 1 cup yogurt. Add the chicken and turn to coat. Cover with plastic wrap and let marinate in the refrigerator overnight.

2. Light a charcoal fire or preheat your gas grill on high. Oil the grill's cooking surface. Let the coals burn down to a medium-hot fire or adjust the gas grill burners to medium-high.

3. Remove the chicken from the marinade and place it on the grill. Cook until no longer pink at the bone, about 12 minutes per side, occasionally basting with butter during the last 2 minutes.

4. Transfer the chicken to a platter, top with the onion rings and cilantro, and serve.

MUSTARD BUTTER

½ cup (1 stick) unsalted butter, softened

2 tablespoons coarse-grained mustard

2 tablespoons Dijon mustard

2 tablespoons minced shallot

½ teaspoon white pepper

¾ teaspoon kosher salt

1½ tablespoons fresh thyme leaves, chopped

HERB MIXTURE

2 teaspoons kosher salt

1 teaspoon dried sage, crumbled

1 teaspoon dried oregano, crumbled

1 teaspoon ground ginger

1 teaspoon dried rosemary, crumbled

1 teaspoon dried marjoram, crumbled

1 teaspoon dried thyme, crumbled

1 teaspoon celery seeds

1 teaspoon white pepper

3 pounds chicken quarters, both leg and breast

Bridgehampton, NY

SERVES 4

Karen's Grilled Herb-Crusted
chicken with mustard butter

My neighbor Verla Gabriel shared this recipe from her friend and foodie buddy Karen Lee of Bridgehampton, New York. It looks like a whole lot of ingredients, but you'll see that everything comes together quickly. The mustard butter is outstanding not only in this dish but also on grilled steak and fish.

– ᴄᴏᴏᴏᴠ –

1. Combine the mustard butter ingredients until well blended in a medium bowl. Transfer the mixture to a piece of waxed paper and form it into a 7-inch-long log, using the waxed paper as a guide. Refrigerate, wrapped in the waxed paper, until firm enough to slice. It will keep for up to 2 weeks in the refrigerator and 3 months in the freezer.

2. Combine the herb mixture ingredients in a small bowl.

3. Set up the grill for indirect grilling (see pp. 6–9). Oil your grill's cooking surface.

4. Spread the herb mixture on a sheet of waxed paper. Press the chicken pieces into the herbs, coating them evenly. Place the chicken on the grill directly over the fire and cook until golden, about 4 minutes per side, then move them away from the heat and cook until no longer pink at the bone, another 30 to 45 minutes.

5. Serve the chicken topped with ¼-inch-thick rounds of the mustard butter.

2 cloves garlic, crushed

Juice of 2 limes

1 teaspoon garlic-flavored vinegar

Freshly ground black pepper

One 3-pound chicken, cut into 8 to 10 serving pieces

1. Combine the garlic, lime juice, vinegar, and pepper in a small bowl, then pour into a large zip-top plastic bag. Add the chicken pieces, seal the bag, and squish everything to coat with the marinade. Let marinate in the refrigerator overnight; 2 days is even better.

2. Light a charcoal fire or preheat your gas grill on high. Oil the grill's cooking surface.

3. Remove the chicken from the bag and discard the marinade. Place the chicken on the grill, skin side down, and cook for a total of 30 to 40 minutes, turning the pieces every 5 minutes. The pieces will cook at different rates, the drumsticks, thighs, and wings faster than the breasts, so check them several times for doneness.

4. Remove the chicken when done to a platter. Serve at room temperature.

Carolina's
pollo de limca

Carolina Spissu grew up in Guatemala City but spent a great deal of her adult life in Argentina, where grilling is almost sacred. "This is a little bit Guatemalan, with some Argentina mixed in," she says. "In Argentina, everyone had a *quincho*, which is a built-in outdoor grill. We would use it daily, sometimes three times a day. This chicken has always been one of my favorites." This recipe is so simple, but you won't believe the results.

One 3- to 4-pound chicken, cut into
8 serving pieces

Two 8-ounce bottles Italian salad dressing

¼ cup extra-virgin olive oil

2 tablespoons cider vinegar

2 tablespoons fresh lemon juice

3 cloves garlic, crushed

1 tablespoon cracked black peppercorns

1. Place the chicken in a large zip-top plastic bag. Combine the remaining ingredients in a medium bowl. Divide the marinade in half. Pour half of it into the bag, seal, and squish everything around to coat the chicken. Refrigerate the chicken and the reserved marinade overnight.

2. Light a charcoal fire or preheat your gas grill on high. Oil the grill's cooking surface. Let the coals burn down to a medium fire or adjust the gas grill burners to medium.

3. Fill your cooler with hot water. Remove the chicken from the bag and discard the marinade. Place on the grill and cook for 20 to 30 minutes, turning frequently and basting with the reserved marinade once all the sides have been seared. The wings will be first to get done and the breast last. Remove to a platter.

4. Empty the cooler, put the platter with the chicken in, close the lid tightly, and let steam for 1 hour. Remove from the cooler and serve immediately.

Kenner Patton's
"my chicken"

Kenner Patton from down Birmingham, Alabama, way is famous for this chicken recipe. To hear him tell it, "I will take chicken [whatever your favorite cut is], wash it, marinate it, grill it, then steam it. The marinade is usually a vinegar-based store-bought salad dressing, and I will add virgin olive oil, crushed garlic, vinegar, crushed black pepper, and lemon juice to it. If I have some extra BBQ rub on hand, I'll throw it in, too. Let the chicken marinate in this overnight in a large zip-lock. I then grill it until it is done, basting frequently with another batch of marinade of the same concoction. While the chicken is grilling, I will take a small ice chest and fill it with hot water to get the cooler hot. Once the chicken is finished grilling, I will empty the cooler, take the chicken off the grill, and put it in the cooler for an hour or so. The extra time gives the chicken an opportunity to 'rest' and rehydrate. The result is an extremely moist, tender, and flavorful grilled chicken that is very easy to do."

Moist and flavorful is a gross understatement. It may be some of the best chicken you'll ever taste off the grill. This treatment also works great with quail, Cornish game hens, or any other kind of fowl.

LEMON-GARLIC MARINADE

¼ cup fresh lemon juice

1 tablespoon grated lemon zest

2 tablespoons extra-virgin olive oil

4 large cloves garlic, minced

1 teaspoon dried oregano, crumbled

1 teaspoon dried thyme, crumbled

1 teaspoon kosher salt

½ teaspoon freshly ground black pepper

One 3½- to 4-pound chicken, cut into serving pieces

LEMONY BATH

2 tablespoons extra-virgin olive oil

4 teaspoons fresh lemon juice

1 tablespoon snipped fresh chives or chopped fresh parsley

⅛ teaspoon kosher salt

Mirian's Double
lemon chicken

I first met Mirian at a food writers' symposium at the Greenbrier Hotel in West Virginia. Her enthusiasm for food and life is infectious, and she has become a friend I don't get to see nearly enough. A native of Detroit, she has lived in New York City and now lives on a farm with her husband, David, in western Pennsylvania. This is one of their favorites from the grill, and it has also become one of mine.

– ୧୦୦୬ –

1. In a glass measuring cup, combine the marinade ingredients until well combined. Place the chicken in a zip-top plastic bag, add the marinade, seal, and squish everything around to coat. Let marinate in the refrigerator at least 10 hours, preferably overnight.

2. Set up the grill for indirect grilling (see pp. 6–9). Oil your grill's cooking surface.

3. Remove the chicken from the marinade and pour marinade into a small saucepan. Bring it to a boil and let continue to boil 1 full minute.

4. Arrange the chicken skin side down on hot side of grill and get a good sear on both sides, about 3 minutes per side, with the lid down. Then transfer the chicken to the cooler side of the grill and continue cooking, basting 2 or 3 times with the marinade, until no longer pink at the bone, 12 to 15 minutes more per side. Discard any remaining marinade.

5. Meanwhile, combine the lemony bath ingredients in a small bowl. When the chicken is done, transfer it to a clean platter and pour the bath over it. Serve the chicken hot, warm, or at room temperature.

TEXAS SPICE BBQ SAUCE

½ cup ketchup

¼ cup cider vinegar

2 tablespoons teriyaki sauce

3 tablespoons sriricha hot sauce or Asian chili-garlic sauce

2 teaspoons liquid Maggi® seasoning

3 tablespoons firmly packed light brown sugar

2 tablespoons finely diced sweet onions (1014 or Vidalia, preferably)

¼ cup seeded and finely diced red bell peppers

One 3- to 4-pound chicken, cut into 8 serving pieces

Ray, Cathy, and Kyle's
texas spice chicken

Growing up in Texas, Cathy Cochran-Lewis says, "Outdoor grilling is not only a cooking style but a testament to how truly deep your Texas roots run." The more you depend on the grill for cooking, the deeper your roots. "At our house, we light up the grill almost as much as we turn on the air-conditioning!" This Austin, Texas, family pretty much grills all year long and does a variety of things on their grill. Lately, their son, Kyle, has become the sauce master, approaching this duty almost like a chemist. Grilled vegetables are always a part of this meal.

– ꮯꙨꙨꙶ –

1. Combine the sauce ingredients in a medium bowl. Brush the chicken pieces with about ¼ cup of it, coating the chicken on all sides. Reserve the extra sauce. Place the chicken in a large zip-top plastic bag and let marinate in the refrigerator for at least 1 hour and up to overnight.

2. Set up the grill for indirect grilling (see pp. 6–9). Oil your grill's cooking surface.

3. Place the chicken over direct flames for several minutes on each side to get grill marks, then move away from the heat. Close the lid and cook for 15 to 20 minutes, depending on the thickness of the pieces.

4. Remove the chicken to a platter, mop with the remaining sauce, and serve.

4 to 6 chicken quarters, leg or breast or a combination

CAROLINA CHICKEN MOP SAUCE

1½ cups chicken broth

½ teaspoon red pepper flakes

1 teaspoon black peppercorns

2 to 3 sprigs fresh parsley

1 bay leaf

¼ cup prepared yellow mustard

¼ cup vegetable oil

Kosher salt and freshly ground black pepper

V. F.'s Carolina-Style
mustard barbecued chicken

V. F. Talley, from Fayetteville, North Carolina, was a close friend of my dad's. V. F. and his family owned an independent grocery store that survived until a few years ago even with the pressure of food chains. He had a place on White Lake in southeast North Carolina, and my family was invited down quite a bit. The highlight of the weekends was V. F.'s barbecue chicken with mustard sauce. Even though it's a little more South Carolina than North Carolina, it's mighty good. V. F. and my dad have both passed away, so I include this recipe in memory of their friendship.

– ದಿಯ –

1. Rinse the chicken pieces under cold running water and pat dry with paper towels. Allow to come to room temperature.

2. In a small saucepan, combine the broth, red pepper, peppercorns, parsley, and bay leaf and cook over low heat about 30 minutes. Remove the parsley and bay leaf. Stir in the mustard and heat through. Set aside. (It will keep, refrigerated and tightly covered, up to 2 weeks.)

3. Light a charcoal fire or preheat your gas grill on high. Oil the grill's cooking surface. Let the coals burn down to a medium-low fire or adjust the gas grill burners to medium-low.

4. Lightly brush the chicken on all sides with the oil. Add the remaining oil to the mop. Place skin side down, on the grill, cover, and cook until the skin browns, 10 to 15 minutes. Turn, cover, and cook until the other side browns. Turn and baste with the sauce. Grill 10 minutes, turn, and baste again. Continue cooking, turning, and basting for 1 to 1¼ hours. If cooking with charcoal, replenish the fire as needed. The juices should run clear when the chicken is pierced at the joint with a fork. If the breast quarters are done sooner than the leg quarters, move them to the edges of the fire to prevent overcooking. Move the leg quarters to the hotter part of the grill.

5. Remove the chicken to a platter and keep warm with foil. Return the remaining sauce to low heat and bring to a boil. Add any juices that have accumulated on the platter. Taste and adjust the seasoning with salt and pepper. Pour the sauce over the chicken and serve.

6 chicken leg quarters

6 chicken breast quarters

1 tablespoon unsalted butter

1 onion, chopped

2 bottles Kraft® Original barbecue sauce

½ cup ketchup

⅓ cup honey

⅓ cup fresh lemon juice

¼ cup whole-grain mustard

1 tablespoon cayenne pepper

1. Set up the grill for indirect grilling (see pp. 6–9). Oil your grill's cooking surface.

2. Place the chicken on the grill away from the heat and cover.

3. Meanwhile, melt the butter in a large saucepan over medium heat. Add the onions and cook, stirring, until softened, about 3 minutes. Add the remaining ingredients and slowly bring to a boil, stirring occasionally. Reduce the heat to a simmer and cook for about 15 minutes. Divide the sauce between two bowls. Reserve one to pass at the table.

4. After the chicken has cooked for 1 to 1½ hours, begin to baste them heavily with the sauce every 5 to 10 minutes for another 30 minutes of cooking, until the chicken is no longer pink at the bone. Remove from the grill and serve with the reserved sauce.

Johnny Oystalet's
new orleans firehouse chicken

Ramble by New Orleans Central Fire Station on Decatur Street, in the heart of the French Quarter, and you'll find Engine Company 29. It's where Johnny Oystalet holds court over the flames of the kitchen. When the fire bells go off, he's an operator, fire department speak for the fire engine driver. When not on a call, he's cooking the meals for the company. Now with New Orleans being a food city, you'd better be good at it, although Johnny swears that "if you step up to cook, you're stuck with it."

His barbecued chicken is a firehouse favorite. Even the brass in the department seems to know to visit the station when the chicken is on the grill. Johnny takes simple ingredients and makes them special. Serve this up with macaroni and cheese and baked beans.

GARLICKY MUSTARD-HERB FLAVOR PASTE

2 tablespoons minced garlic

2 tablespoons whole-grain mustard

2 tablespoons finely chopped fresh thyme

2 tablespoons finely chopped fresh rosemary

2 tablespoons coarsely ground white pepper

2 tablespoons fresh lemon juice

2 tablespoons extra-virgin olive oil

Two 4-pound chickens

Olive oil

Kosher salt

Chicken
grilled under bricks

I love cooking chickens this way, and I think you will, too. The flavor seems to intensify, and you get perfectly even cooking, resulting in moist breast and thigh meat. The method is Northern Italian, but much of Europe does this in some form, and you can change the herbs to your liking. I like this particular mix because it gives the birds an earthy, robust taste.

– ⌘ –

1. In a small bowl, combine the flavor paste ingredients.

2. Remove the neck, giblets, and any excess fat from the chickens. Rinse the chickens, inside and out, under cold running water and pat dry with paper towels. Using a chef's knife or kitchen shears, cut out the backbones, then cut the birds in half through the back. Coat each chicken half thoroughly with the paste. Place the halves in a large zip-top plastic bag. If one bag isn't large enough, use two. Press the air out of the bag, seal tightly, massage the paste into the chickens, and refrigerate for 8 to 24 hours.

3. Set up the grill for indirect grilling (see pp. 6–9). Oil your grill's cooking surface.

4. Wrap three bricks in aluminum foil.

5. Remove the chicken from the bag and lightly brush the halves with olive oil. Season with salt. Place the chicken, skin side down, on the grill away from the heat. Place a baking sheet on top of the chicken halves and weight the sheet down with the bricks. Grill the chickens until the skin is crispy and the juices at the joints run clear, 30 to 40 minutes.

6. Using barbecue mitts, carefully remove the bricks and baking sheet. Turn the chickens and grill another 2 to 3 minutes to crisp the other side.

7. Transfer from the grill to a platter, loosely cover with aluminum foil, and let rest for about 5 minutes before cutting the halves in two. Serve immediately.

1 tablespoon kosher salt

1 tablespoon sweet Hungarian paprika

1 tablespoon firmly packed dark
brown sugar

2 teaspoons freshly ground black pepper

¼ teaspoon celery seeds

Two 3½- to 3¾-pound chickens,
backbones cut out and cut in half through
the back

1 cup water

¾ cup distilled white vinegar

¼ cup Worcestershire sauce

ROOT BEER BBQ SAUCE:

MAKES 1½ CUPS

1 cup root beer

1 cup ketchup

¼ cup fresh lemon juice

¼ cup orange juice

3 tablespoons Worcestershire sauce

1½ tablespoons firmly packed dark
brown sugar

1 tablespoon mild-flavored (light) molasses

1 teaspoon liquid smoke

½ teaspoon grated lemon zest

½ teaspoon ground ginger

½ teaspoon garlic powder

½ teaspoon onion powder

Kosher salt and freshly ground black
pepper to taste

2 cups hickory wood chips, soaked 1 hour
in water to cover and drained

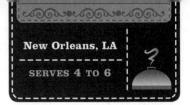

New Orleans, LA

SERVES 4 TO 6

Grilled Smoked Chicken
with root beer barbecue sauce

In the South, you'll see many barbecue sauces based on Pepsi®, Coke®, or Dr Pepper®. All of these sauces are good, with their sweetness and caramel flavors, but the earthiness of root beer made me think that it could be pretty good, too. The chickens get a smoking, which adds to the flavor experience, and the sauce becomes a glaze at the end of the cooking.

- ᧕ᦞᦞᧁ -

1. Mix the salt, paprika, brown sugar, pepper, and celery seeds together in a small bowl. Reserve 4 teaspoons of the spice mixture for the mop mixture. Rub the remaining spice mixture all over the chicken halves. Refrigerate the chickens for 1 hour.

2. Combine the water, vinegar, Worcestershire, and remaining spice mixture in a medium bowl to use as a mop.

3. Combine the BBQ sauce ingredients, except the salt and pepper, in a medium, heavy saucepan. Boil over medium heat, stirring occasionally. Reduce heat to simmer until reduced to 1½ cups, about 20 minutes. Add salt and pepper. (Set aside until ready to use or let cool and refrigerate.)

4. Set up the grill for indirect grilling (see pp. 6–9). Oil your grill's cooking surface. Add 1 cup of the drained wood chips. Fill an aluminum foil drip pan halfway with water.

5. Arrange the chicken, skin side up, on the grill above the drip pan and cover. Use the top and bottom vents to maintain the temperature between 275°F and 325°F. Keep any other vents closed. Grill until almost cooked through, brushing with the mop every 15 minutes, for 1 hour 25 minutes.

6. Begin brushing the chickens with the barbecue sauce and continue grilling until an instant-read thermometer inserted in the thigh away from the bone registers 180°F, about 10 minutes longer. Using tongs, move the chickens directly over the fire. Grill until the sauce sizzles and browns, about 2 minutes. Remove to a platter, cut into quarters, and serve, passing the remaining barbecue sauce separately.

1 tablespoon sugar

1 teaspoon dry mustard

1 teaspoon onion powder

1 teaspoon paprika

1 teaspoon kosher salt

1 teaspoon garlic powder

½ teaspoon ground coriander

½ teaspoon ground cumin

½ teaspoon freshly ground black pepper

One 4-pound or larger chicken

1 tablespoon vegetable oil

One 16-ounce can beer

Vinegar in a spray bottle

Jane's
beer can chicken

Jane Kuntz is one tough lady. I first met Jane and her husband, Chuck, on the golf course. She was feisty and had a mouth on her that kept me in stitches. She had successfully battled cancer once and lived life for all it was worth. A few years later, she had to do battle again and continues to fight today. But on her good days, she's out on the golf course, working in her yard, or having folks over for her famous beer can chicken. It's a fairly standard take on this new grilling classic, but she is the fussiest about it of anyone I know. I think it's that extra attention that makes hers the best. And if you don't think you have time to cook out, remember Jane, who makes the time, when time is truly precious.

– ເວໂຄໂວ –

1. Set up the grill for indirect grilling (see pp. 6–9). Oil your grill's cooking surface.

2. Combine the sugar, mustard, onion powder, paprika, salt, garlic powder, coriander, cumin, and pepper in a small bowl.

3. Remove the neck and giblets and any excess fat from the chicken, rinse it inside and out under cold running water, and pat dry with paper towels. Brush the vegetable oil over the chicken. Take the rub mixture and coat the chicken inside and out with it.

4. When the grill is ready, open the beer can and pour off half the beer. Of course, there's no reason to waste good beer, so drink it—Jane does. Set the half-full can on your countertop and slide the chicken over the top of the can and into the bird's cavity. Transfer the chicken to the grill, keeping the can upright. The legs of the chicken need to touch the grill top for extra stability. Spray the bird with the vinegar every 15 minutes or so. Cover and cook until an instant-read thermometer inserted in the thigh registers 180°F and the juices run clear. This should take 1¼ to 1½ hours.

5. Remove the chicken from the grill. Be careful with the can of beer—it will be hot. Let the chicken rest on the can for about 10 minutes. Pull the chicken off the can and cut the chicken into serving pieces. Serve warm with a favorite sauce, if desired, but Jane's has never needed anything extra.

The "Boss" Grilled Butterflied Chicken

with lemon and herbs, greek style

The Gemini Diner is one of many Greek-run diners in New York City and offers the same bill of fare—anything you could possibly want to eat 24 hours a day. My favorite waiter there is a big Greek guy who everyone simply knows as the "Boss." Even the owners claim not to know his real name.

When things are slow, Boss will come by my table, and, well, BS for a while. We usually talk politics, but food always comes up. I had been trying to get a connection to someone in the Greek section of Queens called Astoria to spit roast a baby lamb for me. "Why you want a lamb?" asked Boss after I had pestered him for a couple of weeks. "Hell, anybody can do lamb, but split chickens, now that's good stuff. Let me tell you how to do that." I wrote down his recipe, and when I got back to North Carolina, I fired up my grill and gave it a whirl. The result is one of my favorite recipes.

Using this method takes a little work but it's fairly simple. You need to remove the backbone of the chicken, which allows the chicken to open up like a book, lay flat on the grill, and cook fast—it's called spatchcocking a bird.

The marinade for the chicken is basic European farmhouse and adds a lively flavor, between the acidity of the lemon juice and the freshness of the herbs.

Don't attempt this with boneless, skinless chicken breasts. You'll end up with nothing but dry, burnt chicken. One of my dad's favorite lines, "The nearer the bone, the sweeter the meat," certainly applies here.

Give this one a try. It's good hot, at room temperature, even cold the next day for lunch or a picnic. You know the "Boss" is always right.

One 3- to 4-pound chicken

Kosher salt and freshly ground black pepper

¼ cup chopped mixed fresh herbs (such as thyme, oregano, basil, and/or rosemary)

¼ cup chopped fresh parsley

½ cup fresh lemon juice (2 to 4 lemons)

½ cup olive oil

tip: A spatula and tongs are helpful in turning the chicken.

You may have some flare-ups to start with; just move the chicken around on the grill or hit the flames with a squirt from a water bottle. Remember that some flame is good and adds to the flavor.

1. Place the chicken on a cutting board, breast side down. With a pair of poultry shears (having shears really makes this a whole lot easier), make a cut on one side of the backbone from the neck to the tail. Duplicate that cut on the other side of the backbone. Throw the backbone in a zip-top plastic bag, seal it, and throw it in the freezer; add other backbones (believe me, you'll be coming back to this recipe) to the bag until you've got enough to make chicken broth.

2. Open the bird up, kind of like a book, and press down on each side. Turn the chicken over and press on both sides again. You should hear a few joints pop and the chicken should lie somewhat flat. Turn the bird over and make two slits toward the end of the bird. Pull the end of each drumstick through each slit. Turn the chicken back over and snip the wing tips if desired. Liberally salt and pepper the chicken.

3. Combine the mixed herbs and parsley in a medium bowl. Stir in the lemon juice, then whisk in the oil.

4. Place the chicken in a 2-gallon zip-top plastic bag and pour the marinade over it. Seal the bag, lay it flat in the refrigerator, and let marinate for 24 hours, turning the bag over a couple of times.

5. Light a charcoal fire or preheat your gas grill on high. Oil your grill's cooking surface.

6. Remove the chicken from the marinade and pat it with paper towels Discard the marinade. Place the chicken, skin side down, over the fire and cook for 12 to 15 minutes.

7. Turn and cook until an instant-read thermometer inserted in the thigh registers 180°F, about another 12 to 15 minutes. Let rest a few minutes and cut into serving pieces.

¼ cup McCormick's® Montreal chicken seasoning®

Two 3-pound chickens, giblets removed

Two 12-ounce cans Coors Light® beer, if doing beer can

1. Liberally sprinkle both birds inside and out with the seasoning.

2. Set up the grill for indirect grilling (see pp. 6–9). Steve uses oak wood chunks instead of charcoal. Oil your grill's cooking surface.

3. *For rotisserie*, position the birds on the spit. Close the lid and start the motor. *For beer can style*, open each can of beer and drink half. Position each chicken firmly over a beer can and place upright on the grill away from the fire. Cover.

4. Either way, cook until an instant-read thermometer inserted in the thigh registers 180°F, about 1½ hours. Transfer to a platter and cut into individual serving pieces.

Steve's Oak-Smoked
rotisserie or beer can chicken

Steve Sancimino is one of the brothers who run Swan Oyster Depot in San Francisco. When I asked the guys about grilling, they all pointed to Steve. "Hey, he's got two brick barbecue grills in his backyard," says younger brother Tom. "Yeah, I love to barbecue, but I don't use gas or charcoal. Just oak wood, man, that's flavor, especially on chickens." When I ask how he starts the wood, he takes off to the back and returns with a wooden clam box. "I let these dry out, then bust 'em into kindling."

"Since I have a rotisserie, I use it a lot, but I do it beer can style, too," says Steve. "Sometimes I think the beer can style is better because of the moist steam that gets into the chicken."

JOHNSON & GUNSTONE
PORT TOWNSEND, WASH.
PRODUCERS OF THE FAMOUS
DISCOVERY BAY
LITTLE NECK CLAMS

Jennifer's Spicy Smoked Almonds *(page 16)*
and Rachel's Bewitching Deviled Eggs *(page 18)*

Grilled Pizza Margherita *(page 20)* | **Grilled Fresh Figs with Country Ham** *(page 22)*

‹ **Brooklyn Jerked Chicken Wings** *(page 28)* **and Fred's Sweet Tea** *(page 320)*
**Sharon Benton's Simply Wonderful Grilled Shrimp Wrapped in Basil
and Prosciutto** *(page 31)* **and Blackberry Limeade** *(page 321)*

OPPOSITE | **Maria Martin's Cowboy Rib-Eye Steaks with Cilantro-Lime Butter** *(page 40)* **and Tony Inscore's Old-Fashioned Panned Squash** *(page 327)*

Skip Skipworth's Santa Maria Barbecue and Santa Maria Salsa *(page 64)* **and Santa Maria-Style Pinquito Beans** *(page 324)*

Monterey Stuffed Flank Steak *(page 54)*

Ben and Jacques's Excellent Grilled and Braised Short Ribs *(page 68)* **served over grits**
Jean Lynn's Beef Brisket, by Way of Kansas City *(page 72)* **and Jean Lynn's Potato Salad** *(page 330)* >

< **Cheese-Stuffed Veal Chops with Rosemary and Sage** *(page 73)*
and Katrina's Mixed Vegetable Grill *(page 291)* | **Hugh's Awesome
Smoked Ribs** *(page 106)*

Opposite | **Jack Daniel's Grilled Country Ham** *(page 119)* **served up with some scrambled eggs for a grillin' good breakfast**

Italian Grilled Pork Chops with Grilled Leeks *(page 104)*

Fred's North Carolina-Style Barbecue *(page 122)*, **Martha and Fred's Fabulous Baked Beans** *(page 322)*, **and Lexington-Style Red Slaw** *(page 334)*

< **Rosemary Skewered Lamb** (*page 132*)
Carla's Pork Tenderloin with Cumin Crust and Mango Salsa (*page 78*)

OPPOSITE | **Verla's Grilled Chicken Salad with Radicchio and Figs** *(page 148)*

Cheesy Grits with BBQ Chicken and Caramelized Onions *(page 144)*

Boris's Grilled Chicken Breasts Stuffed with Ham and Blue Cheese *(page 149)*

OPPOSITE | **Ting's Grilled Shrimp with Tamarind Sauce** *(page 230)*
Chris's Eureka Cedar-Planked Salmon *(page 197)*

OPPOSITE | **Grilled Deconstructed Niçoise Salad** *(page 206)*

Meredith's Grilled Fish Tacos
(page 223)

Grilled Mahimahi with Pineapple Barbecue Sauce and Grilled Sweet Onions *(page 221)*

OPPOSITE | **Frito's Olé Burger** *(page 256)*

Tony Bell's Inside-Out Cheeseburgers
(page 246)

Sandra Dey's Cajun Pork Burgers with Grilled Sweet Potato "Fries" *(page 261)*

< **Garlicky Lemon-Marinated Portobello Burgers with Baby Greens in a Pita** *(page 271)*
Grilled Sausage Tacos San Antonio Style *(page 277)*

OPPOSITE | **"Tube Steaks" College Style** *(page 273)* **with Dad's Hot Dog Chili Sauce** *(page335)*

Assorted barbecue sauces

Belinda's Grilled Pineapple with Pound Cake *(page 295)*

1 cup kosher salt

2 quarts cold water

One 3½-pound chicken

BEAUFORT SPICE RUB

2 tablespoons ground cumin

2 tablespoons curry powder

2 tablespoons chili powder

1 tablespoon ground allspice

1 tablespoon freshly ground black pepper

1 teaspoon ground cinnamon

One 12-ounce can beer

Beaufort's
dancing chicken

Around Beaufort, South Carolina, there is no beer can chicken. There is, however, dancing chicken, which is the way they describe chicken stuck on top of a beer can when it's sitting on the grill. My friend Pete Singletary shared this recipe with me years ago. The method and the spices are a bit different in this part of the world, with curry powder and allspice making an appearance. The quick brine helps you to keep the chicken moist. If you love beer can chicken, you may want to put this recipe on your dance card.

– ເວົ້າໆ –

1. Dissolve the salt in the water in a container large enough to hold the chicken, then immerse the chicken in the brine and chill for 1 hour.

2. Remove the chicken from the brine and rinse under cold running water. Pat dry with paper towels and set aside.

3. Set up the grill for indirect grilling (see pp. 6–9). Oil your grill's cooking surface.

4. Meanwhile, combine the spice rub ingredients in a small bowl. Take 3 tablespoons of it and rub the inside and outside of the chicken with it, including under the breast skin. (Store the remaining rub in a small, tightly covered container for your next turn with Dancing Chicken.)

5. Open the beer can and discard (or take a swig of) ¼ cup of the beer. Punch 2 large holes in the top of the can with a bottle opener. Slide the chicken over the can so the drumsticks reach down to the bottom of the can and the chicken stands upright. Place the chicken away from the heat, using the drumstick ends to steady it. Cover the grill and roast, rotating the chicken 180°F after 35 to 45 minutes.

6. Continue roasting another 35 to 45 minutes, until an instant-read meat thermometer inserted in the thickest part of the thigh away from the bone registers 180°F and the juices run clear.

7. Transfer the chicken, using tongs and wearing ovenproof gloves, to a cutting board, keeping the can upright. Let rest 15 minutes, then carefully (the liquid in the can will still be hot) lift the chicken off the can and onto a cutting board and cut into serving pieces.

One 4-pound chicken

Kosher salt and freshly ground black pepper

Six 6-inch sprigs fresh rosemary

2 cups Mark's Favorite Marinade (recipe below), or more as needed

Mark Cheeseman's
roasted chicken

Serious griller Mark Cheeseman from Alabama way really shows his flair with this recipe. The key is his marinade, which is really a basting sauce or, as it is known in the pork world, "a mop." All *you* need to know is that it adds volumes of flavor to ordinary chicken or any kind of poultry.

– ༒ཀ –

1. Set up the grill for indirect grilling (see pp. 6–9). Oil your grill's cooking surface.

2. Meanwhile, remove the giblets and neck from the chicken cavity and set aside. Rinse the chicken under cold running water and pat dry with paper towels. Sprinkle inside and out with salt and pepper to taste and insert the rosemary sprigs into the cavity.

3. Place the chicken on a standing grill rack set away from the heat, and grill until an instant-read thermometer inserted in the thigh away from the bone registers 180°F, 1 to 1¼ hours and the juices run clear, basting with the marinade every 15 minutes.

4. Remove from the grill rack and let rest for 10 minutes before cutting into serving pieces.

---

mark's favorite marinade
MAKES ABOUT 1 QUART

This marinade can be stored in an airtight container in the refrigerator for several weeks. Shake well before you use.

1 cup vegetable oil

½ cup soy sauce

⅓ cup red wine vinegar

¼ cup fresh lemon juice

3 tablespoons Worcestershire sauce

4 cloves garlic, minced

1½ tablespoons dry mustard

1 tablespoon dried parsley flakes

1 tablespoon dried rosemary

2 teaspoons freshly ground black pepper

1½ teaspoons dried oregano

1½ teaspoons salt

Combine all the ingredients in a large bowl with a wire whisk.

8 cups water

⅓ cup coarse kosher salt

¼ cup rice or distilled white vinegar

¼ cup soy sauce

8 star anise, broken

Two 3-inch cinnamon sticks, broken

1 tablespoon sugar

2 teaspoons fennel seeds, crushed

One 3- to 3½-pound chicken

Asian Spice-Brined
grill-roasted chicken

If you have been buying those spit-roasted chickens from your supermarket's deli, you have been limited to plain, lemon-garlic, and probably barbecue flavors for choices. Roasting a whole chicken on the grill is so easy that I beg you to try this recipe. Why? First, you will get a great Asian twist, and second, it's so good I bet you will leave the store-bought behind and make your own on a regular basis—try any flavor combination you want.

–⌒◠◡◠⌒–

1. In a large bowl, combine the water, salt, vinegar, soy sauce, star anise, cinnamon, sugar, and fennel seeds. Stir until the salt is dissolved.

2. Rinse the chicken under cold running water inside and out. Remove any fat from the cavity. Carefully add the chicken to the brine. Cover with plastic wrap and let soak in the refrigerator for 6 to 8 hours, turning the chicken occasionally.

3. Remove the chicken from the brine; discard the brine. Rinse the chicken and pat dry with paper towels.

4. Set up the grill for indirect grilling (see pp. 6–9). Oil your grill's cooking surface.

5. Place the chicken, breast side up, on the grill rack over a drip pan. Cover and grill until an instant-read thermometer inserted at the thigh registers 180°F and the juices run clear, 1¼ to 1½ hours.

6. Transfer the chicken to a platter. Cover with aluminum foil and let rest for 10 minutes before cutting into serving pieces.

Two 1- to 1½-pound Cornish game hens, backbones removed and split in half

Kosher salt and freshly ground black pepper

2 cups hickory or other mild smoking chips, soaked in water for 30 minutes or more

½ cup vegetable oil

1 cup mayonnaise

1 cup cider vinegar

1 tablespoon fresh lemon juice

1 tablespoon prepared horseradish

1½ tablespoons cracked black pepper

½ teaspoon kosher salt

¼ teaspoon cayenne pepper

1. Set up your grill for indirect cooking (see pp. 6–9). Oil your grill's cooking surface.

2. Salt and pepper the hens. Add the soaked chips to the grill. Position the hens away from the fire. Adjust your vents to almost closed and cover. Smoke until an instant-read thermometer inserted into the thickest part of the thigh away from the bone registers 180°F and the juices run clear, 2 to 2½ hours, basting with the oil and seasoning again with salt and pepper after 1 hour. If cooking with charcoal, replenish your fire as needed.

3. Meanwhile, in the largest bowl you have, combine the mayonnaise, vinegar, lemon juice, horseradish, cracked black pepper, salt, and cayenne. (This can be prepared up to 4 days in advance.) Refrigerate until the hens are done.

4. Ladle out a little sauce, then place the smoked hens in the bowl with the remaining sauce and toss to coat. Let them sit a few minutes, then drain and serve with the reserved sauce on the side.

Nikki Parrish's Smoke-Roasted
cornish game hens alabama style

To think that a ballet dancer could be a pro at the grill, well, I wouldn't have believed it until I met Nikki Parrish. Nikki grew up in a small northern Alabama town, Cullman to be exact. While her dad was building one of the most respected cattle stockyards in the country, her mom was running Nikki to Birmingham for ballet lessons. "Mother was a good cook, not very adventuresome, like many that were born during the Depression, but she impressed on me the need to serve tasty vittles." Marriage took her to Richmond and performances with the Richmond Ballet Company. Her white-sauced Cornish hens quickly became a hit with friends. "The white sauce is a taste of home for me. This is a goosed-up version of what I knew in Alabama. It's great for that first time at home dinner date," she says. "It usually proves that I'm a force to be dealt with, not just some girly-girl. These hens truly are hard to beat."

Only in northern Alabama will you see this kind of sauce paired with barbecue—and don't snicker about the mayonnaise until you've tasted it.

Nikki uses a space ship looking grill for her smoking.

SOUTHEAST MARINADE

2 Thai or Serrano chiles, seeded

3 tablespoons chopped shallots

¼ cup finely chopped fresh cilantro

2 tablespoons peeled and minced fresh ginger

1 tablespoon chopped garlic

1 teaspoon chopped fresh lemongrass (use the tender inner stalks) or dried, or substitute finely grated lemon zest

¼ cup Asian fish sauce (you can find this in the Asian section of most supermarkets)

½ cup unsweetened coconut milk

3 tablespoons canola oil

1 tablespoon sugar

4 Rock Cornish game hens

Southeast Asian
rock cornish game hens

Nancie McDermott, author of *Real Thai* and *Everyday Vietnamese Cooking*, put her two cents into this recipe with her vast knowledge of Southeast Asian flavors. If you're feeling flush and can find poussins, which are very young and tender chickens, by all means enjoy them as a special treat. Does this recipe also work with plain old chicken? You bet.

– ✤ –

1. In a food processor or blender, combine the chiles, shallots, cilantro, ginger, garlic, and lemongrass, and pulse until finely chopped. Add the fish sauce, coconut milk, oil, and sugar, and continue to pulse until smooth.

2. Rinse the game hens under cold running water and pat dry with paper towels. In each of two large zip-top plastic bags, place two game hens. Divide the marinade between the two bags. Seal, squish everything around to coat the hens, and let marinate in the refrigerator overnight, turning the bags a few times.

3. Set up the grill for indirect grilling (see pp. 6–9). Oil your grill's cooking surface.

4. Remove the birds from the marinade and place the marinade in a saucepan over medium-high heat. Bring to a boil and boil 1 to 2 minutes. Remove from the heat and let cool slightly. Place the game hens on the grill, breast side down directly over the fire. Sear the hens for about 2 minutes, then turn and sear the backs for 2 minutes. Move the birds away from the fire and close the lid. About every 8 minutes, rotate the birds and brush with the marinade. Cook for a total of 1 to 1½ hours, until an instant-read meat thermometer inserted at the thigh away from the bone registers 180°F and the juices run clear. Remove the game hens to a platter and serve.

6 cups white cranberry juice cocktail

½ cup pure maple syrup

¼ cup coarse kosher salt

Two 1¼- to 1½-pound Cornish game hens

Chopped fresh herbs (optional)

Lee's
maple-cranberry game hens

Lee Flucher likes to drive his Gloucester, Massachusetts, neighbors crazy with hunger when he throws this recipe on the grill. "Heck, it's just local stuff, cranberries and maple syrup. Anybody can do it." His brine of cranberry juice and maple syrup brings a unique taste to the slow-cooked hens. The sweet-tart combination almost generates a pork essence, as well as keeps the birds moist. And, boy, does it smell great when it's cooking.

– ᘓᘔᘕᗐᘔᗐᘚ –

1. Make the brine in a large bowl by combining the cranberry juice, maple syrup, and salt. Stir until the salt is dissolved.

2. Rinse the game hens under cold running water inside and out, and cut away any excess fat from cavities. Carefully add the hens to the brine, cover with plastic wrap, and let marinate in the refrigerator for 4 hours (but no longer), turning the hens occasionally.

3. Remove the hens from the brine, discarding the brine. Rinse the hens and pat dry with paper towels. Twist the wing tips under the backs and tie the legs of each hen together.

4. Set up the grill for indirect grilling (see pp. 6–9). Oil your grill's cooking surface.

5. Place the game hens, breast side up, on the grill over a drip pan and cover. After 40 minutes, cut the strings and cover them loosely with aluminum foil. Put the lid down and grill until an instant-read thermometer inserted into the thickest part of the thigh away from the bone registers 180°F and the juices run clear, 1 to 1¼ hours total. Add additional coals to your fire as needed.

6. Transfer the hens to a platter, cover, and let rest for 10 minutes. If desired, serve garnished with herbs.

GREEK STYLE MARINADE

¼ cup fresh lemon juice

¼ cup extra-virgin olive oil

2 tablespoons chopped fresh oregano

2 tablespoons chopped fresh mint

1 tablespoon minced garlic

1 tablespoon lemon-pepper seasoning

---

1 boneless, skinless turkey breast (about 2 pounds)

2 medium white onions

2 large green bell peppers

Extra-virgin olive oil

Kosher salt

Birmingham, AL

SERVES 6 TO 8

Greek-Inspired
turkey kebobs

You think Greek-style spices only apply to some cuts of lamb? I'm out to show you differently. This marinade flavors turkey breast in a magnificent way. You could leave the turkey breast whole and grill it much like you would a London broil, but cutting it into kebobs lets the marinade soak more deeply into the meat, giving you more flavor with every bite.

– ৵৩৶ৎ –

1. In a small bowl, whisk together the marinade ingredients. Set aside.

2. Rinse the turkey breast under cold running water and pat dry with paper towels. Cut into 1½-inch chunks. Place in a large zip-top plastic bag, pour the marinade over, and squish to coat. Seal the bag and place in the refrigerator at least 4 hours or overnight, turning occasionally.

3. Light a charcoal fire or preheat your gas grill on high. Oil the grill's cooking surface.

4. Meanwhile, cut the onions and bell peppers into 1½-inch chunks. Remove the turkey from the marinade and discard the marinade. Thread the turkey and vegetables alternately onto the skewers. Brush lightly with olive oil and sprinkle with salt.

5. Place the skewers on the grill and cook until the meat is firm to the touch and the vegetables are tender, 6 to 8 minutes, turning once.

6. Remove from the grill, let cool slightly, remove the turkey and vegetables from the skewers, and serve immediately.

SWEET CHILE RUB

3 tablespoons firmly packed light brown sugar

4½ teaspoons kosher salt

4½ teaspoons ancho chile powder or regular chili powder

4½ teaspoons paprika

4½ teaspoons ground cumin

2¼ teaspoons freshly ground black pepper

One 10- to 12-pound turkey

½ onion

½ orange

Kosher salt and freshly ground black pepper

Lexington-Style North Carolina Barbecue Sauce (p. 302) or Eastern North Carolina-Style Barbecue Sauce (p. 304)

Smoked
turkey bbq

Turkey, when handled right, can make an excellent substitute for pork when you crave that barbecue flavor and texture but need to cut down on the fat. I first used this recipe for a cooking class in Chapel Hill and had the audacity to call it low-fat barbecue. The 50-plus students I had were so enamored with it that they wondered why we ever made barbecue from pork shoulders. The key is to inject the turkey with an apple juice–based fluid, which will keep it moist throughout the smoking and helps it to develop good smoke flavor. This dish may surprise you. Use this recipe as you would chopped barbecue pork, for sandwiches or served with your favorite side for barbecue.

– ᏸᎧᏺᏸ –

1. Combine the rub ingredients in a small bowl.

2. Rinse the turkey under cold running water and pat dry with paper towels. Cut away any excess fat and discard the innards. Place the onion and orange in the cavity and season the cavity with salt and pepper. Generously pat the chile rub all over the outside of the turkey.

3. Set up the grill for indirect grilling (see pp. 6–9). Oil your grill's cooking surface.

4. Place the turkey on the grill, close the lid, and cook, keeping the grill temperature at about 300°F, until an instant-read meat thermometer inserted into the thickest part of the thigh away from the bone registers 180°F and the juices run clear, about 2 hours. Move the turkey around as necessary to allow all sides to cook evenly, and replenish the fire as needed if cooking with charcoal.

5. Remove to a cutting board and let rest for 10 minutes, then slice or pull into shreds. Place in a large bowl and toss with as much of the sauce as you prefer. Serve immediately. This also freezes well for up to 3 months.

Breast from 1 wild turkey (4 to 5 pounds)

1 bottle Italian dressing

1. Cut the breast crosswise into 1½-inch-thick strips. Place in a large zip-top plastic bag and pour the Italian dressing over the meat. Seal the bag, squish everything around to coat the turkey, and let marinate in the refrigerator overnight.

2. Light a charcoal fire or preheat your gas grill on high. Oil the grill's cooking surface. Let the coals burn down into a low fire or adjust the gas grill burners to low.

3. Remove the breast strips from the bag and discard the marinade. Place the breast strips on the grill. Cook for about 4 minutes, then turn and cook 3 minutes longer. Be careful not to overcook the strips as they will become dry and tough. The strips are done when they're opaque throughout. Remove to a platter and serve immediately.

Kevin Rouse's
grilled wild turkey breast

Kevin Rouse is one of those guys for whom hunting is born in the bone. He combs through the valleys and mountains of East Tennessee, hunting deer and wild turkey. I had never had grilled wild turkey until Kevin and I met at a Sunday school party in Morristown, Tennessee. "Pretty easy. I just cut the breast into strips and pour Italian dressing over them," he told me, almost embarrassed. He shouldn't have been. The turkey loses some gaminess this way, but it still has a flavor all its own. Even if you don't have a hunter in the family, wild turkeys are increasingly available at specialty butchers and food stores. This recipe also takes to regular turkey.

Wild turkey tenderloins

Kevin takes his Sunday school class to the wild side.

6 semiboneless quail, defrosted if
necessary

RASPBERRY-HERB MARINADE

1 tablespoon raspberry vinegar

3 tablespoons olive oil

2 tablespoons chopped fresh parsley

1 tablespoon chopped fresh thyme

Kosher salt and freshly ground black
pepper

RASPBERRY-MUSTARD VINAIGRETTE

1/2 pint raspberries

2 tablespoons finely chopped shallots

1/4 cup raspberry vinegar

1 tablespoon Dijon mustard

1 tablespoon honey

1 tablespoon chopped fresh parsley

1 cup canola oil

Kosher salt and freshly ground black
pepper

Juice of 1 lemon

1 1/2 cups warm cooked lentils

Grilled Quail with

raspberry-mustard vinaigrette

Frank Stitt is one of America's greatest chefs, and he proves it nightly at his three Birmingham, Alabama, restaurants. Frank grew up in Cullman, north of Birmingham, a rural community of farmers and ranchers. His parents taught him early about using what the land has to offer. Quail were a sure sign of autumn, and Frank's family always liked the way they tasted over charcoal. I've taken this inspiration from one of his more complicated quail dishes and simplified it for us mortals at the grill. You'll find quail in the frozen food section, usually semiboneless.

– ᏣᏬᏬᏫ –

1. Use kitchen shears to cut the quail up the backbone so that it will lie flat on the grill.

2. Combine the marinade ingredients in a small bowl. Pour this over the quail in a large glass baking dish and let marinate at room temperature for about 45 minutes.

3. Light a charcoal fire or preheat your gas grill on high. Oil the grill's cooking surface.

4. Remove the birds from the marinade. Salt and pepper them liberally and place the birds leg side up on the grill. Cook for 5 minutes, then turn and baste with some of the remaining marinade. Cook until the quail are just done, about 5 minutes; they should still be pink inside. Remove from the grill, tent with aluminum foil, and let rest.

5. To make the vinaigrette, crush the raspberries in a small bowl. Add the shallots, vinegar, mustard, honey, and parsley, and whisk together. Slowly whisk in the oil until the vinaigrette thickens. Taste and season with salt and pepper and add lemon juice to taste.

6. Reheat the lentils if necessary and spoon onto a serving platter. Place the cooked quail over the lentils and drizzle with the vinaigrette. Serve immediately.

HOISIN-SESAME BBQ SAUCE

¼ cup hoisin sauce

2 tablespoons sesame seeds

3 tablespoons Asian chili-garlic sauce

3 tablespoons toasted sesame oil

3 tablespoons honey

1 teaspoon ground ginger

---

8 semiboneless quail, defrosted if necessary

One 14.5-ounce can chicken broth

2 teaspoons cornstarch

Sliced scallions (white and green parts) for garnish

Fred's Backyard, NC

SERVES 4

My Asian
grilled quail

Most of the time I grill quail over direct heat, but when I'm working the little birds in a sweet-hot marinade such as this, I like indirect. The quail stay on the grill longer and soak in more smokiness, which really gives this Asian marinade/sauce time to bond with the bird and maximize flavor.

– ⸎⸎⸎ –

1. In a large zip-top plastic bag, combine the sauce ingredients. Gently squeeze the bag to blend, then add the quail and seal the bag. Squish them around in the marinade to coat and let marinate in the refrigerator for 30 minutes, turning the bag a couple of times.

2. Remove the quail from the marinade, reserving the marinade.

3. Set up the grill for indirect grilling (see pp. 6–9). Oil your grill's cooking surface.

4. Arrange the quail away from the fire, close the lid, and cook until an instant-read thermometer inserted in the thickest part of the thigh registers 160°F, about 30 minutes.

5. Meanwhile, pour the marinade into a small saucepan. Set aside ¼ cup of the chicken broth, and add the remaining broth to the saucepan. Bring to a boil over medium-high heat and let continue to boil, stirring occasionally, for 5 minutes.

6. Whisk together the cornstarch and reserved ¼ cup broth until smooth. Whisk into the marinade, bring back to a boil, whisking constantly, and let boil for 1 minute.

7. Serve with the quail garnished with scallions, if desired. Serve immediately, passing the sauce at the table.

8 semiboneless quail, defrosted if necessary

Kosher salt and freshly ground black pepper

24 freshly shucked oysters

16 small sprigs fresh thyme

8 strips thick-cut applewood smoked bacon

Hugh's Sugarland Grilled
quail stuffed with oysters

If you live around Sugarland, Texas, you better have a pretty good bird dog because when quail season comes you'll see more of that dog than you will your significant other. Born and raised around Sugarland, Hugh Lynn is an avid quail hunter. He likes to wrap quail in bacon and season them with a little thyme. I decided to take his method one step further by stuffing these juicy little birds with some Gulf Coast oysters. Served on top of a heaping spoonful of grits, this is almost heaven on earth.

– ᴄᏮᏮ –

1. Wash the quail under cold running water and pat dry with paper towels. Sprinkle inside and out with salt and pepper. Put 3 oysters in each quail cavity. Tuck a sprig of thyme under each wing and tie the legs together with kitchen twine. Wrap each bird with a strip of bacon and secure it with toothpicks or more twine.

2. Light a charcoal fire or preheat your gas grill on high. Oil the grill's cooking surface.

3. Place the quail on their side on the grill and cook until the bacon has browned and gotten somewhat crisp, 8 to 9 minutes. Turn the birds to the other side and cook 8 minutes more. Finally, turn the quail breast side down and cook about another 8 minutes. Quail are best eaten medium. If the bacon begins to get too brown, move the quail to a cooler part of the grill.

4. Remove the quail to a platter and let rest for 5 minutes. Pour any accumulated juices over the quail and serve over grits.

BOURBON-THYME MARINADE

¼ cup vegetable oil

2 tablespoons bourbon

2 tablespoons fresh lemon juice

1 tablespoon balsamic vinegar

1 tablespoon finely chopped fresh thyme

2 teaspoons grated lemon zest

½ teaspoon kosher salt

¼ teaspoon freshly ground black pepper

4 butterflied squabs (about 1 pound each), defrosted if necessary

Vegetable oil

MAPLE-MUSTARD SAUCE

¼ cup maple syrup

2 tablespoons bourbon

2 tablespoons Dijon mustard

Squab Bathed in
bourbon and mustard

I love squab—it's rich, earthy, and awesome when cooked over a live fire. Squab is the veal of the poultry world. These are young birds, usually 4 weeks old, have never flown, and are extremely tender. Like many dark-fleshed birds, bourbon and mustard seem to best bring out its flavor, but also try the Chinese Asian-Style Rub (p. 299) for an international twist. Squab typically is not a supermarket item, but sometimes you will find it in the frozen section. Most specialty stores carry it, and it can be ordered from Internet gourmet retailers. They're usually sold butterflied. If you can't get a hold of it, try this recipe with quail or duck instead.

- ᦥᧁᧁᨽ -

1. In a small bowl, combine the marinade ingredients.

2. Place the squabs in a large zip-top plastic bag and pour in the marinade. Seal the bag, then squish the birds around in the marinade to coat them evenly and let marinate in the refrigerator for at least 2 hours and up to 12 hours, turning the bag occasionally.

3. Remove the squabs from the bag and discard the marinade. Pat them dry with paper towels and lightly brush with vegetable oil.

4. Set up the grill for indirect grilling (see pp. 6–9). Oil your grill's cooking surface.

5. Meanwhile, combine the sauce ingredients in a small bowl.

6. Place the squabs on the grill away from the fire, skin side down, close the lid, and cook until the skin is golden brown and the juices are still slightly pink, 35 to 40 minutes, turning once. During the last 10 minutes of cooking, brush on the sauce frequently.

7. Remove the squabs to a platter, brush again with the sauce, and serve immediately.

4 boneless duck breast halves

SHERRIED BOURBON MARINADE À L'ORANGE

Grated zest and juice of 1 large orange

⅓ cup dry sherry

⅓ cup bourbon

2 tablespoons grated shallots

1 tablespoon Worcestershire sauce

¼ teaspoon kosher salt

Freshly ground black pepper

1 to 1½ cups peach preserves or orange marmalade, gently heated until liquid

South Louisiana Likkered-Up

orange-glazed grilled duck breasts

Where duck blinds are as thick as trees, you'll find good ways to cook duck. Around the bayous of Louisiana the consensus is that duck breast must be marinated in sherry and bourbon, grilled to medium-rare, and glazed for a sweet touch. I find that either a peach preserve or an orange marmalade works nicely. It cuts the fat, as does the bourbon, for an incredibly rich and luxurious finish.

– ꙮ –

1. Rinse the duck breasts and pat dry with paper towels. Place in a large zip-top plastic bag. Combine the marinade ingredients in a small bowl and pour into the bag. Seal the bag and squish everything around to coat the duck. Let marinate in the refrigerator overnight, turning the bag several times.

2. Light a charcoal fire or preheat your gas grill on high. Oil the grill's cooking surface. Any time you're grilling duck breasts, there is a chance the fire will flare up. Have a spray bottle full of cold water handy to put out the flames.

3. Remove the breasts from the marinade, pat dry, and place them on the grill skin side down. Cook until the skin is browned and crispy, 4 to 6 minutes. If you get a flare-up, move the breasts away from the flames and use your water bottle to extinguish it. Turn the breasts, brush the cooked side with the preserves, and cook another 5 minutes for medium-rare, which is perfect for duck breasts. Brush the other cooked side with the preserves, and let sit on the grill another minute to set the glaze.

4. Remove the breasts to a platter. Brush once again with the preserves and pass what remains at the table. Serve immediately.

4 boneless duck breast halves

2 teaspoons kosher salt

½ teaspoon freshly ground black pepper

¼ teaspoon cayenne pepper

4 cloves garlic, sliced

¼ cup chopped andouille sausage or tasso

¼ cup (½ stick) unsalted butter, melted

¼ cup cane syrup

1 tablespoon Tabasco sauce

Andouille-Stuffed
duck breast with cane syrup glaze

Duck is one of my favorite things to put on the grill, and I was lucky to get this recipe from Louisiana native Sandra Dey. Duck, quail, and other game birds are a way of life in Louisiana, and people there know how to fix them right. "The procedure of cutting pockets in meat or poultry and stuffing it with garlic and seasoning is very popular in Cajun country," says Sandra. "Adding andouille and a cane syrup glaze makes this everyday practice a little more special when paired with duck. This goes over big every time I serve it." It certainly has been a hit at my house. Serve it with grilled sweet potatoes or a salad of mixed baby greens. Cane syrup is a big deal in Louisiana and has become more widely available across the country in specialty markets and natural-food stores.

– ⌒⌒⌒ –

1. Score the skin on the duck; turn it over and cut 4 to 6 slits in the underside of each breast. Combine the salt, black pepper, and cayenne in a small bowl and mix well. Sprinkle a pinch of the seasoning mix in each pocket, using your finger to work it in evenly. Insert a slice of garlic and some andouille in each slit. Rub any remaining seasoning over the outside of the duck. Refrigerate them until ready to grill.

2. Combine the melted butter, cane syrup, and Tabasco in a small bowl and mix well; set aside.

3. Light a charcoal fire or preheat your gas grill on high. Oil the grill's cooking surface. Let the coals burn down to a medium-hot fire or adjust the gas grill burners to medium-high.

4. Place the breasts skin side down on the grill and cook 15 minutes, moving the duck if flames flare up; watch closely to prevent burning. Turn the breasts over and cook 5 to 7 minutes longer, brushing each side a few times with cane syrup glaze during the last 5 minutes.

5. Heat any remaining glaze. Slice the duck and drizzle with the glaze.

7 from water to flame:

fish and shellfish

My two loves are cooking anything over an outdoor flame and seafood cookery.

Grilling seafood is not difficult. Start with a clean grill—I mean a spotlessly clean grill. Lubricate the grill's cooking surface and the seafood in some manner, and make sure the grill's surface is hot. A light coating of mayonnaise on a piece of fish makes all the difference in it not sticking to the grill. Have at hand a good metal spatula. Start with a seafood item that can hold up to grilling. Super-thin pieces of fish and 100-count **shrimp** aren't good choices.

Forget "10 minutes per inch" or "cook until flakey." Both will leave you with overcooked, dry fish. Think in terms of 8 minutes per inch, and watch for the natural separation in the fish's surface for a true indication of doneness. Many popular fish for the grill, such as **tuna and salmon**, are actually better when undercooked slightly, more of a medium doneness.

Whole small fish are also loads of fun to cook on the grill. Trout, whether you caught it or not, takes to the grill like it does to a mountain stream.

Brining shrimp is a good way to protect them from overcooking, but buying the right size shrimp helps as well. Twenty-six-count-per-pound shrimp (please don't go by labels such as large, medium, etc.—they're not standardized) are perfect for the grill, cooking through quickly enough that the outsides don't get tough. And leave the shell on. Not only does it protect the shrimps' flesh, but the shell itself adds all kinds of flavor.

Buy your fish and shellfish from a reputable fishmonger. Know that ice is the "gold standard" of any seafood shop. Let your senses be your guide. Ammonia smell? You should leave. Fish are like people when they age—the flesh doesn't spring

> ### Tips for Buying Frozen
> If buying frozen fish and shellfish products, avoid any bags with rips or tears. Also look for evidence of mishandling, like excessive ice crystals and freezer burn, which add a gray tint to the flesh.

back as fast when pushed down and they get age spots. If you see a rainbow effect on fillets, avoid them. Also, remember that there is very little "fresh" fish or shellfish out there. Most of it is caught and quick-frozen out at sea and many times this product is better than "fresh." And if you buy it frozen, at least you will know how long it has been thawed.

½ cup good-quality mayonnaise

1 tablespoon chopped fresh dill

1 tablespoon grated lemon zest

Six 6- to 8-ounce 1-inch-thick steelhead salmon fillets, with skin on

1. Stir together the mayonnaise, dill, and lemon zest in a small bowl. Spoon equal amounts on each fillet and, using your hands, completely cover the fish with the mixture. Let set at room temperature while you get the fire going.

2. Light a charcoal fire or preheat your gas grill on high. Oil the grill's cooking surface. Let the coals burn down to a medium-hot fire or adjust the gas grill burners to medium-high.

3. Place the fillets, flesh side up, on the grill. Cook for about 4 minutes, carefully turn, and cook for another 4 minutes for medium or to your desired degree of doneness.

Evita's Dilled
steelhead salmon

Winnipeg, Canada, may not seem like year-round grilling country, but for Evita Smordi, a Holocaust educator, it is. "People enjoy entertaining here and we don't let a little cold get in the way of good barbecue flavor." The mayonnaise acts as an insulator for the moisture in the fish, as well as lubrication between the fish and the grill. Fish just won't stick when done this way.

1 quart water

1 cup firmly packed light brown sugar

1 cup granulated sugar

¼ cup kosher salt

Six 5- to 6-ounce salmon fillets, with skin on, any pin bones removed

3 cups or more alder wood chips, soaked in water for 30 minutes and drained

1. In a large bowl, combine the water, both sugars, and salt. Stir until the sugars and salt dissolve, then add the salmon, skin side up, to the brine, pressing to submerge it. Cover with plastic wrap and refrigerate overnight.

2. Remove the salmon from the brine and discard the brine. Rinse the salmon under cold running water. Place the salmon, skin side down, on a rack and let stand until the top is dry to touch, about 1 hour. Do not pat dry.

3. Light a charcoal fire or preheat your gas grill on high. Oil the grill's cooking surface. Let the coals burn down to a medium fire or adjust the gas grill burners to medium.

4. Add the smoking chips. Place together three 10x12-inch pieces of aluminum foil and, with a wooden skewer, pierce with 6 to 8 holes. Set two fillets, skin side down, on each piece of foil, and transfer the foil and salmon to the grill. Cook until the salmon is firm and a glaze begins to form over the surface of the salmon. This could take at least 30 minutes but no more than an hour, depending on your grill. You may need to replenish your fire.

5. Remove the salmon from the foil and transfer to a platter. Serve warm or at room temperature.

Jordy's
home-smoked salmon

Smoking salmon at home is easier than you think, but you won't have the exact same results of purchased smoked salmon. The flavor will be bold but not strongly flavored with wood smoke. The fish is done when it is firm to the touch. It's fine to make it a day in advance; just wrap in plastic wrap and refrigerate. If you have any left over, it makes an awesome salmon cake. Jordy, one of the fishmongers at the incredible Wild Edibles fish store at Grand Central Terminal in Manhattan, taught me the particulars of this dish.

Wild vs. Farm-Raised Salmon

With all the talk about farm-raised salmon vs. wild caught and their taste differences, this is a recipe that makes the most of the flavor of farm raised. I wouldn't use premium wild-caught king salmon here because the flavor would almost be too strong. Farm-raised salmon has a delicate flesh that takes to the smoke in a pleasing way. As much as I like and encourage the use of wild-caught seafood, this is one case where farm raised is probably the best.

¼ cup chopped fresh dill

1 teaspoon kosher salt, plus more to taste

1 teaspoon freshly ground black pepper

1 whole salmon (4 to 6 pounds), without
the head or tail, butterflied (ask your fishmonger to do this)

MARTINI MARINADE

2 cups gin

½ cup dry vermouth

¼ cup olive oil

2 teaspoons dried thyme

1 bay leaf

2 teaspoons onion powder

Juice of 1 lemon

Vegetable spray

Martini
salmon

Here's another recipe from the wilds of Northern California's salmon country. It takes the vibrancy of a martini and the richness of grilled salmon
and serves up a kickin' fish dish. Alder wood is the traditional smoking
wood for salmon. It's worth the effort to try to find some as it gives a
pleasant, smooth finish to the salmon.

– ᴄᷜᴼᴼᴳᷠ –

1. Mix the dill, salt, and pepper together in a small bowl. Rub this into
the flesh of the salmon and place it in a large baking dish. Cover with
plastic wrap and place in the refrigerator for 2 to 3 hours.

2. In medium bowl, combine the marinade ingredients. Taste and add salt
if necessary. Remove the fish from the refrigerator and pour the marinade
over it. Return the salmon to the refrigerator for another 3 hours.

3. Set up the grill for indirect grilling (see pp. 6–9). Oil your grill's
cooking surface.

4. Remove the salmon from the refrigerator about 30 minutes before
cooking. Pour off the marinade into a medium saucepan and warm over
medium-low heat. Take a piece of aluminum foil large enough for the
salmon to fit on and place it on your grill away from the fire. Lightly coat
with vegetable spray. Add your smoking chips if using. Place the salmon,
flesh side down, on the foil and cook for 30 minutes with the lid down.

5. Carefully turn the salmon. You will probably need someone to help
you or at least two big spatulas in order to do this successfully. Brush the
salmon with the warm marinade and cook another 30 minutes with the lid
down until opaque almost to the center, replenishing the fire as necessary.

6. Remove to a platter and serve. A cake or pie spatula works nicely to
remove servings from the salmon.

Fort Bragg, CA

SERVES 6

LEMON BASTING SAUCE

1 cup (2 sticks) unsalted butter

⅓ cup fresh lemon juice

2 tablespoons chopped fresh parsley

1½ teaspoons soy sauce

1½ teaspoons Worcestershire sauce

1 teaspoon dried basil

½ teaspoon garlic powder

Kosher salt and freshly ground black pepper

Six 6- to 8-ounce center-cut salmon fillets, any pin bones removed

Olive oil

Dodie's Salmon Cream Sauce (p. 315; optional)

1. Melt the butter in a small saucepan over medium heat, then whisk in the lemon juice, parsley, soy sauce, Worcestershire, basil, and garlic powder. Taste and season with salt and pepper. Keep warm.

2. Light a charcoal fire or preheat your gas grill on high. Oil the grill's cooking surface.

3. Liberally salt and pepper the salmon fillets. Drizzle with olive oil on both sides. Place the salmon on the grill, skin side up, and cook for 2 minutes. Turn and continue cooking for another 8 minutes for medium or to your desired degree of doneness, basting with the sauce the entire time. Remember, salmon is best when slightly undercooked.

4. Transfer to a platter and serve with the cream sauce, if desired.

Gene's World-Famous
salmon barbecue

One of the most unusual barbecue festivals takes place in the tiny fishing village of Fort Bragg, California. Billed as the world's largest salmon barbecue, more than 5,000 people will spend a Fourth of July weekend eating perfectly grilled king salmon. This event is a benefit for the Salmon Restoration Association, and it provides the primary funding for two local fish hatcheries charged with the responsibility of replenishing the once great numbers of salmon that flourished in Northern California's waters. Of course, being this close to wine country, chilled California wines and microbrew beers wash all this goodness down.

My friend Gene Mattiuzzo, who I consider the mayor of Noyo Harbor, passed along this recipe for what he swears is the original basting sauce for the salmon barbecue. "The proportions have changed a bit over the years, but this is the one they started with," says Gene. The seafood business is important to Gene, not only because he's a sales manager at Caito Fisheries on the harbor but also because these are people he's grown up with and who are his closest friends. Fishermen of all types are the last of the hunters and gatherers in this country, so, I say, let's eat more wild seafood. By the way, Noyo Harbor and, just down the road, Mendocino doubled as Cabot Cove, Maine, in the television show *Murder She Wrote*.

SALMON SPICE RUB

3 tablespoons firmly packed light brown sugar

1 tablespoon paprika

1 tablespoon smoked paprika

2 teaspoons kosher salt

1½ teaspoons freshly ground black pepper

1 teaspoon chopped fresh thyme

Six 7-ounce salmon fillets, any pin bones removed

Olive oil

Grilled Portobello Hash (p. 285)

1 lemon, cut into 6 wedges

Fresh basil leaves (optional)

Tom Douglas's
pit-roasted salmon

On my first trip to Seattle I had but one concern—to eat in each of Tom Douglas's restaurants. I had heard reports from people I trust about food that I would not be disappointed with anything that I ordered. Over the course of four days, I managed to eat in all four of them. Is one better than another? No, they're just delightfully different, with a little bit of down-home influence coupled with Pacific Rim-Northwest products and even some Middle Eastern flavors.

I love the way Tom prepares this salmon, which he serves at his predominantly seafood restaurant, Etta's, named for his daughter. He gave me the gist of the recipe as he was cooking at a culinary event at Pikes Market. The smoked paprika is the key ingredient and can be found at larger supermarkets and specialty-food stores. I think you'll like this.

– ೆೋಲ –

1. Combine the spice rub ingredients in a small bowl. The rub can be made up to 2 days in advance and stored, tightly covered, at room temperature. It is also good on tuna and halibut.

2. Sprinkle both sides of the salmon fillets with all of the rub, then brush the fish with oil on both sides.

3. Light a charcoal fire or preheat your gas grill on high. Oil the grill's cooking surface. Let the coals burn down to a medium-hot fire or adjust the gas grill burners to medium-high.

4. Grill the fillets for 10 to 12 minutes total, turning them once, for medium or to your desired degree of doneness. The sugar in the spice rub can burn easily, so watch the fillets closely.

5. Remove from the grill to individual plates. Spoon the portobello hash over each fillet and garnish with lemon wedges and fresh basil, if desired.

BALSAMIC GLAZE

½ cup balsamic vinegar

½ cup dry white wine

2 tablespoons fresh lemon juice

2 tablespoons firmly packed dark brown sugar

Salt and freshly ground black pepper

Six 5- to 6-ounce salmon fillets, any pin bones removed

Olive oil

Grilled Salmon
fillets with balsamic glaze

The sweet and sour notes in the glaze marry well with the deep richness of the salmon. If you make the glaze ahead of time, you can plate this spectacular entrée in the middle of a busy workweek.

– ❧❧ –

1. Combine the vinegar, wine, lemon juice, and brown sugar in a medium saucepan, bring to a boil, and let continue to boil until reduced to ⅓ cup, about 15 minutes. Season with salt and pepper. (This will keep in an airtight container in the refrigerator up to 1 week. Rewarm over very low heat before using.)

2. Light a charcoal fire or preheat your gas grill on high. Oil the grill's cooking surface. Let the coals burn down to a medium fire or adjust the gas grill burners to medium.

3. Brush the salmon lightly with oil and sprinkle with salt and pepper. Grill, flesh side down first, about 5 minutes per side for medium or to your desired degree of doneness.

4. Transfer the salmon to a platter. Drizzle with the warm glaze and serve immediately.

½ cup chopped fresh dill

½ cup chopped shallots

2 cloves garlic, chopped

2 scallions (white and green parts), chopped

3 tablespoons freshly ground black pepper

2 tablespoons olive oil

Juice of 1 lemon

1 tablespoon your favorite rib rub

Eight 6-ounce salmon fillets, any pin bones removed

Kosher salt

Lemon wedges

1. Combine the dill, shallots, garlic, scallions, pepper, oil, and lemon juice in a medium bowl. Use your hands to mix it thoroughly.

2. Sprinkle the rub evenly over the salmon fillets on both sides. Generously spread the dill mixture over the flesh side of each fillet and let sit at room temperature while your grill is getting ready.

3. Light a charcoal fire or preheat your gas grill on high. Oil the grill's cooking surface.

4. Remove the cedar planks from the water and season them liberally with salt. Place on the grill and heat until they start to crackle and smoke, about 5 minutes, then place the salmon on them, close the lid, and cook without turning the fillets for 10 to 12 minutes for medium or to your desired degree of doneness. The planks may catch on fire, so keep an eye out and use a spray bottle filled with water to extinguish any flames.

5. When the salmon is done, remove the planks from the grill and transfer the salmon to a platter. Serve immediately with lemon wedges.

Northwest
wood-planked barbecue salmon

If New Orleans has its redfish and its blackfish, then the Northwest states have cedar-planked salmon. Cedar-planking actually was a widely used method in the 19th and early 20th centuries, not just with fish but with poultry and meats as well. It adds a special and local flavor to fish that's different from normal smoking or grilling. It seems in the past year or two that planking fish has become quite popular. Try cedar and salmon first, then strike out from there with other woods—like cherry and maple—and other fish. Large supermarkets, seafood markets, and kitchen stores carry the planks. You can usually fit four fillets on a plank. Remember that your planks need to soak in water 4 to 6 hours before you plan to use them. You should be able to get two or three uses out of each cedar plank. Be sure to scrub them after each use.

¼ cup olive oil

1 tablespoon of any of the barbecue seasonings from Chapter 10, or your favorite store-bought brand

Four 6-ounce salmon fillets, any pin bones removed

1 cup fresh dill fronds, chopped

½ cup chopped shallots

2 cloves garlic, chopped

2 scallions (white and green parts), chopped

2 tablespoons cracked black peppercorns

Juice of 1 lemon

Sea salt

Lemon wedges

1. Light a charcoal fire or preheat your gas grill on high. Oil the grill's cooking surface.

2. Take 2 tablespoons of the olive oil and brush both sides of the cedar planks with it. Sprinkle the seasoning evenly over the cut side of the fillets.

3. Combine the dill, shallots, garlic, scallions, cracked pepper, the remaining 2 tablespoons olive oil, and the lemon juice to make a paste. Spread equally and generously over the flesh side of each salmon fillet.

4. Sprinkle the planks with sea salt and place on the grill. Close the lid and let heat for about 5 minutes, until they start to crackle and smoke. Lift the lid and place the salmon fillets, skin side down, on the planks. Close the lid and cook without turning for 10 to 12 minutes for medium or to your desired degree of doneness. The planks may catch on fire, so keep an eye out and use a spray bottle filled with water to extinguish any flames.

5. Remove the planks from the grill and transfer the salmon to a platter. Arrange the lemon wedges around and serve immediately.

Chris's Eureka
cedar-planked salmon

Chris Smiley is a 20-something from Eureka, California, which might as well be in Oregon for its lack of California trappings. When I first heard about Chris, it was for his cioppino recipe, which is the best I've ever put in my mouth, but this salmon recipe is first-rate. I've always thought the cedar-plank thing a bit of a gimmick until I tasted this. The seasoning and paste seem to bring out the cedar flavor. You'll need two planks for this recipe and, remember, they need to soak in water 4 to 6 hours before you use them, so plan accordingly.

8 ounces soft goat cheese, at room temperature

½ cup heavy cream

⅓ cup chopped fresh cilantro

Kosher salt and freshly ground black pepper

Two 15-ounce cans black beans, drained, reserving ½ cup of the liquid

1 tablespoon olive oil, plus more for brushing

1 tablespoon chili powder

Six 5-ounce salmon fillets, any pin bones removed

Six burrito-size flour tortillas

Cucumber-Cilantro Salsa (recipe below)

Lime wedges

cucumber–cilantro salsa

MAKES ABOUT 3 CUPS

This is a super surprising salsa. Any grilled fish will take nicely to it, but chicken and even grilled veal gets excited when coupled with this salsa.

2 cups peeled, seeded, and finely chopped cucumber

¾ cup seeded and finely chopped red bell peppers

⅔ cup finely chopped red onions

½ cup chopped fresh cilantro

2 tablespoons red wine vinegar

2 tablespoons olive oil

Kosher salt and freshly ground black pepper to taste

Combine all the ingredients in a large bowl. This can be prepared up to 4 hours ahead. Cover with plastic wrap and refrigerate, if necessary.

Tucson Grilled
salmon burritos with cucumber salsa

This Southwest take on salmon comes from Alma Jenkins of Tucson, Arizona. She tells me it's similar to a dish at the Ventana Canyon Resort in Tucson. Lighter and more flavorful than the standard Cal-Mex burritos, which are stuffed with everything and way too big for most appetites, these burritos accent the salmon with crisp, fresh flavors. Whether you like burritos or salmon, this recipe is a winner.

– ເອວັ –

1. Light a charcoal fire or preheat your gas grill on high. Oil the grill's cooking surface. Let the coals burn down to a medium-hot fire or adjust the gas grill burners to medium-high.

2. Cream together the goat cheese, cream, and cilantro in a medium bowl to blend. Season to taste with salt and pepper.

3. Heat up the beans in a medium saucepan with the reserved bean liquid over medium-high heat, then set aside.

4. Mix the oil and chili powder together in a small bowl. Sprinkle the salmon with salt and pepper, then coat with the chili paste. Place the fillets on the grill and cook about 4 minutes per side for medium or to your desired degree of doneness. Transfer to a platter.

5. Brush the tortillas lightly with oil. Cook on the grill for about 1 minute per side. Remove from the heat to a warm plate.

6. Place 1 tortilla on a work surface. Spoon ¼ cup of the beans, then ¼ cup of the goat cheese mixture in center of the tortilla. Top with 1 salmon fillet, then fold the sides of the tortilla over the filling and roll up to enclose completely. Repeat with the remaining tortillas, beans, cheese mixture, and salmon. Spoon some salsa on top of each burrito. Serve with lime wedges and pass the remaining salsa separately.

SESAME-LIME MARINADE

½ cup rice vinegar

½ cup fresh lime juice (from about 6 limes)

¼ cup toasted sesame oil

¼ cup canola oil

Eight 6- to 8-ounce center-cut salmon fillets, with skin on, any pin bones removed

Touch Your Way to Grilling Greatness

Fish steaks and fillets firm up as they cook almost exactly as beef. Learn to use your fingertip to gauge doneness and you'll be grilling like a pro.

Grilled Salmon with

sesame-lime marinade

Like most fish, salmon likes a dose of citrus, in this case to counterbalance its richness. It's even comfortable with a little more acid than other sea dwellers. This short recipe takes no time to put together and cooks quickly, but most important, it converts salmon haters into salmon lovers.

– ◦◦◦ –

1. Combine the marinade ingredients in a small bowl. Place the fillets in a large zip-top plastic bag and pour the marinade over. Seal the bag and squish everything to coat the fillet. Let marinate in the refrigerator for at least 2 hours but no longer than 3 hours.

2. Light a charcoal fire or preheat your gas grill on high. Oil the grill's cooking surface. Let the coals burn down to a medium-hot fire or adjust the gas grill burners to medium-high.

3. Remove the fillets from the marinade and discard the marinade. Place the fish on the grill, skin side up, cook for about 6 minutes, and turn. Cook another 6 minutes for medium or to your desired degree of doneness. (If your fish fillet is less than 1 inch thick, cook 4 to 5 minutes on each side for medium.) Transfer to a platter and serve.

Salt and freshly ground black pepper

Four 8-ounce 1-inch-thick wild-salmon steaks

2 tablespoons fresh lemon juice

2 tablespoons unsalted butter, melted

¼ cup shredded dill-flavored Havarti cheese

Seth and Aaron Israel's
grilled salmon steaks with havarti cheese

Brothers Seth and Aaron Israel both migrated to San Francisco from Richmond, Virginia. That's not surprising, since their mother, Susan Israel, was Oregon bred before moving to the East Coast. Although they live in different parts of the city and have different lives (one works with the Sierra Club, the other in finance), they get together from time to time to cook and entertain friends. This recipe is one of their friends' favorites and is always in demand at their get-togethers. I was skeptical of the cheese at first, but it adds a nice twist. They insist on using only wild salmon.

– ᥣᥣᥱᥣᥱ –

1. Light a charcoal fire or preheat your gas grill on high. Oil the grill's cooking surface.

2. Salt and pepper the salmon steaks. Combine the lemon juice and butter in a small bowl, and brush some on both sides of the steaks. Place on the grill and cook for about 5 minutes, basting frequently. Turn the steaks, continue basting, and cook for another 3 minutes, then top each steak with 1 tablespoon of the cheese. Cook another 1 to 2 minutes, until the cheese melts. Remove from the grill and serve immediately.

4 to 6 apple, alder, or pecan wood chunks
or 4 cups wood chips

One 4- to 6-pound whole salmon

10 sprigs fresh rosemary

20 sprigs fresh thyme

2 lemons, thinly sliced

1 tablespoon coarse sea salt

1 teaspoon cracked black peppercorns

2 tablespoons unsalted butter, melted

CHIVE CREAM SAUCE

One 8-ounce container sour cream

2 tablespoons milk

3 tablespoons finely snipped fresh chives

Lemon wedges

Fresh herb sprigs

Herb-Grilled
salmon with chive cream sauce

I am tempted to call this my Wal-Mart℠ salmon because I found frozen and vacuum-sealed whole salmon for sale there and decided to develop a recipe using it. This is a fabulous way to feed a crowd, especially at a holiday gathering. The herbs and the gentle flavor of the lighter smoke woods will please just about anyone. Don't let the length of this recipe put you off; it all comes together quickly.

– ⌒⊚⌒ –

1. At least 1 hour before grilling, soak the wood chunks or chips in water to cover. Drain before using.

2. Rip off a large piece of heavy aluminum foil, one that's slightly larger than the salmon when folded in half. Place half the rosemary and thyme and one-third of the lemon slices on the doubled foil. Place the salmon on top and season the cavity with the salt and pepper. Place another third of the lemon slices and the remaining rosemary and thyme in the cavity, then the remaining lemon slices in the cavity. Brush the fish with the melted butter.

3. Set up the grill for indirect grilling (see pp. 6–9). Oil your grill's cooking surface. Add the wood chips and allow them to start smoking.

4. Meanwhile, whisk together the sauce ingredients in a small bowl and refrigerate for at least 1 hour to let the flavors develop.

5. Place the salmon with the foil on the grill rack away from the heat over a drip pan. Cover the grill and cook for 40 to 50 minutes, until the fish gives way easily when poked with a fork. If cooking with charcoal, replenish your fire if necessary.

6. Remove the fish from the grill. Let rest, covered with foil, for 5 minutes, then serve with the cream sauce, garnished with lemon wedges and fresh herbs.

1 side of salmon, skinned and any pin bones removed

Kosher salt and freshly ground black pepper to taste

Flour for dredging

1 cup water

1 tablespoon Worcestershire sauce

1 tablespoon unsalted butter, melted

Blanche Wheeler's
salmon roast

In Oregon, salmon is king. While the rest of us cook up salmon steaks and fillets, Oregonians are likely to prepare a side of salmon in place of a Sunday pot roast. In and around Portland, folks pointed me to Una-Blanche Wheeler for the best salmon roast. She was much too modest to share her recipe, but her daughter, Susan, was proud enough of her mom's roast to get it for me. It's so simple and good you'll wonder why you've never made salmon like this before. Make sure your grates are clean for this one—you might even want to cook it on top of a sheet of aluminum foil.

– ᥒᥱ᥯ᥱ᷒ –

1. Set up the grill for indirect grilling (see pp. 6–9). Oil your grill's cooking surface.

2. Liberally salt and pepper the salmon. Dredge it lightly on both sides with flour, tapping off any excess.

3. Place the salmon, seasoned side up, on the grill away from the heat. Close the lid and cook for about 10 minutes.

4. Meanwhile, combine the water, Worcestershire, and butter in a small bowl. After the first 10 minutes, baste the salmon with the mixture. Continue to baste every 10 minutes until the salmon is done; roasting it slowly like this will usually take 45 minutes to 1 hour, depending on how you like your salmon. If cooking with charcoal, replenish your fire if necessary.

5. Transfer the salmon to a platter and let rest for about 10 minutes, then carve as you would a beef roast and serve.

4 plum tomatoes

1 teaspoon salt

1 teaspoon freshly ground black pepper

2 teaspoon balsamic vinegar

1 tablespoon chopped fresh basil or oregano

1½ cups good-quality mayonnaise

Juice of 2 lemons

Four 5- to 6-ounce salmon fillets, any pin bones removed

8 slices of your favorite bread (French works well)

4 pieces green-leaf lettuce

8 slices smoked bacon, fried until crisp and drained on paper towels

Dennis and Fred's
grilled salmon blt

More than a dozen years ago, I was working on a test shot with New York City food photographer Dennis Gottlieb. He wanted to do a marketing piece with a sandwich photograph. I came up with this idea, which, after we got the sandwich on film, we heartily ate. Marinated tomatoes (even winter tomatoes taste good when done this way), lemony mayonnaise, good-quality, thick-cut bacon, and grilled salmon add up to one extraordinary sandwich. It wasn't long after Dennis sent out his mailer that we both noticed the number of salmon BLTs showing up on menus around the city.

– දිගිරිකි –

1. Cut each tomato into 4 to 5 slices lengthwise. Place them in a bowl and sprinkle with the salt, pepper, and vinegar. Add the basil and toss to combine. Let stand at room temperature.

2. Combine the mayonnaise and lemon juice in a measuring cup.

3. Light a charcoal fire or preheat your gas grill on high. Oil the grill's cooking surface.

4. Place the salmon fillets, skin side up, on the grill and cook for about 5 minutes. Carefully turn over and cook another 3 minutes for medium or to your desired degree of doneness. Transfer the fish to a platter.

5. Toast the bread, if desired, then spread the lemon mayonnaise on each piece. Place one lettuce leaf on four of the slices of bread. Place a salmon fillet on top of each lettuce leaf. Top with two slices of bacon. Equally divide the marinated tomatoes between the sandwiches. Top with the remaining bread. Cut in half and serve.

Four 2-inch-thick center-cut salmon fillets, any pin bones removed

Your favorite barbecue rub seasoning (Bob uses Dizzy Pig®)

½ cup (1 stick) unsalted butter

¼ cup firmly packed light brown sugar

¼ cup maple syrup

Vegetable spray

Bob Trudnak's
maple-glazed salmon

Bob Trudnak got his start at grilling when he was in art school in Philadelphia getting a photography degree. He was "sick of eating noodles and spaghetti," so he got a Weber and put it in an alley in center city Philadelphia. He started by grilling shark steaks with his roommate. Since they didn't have a lot of money, they began going to the Jersey shore to night fish. They really got excited when they caught a bluefish, which became their favorite. Now that he can afford to buy food, he especially likes to grill homemade sausages and this salmon.

– ୧୬ଡ଼ୄ –

1. Season the salmon with the barbecue rub at least 30 minutes before you plan to cook.

2. Place the butter, brown sugar, and maple syrup in a small saucepan over medium heat and cook, stirring, until the butter has melted, the sugar has dissolved, and the mixture has thickened slightly, about 10 minutes. Keep warm over low heat.

3. Light a charcoal fire or preheat your gas grill on high. Oil the grill's cooking surface. Let the coals burn down to a medium fire or adjust the gas grill burners to medium.

4. Spray the skin side of the salmon fillets with vegetable spray, then place skin side down on the grill and let cook for about 4 minutes. Begin brushing the salmon with the maple syrup glaze about every 4 minutes, and cook for a total of about 20 minutes for medium or to your desired degree of doneness. Brush the glaze over the salmon one last time before removing it from the grill to a platter. Serve immediately.

TERIYAKI MARINADE

¾ cup teriyaki sauce

2 tablespoons soy sauce

2 tablespoons firmly packed light brown sugar

1 tablespoon dry sherry or white wine

1 tablespoon rice vinegar

1 tablespoon vegetable oil

1 teaspoon toasted sesame oil

3 cloves garlic, minced

One 1-inch piece fresh ginger, peeled and finely chopped

2 scallions (white and green parts), finely chopped

Pinch of red pepper flakes or to taste

Four 8-ounce tuna steaks

Salinas, CA

SERVES 4

Martha's Evacuation
teriyaki-marinated tuna steak

I love this story from Martha Rau of Salinas, California. She, her husband, and her son and his family had rented a house on the Outer Banks of North Carolina. They got in one meal before Hurricane Felix forced their evacuation, and this grilled marinated tuna was it. There's not a whole lot of ways off that island, and you really don't want to be caught there staring at one of the Atlantic's monstrous storms.

This grilled tuna has an Asian flair with a little bit of kick. The marinade is easy to put together, and tuna does so beautifully when cooked over glowing coals.

– ⌒⌒ –

1. In a large bowl, combine the marinade ingredients.

2. Place the tuna steaks in a large zip-top plastic bag. Add the marinade, seal the bag, and squish everything around to coat the fish. Let marinate in the refrigerator at least 1 hour and up to 2 hours, turning several times.

3. Light a charcoal fire or preheat your gas grill on high. Oil the grill's cooking surface. Let the coals burn down to a medium-hot fire or adjust the gas grill burners to medium-high.

4. Place the fish on the grill and cook about 5 minutes per side for medium-rare or to your desired degree of doneness. Transfer to a platter and serve immediately.

6 tablespoons white wine

1 cup plus 2 tablespoons balsamic vinegar

2 tablespoons sugar

1 teaspoon freshly ground black pepper

1½ pounds ripe tomatoes, cut into
½-inch dice

2 teaspoons olive oil

2 teaspoons kosher salt

¾ pound haricots verts or thin green
beans, ends trimmed

1 teaspoon fresh lemon juice

Six 6-ounce tuna steaks, cut 1 inch thick

¼ cup loosely packed fresh basil leaves,
very thinly sliced

½ cup pitted niçoise olives, drained

Grilled Deconstructed
niçoise salad

This is in no way a traditional salad niçoise, but it does have some of
the key elements you'll find in that popular bistro dish. Using the grill,
we're going to add more flavor to the tuna and the green beans. For me,
balsamic vinegar is a go-to seasoning—if I can't think of anything else to
do, I grab my bottle of balsamic and start there. Cooking it down into a
glaze is a particularly nice option, which is what I've done to flavor the
tuna in this recipe.

– ᥒᥨᥩᥢ –

1. Combine the wine, vinegar, sugar, and ¼ teaspoon of the pepper in a
small saucepan over medium-high heat. Simmer until slightly thickened
and syrupy, 25 to 30 minutes. Remove from the heat.

2. Combine the tomatoes, 1 teaspoon of the oil, ½ teaspoon of the salt,
and another ¼ teaspoon of pepper in a medium bowl. Toss and set aside.

3. Light a charcoal fire or preheat your gas grill on high. Oil the grill's
cooking surface. Let the coals burn down to a medium-hot fire or adjust
the gas grill burners to medium-high.

4. Combine the haricots verts, lemon juice, the remaining 1 teaspoon oil,
and another ½ teaspoon of salt and ¼ teaspoon of pepper in a large bowl
and toss well. Place the beans on the grill perpendicular to the grate and
cook, turning, until just limp and lightly charred, 2 to 4 minutes. Transfer
to a serving platter.

5. Sprinkle the remaining 1 teaspoon salt and ¼ teaspoon pepper on both
sides of the tuna steaks. Brush the balsamic glaze over the tops and sides
of the steaks and place, glazed side down, on the grill. Cook, brushing
with more glaze, until lightly charred, about 3 minutes per side for rare,
6 to 7 for well done. Transfer to the platter with the beans.

6. Add the basil to the tomatoes, toss, and spoon over the tuna. Add the
olives to the platter and serve immediately.

6 tuna steaks, cut 1½ inches thick (about 1½ pounds total)

LEMON-BASIL MARINADE

Finely grated zest and juice of 1 large lemon

¼ cup chopped fresh basil

¼ cup olive oil

1 teaspoon kosher salt

½ teaspoon freshly ground black pepper

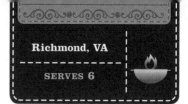

Richmond, VA

SERVES 6

Jacky Robinson's

lemon-basil grilled tuna

I like calling Jacky Robinson of Richmond, Virginia, a renaissance woman. She's a foodie, an art buff, and one of the most intriguing interior decorators you'll ever come across. This grilled tuna is a different take from the usual Asian or Mediterranean flavors typically bestowed on tuna. This seasoning mix lets the true flavor of tuna stand out by accenting its mild and delicate taste.

– ⌀⌀⌀ –

1. Place the tuna steaks in a large zip-top plastic bag.

2. In a small bowl, combine the marinade ingredients. Pour over the steaks, seal the bag, and squish everything around to coat the steaks. Let marinate in the refrigerator 1½ hours, turning the steaks once.

3. Light a charcoal fire or preheat your gas grill on high. Oil the grill's cooking surface. Let the coals burn down to a medium-hot fire or adjust the gas grill burners to medium-high.

4. Place the steaks on the grill and cook, with the cover down, about 6 minutes per side for medium or to your desired degree of doneness. Transfer to a platter and serve immediately.

FRED'S TOMATO COMPOTE

2 pounds ripe plum tomatoes

2 tablespoons olive oil

2 large cloves garlic, crushed

4 teaspoons red wine vinegar

¼ cup chopped fresh chives

Kosher salt and freshly ground black pepper

SWORDFISH

2 teaspoons kosher salt

1 teaspoon freshly ground white pepper

1 teaspoon ground cumin

½ teaspoon garlic powder

¼ teaspoon ground nutmeg

Four 8-ounce swordfish steaks

Olive oil

Frank's Spiced Grilled

swordfish with fred's tomato compote

Northern Californian swordfish fisherman Frank Bertoni suggests this simple preparation for swordfish steaks. The tomato compote is my idea. Frank would just put a little marinara sauce on the side to dip the fish in. If you want to go that route, just add a bit of vinegar to your marinara; the acid seems to round out all the flavors.

– ත්ෆ්ව –

1. For the compote, blanch the tomatoes in a large pot of boiling water until the skins begin to loosen, about 40 seconds. Using a slotted spoon, transfer them to a large bowl of ice water and let cool, then drain. Peel, seed, and chop the tomatoes.

2. Heat the oil in a large, heavy skillet over medium-high heat. Add the tomatoes and garlic and cook, stirring, just until softened, about 2 minutes. Remove from the heat and stir in the vinegar. Let cool to room temperature or cover with plastic wrap and refrigerate for up to a day.

3. For the swordfish, combine the salt, white pepper, cumin, garlic powder, and nutmeg in a small bowl.

4. Light a charcoal fire or preheat your gas grill on high. Oil the grill's cooking surface. Let the coals burn down to a medium-hot fire or adjust the gas grill burners to medium-high.

5. Brush the swordfish with oil. Sprinkle each steak liberally with the spice mixture, then place on the grill and cook until opaque in the center, about 4 minutes per side. Transfer to plates.

6. Stir the chives into the tomato compote. Season to taste with salt and black pepper, then spoon over the fish and serve.

½ cup (1 stick) unsalted butter

1 cup chopped pecans

Sea salt

White pepper

4 center-cut swordfish steaks, about
1 inch thick

Olive oil

1. Place the butter in a cold sauté pan. Turn
the heat to medium-low heat and slowly
melt the butter. Add the pecans and let them
brown and become toasted as the butter
slowly browns. Season lightly with salt and
white pepper. You will need to watch the
pan closely as the butter can burn quickly.
When the butter reaches the desired color—
like dark caramel—remove from the heat,
cover, and set aside. If needed, gently reheat
before using it to top the fish.

2. Light a charcoal fire or preheat your gas
grill on high. Oil the grill's cooking surface.
Let the coals burn down to a medium fire or
adjust the gas grill burners to medium.

3. Brush the fish steaks on both sides with
olive oil. Season with salt and white pepper.
Place on the grill and cook until opaque all
the way through, about 5 minutes per side.

4. Transfer the steaks to a platter. Top with
the warm brown butter and pecans and
serve immediately.

Chicago, IL

SERVES 4

Elizabeth's Nantucket
swordfish with browned butter and sautéed pecans

In 1983, Elizabeth Karmel packed her bags and went to Nantucket to work
for the summer. She remembers how the fashionable dish on the island at
the time was swordfish with béarnaise sauce. This Southern transplant,
now living in Chicago, decided to improve on the dish from her "summer
of fun" and started by grilling the fish. She wanted a sauce that was as rich
as the béarnaise but without the trouble. This is the result, a marriage of
tastes that seems more complex than it is to make. That classic Southern
nut, the pecan, adds some crunch. Elizabeth tells me that the sauce can be
made in advance and gently reheated just before serving. This recipe will
also work with any firm whitefish, such as tilapia or sturgeon.

CUCUMBER-LIME SALSA

1 lime

One ¼-pound Kirby cucumber, peeled, cut in half lengthwise, seeded, and cut into ¼-inch dice (¾ cup)

1 tablespoon finely chopped fresh cilantro

1 tablespoon finely chopped scallion greens

1 teaspoon finely chopped jalapeño or Serrano chile (include the seeds)

1 teaspoon sugar or to taste

¼ teaspoon kosher salt

SWORDFISH

¼ cup fresh lime juice

1 tablespoon honey

1 tablespoon vegetable oil, plus more for brushing pan

2 teaspoons ground coriander

Four 6-ounce 1-inch-thick swordfish steaks

Kosher salt and freshly ground black pepper

Raleigh, NC

SERVES 4

Grilled Swordfish with
cucumber-lime salsa

In the Florida Keys, I ran in to an interesting cucumber-based salsa at a private party. The caterer was using it with spiny lobster, but I thought it too good to save for special foods. Knowing that citrus, and lime especially, heightens the flavor of swordfish, I decided to pair the two. My neighbors in Raleigh, who are my main tasters/guinea pigs, declared it brilliant, and some of them are not great fish lovers. Make this in summer, when cukes are at their peak.

– ৩৬৩৬ –

1. To prepare the salsa, remove the peel, including all the white pith underneath, from the lime with a sharp paring knife. Cut the segments free from the membranes and finely chop them. In a small bowl, combine the lime with the remaining salsa ingredients. The salsa can be made up to 2 hours ahead and kept, covered, in the refrigerator.

2. For the swordfish, stir together the lime juice, honey, oil, and coriander in a shallow baking dish. Add the swordfish, turning to coat evenly with the mixture, and let marinate at room temperature, turning the steaks once, for 5 minutes. Don't marinate them any longer than that, as the acid in the lime juice will begin to cook the fish.

3. Light a charcoal fire or preheat your gas grill on high. Oil the grill's cooking surface. Let the coals burn down to a medium-hot fire or adjust the gas grill burners to medium-high.

4. Remove the swordfish from the marinade and season both sides with salt and pepper. Grill until opaque all the way through, 3 to 4 minutes per side. Serve immediately, topped with the salsa.

CITRUS-MOLASSES GLAZE

½ cup white wine vinegar

½ cup orange juice

½ cup fresh lime juice (about 4 limes)

¼ cup unsulfured molasses

1½ teaspoons ground cumin

1½ teaspoons chili powder

1 clove garlic, minced

3 large lemons, cut in half and each half cut into 4 wedges

18 bay leaves

2¼ pounds swordfish steaks, trimmed of skin and cut into 2-inch cubes

12 cherry tomatoes

1½ teaspoons kosher salt

¼ teaspoon freshly ground black pepper

Jackie's Citrus
molasses-glazed swordfish kebobs

Frank Bertoni is an old-style fisherman who believes that if you treat the ocean fairly, it will sustain you for a lifetime. Frank fishes out of Noyo Harbor in Fort Bragg, California. Depending on the season, he might be after Dungeness crab, octopus, squid, or swordfish. Frank has always line-caught swordfish. For a few years, eating swordfish was politically incorrect, but the balance has tipped and swordfish is now more abundant. Jackie, Frank's wife, is a first-rate cook, and this recipe is one of many that she has developed to enjoy the rewards of Frank's labors.

– ᴇᴏᴏᴏᴠ –

1. Combine the glaze ingredients in a small saucepan, bring to a boil, and let boil for 2 minutes. Remove from the heat and set aside.

2. On each of 6 long metal skewers, arrange 4 lemon wedges, 3 bay leaves, 3 pieces of fish, and 2 tomatoes. The kebobs can be prepared up to this point, covered with plastic wrap, and refrigerated for up to 6 hours before cooking.

3. Light a charcoal fire or preheat your gas grill on high. Oil the grill's cooking surface. Let the coals burn down to a medium-hot fire or adjust the gas grill burners to medium-high.

4. Sprinkle the kebobs with the salt and pepper and spoon the glaze over them. Place the kebobs on the grill and cook until the fish is opaque in the center and the outside is lightly charred, 3 to 4 minutes per side, brushing with the glaze several times while cooking. Remove the skewers from the fire and serve immediately.

BLACK-EYED PEA SALAD

2 tablespoons vegetable oil

½ cup finely diced smoked ham

½ cup finely diced yellow onions

½ cup finely diced celery

½ cup finely diced red bell peppers

One 15-ounce can black-eyed peas, rinsed and drained

1 tablespoon sugar

1 tablespoon cider vinegar

Freshly ground black pepper

4 wahoo steaks (6 to 8 ounces each), cut about 1 inch thick

Vegetable oil

Kosher salt and freshly ground black pepper

½ cup tomato-based barbecue sauce of your choice

Carolina Wahoo with
black-eyed pea salad

Off the coast of North Carolina the waters are filled with wahoo, one of the world's great sport fish. It loves to fight and is difficult to land. In Hawaii the fish is called *ono*, which means delicious. Wahoo is firm, very meaty, and a lot like tuna in texture. Being a member of the mackerel family, its flesh is dark but it's not oily or overly fishy.

The inspiration for this dish came from Ben Barker, chef-owner of the Magnolia Grill in Durham, North Carolina. You could skip the black-eyed pea salad, but it really does complete the dish. If wahoo is not available, use swordfish or tuna.

– ꙮꙮ –

1. To make the salad, in a medium skillet over medium-high heat, warm the oil, then add the ham and cook for 2 to 3 minutes, stirring a few times. Add the onions and cook, stirring a few times, until translucent, 4 to 5 minutes. Add the celery and bell peppers and cook for 3 to 4 minutes more, stirring occasionally. Add the peas, sugar, and vinegar and simmer for 2 to 3 minutes. Season with pepper and set aside to cool.

2. Light a charcoal fire or preheat your gas grill on high. Oil the grill's cooking surface. Let the coals burn down to a medium fire or adjust the gas grill burners to medium.

3. Meanwhile, lightly brush both sides of the fish steaks with oil and season with salt and pepper. Brush the steaks with the barbecue sauce. Place the steaks on the grill and cook until opaque all the way through but still moist, 8 to 10 minutes total, turning once. Brush with additional sauce after turning.

4. Transfer to a platter and serve immediately with the salad.

5 pounds mackerel or trout, with the skin, cut into 1½-inch-thick steaks

1½ cups water

⅓ cup firmly packed light brown sugar

3 tablespoons kosher salt

¼ teaspoon cayenne pepper

Hickory chunks

Pine Knoll
smoked mackerel

Down at my buddy Hugh Lynn's beach cottage at Pine Knoll Shores, North Carolina, we would smoke mackerel from time to time. It was a great way to preserve the abundance of Spanish mackerel that can be caught in that area. Trout also works well with this method, as would bluefish. Hugh has one of those bulletlike water smokers, but I've adapted this recipe to a more conventional kettle grill or any grill that you can set up to smoke. This smoked fish is wonderful for lunch over salad greens or on top of cream cheese that's been spread on baguette toasts.

– ᘓᕼᕼᕼᕼᕼ –

1. Place the fish in a few large zip-top plastic bags. In a medium bowl, combine the water, sugar, salt, and cayenne, stir until the salt and sugar dissolve, then pour over the fish. Seal the bags and squish everything to coat the fish. Let marinate in the refrigerator for 8 hours, turning the bags occasionally.

2. Soak the hickory chunks in water for at least 1 hour.

3. Set up the grill for indirect grilling (see pp. 6–9). Oil your grill's cooking surface.

4. Place the drained hickory chunks on the coals. Set a small aluminum pan filled with water in the grill away from the flames. Remove the fish from the marinade and discard the marinade. Place it on the grill away from the fire and smoke, with the lid down, for about 3 hours, maintaining a temperature of 200°F to 250°F and replenishing the coals as necessary if cooking with charcoal. The fish will be opaque to the center when done.

FRESH GINGER-GARLIC FLAVOR PASTE

3 cloves garlic, peeled

1 teaspoon black peppercorns

2 tablespoons chopped fresh cilantro

1 quarter-size slice fresh ginger, crushed

1½ tablespoons tamari or low-sodium soy sauce

One 2-pound snapper or striped bass, dressed

CHILE-LIME SAUCE

3 Serrano chiles, seeded and finely chopped

3 cloves garlic, peeled

2 tablespoons chopped fresh cilantro

1 teaspoon sugar

¼ teaspoon kosher salt

½ cup fresh lime juice

⅓ cup low-sodium chicken broth

Vegetable oil

If You're Using Banana Leaves

If using a banana leaf for this recipe or any other, rinse it under cold running water to clean. Plunge the leaf into a pot of boiling water for a few seconds to soften and make pliable. Remove the leaf and wipe dry. With a knife or scissors, remove the thick spine of the leaf and place the leaf with its glossy side down on a work surface. Proceed with your recipe.

Grilled Fish in Foil with

chile-lime sauce

This recipe is based on the popular use of banana leaves to grill fish throughout Asia. Aluminum foil is obviously much more available in this country and is a perfectly good substitute. If you have access to banana leaves, by all means use them as the wrapper.

– ᶜᵔᵔᵔᵔᵛ –

1. In a food processor, combine the garlic, peppercorns, cilantro, and ginger. Pulse to combine, then process into a fine paste. Transfer to a bowl and stir in the tamari.

2. Rinse the fish under cold running water and pat dry with paper towels. Rub the garlic paste over the entire fish, including the inside. Let marinate at room temperature for 30 minutes.

3. Meanwhile, place the chiles, garlic, cilantro, sugar, and salt in a mortar or food processor and work into a smooth paste. Transfer the mixture to a small saucepan over medium-high heat. Add the lime juice and broth and bring to a boil. Remove from the heat and let cool.

4. Light a charcoal fire or preheat your gas grill on high. Oil the grill's cooking surface.

5. Take a piece of aluminum foil about 6 inches longer and 3 times wider than the fish or a banana leaf. Oil the surface where you plan to put the fish. Place the fish on it, fold over the wide sides and then the ends. Use a toothpick if using a banana leaf. Set the packet on the grill and cook for about 8 minutes. Carefully turn the packet over and cook 8 minutes longer.

6. Transfer to a platter and carefully open the packet. Use a large spoon to divide the fish into 4 servings and to transfer to dinner plates. Serve with the sauce.

6 Chilean sea bass fillets or halibut fillets

Olive oil for brushing

Kosher salt and freshly ground black pepper

3 shallots, thinly sliced

3 to 4 cloves garlic, to your taste, chopped

3 to 4 tablespoons capers, to your taste, drained and rinsed

9 to 12 oil-packed sun-dried tomatoes, to your taste, chopped

12 to 15 black olives (Greek or Kalamata), to your taste, pitted and thinly sliced

Juice and grated zest of 2 lemons

$\frac{1}{2}$ cup white wine

$1\frac{1}{2}$ teaspoons paprika

Leif and Myra's
"foiled" sea bass

Leif and Myra Daleng from Richmond, Virginia, are great hosts. Leif is originally from Norway and loves to talk about his home country. Myra is the director of dance at the University of Richmond. Put them together, and their happiness and charm will infect you. I enjoyed this recipe—bold and robust, full of Mediterranean goodness—at their home. Cooking it in foil helps keep the fish moist and the flavors concentrated. The hint of smoke from the grill makes it perfect. Leif and Myra served it with wonderful Grilled Potato and Feta Pancakes, which you'll find on p. 286.

– දිංගින –

1. Light a charcoal fire or preheat your gas grill on high. Oil the grill's cooking surface. Let the coals burn down to a medium-hot fire or adjust the gas grill burners to medium-high.

2. Brush each side of the fish lightly with olive oil and place each fillet in the center of a piece of nonstick aluminum foil large enough to enclose the fish; season with salt and pepper. Evenly sprinkle the shallots, garlic, capers, sun-dried tomatoes, olives, and lemon zest over the fish, then sprinkle with the lemon juice, wine, and paprika.

3. Fold the foil to enclose the fish loosely, sealing the edges firmly so the juices will not escape. Place the parcels on the grill and cook for 12 to 15 minutes. Remove the fish from the foil and serve.

½ cup (1 stick) unsalted butter, melted

¼ cup dry white wine

1 tablespoon capers, drained and rinsed

1 tablespoon chopped fresh sage

1 tablespoon chopped fresh thyme

2 tablespoons unsalted butter, softened, or vegetable spray

Four 12x16-inch sheets parchment paper, folded in half, and cut into as large a half-heart shape as possible so you have a heart when it opens

Four 4- to 5-ounce petrale, sole, halibut, or Chilean sea bass fillets

Gary Spratt's
grilled fish in parchment

Gary Spratt lives in the heart of Napa Valley's wine country, Rutherford, California. Gary has taken a classic and underused method of cooking fish and adapted it for the grill and his Napa lifestyle. Cooking in parchment is an excellent way to prepare fish, almost steaming the critter and adding moist flavor to boot. Gary has taken the process one step further, extending the normal cooking time and scenting that steam with gentle smokiness. Watch your heat levels—too hot a fire will cause the parchment to catch fire and burn, which will pretty much screw up your meal. It's the low, slow heat that really makes this work.

– ⌘ –

1. Combine the melted butter, wine, capers, sage, and thyme in a small bowl.

2. Take the softened butter and smear over one side of each of the parchment hearts.

3. Place a piece of fish on each of the parchment hearts. Spoon an equal amount of the herbed mixture over each of the fish and, beginning at one edge, fold and crimp the parchment, closing to make a packet.

4. Set up the grill for indirect grilling (see pp. 6–9). Oil your grill's cooking surface.

5. Place the packages on the grill away from the heat. Close the grill and cook for about 30 minutes.

6. Remove each packet to a dinner plate and serve immediately. Part of the pleasure is to cut into the packet and enjoy the aroma of the fish and the seasonings.

ORANGE-FENNEL SALSA

2 tablespoons olive oil

3 tablespoons white wine vinegar

2 tablespoons chopped fresh cilantro

2 teaspoons soy sauce

2 teaspoons peeled and minced fresh ginger

2 teaspoons sugar

3 oranges

1 medium fennel bulb, trimmed and cut into matchstick-size strips

½ medium red onion, thinly sliced

Kosher salt and freshly ground black pepper

- - - - - - - - - - - - - - - - - - - -

3 tablespoons olive oil

1 tablespoon soy sauce

1 clove garlic, thinly sliced

Salt and freshly ground black pepper

Four 6- to 8-ounce rockfish or Chilean sea bass fillets

Grilled Fish with

orange-fennel salsa

Orange and fennel like to play together in salads, so why not a salsa? The result, served with a mildly flavored fish, is superb and visually stunning. This is a favorite of my seafood grilling classes, and I think it will become one of yours. If you see blood oranges in the market, substitute them for an upscale twist.

- ᴇᴏᴏ૭ꙷᴠ -

1. Whisk the oil, vinegar, cilantro, soy sauce, ginger, and sugar together in a medium bowl.

2. Cut the peel and white pith from the oranges and discard. Holding each orange over a medium bowl to catch the juices, cut between membranes to release the segments into the bowl. Add the fennel and onions; toss gently. Season with salt and pepper. (This can be prepared up to 3 hours ahead. Cover and refrigerate until ready to serve.)

3. Light a charcoal fire or preheat your gas grill on high. Oil the grill's cooking surface. Let the coals burn down to a medium-hot fire or adjust the gas grill burners to medium-high.

4. Combine the oil, soy sauce, and garlic in glass pie dish. Turn the fish in the mixture to coat. Sprinkle with salt and pepper. Grill until just opaque in the center, turning the fish just once, about 3 minutes per side.

5. Transfer to serving plates, spoon the salsa over, and serve immediately.

1 ½ teaspoons red pepper flakes

½ teaspoon garlic salt

¼ teaspoon sea salt

Four 6- to 8-ounce halibut fillets, cut
1 inch thick

CAPER BUTTER

½ cup (1 stick) unsalted butter

Juice of ½ lemon

1 tablespoon capers, more to taste,
drained and rinsed

1. Combine the red pepper, garlic salt, and
sea salt in a small bowl. Sprinkle liberally
over one side of each of the fillets and pat it
in so it adheres.

2. Light a charcoal fire or preheat your gas
grill on high. Oil the grill's cooking surface.
You're going to want to cook over a very
hot fire.

3. Meanwhile, melt the butter in a small
saucepan over low heat. Add the lemon juice
and capers, and stir to combine. Keep warm.

4. Place the halibut, seasoned side down,
on the grill. Cook for about 4 minutes; turn
and cook until just opaque in the center,
about another 4 minutes.

5. Transfer the fillets to a platter, pour
over the caper butter sauce, and serve
immediately.

Tom Sancimino's
crispy grilled halibut with caper butter

Swan Oyster Depot of Polk Street is one of my favorite hangouts in San
Francisco. The seafood salads and oyster cocktails are second to none, and
the only hot food they serve, New England clam chowder, is better than
any I've had in Boston. This is a family business. Tom is the youngest of
the four brothers, all of whom keep the atmosphere boisterous. From past
visits I knew all the boys grilled and I figured I'd find something good
and unusual.

Tom cooks this halibut without any oil to get a nice caramelized surface
and to toast the red pepper flakes. This is a delicious way with fish, but
your grill must be really clean to do it this way. If in doubt, drizzle a little
oil on each side of the fish.

Tom is obviously the best-looking of the brothers.

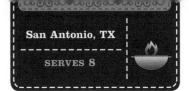

2 tablespoons coriander seeds

2 tablespoons cumin seeds

2 tablespoons yellow mustard seeds

½ cup olive oil

¼ cup shredded fresh mint leaves

Eight 6-ounce wild striped bass fillets, with skin on

Kosher salt and freshly ground black pepper

Grilled Wild
striped bass with an indian twist

There are hints of the subcontinent here. While visiting with Indie Reddy (check out her Grilled Chicken Tikka on p. 156), she talked at length about her mother's spices, which she ground daily in India and would blend with oils. Would it work for fish? It certainly does with wild striped bass.

– ເອີ⊙ຜ –

1. Place a medium saucepan over medium heat, add the coriander, cumin, and mustard seeds, and toast until fragrant, shaking the pan a few times. Transfer them to a spice grinder and coarsely grind. In a small bowl, combine the olive oil, toasted spices, and mint.

2. Light a charcoal fire or preheat your gas grill on high. Oil the grill's cooking surface. Let the coals burn down to a medium-hot fire or adjust the gas grill burners to medium-high.

3. Season the fish with salt and pepper. Pour ¼ cup of the spiced oil into a small bowl and use it to brush the fillets on both sides, coating them well with the spices. The rest of the spiced oil can be stored in an airtight container in the refrigerator for up to 3 weeks. Grill the fish, skin side down, until deep brown and crusty, about 5 minutes. Turn the fillets and grill until just opaque at the center, about 4 minutes longer. Serve immediately.

MISO-MUSTARD SAUCE

2 teaspoons water

1 teaspoon Chinese hot mustard or Dijon mustard

⅓ cup white miso

3 tablespoons rice vinegar

2 tablespoons mirin (sweet rice wine)

4 teaspoons sugar

1 teaspoon soy sauce

Four 5- to 6-ounce Chilean sea bass fillets

8 scallions, roots trimmed

Olive oil

Kosher salt and freshly ground black pepper

2 tablespoons sesame seeds, toasted in a dry skillet over medium heat until light brown

New York, NY

SERVES 4

Grilled Sea Bass and
scallions with miso-mustard sauce

A recipe that called for miso used to entail a trip to an Asian market but not anymore. Most large supermarkets now stock it, usually where you find the tofu. The other ingredients called for here should also be easy to find in most Asian food sections. The restaurant Nobu in New York City made miso-glazed fish popular with its miso-glazed black cod. This recipe is a little more manageable at home, with a mustard twist.

– ത@ை –

1. Whisk the water and mustard together in a small bowl until smooth. Combine the miso, vinegar, mirin, sugar, and soy sauce in a small saucepan and place over medium heat. Stir until smooth and cook, continuing to stir, for about 3 minutes. Whisk in the mustard mixture. (This can be made a day ahead and kept, tightly covered, in the refrigerator. Rewarm over low heat before using.)

2. Light a charcoal fire or preheat your gas grill on high. Oil the grill's cooking surface. Let the coals burn down to a medium-hot fire or adjust the gas grill burners to medium-high.

3. Brush the fish and scallions with oil. Sprinkle both with salt and pepper. Place the fish and scallions on the grill and cook the fish until just opaque in the center, turning just once, about 4 minutes per side. Grill the scallions until they begin to brown, about 3 minutes per side.

4. Divide the fish and scallions between 4 plates. Spread the miso sauce over the fish, sprinkle with the sesame seeds, and serve immediately.

PINEAPPLE BARBECUE SAUCE

¼ cup chopped pineapple

2 tablespoons seeded and minced jalapeño

2 tablespoons firmly packed light brown sugar

1 cup of your favorite barbecue sauce (I like Bone Sucking Sauce™)

Four 6-ounce mahimahi fillets

2 large Vidalia or other sweet onions, cut ½ inch thick

2 tablespoons olive oil

Kosher salt and freshly ground black pepper

2 tablespoons peanut oil

2 tablespoons unsalted butter

2 tablespoons fresh lime juice

2 tablespoons chopped fresh cilantro

Grilled Mahimahi with pineapple barbecue
sauce and grilled sweet onions

The Hawaiian restaurant that plated a dish similar to this wouldn't give up the recipe, so, of course, I went to tinkering. The result is a better sauce and probably a simpler recipe with just as much flavor and excitement as the restaurant version. Mahimahi is almost as common as cod in fish counters today. It's meaty but not oily or fishy and holds up to grilling. This barbecue sauce also partners well with pork or chicken. And do grill the onions—they really make the dish.

- ⌇⌇ -

1. Combine the pineapple, jalapeño, and brown sugar in a small saucepan over high heat and cook, stirring, until the pineapple begins to caramelize, about 5 minutes. Pour in the barbecue sauce and cook another 2 minutes. Pour the mixture into a blender or use a hand-held blender to process until smooth. Let cool and set aside ¼ cup for basting on the grill.

2. Place the mahimahi in a baking dish and pour the sauce over, completely coating the fish. Cover with plastic and refrigerate for 2 hours.

3. Light a charcoal fire or preheat your gas grill on high. Oil the grill's cooking surface.

4. Brush the onion slices with the olive oil and season with salt and pepper. Place the onions on the grill and cook for about 3 minutes per side. They should still be slightly firm but warm through. Remove from the grill and tent with aluminum foil.

5. Remove the mahimahi from the sauce and pat dry. Brush each with the peanut oil and season with salt and pepper. Place on the grill and cook for about 4 minutes per side, basting with the barbecue sauce. Remove from the grill and tent with foil.

6. Place the remaining barbecue sauce in a small saucepan, bring to a boil, then reduce the heat to a simmer. Stir in the butter, lime juice, and cilantro. Puddle some of the sauce on 4 serving plates. Top with the grilled fish and some onion rings and serve immediately.

FRESH LIME FAJITA MARINADE

3 tablespoons fresh lime juice

2 tablespoons vegetable oil

1 tablespoon minced garlic

1 teaspoon ground cumin

1 teaspoon kosher salt

¼ teaspoon red pepper flakes

Four 6-ounce skinless red snapper fillets

BLACK BEAN SALSA

1 pound ripe plum tomatoes, cored
and diced

1 medium ripe avocado, peeled, pitted,
and finely diced

½ cup canned black beans, rinsed and
drained

¼ cup finely diced red onions

1/4 cup finely chopped fresh cilantro

2 tablespoons fresh lime juice

1 tablespoon vegetable oil

1 tablespoon seeded and minced jalapeño

1 teaspoon minced garlic

½ teaspoon kosher salt

Vegetable oil

Eight to ten 10-inch flour tortillas

½ head Savoy cabbage, cored and finely
shredded

Mahimahi Fajitas with
black bean salsa

When I make fajitas at home, I almost always make them with fish,
and mahimahi is an excellent choice. It can stand up to grilling and
absorbs other flavors without losing its own. This recipe also works well
with shrimp.

— ✑✑✑ —

1. In a small bowl, whisk together the marinade ingredients.

2. Place the fish in a large zip-top plastic bag and pour in the marinade.
Squish everything around to coat the fish. Seal the bag and let marinate in
the refrigerator for 30 minutes.

3. Meanwhile, in a medium bowl, combine the salsa ingredients. Taste
and adjust the seasonings to your taste with more salt and lime juice,
if desired.

4. Remove the fillets from the bag and discard the marinade. Lightly
brush or spray both sides with vegetable oil.

5. Light a charcoal fire or preheat your gas grill on high. Oil the grill's
cooking surface.

6. Place the fillets on the grill and cook until the fish begins to flake, 3 to
4 minutes, turning once. Remove from the grill to a platter. Separate into
large flakes using two forks.

7. Place the tortillas on the grill and heat for about 1 minute without
turning. Wrap in a clean kitchen towel or aluminum foil to keep warm.

8. Assemble the fajitas by placing cabbage and the fish on the warm
tortillas and topping with the salsa. Serve immediately.

2 teaspoons ground ancho chile powder

½ teaspoon ground cumin

3 cloves garlic, minced

½ teaspoon kosher salt

¼ teaspoon freshly ground black pepper

2 tablespoons olive oil

3 pounds firm-fleshed whitefish fillets
(halibut, snapper, mahi-mahi, cod)

2 dozen 6-inch corn tortillas

2½ cups shredded green cabbage

2½ cups shredded red cabbage

Lime-Cilantro Sour Cream Sauce (recipe
at right)

Meredith Deeds's Pico de Gallo (p. 317)

4 limes, quartered

Meredith's
grilled fish tacos

A grilled fish taco is a beautiful thing to eat. San Diego and points south are where they originated. Although many of the fish tacos in the area are fried, the grilled ones really stand out and are much lighter. Meredith Deeds grew up in San Diego and taught me the ins and outs of the fish taco. These are an adaptation of her mom's recipe.

1. In a small bowl, combine the ancho powder, cumin, garlic, salt, and pepper and stir to mix. Add the oil and whisk until a loose paste is formed. Rub the fish with the spice paste and let marinate in the refrigerator for at least 30 minutes and up to 4 hours.

2. Light a charcoal fire or preheat your gas grill on high. Oil the grill's cooking surface. Let the coals burn down to a medium-hot fire or adjust the gas grill burners to medium-high.

3. Grill the fish until just cooked through, 3 to 4 minutes per side. Transfer to a cutting board and coarsely chop.

4. Divide the tortillas into 2 stacks and wrap each in aluminum foil. Place on the grill until heated through, about 5 minutes.

5. In a large bowl, combine the green and red cabbage.

6. To assemble the tortillas, take 2 tortillas, top it with chunks of fish, a dollop of the sauce, a spoonful of the Pico de Gallo, and some of the cabbage. Squeeze a wedge of lime over the filling, fold the tortillas, and eat.

lime-cilantro sour cream sauce
MAKES A GENEROUS 1½ CUPS

Use this sauce in place of tartar sauce or cocktail sauce with other grilled fish, scallops, or shrimp. It's also good with any of the fajita recipes in this book.

1 cup sour cream

½ cup mayonnaise

3 tablespoons minced fresh cilantro

Grated zest of 1 lime

1 tablespoon fresh lime juice

Combine all the ingredients in a 2-cup measuring cup and whisk until smooth. Refrigerate up to 4 hours until ready to use.

½ cup (1 stick) unsalted butter, at room temperature

2 cloves garlic, minced

6 catfish fillets, 5 to 7 ounces each

2 tablespoons lemon-pepper seasoning

Garry's Yazoo City
lemon-garlic grilled catfish

At first glance, Garry Roark seems an unlikely fellow to prepare superior barbecue, but that's what he does. He and his wife own a bed and breakfast in Yazoo City, Mississippi, but their hobby and new love has been entering barbecue contests around the country. But his skills are not limited to pork. He lives in the middle of catfish country, and I think you'll be thrilled with this simple grilled catfish preparation.

– ⟲⟳ –

1. Combine the butter and garlic in a small bowl, mixing well to combine. Coat both sides of the fillets with some of the butter mixture. Sprinkle evenly with the lemon pepper.

2. Light a charcoal fire or preheat your gas grill on high. Oil the grill's cooking surface. Let the coals burn down to a medium-hot fire or adjust the gas grill burners to medium-high.

3. Place the fillets on the grill and cook about 6 minutes. Turn and spread the remaining butter mixture over the fillets. Cook about 5 minutes longer, until the fish is firm and completely opaque. Remove to a platter and serve immediately.

2 pounds catfish or grouper fillets

Juice of 4 limes

1/2 cup dark rum

Olive oil

MIKE MIGNETTI'S JERK SEASONING

1 tablespoon dried parsley

1 tablespoon granulated onion

2 teaspoons ground thyme

2 teaspoons light brown sugar

2 teaspoons granulated garlic

2 teaspoons cayenne pepper

1 1/2 teaspoons kosher salt

1 teaspoon ground allspice

1 teaspoon red pepper flakes

1 teaspoon ground nutmeg

1/4 teaspoon ground cinnamon

1/4 teaspoon freshly ground black pepper

1/4 teaspoon ground star anise

Rummy Lime
jerk catfish

I was looking for a new take on catfish, which really holds up to grilling. Michael Mignetti of Tequesta, Florida, had given me a jerk seasoning recipe, and I decided that a quick bath in some rum and lime juice might add to the Caribbean effort. The result is something Hemingway might have loved. Most any firm, thick whitefish will work in place of the catfish. I've made this with grouper many times because it is plentiful on the East Coast and usually a good value. This jerk seasoning also works well with chicken and pork.

- ᐧᗜᗤᗢᑊ -

1. Pat the fish fillets dry with paper towels, place them in a glass baking dish, and pour over the lime juice and rum. Let marinate in the refrigerator for no more than 15 minutes.

2. Meanwhile, combine the jerk seasoning ingredients in a small bowl.

3. Remove the fish from the marinade and discard the marinade. Sprinkle the fish with enough of the jerk seasoning on both sides to nicely coat. (Any left over will keep in an airtight container for up to a month.) Cover and let the fish sit in the refrigerator for another hour.

4. Light a charcoal fire or preheat your gas grill on high. Oil the grill's cooking surface. Let the coals burn down to a medium-hot fire or adjust the gas grill burners to medium-high.

5. Remove the fish from the refrigerator and brush with olive oil. Place the fish on the grill, cover, and cook until just opaque at the center, 3 to 4 minutes per side. Transfer to a platter, let rest for a few minutes, then serve.

Four 18-inch squares heavy-duty
aluminum foil

Vegetable cooking spray

4 trout fillets (about 2 pounds total)

1 cup dry white wine

¹/₂ cup vegetable oil

One 4-ounce can mushroom stems and
pieces, drained

¹/₄ cup chopped onions

2 tablespoons chopped fresh parsley

2 tablespoons fresh lemon juice

2 teaspoons kosher salt

¹/₄ teaspoon dried thyme

Grilled
lake trout

If you fish, you need to keep this recipe handy. It's great for rainbow and
all other kinds of stream trout, as well as bigger lake trout and most freshwater fish, so long as they're not too bony. By cooking these thin fillets in
foil, you preserve their moisture through the steam that builds up, but you
also get a wisp of smokiness from the fire. It's great campsite fare.

– ଏଓଓ୬ –

1. Light a charcoal fire or preheat your gas grill on high. Oil the grill's
cooking surface. Let the coals burn down to a medium-hot fire or adjust
the gas grill burners to medium-high.

2. Meanwhile, coat the foil squares with the spray on one side. Place a
fillet on each square and bring up the edges of the foil on all sides.

3. Combine the wine, oil, mushrooms, onions, parsley, lemon juice, salt,
and thyme in a medium bowl, then pour it evenly over each of the fillets.
Close the foil around the fish, sealing it up tightly. Place the packets on the
grill and cook, with the lid down, until just opaque in the center, about
15 minutes. Remove from the grill and serve immediately.

LEMON-SAGE BUTTER

¾ cup (1½ sticks) unsalted butter

2½ tablespoons grated lemon zest

1½ tablespoons chopped fresh sage

Kosher salt and freshly ground black pepper

12 dressed trout, butterflied

Lemon wedges

Grilled Trout with
lemon-sage butter

Lemon is a no-brainer with most fish. But sneak a little sage into the mix, especially with trout, bluegills, or other freshwater fish, and you add another dimension of flavor. Trout takes amazingly well to the grill—maybe it's the idea of freshly caught fish and crisp outdoor air beside a mountain stream. Whatever it is, it certainly tastes good.

– ↷↶ –

1. Melt the butter in a small saucepan over medium-low heat. Remove from the heat, stir in the lemon zest and sage, and season to taste with salt and pepper.

2. Light a charcoal fire or preheat your gas grill on high. Oil the grill's cooking surface. Let the coals burn down to a medium-hot fire or adjust the gas grill burners to medium-high.

3. Brush the flesh and skin sides of the fish with the butter mixture. Sprinkle with salt and pepper on all sides. Close the fish and secure with toothpicks. Place on the grill and cook until just opaque in the center, about 4 minutes per side.

4. Remove from the grill and pull out the toothpicks. Serve immediately, passing lemon wedges on the side.

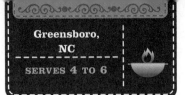
½ cup (1 stick) unsalted butter, melted

½ teaspoon garlic powder

1 tablespoon Worcestershire sauce

1 teaspoon lemon-pepper seasoning

Juice of 1 lemon

3 pounds amberjack fillets

Dad's Barbecued
amberjack

The only trophy that was mounted on a wall at home was Dad's amberjack. Amberjack is a beautiful fish and quite a fighter when hooked, making it one of the great sport fish. Dad would take clients down to Florida for a week of fishing each year, and one year he came back with this recipe that the cook at the fish camp used to grill amberjack. I also use this basting sauce on tuna and grouper.

– ⊷⊶ –

1. Combine the butter, garlic powder, Worcestershire, lemon pepper, and lemon juice in a small bowl.

2. Light a charcoal fire or preheat your gas grill on high. Oil the grill's cooking surface.

3. Grill the fish, basting with the sauce once each side has been seared, until the fish is firm and cooked to the center, about 20 minutes total.

8 cups ice water

⅓ cup coarse kosher salt

1 cup dry white wine

6 bay leaves

2 lemons (1 chopped, 1 cut into wedges)

½ teaspoon black peppercorns

2 pounds jumbo or larger shrimp, with shells on

¾ cup extra-virgin olive oil

6 cloves garlic, finely chopped

1 loaf French or ciabatta bread, sliced

Grilled Brined
shrimp with garlic oil

When I ask in my seafood grilling classes what gives them the most trouble, grilled shrimp is the most complained about. It is so easy to cook shrimp into rubbery little lumps. To avoid this grilling catastrophe, first you have to start with the right size shrimp. The larger ones, 16 count or fewer per pound, are perfect. They are big enough not to fall between the grates and easier to turn with your tongs. More important, they don't cook in the blink of an eye. Brining the shrimp gives you an even bigger fudge factor by adding moisture as well as sneaking in some welcome flavor to boot. This is one of my students' favorites.

– ᘓᗴᗶᕉ –

1. Stir 1 cup of the water and the salt together in a small saucepan over high heat until the salt dissolves, about 5 minutes. Pour into a large heatproof bowl. Mix in the wine, 1 of the bay leaves, the chopped lemon, peppercorns, and remaining ice water. Add the shrimp and let set in the brine for at least 15 minutes and up to 30 minutes.

2. Light a charcoal fire or preheat your gas grill on high. Oil the grill's cooking surface. Let the coals burn down to a medium-hot fire or adjust the gas grill burners to medium-high.

3. Whisk the oil and garlic together in a small bowl.

4. Drain the shrimp and rinse, then drain well again. Using kitchen scissors, cut the shells down the center and devein, leaving the shells on. Grill the shrimp until a little charred and just opaque, 3 to 4 minutes per side. Grill the bread until it begins to brown, about 2 minutes per side.

5. Transfer the shrimp to a clean large bowl. Add half the garlic oil and toss to coat. Mound the shrimp on a platter. Garnish with the remaining bay leaves (but warn your guests they're for show only) and the lemon wedges. Serve with the grilled bread and remaining garlic oil for dipping.

1 1/2 pounds 8- to 12-count shrimp, soaked in a mixture of 1 tablespoon sea salt dissolved in 1 1/2 cups water for 5 minutes, then drained

TAMARIND SAUCE

1 tablespoon tamarind from a pliable block

1/3 cup water

1 tablespoon peanut oil

1 tablespoon chopped fresh cilantro

1 tablespoon minced garlic

1 tablespoon sriracha or other Asian hot sauce

1 1/2 tablespoons palm sugar or sugar in the raw

1 tablespoon Asian fish sauce

2 jalapeños, cut in half lengthwise, seeded, and cut into thin strips across

Fresh cilantro leaves

Ting's Grilled
shrimp with tamarind sauce

Ting, an industrial engineer who came to the U.S. from Thailand for his graduate work, was my dormmate at North Carolina State University. He treated us to Thai food long before it had made its mark on this country.

In this dish, he brines the shrimp before grilling them. I added the split shell technique. This has heat but in a balance of sweet, salt, and sour, typical of Southeast Asian cooking. Tamarind is a pod-based fruit that is very sour when dried but more sweet and sour when left semidried. While it is more readily available in the pod, buying a block of it will save you a lot of time. Any Asian market will have sriracha, palm sugar, and fish sauce. This makes for nice finger food for a party. Serve with plenty of hot rice.

– ༖༅྅ –

1. Light a charcoal fire or preheat your gas grill on high. Oil the grill's cooking surface. Let the coals burn down to a medium-hot fire or adjust the gas grill burners to medium-high.

2. Combine the tamarind and water in a small bowl by rubbing with your fingers to dissolve the pulp. Pour through a sieve, pressing hard on the solids. Discard the solids.

3. Heat the oil in a small, heavy saucepan over medium heat until hot but not smoking, then cook the cilantro and garlic, stirring, until fragrant. Stir in the hot sauce, 3 tablespoons of the tamarind juice, the palm sugar, and fish sauce. Simmer until thickened to the consistency of a light syrup—it should coat the back of a spoon—about 3 minutes.

4. Snip the shells of the shrimp with kitchen shears down the center of the back, from the wide end to the second-to-last tail section. Butterfly them in their shells, making a deep incision along the length of the back where the shells are cut, and devein. Grill the shrimp on their sides until the shells are pink and slightly charred, and they are just cooked through, 3 to 4 minutes per side.

5. Remove to a serving dish. Spoon the warm tamarind sauce over them, garnish with the jalapeños and cilantro, and serve immediately.

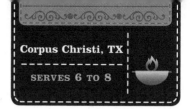

1½ pounds 24- to 26-count shrimp, peeled and deveined, with tails left on

¾ cup Cilantro-Pine Nut Pesto (recipe at right)

1. Place the shrimp in a large bowl and toss with 6 tablespoons of the pesto. Set aside to marinate at room temperature for 30 minutes.

2. Light a charcoal fire or preheat your gas grill on high. Oil the grill's cooking surface.

3. Thread the shrimp crosswise onto long metal skewers, 5 or 6 to a skewer. Grill the skewers in batches 3 inches from the heat source for 3 minutes per side.

4. Remove the shrimp from the skewers and place in a clean bowl. Toss with the remaining 6 tablespoons pesto and serve immediately.

Cilantro-Pine Nut
pesto grilled shrimp

These marinated shrimp are based on a recipe from Corpus Christi, Texas, with some help from Mark Cheeseman, and one that has excited my cooking school classes. It couldn't be simpler to do, especially when you realize the flavor impact that comes from the pesto. Just remember not to overcook the shrimp. Try serving these over pasta that's been tossed with a little of the pesto.

cilantro-pine nut pesto MAKES ABOUT ¾ CUP

This condiment is perfect with basic grilled fish, shrimp, chicken, and even beef.

3 cups loosely packed fresh cilantro leaves, rinsed and patted thoroughly dry

2 tablespoons pine nuts

1 teaspoon minced garlic

Pinch of ground cumin

Kosher salt and freshly ground black pepper to taste

½ cup extra-virgin olive oil

1. Place the cilantro in a food processor and pulse until coarsely chopped. Add the pine nuts, garlic, and cumin, season with salt and pepper, and pulse until the mixture is well chopped but not pureed.

2. With the machine running, slowly drizzle in the olive oil through the feed tube and process until the mixture is smooth and well combined. Use immediately or transfer to a glass jar with a lid and refrigerate for up to 3 days.

HONEY-BALSAMIC MARINADE

½ cup balsamic vinegar

½ cup white wine

¼ cup soy sauce

¼ cup honey

¼ cup your favorite barbecue dry rub

1½ pounds 24- to 26-count shrimp, peeled and deveined

CUCUMBER SAUCE

1 pound cucumbers, peeled and seeded

½ cup mayonnaise

½ cup sour cream

Dash of Tabasco sauce

1 teaspoon kosher salt

1 teaspoon freshly ground black pepper

1 tablespoon cider vinegar

1 teaspoon Dijon mustard

1 teaspoon minced garlic

The Pitmaster's Honey-Balsamic Marinated

grilled shrimp with cucumber sauce

Troy Black, from just outside Birmingham, Alabama, designs landscapes during the week, but, come the weekend, he's on the barbecue competition circuit. He just joined the circuit a few years ago, but he's already a force to be reckoned with. His pulled pork and ribs place in the top three most all the time. I asked him what he cooks for his family. "Usually seafood, and they love my shrimp." So, from a champion pitmaster, here's some great-tasting shrimp.

– ⌐⌐⌐ –

1. Combine the marinade ingredients in a medium bowl, Place the shrimp in a large zip-top plastic bag and pour in the marinade. Seal the bag and squish everything around to coat the shrimp. Let marinate in the refrigerator for about 3 hours, turning the bag a couple of times.

2. Light a charcoal fire or preheat your gas grill on high. Oil the grill's cooking surface. Let the coals burn down to a medium-hot fire or adjust the gas grill burners to medium-high.

3. Meanwhile, combine the sauce ingredients in a blender and process until smooth. Keep cold until needed but make no more than 1 hour in advance.

4. Skewer the shrimp on metal skewers and cook on the grill until pink, about 3 minutes per side.

5. Remove the shrimp from the skewers and serve with the sauce poured over the top or on the side for dipping.

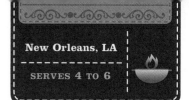

1 pound 24- to 26-count shrimp, peeled and deveined, leaving the tails on

One 10-ounce package frozen whole okra, defrosted, or small fresh okra, bottoms trimmed

24 cherry tomatoes

Eight 12-inch wooden or metal skewers, soaked in water for 1 hour if wooden

1 tablespoon Creole seasoning

2 tablespoons olive oil

1 teaspoon garlic powder

¼ teaspoon freshly ground black pepper

⅛ teaspoon cayenne pepper

Creole
shrimp kebobs

Only in the South will you ever see this combination of shrimp and okra on a stick. It sounds odd, but you won't be disappointed. "Hollywood," the oyster shucker at the Acme Oyster Bar in New Orleans, told me about these kebobs.

– ౿ఁ౨ఁ౷ –

1. Thread 1 shrimp, 1 okra, and 1 tomato alternately on a skewer 3 times. Place on a baking sheet. Repeat with the remaining shrimp, okra, and tomatoes.

2. Whisk together the Creole seasoning, oil, garlic powder, black pepper, and cayenne in a small bowl. Brush this liberally on the kebobs. Cover the kebobs with plastic wrap and refrigerate for 20 to 30 minutes.

3. Light a charcoal fire or preheat your gas grill on high. Oil the grill's cooking surface. Let the coals burn down to a medium-hot fire or adjust the gas grill burners to medium-high.

4. Remove the kebobs from the refrigerator and place on the grill. Cook about 5 minutes per side, until the shrimp have curled but are not overcooked. If your fire is hotter than expected, this could take only 3 minutes per side. Remove from the grill and serve immediately.

1 ½ pounds 16-count shrimp

BASIL-CILANTRO MARINADE AND DIPPING SAUCE

Grated zest of 1 large lime

Juice of 2 large limes

4 cups tightly packed fresh basil leaves (from about 1 large bunch)

2 cups tightly packed fresh cilantro leaves (from about 1 ¼ bunches)

2 large cloves garlic, peeled

1 jalapeño, seeded

1 ½ teaspoons peeled and grated fresh ginger

½ teaspoon kosher salt

¼ teaspoon freshly ground black pepper

1 cup plain nonfat yogurt

Freshly ground black pepper

½ teaspoon kosher salt

Get-Their-Attention Spicy Shrimp
with basil-cilantro dipping sauce

I've used this recipe to start many a grilled seafood cooking class. It was designed to capture the class's tastes buds quickly. It's sort of an upscale shrimp cocktail, but the flavor is explosive. Shrimp continues to befuddle many grillers, and this is another method to ensure your success. Follow the method closely. Grilling shrimp in their shells is one of the best ways to increase their flavor and keep them moist. The biggest trick in grilling shrimp is not to overcook them. While cutting the slit down the back of the shells allows you to easily remove the vein, it also gives you a peek inside the shrimp, helping you to judge when they're done. Remember, shrimp should take a lazy C shape and never get tightly coiled.

– ᥴᡠᡣᡖᠪᡡᥟ –

1. Using scissors, cut off the legs of the shrimp close to the body, leaving the shells intact. Cut a slit down the back of the shells into the flesh, leaving the section at the tail intact. Remove the vein. Transfer to a large zip-top plastic bag.

2. In a food processor or blender, process the lime zest and juice, basil, cilantro, garlic, jalapeño, ginger, salt, and pepper until finely chopped, about 1 minute. Add yogurt and process to combine. Pour 1¼ cups of the yogurt mixture over the shrimp, seal the bag, and squish to coat everything. Refrigerate for 2 to 3 hours, turning the bag several times. Pour the remaining ¾ cup of marinade into a small bowl, cover, and refrigerate.

3. Light a charcoal fire or preheat your gas grill on high. Oil the grill's cooking surface. Let the coals burn down to a medium-hot fire or adjust the gas grill burners to medium-high.

4. Remove the shrimp from the marinade and discard the marinade. Season both sides of the shrimp with pepper and salt. Place on the grill and cook until the shrimp are opaque and lightly charred, 3 to 4 minutes per each side.

5. Remove from the grill and serve with the reserved marinade as a dipping sauce.

½ cup (1 stick) unsalted butter

Juice of 2 large limes

2 ounces white liquor

½ cup kecap manis

2 pounds 24- to 26-count shrimp

1. Melt the butter in a small saucepan. Take it off the heat (never allow high-proof moonshine to get close to open flames because even its fumes are highly flammable), and add the lime juice, liquor, and kecap manis. Toss the shrimp with half the sauce in a large bowl and let marinate for about 20 minutes.

2. Light a charcoal fire or preheat your gas grill on high. Oil the grill's cooking surface.

3. Grill the shrimp in two batches if necessary, 2 to 3 minutes per side, until pink and showing a little char. Put them on plates or into a communal bowl, and serve the reserved sauce on the side for further dipping.

When You Need to Substitute

When you're fresh out of kecap manis, sorghum or cane syrup are respectable stand-ins if you add some cayenne pepper and maybe a bit of ground ginger. If you don't have a line on a supply of local moonshine, try bourbon or the Brazilian cane sugar brandy called *cachaça* (the wallop behind the caprihinia).

Indonesian
bootleg shrimp

Matt Rowley is a close friend from Philadelphia who imports cheese for a living and cooks for the fun and pleasure of his friends. His latest project has been a book on the state of moonshine, or bootleg liquor, in this country.

This is an authentic Indonesian recipe, except for the alcohol, which you can easily omit. It relies on a sweet, thick Indonesian soy sauce widely available from Asian grocers and showing up increasingly in large supermarkets. "Since discovering that sneaky barbecuers use ABC® brand kecap manis instead of the more expensive molasses in their grilling sauces, I've always kept a bottle in the larder for impromptu entertaining—and rave reviews," says Matt.

The shrimp can be heads-on or heads-off, shelled or not, depending on your taste and the formality of the gathering, but I prefer it with the shells on—they capture and hold the sauce, making this messy but tasty eating that cries out for beer.

SCAMPI MARINADE

2 tablespoons extra-virgin olive oil

2 tablespoons dry white wine

1 1/2 tablespoons finely minced garlic

1/4 teaspoon paprika

Pinch of red pepper flakes

Kosher salt and freshly ground black
pepper to taste

1 tablespoon coarsely chopped fresh
flat-leaf parsley

2 pounds 24- to 26-count shrimp, peeled
and deveined, leaving the tails on

1 tablespoon coarsely chopped fresh
flat-leaf parsley

3 lemons, cut in half

Grilled
scampi on a stick

If you love scampi cooked in a pan, you will be thrilled at how well the flavors transfer to the grill. My friends and neighbors, both in the South and New York, can't get enough of this grilled twist on a classic. It's also a nice choice for appetizer skewers.

– ⟡⟡⟡ –

1. In a large bowl, combine the marinade ingredients. Add the shrimp and toss well to coat. Let marinate in the refrigerator, covered, for 1 hour.

2. Light a charcoal fire or preheat your gas grill on high. Oil the grill's cooking surface.

3. Thread 4 to 6 shrimp, crosswise, on each of 4 to 6 metal skewers. Grill the shrimp 3 inches from the heat source, brushing them with any remaining marinade, until just cooked through, 3 to 4 minutes per side. Do not overcook them.

4. Arrange the skewers on a large platter, sprinkle with the parsley, and serve with the lemon halves for squeezing.

¼ cup extra-virgin olive oil

2 cloves garlic, finely chopped

1 small shallot, finely chopped

Sea salt and freshly ground black pepper

1½ pounds 8- to 16-count shrimp, head on if available

HONEY-MUSTARD-BALSAMIC VINAIGRETTE

1 tablespoon whole-grain mustard

1 tablespoon honey

¼ cup balsamic vinegar

¾ to 1 cup extra-virgin olive oil

1 tablespoon finely chopped shallot

1 clove garlic, finely chopped

Sea salt

Cracked black peppercorns

Michael, Rebecca and Laila Sofia spend evenings grilling at the beach.

Michael Mignetti's Jumbo Grilled Shrimp with
honey-mustard-balsamic vinaigrette

I met Michael Mignetti, his wife, Rebecca, their cutie-pie daughter, Laila Sofia, and the trick dog, Indica, all because I needed special hand surgery that is only done in Jupiter, Florida, and Michael's mother-in-law, Terry, worked for the surgeon. Michael is the chef at a popular restaurant in the area called Too Bizarre. Michael started his career at Legal Seafood in Boston and was sent to California to do clambakes for, most notably, the cast and crew of *ER* and *The West Wing*. Michael was so open and enthusiastic about cooking that I asked what he grilled for his friends and family at home. "I love to do super big shrimp and veggies with a simple vinaigrette. We really like to hit the beach or take a boat ride to an island and just enjoy the peace and calm."

The key to this dish is the jumbo shrimp, with their heads on if you can get them in your area. The heads actually help season the rest of the shrimp.

– ᘓᘒᘓᘗᘒᘐ –

1. In a shallow baking dish, whisk together the oil, garlic, shallot, and salt and pepper to taste. Add the shrimp, tossing to coat. Set aside at room temperature for 30 minutes or refrigerate up to 2 hours.

2. Meanwhile, make the vinaigrette. In a small bowl, whisk together the mustard, honey, and vinegar. Slowly drizzle in the oil, whisking constantly. Stir in the shallot and garlic. Taste for salt and pepper.

3. Light a charcoal fire or preheat your gas grill on high. Oil the grill's cooking surface.

4. When the grill is ready, remove the shrimp from the marinade and discard the marinade. Place on the grill and cook until opaque all the way through, about 3 minutes per side. Do not overcook the shrimp because they will be tough. Remove the shrimp from the grill to a serving platter. Whisk the vinaigrette again if necessary, drizzle over the shrimp, and serve with plenty of napkins.

TEQUILA MARINADE

¹/₃ cup tequila

2 tablespoons extra-virgin olive oil

2 tablespoons fresh lime juice

1 tablespoon minced garlic

1 tablespoon minced jalapeño, with the seeds

1 teaspoon ground coriander

¹/₂ teaspoon freshly ground black pepper

1¹/₂ pounds 24- to 26-count shrimp, peeled and deveined

Kosher salt

2 limes, cut into wedges

Honeymoon
tequila shrimp

During one of my cooking classes at A Southern Season in Chapel Hill, North Carolina, I was begged by a couple to create a tequila-marinated grilled shrimp because they had enjoyed the dish. Here's what I came up with, which got an A+ from the tequila-shrimp-deprived couple.

– ᦦᧁᦧ –

1. Whisk together the marinade ingredients in a small bowl.

2. Place the shrimp in a large zip-top plastic bag, then pour in the marinade and seal. Squish the marinade with the shrimp and turn the bag over. Let marinate in the refrigerator for at least 30 minutes but no longer than 45 minutes.

3. Remove the shrimp from the bag and discard the marinade. Skewer the shrimp and season lightly with salt. Return to the refrigerator until your fire is ready.

4. Light a charcoal fire or preheat your gas grill on high. Oil the grill's cooking surface.

5. Place the skewers on the grill and cook until the shrimp are just opaque in the center and firm to the touch, 2 to 4 minutes total, turning once.

6. Transfer to a platter and serve warm with the lime wedges.

Know Your Alphabet

You do not want to overcook shrimp. When they begin to form a lazy C, they are just moments away from being done.

THAI PEANUT SAUCE

1 tablespoon peeled and finely chopped fresh ginger

2 cloves garlic, chopped

1 teaspoon Thai red curry paste

1 cup chunky peanut butter

3 tablespoons sugar

2 teaspoons Thai fish sauce

¾ cup unsweetened coconut milk

APRICOT GLAZE

1 cup apricot preserves

1 cup cider vinegar

½ teaspoon freshly ground black pepper

1 star anise

½ teaspoon ground coriander

2 tablespoons chopped fresh cilantro

---

1 pound 24- to 26-count shrimp, peeled and deveined

2 tablespoons olive oil

Kosher salt and freshly ground black pepper

4 burrito-size tortillas

Grilled Shrimp Wraps with
thai peanut sauce and apricot glaze

This is a fun dish I developed for a cooking class. It's served on a tasty Thai-style peanut sauce that is also good with chicken satays and pork tenderloin. The apricot glaze can do double duty with pork chops. This is a faultless summer lunch and, if you cut the wraps into thirds and secure them with toothpicks, it makes for wonderful finger food at a party, serving 14 as an appetizer. Whatever way you choose, make sure to serve them with additional peanut sauce for dipping. For a real Asian flair, make these wraps with spring roll wrappers instead of tortillas. Thai curry paste, fish sauce, and coconut milk are available in the Asian section of many large supermarkets.

- ᘒᘛᕟᕥᕑ -

1. To make the peanut sauce, place the ingredients in a food processor and pulse to combine, then process until smooth. Pour into a small bowl and set aside. This can be made up to a day ahead and refrigerated, covered with plastic wrap.

2. Up to 1 hour ahead, make the glaze. Place the preserves, vinegar, pepper, star anise, and coriander in a small saucepan over medium-high heat and bring to a boil, stirring. Reduce the heat to a simmer and cook until syrupy, about 5 minutes, stirring a few times. Pour into a small bowl. Remove the star anise and stir in the cilantro. Set aside.

3. Light a charcoal fire or preheat your gas grill on high. Oil the grill's cooking surface.

4. Place the shrimp in a medium bowl with the oil and season with salt and pepper. Toss to coat. Grill the shrimp for about 3 minutes per side. Remove from the grill to a bowl. Place the tortillas on the grill and cook for about 30 seconds on each side.

5. Spread each tortilla with about 1 tablespoon of the peanut sauce. Equally divide the shrimp between the tortillas, and spoon 1 tablespoon of the glaze over the shrimp. Roll up and serve at once, with the remaining peanut sauce on the side for dipping.

½ cup (1 stick) unsalted butter

¼ cup fresh lemon juice

1 tablespoon grated lemon rind

¼ cup chopped fresh chives

2 tablespoons chopped fresh tarragon or 2 teaspoons dried

Kosher salt and freshly ground black pepper

4 live lobsters (each about 1½ pounds)

Drew's Grilled
lemon-tarragon lobster

I assisted restaurateur Drew Nieporent with this recipe when he was demonstrating it on a national television show. I've changed it a bit from what we did to make it a little easier for folks at home to deal with the lobster. This is one of those recipes that just screams summer. It makes you want to be out on the beach with some corn on the cob and vine-ripe tomatoes.

– ✦✦✦ –

1. Light a charcoal fire or preheat your gas grill on high. Oil the grill's cooking surface. Let the coals burn down to a medium-hot fire or adjust the gas grill burners to medium-high.

2. In a small saucepan over low heat, combine the butter, lemon juice, and lemon rind, and stir until the butter melts. Mix in the chives and tarragon, season with salt and pepper, and remove from the heat.

3. Meanwhile, bring a large pot of water to a rollicking boil. Drop the lobsters in headfirst. Cover the pot and cook for 2 minutes.

4. With tongs, transfer the lobsters to a work surface. Using a large, heavy knife or cleaver, split the lobsters in half lengthwise. Scoop out and discard the gray intestinal tract, gills, and sand sack from the head. Leave any red roe or green tomalley intact, if desired. Crack the claws. Brush the cut side of the lobsters with 2 tablespoons of the butter sauce.

5. Place the lobsters on the grill, cut side down, and cook for 4 minutes. Turn and grill another 4 minutes. Turn again so the cut side is down and grill until the lobster meat is just opaque but still juicy, about 2 minutes.

6. Transfer the lobsters to a platter, brush lightly with the sauce, and serve immediately, passing the remaining sauce on the side.

2 dozen live blue crabs

Kosher salt

Cayenne pepper

1 pound (4 sticks) unsalted butter

3 tablespoons Zatarain's® Concentrated Liquid Crab & Shrimp Boil (available in many supermarkets and on the Internet)

1 tablespoon lemon-pepper seasoning

1 teaspoon garlic powder

1 tablespoon Worcestershire sauce

1 teaspoon paprika

6 lemons

Henry's
barbecue crabs

Marcelle Bienvenu honors her friend, Henry Mayer, in sharing his recipe for barbecued crab. Marcelle, Henry, and his wife, Phyl, kept up with each other over several decades. Marcelle likes to tell stories about how Henry loved to put you on the spot with out-of-the-blue questions and singing Frank Sinatra songs, always off-key.

These crabs are legendary in South Louisiana. Check out Henry's New Orleans-Style Field Pea Casserole (p. 325) for an excellent dish to go alongside. I do need to warn you that you dress these crabs live, so this recipe is not for the faint of heart.

– ∽⊙⊙⌒ –

1. Run very hot tap water over the live crabs. This will stun them so they can't pinch. Pull the back off the crab, clean out the dead man fingers, which are gray and spongy, and the curly inner sand sack. Crack the claws, but do not remove the shells.

2. Sprinkle the crabs generously with salt and cayenne. Combine the butter, liquid boil, lemon pepper, garlic powder, Worcestershire, and paprika in a medium saucepan. Ream the lemons, cut the halves in half, and add the juice and lemon pieces to the butter mixture. Warm over low heat until the butter is melted.

3. Using a basting brush, brush about one-third of the sauce all over the crabs.

4. Light a charcoal fire or preheat your gas grill on high. Oil the grill's cooking surface. Let the coals burn down to a medium-low fire or adjust the gas grill burners to medium-low.

5. Place the crabs, cavity side down, on the grill and close the lid. Cook for about 10 minutes. Turn the crabs over and brush with more butter sauce. Close the lid and cook for another 10 to 15 minutes. Time will vary according to the heat of the fire and the size of the crabs. Brush the remaining butter sauce on the crabs and serve immediately with lots of napkins and cold beer.

POACHING LIQUID

3 quarts water

2 tablespoons fennel seeds

2 tablespoons black peppercorns

2 tablespoons cumin seeds

1 tablespoon anise seeds

1 tablespoon red pepper flakes

2 teaspoons salt

5 bay leaves

1 stalk celery, broken in half

8 cloves garlic, peeled

4 pounds frozen cleaned octopus, defrosted

LEMON-GARLIC MARINADE

4 cloves garlic, crushed

½ teaspoon red pepper flakes

2 bay leaves, crushed

1 tablespoon dried oregano

⅓ cup olive oil

1 lemon, zest removed with a vegetable peeler and coarsely chopped

SALAD

⅓ cup extra-virgin olive oil

Juice of 1 lemon

¼ cup white balsamic vinegar

2 cloves garlic, minced

1 tablespoon capers, rinsed and chopped

10 Kalamata olives, pitted and coarsely chopped

2 tablespoons golden raisins, plumped in hot water for 20 minutes and drained

Kosher salt and freshly ground black pepper

3 cups arugula

1 cup torn radicchio

8 torn fresh basil leaves

Durham, NC

SERVES 4 TO 6

Zuk's Grilled
octopus salad

Glenn Lozuke, the chef de cuisine at Magnolia Grill in Durham, North Carolina, is originally from New Jersey, where he grew up eating octopus and home-cured meats. This is, hands down, the best grilled octopus I have eaten anywhere in this country. Poaching is the key to tenderness in this preparation, along with the acidity of the marinade. No beating the octopus with a stick to tenderize, as it is sometimes done in the Mediterranean.

- ❧ -

1. Combine the poaching liquid ingredients in a large stockpot and bring to a boil. Add the octopus, reduce the heat to medium-low, and simmer until tender, 1 to 1½ hours. The meat is done when you can cut the thickest part of the tentacle with a butter knife. Remove from the poaching liquid and let the octopus cool for 15 minutes. Using your hands or a clean dishtowel, remove all the skin.

2. Combine the marinade ingredients in a medium bowl. Add the octopus, tossing to coat. Set aside at room temperature for 1 hour.

3. Combine the oil, lemon juice, vinegar, garlic, capers, olives, and raisins in a medium bowl. Salt and pepper to taste. Set aside.

4. Light a charcoal fire or preheat your gas grill on high. Oil the grill's cooking surface.

5. Remove the octopus from the marinade, letting the excess drain back into the bowl. Discard the marinade. Season the octopus with salt and pepper and place on the grill. Cook for 5 to 7 minutes total, turning so that all the sides get slightly golden and crispy.

6. Remove to a cutting board, then cut the tentacles at an angle into ½-inch-thick pieces. Toss with the salad dressing. Add the arugula, radicchio, and basil, tossing well to combine. Serve immediately.

2 tablespoons unsalted butter

2 cloves garlic, finely chopped

1 medium yellow onion, chopped

1 rib celery, finely diced

1/2 green bell pepper, seeded and
finely diced

One 10-ounce box frozen chopped
spinach, thawed, drained, and pressed
to remove all the liquid

1/2 cup milk

36 Gulf Coast oysters, in shell

1/4 to 1/2 cup shredded mozzarella cheese

3 tablespoons plain dry breadcrumbs

Lemon wedges, if desired

Opening Oysters Hollywood's Way

Most of us have been taught
to open an oyster through the
hinge on the back of the shell.
If you will notice, the true hinge
is not directly at the end of the
oyster. Hollywood showed me
that by approaching the oyster's
hinge from the side, rather
than the back, you can slide
the oyster knife right into the
sweet spot that pops the shell.
That positioning also makes it
easier to keep the knife flat and
against the top shell to sever
the oyster's muscle.

Hollywood's Take on Grilled
oysters rockefeller

"Hollywood," as everybody in New Orleans knows him, is the master of
the oyster bar at the Acme restaurant in the French Quarter. "I've been
doing this for 30 years and I ain't never seen a pretty oyster, but taste,
there's nothing like 'em." He is passionate about Gulf Coast oysters and
even more so about the proper way to open one. "I've been lobbying the
state to certify peoples that open oysters. It is an art, just like being a sushi
chef," he bellows. After he showed his technique and schooled me on the
New Orleans way to eat a raw oyster (a drop of hot sauce, then slurp it
out without your mouth touching the shell), I asked him about his grilled
oysters Rockefeller, which I had heard about all over the Quarter. "Damn
man, they is good, my neighbors and friends can't git enough," answers
Hollywood, with his eyes just sparkling. So here it is—one of the best oysters Rockefeller I've ever had, and I think you will agree.

– ꕥꕥꕥ –

1. Light a charcoal fire or preheat your gas grill on high. Oil the grill's
cooking surface. Let the coals burn down to a medium-hot fire or adjust
the gas grill burners to medium.

2. Melt the butter in a large skillet over medium heat. Add the garlic and
cook until you just smell it. Add the onions, celery, and bell peppers and
cook, stirring, until soft, about 5 minutes. Stir in the spinach and milk,
and cook, stirring a few times, another 5 minutes. Remove from the heat.

3. Shuck the oysters as if you were serving them on the half shell. Pour
any liquor from the oysters into the spinach mixture. Place the oysters on
a baking sheet. Add about 1 tablespoon of the spinach mixture to each
oyster. (You may not use up all the spinach mixture.) Top with some cheese
and breadcrumbs. Place the oysters on the grill, cover, and cook until the
cheese is bubbling and beginning to brown, about 5 minutes.

4. Remove the oysters to a platter and serve with lemon wedges, if
desired.

8 the ground pounders:

burgers, dogs, and sausages

There are few pleasures in life better than a perfectly grilled burger.

From Texas to Wisconsin, you'll encounter some mighty fine sausages that have been smoked or grilled to perfection. This is the simple life on the grill, yet it can all be new and exciting.

Getting the Best Burgers

Burgers mean more than beef. Pork, turkey, lamb, and fish can be ground and pattied into wonderful treats.

For a **beef burger**, everything begins with the meat. Chuck is perfect for hamburgers, a great balance of fat vs. lean (you want to have around 20 percent fat, unless you prefer your burgers dry). I usually like to mix in ground sirloin, which is always available, but ground tri-tip or hanger steak will add volumes of taste to your burgers. Never be rough with good meat. Lightly combine the meat and seasoning (your hands are the best tool for this), and take care when making the patties not to press any harder than needed for the burger to retain its shape. Make certain the grill and its cooking surface are hot and have been oiled. Nothing is more disappointing than leaving part of your burger on the grill. A hot grill will help prevent this problem. And please, never push on a burger with a spatula. You are driving out the juices that will make your burger great. Why then do restaurants do it? Speed. It does force heat through the burger but at a great cost. Only turn your burgers once, and let them rest a minute after coming off the grill. To prevent the middle from swelling as the outer edge of the patty shrinks, grilling guru John Willingham suggests poking your finger through the center of the burger. My grilling buddy and expert Elizabeth Karmel makes a thumbprint depression in the center of the burger to keep it flat and cooking evenly. I use a deli container that has a convex bottom to shape my patties, so they come out with a good surface depression. Any of these methods will make your burgers better.

Much has been said about undercooked burgers. The FDA likes the 160°F mark for beef burgers, 155°F for pork, and at least 160°F for burgers made from poultry. I like my beef burgers more medium with some pink in the middle (about 150°F). Of course, I also eat raw oysters. Decide on your own level of risk.

Sensational Sausages

Sausages, which include hot dogs, should cook over a lower heat than most of us use on the grill. To get that perfect crispness to a hot dog, grill them slowly over medium heat. The same applies to most cooked, uncooked, and smoked sausages like **kielbasa and bratwurst**. Raw sausages are much better when cooked over indirect heat. The Texas way is to smoke them for 1 to 2 hours. Cooked sausages will take about 5 to 7 minutes over direct heat and uncooked generally need 20 to 25 minutes over indirect heat.

The Perfect-Size Burger

One-third of a pound of meat seems to be the best weight for burgers made at home. A burger that size cooks evenly and fills out most hamburger buns nicely.

1½ pounds ground beef chuck or cubes of chuck

1 Vidalia onion, sliced

¼ cup crumbled blue cheese

Kosher salt and freshly ground black pepper

4 hamburger buns, buttered and grilled

Lettuce, sliced tomatoes, and condiments

Tony Bell's
inside-out cheeseburgers

Tony is originally from the Atlanta area, where she learned to make these burgers. She and her husband, Steve, now fire up their grill in Johnson City, Tennessee. After Tony cooked these burgers for me the first time, it was two years before I'd make anything but this recipe when I wanted a burger.

These inside-out cheeseburgers are fun to make and eat. If you or the kids don't like blue cheese, then use shredded Cheddar or any cheese you like. Be careful with the salt. Use a cup deli container (the short 2-inch-high ones) as a mold, which makes a perfect bun-size burger.

– ꙮ –

1. In a medium bowl, toss the meat to lightly loosen it. Divide the beef into 8 equal portions. Using a container or mold, lightly press in one portion. Put a few onion rings on top of the meat, then top with 1 table-spoon of the blue cheese. Place a second portion of beef on top of the now cheese-and-onion-covered patty and press lightly to form a ham-burger. Flip the mold over to release the burger. Indent the center of the hamburger slightly. Sprinkle with pepper and salt if you think necessary, being mindful that the cheese is salted. Repeat with the remaining meat, onions, and blue cheese, and refrigerate, covered with plastic wrap, until ready to cook.

2. Light a charcoal fire or preheat your gas grill on high. Oil the grill's cooking surface. You're going to want to cook over a very hot fire.

3. Place the burgers on the grill and cook 3 to 5 minutes (3 minutes for rare and 5 minutes for medium), then turn the burgers and cook the same amount of time on the other side. Remember: If you wanted to eat a hockey puck, you could have gone to a fast-food place. Don't overcook your burgers.

4. Serve on hamburger buns, with lettuce, tomato, and your favorite hamburger fixings.

2 pounds ground beef chuck

¼ cup chopped shallots

2 tablespoons chopped fresh chives

1 tablespoon Dijon mustard

1 tablespoon Worcestershire sauce

1 tablespoon Montreal steak seasoning

2 large egg yolks

1 slice truffle mousse pâté, about
1 inch thick

1½ tablespoons truffle butter

6 hamburger buns (I like potato rolls)

Lettuce

Tomato slices

1. Using your hands, gently combine the beef, shallots, chives, mustard, Worcestershire, steak seasoning, and egg yolks in a large bowl. Make 6 patties 1 to 1½ inches thick.

2. Take the truffle mousse pâté and cut it into six 1-inch cubes. Dig a little hole in the center of each burger, press in the pâté, and push the hamburger meat back over the pâté. Cover with plastic wrap and refrigerate for about 30 minutes.

3. Light a charcoal fire or preheat your gas grill on high. Oil the grill's cooking surface. Let the coals burn down to a medium-hot fire or adjust the gas grill burners to medium-high.

4. Place the burgers on the grill and cook for 6 to 8 minutes per side for medium or to your desired degree of doneness.

5. Remove from the grill to a platter and place about 1 teaspoon of the truffle butter on each patty. Quickly toast the buns on the grill, 1 to 2 minutes, cut side down. Place a patty on the bottom bun. Dress with lettuce and tomato, if desired, and cover with the top bun.

The Gilded
hamburger

New York City and especially Manhattan can get very obsessive about things, especially when it comes to food. Hamburgers have always held a special place in New Yorkers' tummies. The great hamburger emporiums like J. G. Mellon and the Corner Bistro have given way to the Burger Joint and the Shake Shack. But here we're still talking about hamburgers that cost less than $5. Among some of the higher-end restaurants, it has become a battle of how expensive a hamburger can get. I guess the 21 Club started the craze with its 21 Burger decades ago, but the battle was joined by D. B. Bistro Moderne with a $50 burger stuffed with braised short ribs, foie gras, and truffles. Then the Old Homestead Steakhouse entered the act, making a similar burger but using the most expensive beef in the world, Japanese Kobe. And the price of a burger headed toward $100. Cha-ching. Ego or flavor, either way, it's a bit ridiculous. Here's my version of an upscale, rich man's burger, which, yes, will cost you a few more dollars than the classic, but it's probably worth the extra expense and is a whole lot cheaper than enjoying it in one of these restaurants. I'll let you be the judge.

1 pound ground beef, chuck preferred

1 tablespoon Worcestershire sauce

1 tablespoon ketchup

Freshly ground black pepper

4 hamburger buns

Lettuce and sliced tomato and onion as desired

Your favorite burger condiments

1. In a large bowl, using your hands, gently mix together the beef, Worcestershire, ketchup, and several grindings of pepper. Form into 4 patties about ¾ inch thick. Cover with plastic wrap and refrigerate for a couple of hours to let the flavors develop.

2. Light a charcoal fire or preheat your gas grill on high. Oil the grill's cooking surface.

3. Remove the burgers from the refrigerator and place on the grill. Cook about 5 minutes on one side, but turn if you see juices coming out the top of the burgers before the time is up. Cook on the other side for another 5 to 6 minutes for medium or to your desired degree of doneness.

4. Remove from the grill and place one on each bun (you might want to toast your buns on the grill for a minute per side). Serve with the fixings.

RiRi's
burgers

"RiRi" is Marie Inscore's "grandmother name". She likes to spoil her grandchildren with these special burgers that get made both at her home in Rocky Mount, North Carolina, and her beach cottage on the coast. Sometimes it doesn't take much to give something an extra-special flavor and that's what Marie does here, with the addition of Worcestershire to her hamburger meat. You can double or triple the recipe to fit your needs. As a connoisseur of hamburgers, I give this one a big thumbs up.

Marie's grandson Phillip enjoying one of her burgers on the beach.

1½ pounds coarsely ground Grade A Angus beef

1 teaspoon ground allspice

½ cup KC Masterpiece Original Flavor barbecue sauce

2 tablespoons unsalted butter, melted

Hamburger buns

Lettuce, sliced tomato, and burger condiments

Susan's
south dakota-style hamburgers

South Dakotan Susan Dracy-Nerland talked me through this recipe. "Since I used to live in Springfield, Missouri, I guess there's some of that state in the burgers as well."

– ⁓ –

1. Light a charcoal fire or preheat your gas grill on high. Let the coals burn down to a low fire or adjust your gas grill burners to low.

2. In a large bowl, using your hands, gently mix together the ground beef, allspice, and barbecue sauce. Form into 4 burgers. Brush the top of each patty with melted butter. Take the remaining butter and brush the grill's cooking surface.

3. Place the burgers on the grill and cook for a total of 15 minutes for medium, turning once, or to your desired degree of doneness. Do not press down on the burgers with a spatula because this causes the juices to escape. When cooked to your liking, remove from the grill and serve on buns with your favorite toppings and condiments.

1 pound ground beef chuck

1 small onion, minced

1 large egg, beaten

½ cup plain dry breadcrumbs

1 teaspoon kosher salt

1 tablespoon freshly ground black pepper

1 tablespoon sugar, preferably raw
and brown

2 tablespoons soy sauce

HOMESTYLE TERI SAUCE

1 cup soy sauce

¼ cup sugar, preferably raw and brown

½ tablespoon peeled and grated
fresh ginger

1 clove garlic, minced

¼ cup minced scallions (white and green
parts)

½ teaspoon Accent® seasoning

Mayonnaise

6 crusty rolls

Sliced onion

¼ head iceberg lettuce

Sliced tomato

John T's
hawaiian excuse

John T Edge, food writer and executive director of Southern Foodways Alliance, will do just about anything to get a great food story, but I never really thought that he would actually go to Hawaii for a burger recipe. This burger is similar to one that he ate at Diamond Head Market and Grill. What makes it different is the addition of sugar. John T explained to me that sugar was regularly added to burgers in Ohio, and drive-ins like Swensons in Akron still put a touch of sugar in their burgers.

– ເວລ –

1. In a large bowl, using your hands, combine the chuck, onions, egg, breadcrumbs, salt, pepper, sugar, and soy sauce. Form into 6 patties about 1 inch thick. Cover with plastic wrap and refrigerate until ready to cook.

2. Light a charcoal fire or preheat your gas grill on high. Oil the grill's cooking surface. Let the coals burn down to a medium-hot fire or adjust the gas grill burners to medium-high.

3. Meanwhile, combine the sauce ingredients in a small bowl and set aside.

4. Grill the burgers for 2 to 3 minutes per side for medium or to your desired degree of doneness. Remove from the grill.

5. To assemble, spread mayonnaise on the top bun. Spread both sides of the burgers with a thin coating of teri sauce. Place the patties on the bottom buns. Top with onion, lettuce, tomato, and the crown bun. Serve immediately.

1 pound ground beef sirloin

¾ cup grated onion

1 tablespoon plus 1 teaspoon sugar

3 tablespoons soy sauce

½ teaspoon coarsely ground black pepper

1½ teaspoons toasted sesame oil

1 tablespoon plus 2 teaspoons dry sherry

2 cloves garlic, minced

Toasted and buttered hamburger rolls

2 scallions (white and green parts), thinly sliced

Korean
burgers

A New York friend, William Smith, introduced me to Korean barbecue and sweet potato vodka in a small Korean restaurant in the East Village. Korean barbecue is marinated and grilled with a sweet, salty, and tangy end result. This burger captures all those notes.

– ᏜᎧᏇᏽ –

1. In a medium bowl, using your hands, gently mix together the beef, ½ cup of the onion, 1 teaspoon of the sugar, 1 tablespoon of the soy sauce, the pepper, 1 teaspoon of the sesame oil, 1 tablespoon of the sherry, and 1 clove of the garlic. Form into 4 patties, each ¾ inch thick. Cover with plastic wrap and refrigerate until ready to cook.

2. In a small bowl, mix together the remaining ¼ cup onion, 1 tablespoon sugar, 2 tablespoons soy sauce, ½ teaspoon sesame oil, 2 teaspoons sherry, and 1 clove garlic. Set aside.

3. Light a charcoal fire or preheat your gas grill on high. Oil the grill's cooking surface. Let the coals burn down to a medium-hot fire or adjust the gas grill burners to medium-high.

4. Cook the burgers to your desired degree of doneness, 3 to 5 minutes per side for medium-rare.

5. Serve on the buns topped with the onion-soy sauce mixture and scallions.

2 pounds lean ground beef

1 green bell pepper, seeded and minced

½ cup chopped scallions (white and green parts)

3 cloves garlic, minced

2 teaspoons ground cumin

2 teaspoons dried oregano

1 teaspoon dried thyme

1 teaspoon paprika

½ teaspoon kosher salt

6 potato hamburger buns, buttered and toasted

6 slices ripe tomato

6 tablespoons sour cream (optional)

Pableaux's
cajun hamburgers

Pableaux Johnson, a food and travel writer from New Orleans, shared this recipe with me. Now I don't really think of hamburgers as Cajun, but after one bite of this, I really didn't care.

– ౿ఎలిౙఎ –

1. Light a charcoal fire or preheat your gas grill on high. Oil the grill's cooking surface.

2. Using your hands, gently combine the ground beef, bell pepper, scallions, garlic, cumin, oregano, thyme, paprika, and salt together gently in a large bowl. Shape into six ⅓-pound patties.

3. Place the patties on the grill and cook for about 8 minutes, turn, and cook another 8 minutes for medium. Adjust the time up or down for rare or well done.

4. Place one patty on each of the toasted buns; add a tomato slice and 1 tablespoon of sour cream. Serve immediately.

2 canned chipotle chiles in adobo sauce

2 pounds lean ground beef

2 teaspoons Montreal steak seasoning

5 ounces medium-sharp Cheddar cheese, cut into 4 thick slices

4 sesame seed hamburger buns

Toppings (tomato slices, red onion slices, romaine lettuce leaves, yellow mustard, mayonnaise)

Spicy
cheddar stuffed burgers

When I was in San Antonio, Texas, there seemed to be a distinct desire to put chipotle chiles in most everything. Where I really found them to be tasty was in a hamburger. So here's my burger ode to San Antonio.

– ᏮᏗᏮᏬᏯ –

1. Place the chipotles in a blender or food processor and process until smooth.

2. Using your hands, gently combine the chipotle puree, ground beef, and steak seasoning in a large bowl until well blended. Do not overwork the meat mixture. Shape into eight 4-inch patties about 1 inch thick. Place 1 cheese slice on each of 4 patties. Top with the 4 remaining patties, pressing the edges together to seal. Cover with plastic wrap and refrigerate for at least 30 minutes.

3. Light a charcoal fire or preheat your gas grill on high. Oil the grill's cooking surface. Let the coals burn down to a medium-hot fire or adjust the gas grill burners to medium-high.

4. Place the burgers on the grill and cook until the beef is no longer pink, 7 to 8 minutes per side.

5. Serve the burgers on the buns with the desired toppings.

1 pound ground beef chuck

1 small red onion, finely diced

8 slices crispy cooked bacon, crumbled

2 tablespoons Worcestershire sauce

1 jalapeño, seeded and finely diced

1 large egg, beaten

1 small, ripe avocado, peeled, pitted, and cut into ½-inch dice

Toasted sesame seed buns

Sour cream

Stuffed
guacamole and bacon burgers

I've always enjoyed guacamole and bacon burgers but thought they were incredibly messy to eat. My sister and I thought that if we could stuff cheese and onions in a burger, why not avocado and bacon? It's actually better this way and keeps all the goodness in your mouth, not on your clothes.

– ꞏꙭꙭꙭ –

1. In a large bowl, using your hands, gently combine the beef, onion, bacon, Worcestershire, jalapeño, and egg until well mixed. Gently fold in the avocado. Form the mixture into 4 patties, each about ½ inch thick. Cover with plastic wrap and refrigerate until ready to cook.

2. Light a charcoal fire or preheat your gas grill on high. Oil the grill's cooking surface. Let the coals burn down to a medium-hot fire or adjust the gas grill burners to medium-high.

3. Cook the burgers to your desired degree of doneness, 2 to 4 minutes per side for medium-rare.

4. Serve on toasted sesame seed buns, topped with a generous dollop of sour cream.

1 ½ pounds ground beef chuck

1 tablespoon Worcestershire sauce

¾ teaspoon garlic salt

1 teaspoon freshly ground black pepper

4 slices American cheese

4 buns

Condiments and garnishes of your choice

I Love
jucy lucy burgers

John T Edge loves iconic American foods. So much, in fact, he's written a series of books on the subject. While at a symposium in Natchez, Mississippi, I pestered him for his favorite hamburger recipe. "The Jucy Lucy, no doubt," exclaims John. Then he goes on to give me some history. The Jucy Lucy burger, as you might think, is basically a stuffed cheeseburger. Its most famous incarnation is at Matt's, a Powderhorn section neighborhood bar in Minneapolis. John cautions that you don't necessarily need your best Cheddar cheese here and I tend to agree. A slice of processed American cheese—you know, the kind where you have to unwrap each slice—really is the best and, as John says, "will achieve the proper fluidity." Grab some napkins, fire up your grill, and give these burgers a try.

– ༄ –

1. Combine the beef with the Worcestershire, garlic salt, and pepper in a medium bowl and mix well. Divide into 8 portions and fashion into thin, round patties, broader than the cheese slices. Place a cheese slice on 4 of the patties. Top each piece of cheese with a remaining patty. Press the edges together very well to seal. Cover with plastic wrap and refrigerate until ready to cook.

2. Light a charcoal fire or preheat your gas grill on high. Oil the grill's cooking surface. Let the coals burn down to a medium-hot fire or adjust the gas grill burners to medium-high.

3. Cook the burgers 3 to 4 minutes per side for medium or to your desired degree of doneness. Remove from the grill and place on buns, dress with your favorite garnishes and condiments, and get busy.

1 pound ground beef chuck

One 8-ounce can refried beans

Kosher salt and freshly ground black pepper

4 hamburger buns

One 15-ounce jar Cheez Whiz

½ cup finely chopped onion

Frito corn chips

Frito's
olé burger

My Dad spent 37 years with Frito Lay®, and I can assure you I've had just about every combination of things you can do with their products. We ate Frito corn chips in every way imaginable. The Frito corn chip was actually born in San Antonio in 1932, so I guess it's only appropriate that in San Antonio you can get a burger that straddles the border, throws on Cheez Whiz®, and tops the whole thing with Frito corn chips. It's different and it's delicious.

– ೲ –

1. Divide the meat into 4 even portions and shape into loose patties. Cover with plastic wrap and refrigerate until you're ready to cook.

2. In a small saucepan, heat the refried beans over medium-high heat until bubbling.

3. Light a charcoal fire or preheat your gas grill on high. Oil the grill's cooking surface. Let the coals burn down to a medium-hot fire or adjust the gas grill burners to medium-high.

4. Cook the burgers for 3 minutes per side for medium or to your desired degree of doneness. Season with salt and pepper to taste. Remove from the grill.

5. Toast the buns and spread Cheez Whiz on each half. Sprinkle a handful of onions over the heel bun and place the patty on top. Spread the patty with beans, toss a handful of Fritos on top, and cover with the crown bun. Serve immediately.

½ cup plain dry breadcrumbs

¼ cup milk

1 pound ground beef round

1 small onion, finely chopped

1 large egg

2 cloves garlic, minced

2 teaspoons ketchup

1 teaspoon sweet paprika

1 teaspoon kosher salt

½ teaspoon coarsely ground black pepper

½ teaspoon ground cumin

½ teaspoon dried oregano

8 dinner rolls

1 small can potato sticks

Lorenzo's
cuban burgers

Fritas are sold throughout Cuba at roadside stands and, of course, migrated with Cuban refugees to this country, where they can be found throughout Little Havana in Miami. *Fritas* are usually little mini burgers, almost like a slider. Highly seasoned with onion, garlic, cumin, and oregano, they are held together with a breadcrumb and milk mixture. I got this recipe from Lorenzo Monteagudo and his wife, Tracy, who left Tampa for the mountains of East Tennessee, where they have opened a small Cuban restaurant, to the delight of the folks in Jefferson County. Once you've tried one of these, you'll want three more.

– ↝↝↜ –

1. Combine the breadcrumbs and milk in a small bowl and set aside.

2. In a medium bowl, gently mix together the beef, half the onions, the egg, garlic, ketchup, paprika, salt, pepper, cumin, and oregano. Fold in the breadcrumb mixture and mix thoroughly. Form into 8 patties, each a little less than ½ inch thick, cover with plastic, and refrigerate until ready to cook.

3. Light a charcoal fire or preheat your gas grill on high. Oil the grill's cooking surface. Let the coals burn down to a medium-hot fire or adjust the gas grill burners to medium-high.

4. Put the burgers on the grill and cook to your desired degree of doneness, 2 to 4 minutes per side for medium.

5. Serve the burgers on dinner rolls, 2 per person. Top with potato sticks (yes, the kind you buy in cans) and the remaining chopped onions.

1½ pounds ground beef chuck

10 saltine crackers, finely crushed

1 cup unsweetened applesauce, drained

Kosher salt and freshly ground black pepper

Hamburger buns

Lettuce

Sliced tomato

Darrell's Mom's
detroit burgers

Darrell told me about these burgers during a photo shoot. I thought he was absolutely nuts when I heard the ingredients. But then, lo and behold, I heard a similar recipe from some folks in Lexington, North Carolina. I tried them, passed some out to my neighbors, and, much to all of our surprises, we thought they were pretty doggone good. I particularly like to use a brat-style mustard with these burgers.

– ⟨⟨◎⟩⟩ –

1. Place the beef, saltines, and applesauce in a large bowl and use your hands to thoroughly mix it all together. Form into 6 hamburger patties, about 1 inch thick. Sprinkle with salt and pepper, then cover with plastic wrap and refrigerate until ready to cook.

2. Light a charcoal fire or preheat your gas grill on high. Oil the grill's cooking surface.

3. Carefully place the burgers on the grill and cook 8 to 10 minutes. Turn and cook another 4 to 5 minutes for medium or to your desired degree of doneness.

4. Remove to a platter. Serve on buns, dressed to your liking.

2 pounds ground beef chuck

12 ounces country sausage, hot or mild, casing removed if necessary

½ cup chopped onions

2 teaspoons hot sauce

1 teaspoon dried sage, crushed

¼ teaspoon seasoned salt

¼ teaspoon freshly ground black pepper

8 hamburger buns

Lettuce

Tomato

Townsend's Famous
pig burger

If you go through Townsend, Tennessee, you might miss the Townsend Grill. It's one of those perfect dives where you know the food is going to be great. They are famous for their burgers and especially this one, and they were pleased to share the recipe with me and now with you.

– ৵৩৫৵ –

1. Combine the beef and sausage in a large bowl. Your hands are the best tools for this. Add the onions, hot sauce, sage, seasoned salt, and pepper and mix thoroughly. Form into 8 hamburger patties. Cover with plastic wrap and set in the refrigerator until ready to cook.

2. Light a charcoal fire or preheat your gas grill on high. Oil the grill's cooking surface. Let the coals burn down to a medium-hot fire or adjust the gas grill burners to medium-high.

3. Remove the pig burgers from the refrigerator. Place on the grill and cook about 8 minutes per side. Be sure these burgers are completely cooked through because of the pork.

4. Transfer the burgers to a platter, then place on buns and dress as desired with lettuce and tomato.

1 1/2 pounds ground venison

1/2 pound ground beef chuck

Kosher salt and freshly ground black pepper

A dash or two of Worcestershire sauce

The usual hamburger fixings

1. In a large bowl, using your hands, gently combine the venison and beef with the salt, pepper, and Worcestershire. Divide into 6 equal balls and shape into patties. Cover with plastic wrap and refrigerate until ready to cook.

2. Light a charcoal fire or preheat your gas grill on high. Oil the grill's cooking surface. Let the coals burn down to a medium-hot fire or adjust the gas grill burners to medium-high.

3. Remove the burgers from the refrigerator and place on the grill while still cold. This will help to keep you from overcooking them. Cook for about 8 minutes per side for medium. Add a couple of minutes per side for more doneness. Remove from the grill and eat with the usual suspects.

Allan Benton's
venison and beef burgers

When I went to Madisonville, Tennessee, to have dinner with Allan Benton and his family, I wound up with a wealth of recipes, including this one. Cook these carefully, as venison is very lean and will dry out quickly. Medium is about as far as you want to take them. The result will be a bold and flavorful hamburger that's a whole lot better for you than beef.

Allan grills on his mountain-view deck when he is not hunting leeks or smoking ham.

1¼ pounds ground pork

¼ cup finely chopped onions

1 large clove garlic, minced

1 teaspoon kosher salt

¼ teaspoon freshly ground black pepper

⅛ teaspoon cayenne pepper

¼ cup mayonnaise

½ teaspoon Tabasco sauce

3 large sweet potatoes, peeled and cut into ⅝-inch-wide sticks

3 tablespoons olive oil

Kosher salt or sugar to taste, whichever you prefer

4 hamburger buns

4 Creole or beefsteak tomato slices

4 lettuce leaves

Lafayette, LA

SERVES 4

Sandra Dey's
cajun pork burgers with grilled sweet potato "fries"

Sandra Dey of Lafayette, Louisiana, is the funniest serious person I've ever met. A consummate foodie, she develops recipes, writes food features, does nutritional analysis, and is a food stylist. I've had the pleasure of knowing Sandra both through Southern Foodways Alliance and on a trip to Umbria with a bunch of other food-crazed folks. I knew she would treat me to something special from the grill. These pork burgers have all the Cajun flavor you'll ever want and are treated with that Louisiana Tabasco kick. Don't just make the pork burgers; the grilled sweet potato fries make an outstanding side dish.

– ഏഏ –

1. Using your hands, gently combine the pork, onions, garlic, salt, and black and cayenne peppers in a large bowl. Shape into 4 patties about 1 inch thick. Cover with plastic wrap and refrigerate until ready to grill.

2. Combine the mayonnaise and Tabasco in a small bowl and mix well. Cover and refrigerate until ready to serve.

3. Parboil the sweet potato sticks in boiling salted water until almost tender but still firm, 4 to 5 minutes; drain. Brush with the olive oil on all sides.

4. Light a charcoal fire or preheat your gas grill on high. Oil the grill's cooking surface. Let the coals burn down to a medium-hot fire or adjust the gas grill burners to medium-high.

5. Place the pork patties and sweet potatoes on the grill and cook about 10 minutes per side, until the potatoes are tender and the pork is cooked all the way through. Remove from the grill and immediately sprinkle the potatoes with salt or sugar.

6. Spread the buns with the mayonnaise and top with the burgers, tomato, and lettuce. Serve with the sweet potatoes on the side.

2 pounds boneless lamb (shoulder or leg), ground twice

1/2 cup dried mushrooms, soaked in hot water to cover until soft, then drained, or 1 cup finely chopped fresh white mushrooms

1 tablespoon minced garlic

2 teaspoons minced fresh rosemary

1 tablespoon kosher salt

1 tablespoon coarsely ground black pepper

8 ounces fontina cheese, cut into 4 slices

Rosemary focaccia, lightly toasted

Tomato Mint Chutney (optional; recipe at right)

Fog City
grilled lamb burgers

The Fog City Diner in San Francisco changed the complexion of the restaurant scene. One of my favorite dishes is their grilled lamb burger filled with mushrooms, garlic, and rosemary. Even if you don't like lamb, I'll bet you'll like this. This is my take on their burger.

1. In a large bowl, gently mix together the lamb, mushrooms, garlic, rosemary, salt, and pepper. Form into 4 patties, each about 1½ inches thick. Cover with plastic wrap and refrigerate until ready to cook.

2. Light a charcoal fire or preheat your gas grill on high. Oil the grill's cooking surface. Let the coals burn down to a medium-hot fire or adjust the gas grill burners to medium-high.

3. Cook the burgers to your desired degree of doneness, 5 to 7 minutes per side for medium. After flipping the burgers the first time, place a slice of cheese on top of each to melt while they finish cooking.

4. Serve on the focaccia, topped with a spoonful of the chutney.

tomato mint chutney   MAKES 1 TO 1½ CUPS
This stuff is great with any kind of grilled lamb.

1¼ pounds ripe plum tomatoes, plunged into boiling water for 1 minute, peeled, and seeded

½ cup sugar

6 cloves garlic, minced

2 teaspoons cayenne pepper

¾ cup cider vinegar

2 tablespoons fresh mint leaves cut into thin ribbons

1 tablespoon kosher salt

¼ cup golden raisins

1. Combine the tomatoes, sugar, garlic, cayenne, vinegar, mint, and salt in a medium, heavy saucepan. Bring to a boil, reduce the heat to low, and simmer, stirring occasionally, until thickened, 15 to 18 minutes. Add the raisins and let the sauce simmer for 10 minutes more.

2. Remove from the heat and allow to cool. This will keep, tightly covered, in the refrigerator for up to 1 week.

2 pounds ground buffalo meat

2 tablespoons Worcestershire sauce

2 cloves garlic, finely chopped

3 tablespoons chopped shallots

1 cup finely diced ham

$1/3$ cup of your favorite barbecue sauce (smoked-flavored sauces don't work as well in this recipe)

1 cup shredded white Cheddar cheese

Kosher salt and freshly ground black pepper

Olive oil

Hamburger buns

Lettuce

Sliced tomato

Cheesy
buffalo burgers

I had the pleasure of working with Jane Fonda back when she was married to Ted Turner. She had just written a cookbook about healthy eating and was championing the use of buffalo. It might have had something to do with the fact that Ted had him a little buffalo ranch in Montana. This burger has been gussied up to add a bit more flavor and moisture. More and more grocery stores are handling buffalo steaks and ground buffalo meat than ever before. Specialty stores such as Whole Foods and Central Market usually carry it.

– ప౦౦ఎ –

1. Gently combine the buffalo meat in a large bowl with the Worcestershire, garlic, shallots, ham, barbecue sauce, and shredded cheese using your hands. Form into 6 patties. Cover with plastic wrap and refrigerate for about 1 hour.

2. Light a charcoal fire or preheat your gas grill on high. Oil the grill's cooking surface.

3. Remove the burgers from the refrigerator. Season with salt and pepper and drizzle with olive oil. Make certain that your grill has been lubricated and is clean. There is so little fat in these burgers that they will stick if given a chance. Place the burgers on the grill and cook for 6 to 7 minutes per side for medium-rare to medium. You don't want to overcook buffalo because it dries out. Remove the burgers to a platter. If you feel you need to cook them longer, place them in a microwave and continue to cook them in 1-minute intervals.

4. Serve with the buns, lettuce, and tomato if desired.

1 pound ground turkey breast

1 pound ground turkey

½ cup minced sun-dried tomatoes

¼ cup minced pitted green olives

¼ cup balsamic vinegar

¼ cup dry red wine

¼ to ½ teaspoon kosher salt, to your taste

¼ teaspoon freshly ground black pepper

12 thin slices Parmesan cheese (a vegetable peeler is the best tool for getting these slices)

6 focaccia rolls

2 cups baby spinach, drizzled with extra-virgin olive oil and balsamic vinegar and tossed

A Sun-Dried Tomato Note

If using dried sun-dried tomatoes, rehydrate by pouring boiling water over them and letting them sit for 20 minutes. If using oil-packed tomatoes, drain them as best you can before chopping them but don't get crazy about it; a little added oil is a good thing in this recipe.

Lynne Rossetto
kasper-influenced turkey burgers

Many of you know Lynn Rossetto Kasper as the voice behind NPR's "Splendid Table." An ultimate food professional, she has made the flavors of the Emilia-Romagna region of Italy her passion. At a conference not too long ago, she and I were complaining about our weight and wondering whether, in our next lives, if we would have perfect metabolisms. In her honor, I developed this lower-fat turkey burger with the flavors of Italy's culinary heart. If you think you don't like turkey burgers, I beg you to try this concoction. Avid haters of ground turkey find this a true joy.

– ᘛᘚ –

1. In a large bowl, using your hands, gently combine the turkey, tomatoes, olives, vinegar, wine, salt, and pepper. Form into 6 patties, about 1 inch thick. Cover with plastic wrap and refrigerate until ready to cook.

2. Light a charcoal fire or preheat your gas grill on high. Oil the grill's cooking surface. Let the coals burn down to a medium-hot fire or adjust the gas grill burners to medium-high.

3. Place the burgers on the grill and cook for about 4 minutes. Turn and cook for at least another 4 minutes but no more than 6 minutes. The turkey burgers must be thoroughly cooked but not overcooked. During the last 2 minutes, add the Parmesan cheese slices to each.

4. Remove from the grill. Place one burger in each bun. Top with the spinach mixture and serve immediately.

2 teaspoons water

2 teaspoons wasabi powder (look for this in the Asian section of most supermarkets)

½ cup sour cream

1 teaspoon Dijon mustard

1 teaspoon sugar

3 tuna steaks, about 1½ pounds total

1 large egg white, lightly beaten

1 tablespoon soy sauce

2 teaspoons sesame seeds, toasted in a dry skillet over medium heat until light brown

2 tablespoons vegetable oil

1 teaspoon salt-free Greek seasoning, like Cavenders®

6 brioche rolls or hamburger buns

Pickled ginger

Tuna Burgers
with a wasabi kick

With my first taste of the fabulous tuna burger served at Danny Meyer's Union Square Café in New York City, I became infatuated with the flavor. I've tried many combinations of tuna burgers, but I always go back to Asian flavoring ingredients. Wasabi is a wonderful side note to the tuna. Be careful not to overprocess the tuna; it should still be chunky, not a smooth paste. These tuna burgers are best served rare to medium-rare to appreciate the full flavor of the seasoning and the fish.

– ⌒⌒ –

1. In a small bowl, mix the water and wasabi powder together to form a paste. Stir in the sour cream, mustard, and sugar.

2. Light a charcoal fire or preheat your gas grill on high. Oil the grill's cooking surface. Let the coals burn down to a medium-hot fire or adjust the gas grill burners to medium-high.

3. Meanwhile, cut the tuna into large chunks, place in a food processor, and pulse just until coarsely ground. Transfer to a large bowl and stir in the egg white, soy sauce, and sesame seeds. With moistened hands, form the mixture into 6 patties, about 1 inch thick. Brush both sides of each burger with the oil and sprinkle the Greek seasoning equally over the burgers.

4. Place the burgers on the grill and cook for 2 to 3 minutes per side or to your desired degree of doneness.

5. Serve on brioche rolls or buns with the wasabi sauce and pickled ginger.

GINGER-MUSTARD MAYONNAISE

¼ cup mayonnaise

1 tablespoon Dijon mustard

1½ teaspoons peeled and finely grated fresh ginger

1 teaspoon soy sauce

SALMON BURGERS

1½ pounds salmon fillet, skin discarded and any pin bones pulled out

⅓ cup fresh breadcrumbs

2 large eggs, beaten

2 tablespoons Dijon mustard

4 teaspoons peeled and finely grated fresh ginger

2 teaspoons soy sauce

Kosher salt and freshly ground black pepper

4 hamburger buns, cut sides toasted lightly

4 thin slices sweet onion

4 slices ripe tomato

Salmon Burgers
with ginger-mustard mayonnaise

Author and Chicago food columnist Don Mauer helped me out with this recipe. I wanted a salmon burger that would hold up on the grill and capture the taste of grilled salmon fillets but without so much binder that it tasted like a school lunchroom croquette. The result is pretty darn good.

– ❦ –

1. Whisk together the mayonnaise ingredients in a small bowl.

2. Finely chop the salmon by hand, or very lightly pulse in a food processor. A chunky texture is what you want. Combine the chopped salmon with the breadcrumbs, eggs, mustard, ginger, soy sauce, and salt and pepper to taste in a medium bowl, working everything together well with your hands. Form into four 3-inch-diameter patties. Cover with plastic wrap and refrigerate for 30 minutes to firm up.

3. Light a charcoal fire or preheat your gas grill on high. Oil the grill's cooking surface. Let the coals burn down to a medium fire or adjust the gas grill burners to medium.

4. Place the burgers on the grill and cook until cooked through, about 4 minutes per side.

5. Transfer the burgers to the buns, top with the mayonnaise, onion, and tomato, and serve up.

½ cup fresh lemon juice

2 tablespoons soy sauce

¼ teaspoon minced garlic

¼ teaspoon freshly ground black pepper

¼ teaspoon hot sauce

¼ cup olive oil

Four 6-ounce fish fillets

¼ cup tartar sauce

Hamburger buns

Sliced tomato

Lettuce leaves

Sea Island
fish burger

Okay. Maybe there's no ground anything here, but this burgerlike fish preparation is wonderful nonetheless. I first enjoyed a sandwich similar to this at the old Cloister Hotel at Sea Island, Georgia, just off the coast from Savannah. The Cloister was an elegant setting, with some of the most upscale food I had ever been around. I ordered this fish sandwich or, as they called it, fish burger, thinking I was taking the food down a notch or two. Absolutely not. This recipe will please the pickiest and most gourmet person in your life.

– ~~~ –

1. Combine the lemon juice, soy sauce, garlic, pepper, hot sauce, and oil in a large zip-top plastic bag. Add the fillets, seal the bag, squish around to coat everything, and let marinate in the refrigerator for 1 hour.

2. Light a charcoal fire or preheat your gas grill on high. Oil the grill's cooking surface. Let the coals burn down to a medium fire or adjust the gas grill burners to medium.

3. Remove the fillets from the marinade; discard the marinade. Place the fillets on the grill and cook until opaque all the way through.

4. Spread tartar sauce on the buns and top with the fillets, then the tomato and lettuce and serve.

Six 6-ounce grouper fillets

1/4 cup good-quality mayonnaise

1 tablespoon lemon-pepper seasoning

1/2 teaspoon freshly ground black pepper

6 potato hamburger buns

6 tablespoons (¾ stick) unsalted butter, at room temperature and very soft

6 slices ripe tomato

6 tablespoons tartar sauce

1. Prepare a charcoal fire or preheat a gas grill on high. Oil the grill's cooking surface. Let the coals burn down to a medium fire or adjust the gas grill burners to medium.

2. Brush the grouper fillets with the mayonnaise. Sprinkle them equally with the lemon pepper and black pepper. Brush the insides of the hamburger buns with the butter.

3. Place the grouper on the grill and cook for about 5 minutes. Turn the fish and add the rolls to the grill, butter side down. Cook the fish another 4 to 5 minutes, until just opaque at the center. (With grouper, the fish starts to separate slightly into large flakes or sections when it's done.) Cook the buns until nicely toasted.

4. Place the grouper on the bottom bun, add a slice of tomato, some tartar sauce, and the top of the bun, and you are ready to eat.

Atlantic Beach, NC

SERVES 6

Robin and Brooks Tilley's
grilled grouper "burgers"

I'll have to admit that eating anything in the shadow of Cape Lookout Lighthouse at the end of Shackleford Banks, one of the Outer Banks of North Carolina, would be a delight. The setting is peaceful, and the smell of charcoal kissing fresh fish is a recipe for pure enjoyment—even if the boat that got you there came close to sinking.

Robin is my little brat sister, who has complained that I have written about all of our relatives and most of her friends but, no, not her, to which I have always replied, "When the time is right, you'll be in print." Well, the time is more than right for these impressive grilled grouper fillets in a bun.

When grilling fish, you need to remember two things. First, make sure your grill's cooking surface is clean—and I do mean *clean*. Second, don't overcook the fish. Sea bass and tilefish are good substitutes if grouper is not available.

1 pound conch meat, cut into ½-inch dice

1 tablespoon fresh lemon juice

1 medium onion, finely chopped

2 cloves garlic, minced

½ cup seeded and finely chopped red bell pepper

2 teaspoons ground allspice

2 teaspoons dried thyme

1 teaspoon Tabasco sauce

1 teaspoon Worcestershire sauce

1 teaspoon kosher salt

½ teaspoon cayenne pepper

½ teaspoon coarsely ground black pepper

½ teaspoon paprika

1 cup plain dry breadcrumbs

Hamburger buns, toasted

Bahamian
conch burgers

In the Florida Keys and the islands of the Bahamas, conch burgers are a local specialty. Conch Cupboard Luncheonette in the Dennis Pharmacy in Key West, Florida, is considered one of the best places to eat any kind of burger and has kept the tradition of conch burgers alive. This recipe is based on an ingredient list I got from a Bahamian conch fisherman. So if you're looking for something off the beaten path, here it is. If you don't live in an area where you can find conch meat fresh, specialty fish markets usually sell it frozen.

– ᕀᑅᖉᐷᐤ –

1. In a food processor, pulse together the conch, lemon juice, onion, garlic, and bell pepper. Add the allspice, thyme, Tabasco, Worcestershire, salt, cayenne, black pepper, and paprika, and pulse until combined. Scrape the mixture into a medium bowl. Add the breadcrumbs and mix well. Form into 4 patties, each ½ inch thick. Cover with plastic wrap and refrigerate until ready to cook.

2. Light a charcoal fire or preheat your gas grill on high. Oil the grill's cooking surface.

3. Place the burgers on the grill and cook until golden brown, 3 to 5 minutes per side, then serve up on toasted buns.

½ cup mayonnaise

1 clove garlic, minced

2 tablespoons chopped fresh basil

2 tablespoons olive oil

1 tablespoon balsamic vinegar

4 large portobello mushrooms, stems removed

Kosher salt and freshly ground black pepper

Ciabatta bread or pita pockets

Well-washed and torn spinach leaves for topping

Grilled
portobello and spinach burgers with basil mayonnaise

When a plain old brown cremini mushroom grows up, it becomes the delicious and steaky-tasting portobello. The folks around Kennett Square, Pennsylvania, the so-called mushroom capital of the world, like to grill their portobellos and top them with a little spinach. How healthy can you get?

– ⌒⌒⌒ –

1. Mix together the mayonnaise, garlic, and basil in a small bowl. Set aside to let the flavors develop.

2. In another small bowl, whisk together the oil and vinegar and brush over the tops of the mushrooms thoroughly. Season with salt and pepper.

3. Light a charcoal fire or preheat your gas grill on high. Oil the grill's cooking surface. Let the coals burn down to a medium-hot fire or adjust the gas grill burners to medium.

4. Cook the mushrooms until tender all the way through, 8 to 10 minutes per side.

5. Serve on toasted ciabatta bread brushed with olive oil or in warm pita pockets. Top with a dollop of the basil mayonnaise and a handful of torn spinach leaves.

8 medium portobello mushrooms, stems removed

LEMON-GARLIC MARINADE

½ cup olive oil

3 large cloves garlic, minced

½ cup fresh lemon juice

¼ teaspoon kosher salt

SHERRY WINE VINAIGRETTE

2 tablespoons extra-virgin olive oil

¼ teaspoon sherry wine vinegar

¼ teaspoon kosher salt

1 bag mesclun salad mix

4 pita pockets

Garlicky Lemon-Marinated
portobello burgers with baby greens in a pita

When I was in culinary school, portobello mushrooms were the lunch "protein" of choice. We all knew how to make them, but they were sort of a welcome relief from the overabundance of food that we had to consume. You make a simple marinade of garlic, olive oil, and lemon juice, add it to some baby greens, shove it in a pita, and you've got a filling lunch that won't slow you down.

- ᘓᗢᗱᘞ -

1. Place the mushroom caps upside down on a baking sheet.

2. Whisk together the olive oil, garlic, lemon juice, and salt, and pour it evenly over the mushrooms. Make sure the marinade pools up in the undersides of the mushrooms. Turn them a few times during their bath so that both sides get liberally coated. Marinate for at least 30 minutes at room temperature.

3. Meanwhile, in a small bowl, combine the vinaigrette ingredients and mix well. Set aside.

4. Light a charcoal fire or preheat your gas grill on high. Oil the grill's cooking surface. Let the coals burn down to a medium-hot fire or adjust the gas grill burners to medium-high.

5. Grill the mushrooms for about 5 minutes per side, longer if you want a slightly crispy crust.

6. Toss the mesclun with the vinaigrette, then serve by placing 2 mushrooms in a warm pita pocket and topping with the dressed mesclun.

¼ cup Worcestershire sauce

1 pound cheap hot dogs

1 tablespoon salt-free Cajun seasoning

Hot dog buns

Hot dog chili (try Dad's Hot Dog Chili Sauce on p. 334)

Hot dog fixings: ketchup, mustard, slaw, pickle relish, chopped onions

Would You Like Some Celery Salt with Your Chili Dog?

If you think these kids are crazy with their spiced-up hot dogs, at Wrigley Field in Chicago most of the hot dog vendors sprinkle celery salt over the dogs and onions as they are being griddled.

"Tube Steaks"
college style

Leave it to a bunch of college students in Birmingham, Alabama, to figure out a way to elevate the simple hot dog to unbelievable heights. Names have been withheld to protect these kids, who fear financial reprisal from their parents if they find out how creative they have become in the pursuit of using their meal money for other adventures.

This simply is a marinated hot dog. As the kids told me, "You would marinate a steak, why not a dog?" No need to use expensive dogs with this recipe—in fact, the cheaper the better.

– ᶜᵕᵒᵕᵕ –

1. In a small baking dish large enough to hold the dogs in a single layer, pour in the Worcestershire. Add the hot dogs and turn to coat. Let marinate while the fire is getting ready.

2. Light a charcoal fire or preheat your gas grill on high. Oil the grill's cooking surface.

3. Sprinkle the dogs with the Cajun seasoning. Place on the grill and cook for a total of about 15 minutes, until hot in the center and some crispy bits on the outside.

4. Transfer to a platter and serve on buns with chili, slaw, relish, onions, and the condiments of your choice.

Porcupine Dogs

Cooking school teacher Sheri Castle mentioned this recipe one day and I just had to include it. Her dad and uncle, who are from the mountains of Boone, North Carolina, have done this to hotdogs "all my life," says Sheri. "I remember it most from camping trips on the Blue Ridge Parkway. I'm the one who started calling them Porcupine hot dogs. And Daddy has been using the same hibachi to grill on since 1959, when he and my mom received it as a wedding present. All the parts are original. We used it outdoors whenever we could, but he also used it all winter by sitting it in the fireplace in our den and letting the smoke go up the chimney."

There is no real recipe here. Basically, you make shallow diagonal cuts all around the hot dog. The cut areas expand and get wonderfully crisp and charred as they cook, adding boatloads to the flavor of the hot dog. Try this with any dog, but it is especially good with Tube Steaks if you cut the dogs before you marinate them.

Sheri's dad with his vintage hibachi keeping an eagle eye on the porcupine dogs.

6 cheap 12-ounce beers

2 pounds fresh bratwurst

2 large onions, roughly chopped

Grainy brown mustard

Hot dog buns

Sauerkraut

1. Light a charcoal fire or preheat your gas grill on high. Oil the grill's cooking surface.

2. Pour the beer in a metal bucket or large stockpot (a bucket is preferred). Add the bratwurst and onions and set over the fire. You can also do this on the stove over medium-high heat. Cook for at least half an hour and up to 2 hours, replenishing the fire as necessary.

3. Carefully remove the pot from the heat and fish out the brats. Put them over a slow to medium fire and cook until brown and crispy, about 15 minutes, turning often.

4. Serve with grainy brown mustard on hot dog buns, with maybe a little sauerkraut.

Sunny's
wisconsin brats

Sunny McDaniel from Lake Geneva, Wisconsin, tells me this is the only way to grill brats. This procedure is sometimes referred to as a "brat fry," even though there is no oil involved. There are a couple of things Sunny wants you to know. Only use grainy brown mustard on your brats—if you use yellow mustard in Wisconsin, they will run you out of town. And heaven forbid you use ketchup on a brat, as her soon-to-be husband once did. It's a testament to her love that she went through with the wedding.

Sunny and her husband, who was foolish enough to use ketchup on a brat.

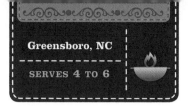
¼ cup water

5 cloves garlic, peeled

1 pound ground beef chuck

⅔ pound ground pork

1 teaspoon baking soda

1½ teaspoons kosher salt

1 teaspoon freshly ground black pepper

½ teaspoon dried thyme

½ teaspoon anise seeds

½ teaspoon dried basil

½ cup low-sodium beef broth

French fries, sliced bread, and mustard if desired

Laura Magheru's
mititei

Mititei are Romanian sausages, and Laura Magheru knows how to make them. Second-generation Romanians, she and her husband settled in Greensboro, North Carolina, to raise their family. These sausages are surprisingly good and really simple to make.

– ⟡ –

1. In a large bowl, combine the water and garlic. Crush the garlic in the water using a fork. Add the beef, pork, baking soda, salt, pepper, thyme, anise, and basil, and stir to combine well. Add the broth and mix well. For each sausage, take ⅓ cup of the mixture and roll it between the palms of your hands into a sausage shape about 4 inches long. Place the sausages in a container, cover, and refrigerate overnight for the flavors to marry.

2. Light a charcoal fire or preheat your gas grill on high. Oil the grill's cooking surface. Let the coals burn down to a medium-hot fire or adjust the gas grill burners to medium-high.

3. Place the sausages on the grill and cook for about 3 minutes per side, until cooked through. Serve with french fries, bread, and mustard, if desired.

Wood chips for smoking, soaked for
30 minutes in water

10 to 12 uncooked pork sausage links,
garlic flavored preferred, 2½ to 3 pounds
total (these should not be small breakfast
links but sausage the size of kielbasa or
bratwurst)

Olive oil as needed

2 cups red wine vinegar

1 cup water

¼ cup sugar

1 large head Savoy cabbage, cored and
thinly sliced

2 cloves garlic, thinly sliced

1 teaspoon mustard seeds

Kosher salt and freshly ground black
pepper

Brown spicy mustard

1. Set up the grill for indirect grilling (see
pp. 6–9). Oil your grill's cooking surface.

2. Add a handful of the drained wood chips
to the fire. Brush the sausages with olive
oil. Poke a few holes in each sausage with
a skewer to prevent them from blowing
up. Place them on the grill away from the
fire, put the lid down, and smoke for 1 to
1½ hours, replenishing your fuel as needed.

3. While the sausages are smoking, combine the vinegar, water, and sugar in a large
saucepan over medium-high heat. Bring
to a boil, stirring, then reduce the heat to
medium and simmer until the sugar has dissolved. Add the cabbage, garlic, and mustard
seeds, and simmer until the cabbage is soft,
usually 15 to 20 minutes. Season with salt
and pepper as needed. This can be used
immediately or kept refrigerated for up to
2 days. Bring to room temperature before
serving.

4. After the sausages have smoked, serve
them with sauerkraut and mustard.

Ralf Brehm's
smoked sausage german style with sauerkraut

The Germans had a huge influence on barbecue and smoked meats in
Texas. In many ways, I think Texans do themselves a disservice, especially
those in south Texas, by not doing a better job of promoting their smoked
sausage, which, to me, are more delightful than beef brisket.

I met Ralf Brehm in New Orleans pre-Katrina. We were at a conference
on sugar that the Southern Foodways Alliance was hosting. Ralf owns
a sign business in Houston, so food is a hobby but I found out that in
his case it's a serious and important part of his life. He originally came
to this country from Coburg in central Germany in 1949 when he was
12 years old. They were supposed to dock in New Orleans but because of
a storm wound up in Mobile. His mom didn't much like Alabama, so after
one night they jumped on the Southern Pacific Railroad and made a home
in Houston.

Ralf's smoked sausages are simple, not a lot of trouble, but all kinds of
good. He uses garlic sausage and specifically those made by Chapel Hill
Sausage Company. Most of us outside of Texas won't be able to get that
brand, but most any uncooked link sausage works perfectly. The second
time I smoked some sausages, I made a quick homemade sauerkraut to go
along with them and found that it was the perfect accompaniment, along
with spicy brown mustard.

1 pound kielbasa sausage, cut into quarters crosswise and halved lengthwise

Four 7-inch-diameter flour tortillas

$\frac{1}{2}$ cup Meredith Deeds's Pico de Gallo (p. 317) or salsa of your choice, well drained

$\frac{1}{2}$ cup guacamole

$1\frac{1}{2}$ tablespoons chopped fresh cilantro

Grilled Sausage Tacos
san antonio style

Germans and Poles have had a great presence in the state of Texas, and nowhere is that seen more than in San Antonio. This combination of sausages and Hispanic flavors works very well together. Many barbecue restaurants throughout the area serve their sausages in tortillas.

– ᥫᩣ –

1. Light a charcoal fire or preheat your gas grill on high. Oil the grill's cooking surface.

2. Grill the sausage pieces 3 inches from the heat source until well browned, about 5 minutes per side.

3. Meanwhile, wrap the flour tortillas in aluminum foil and warm them for a few minutes on the outside edge of the grill.

4. To serve, place 2 sausage halves in the center of a flour tortilla and dollop with 2 tablespoons each of pico de gallo and guacamole. Sprinkle with the cilantro, fold in half, and serve immediately.

9 the garden of eden:
grilled vegetables and fruits

Mom always said, "Eat your vegetables," and instead you probably pushed them around on your plate. ✦✦✦✦✦✦

Vegetables and fruits are now at the heart of healthy eating, yet few of us can figure out a way to get those five servings a day. Let's face it, this stuff can be boring. How many different ways can you steam asparagus? Too many times, the vegetables are an afterthought behind the protein. Well, nothing enriches the vegetable patch like a little grill time.

Vegetables are full of natural sugars just waiting to be exploited for even better flavor. Grilling can also change the way you think about vegetables that are out of season in your area. No tomato in March will ever taste as good as the dead-ripe one in late July, but with some help from the grill, it can go from flavorless to flavorful. And the fruit. I've grilled figs for years but never considered other fruit for some reason. Peaches, pears, nectarines, and pineapples develop a sumptuous taste with a little caramelization from the grill. Toast a slice of pound cake, angel food cake, or sweetened corn bread or biscuit on the grill, top it with your grilled fruit of choice, and you've got a delectable dessert of first rank in no time at all.

Nothing could be simpler than grilling vegetables. Here's one time that it's not essential to oil the grill. But it is essential to oil the vegetables. A toss in olive oil and some kosher salt and freshly ground pepper is all that's needed for a great flavor.

I like cooking sliced vegetables better than whole, so direct heat is my favorite method. Potatoes, turnips, and similar root vegetables may need some indirect heat as well as direct. You should cut your vegetables (and fruit) thick enough so that they won't fall through the grates. Trying to grill vegetables that have been cut too small is an exercise in frustration. You can also purchase a vegetable grilling basket or grilling grates with extremely small holes, but I really think most of us can get by with some sensible slicing.

Fresh, seasonal fruits and vegetables are the best choices for grilling. Grilling previously frozen fruits and vegetables is an iffy proposition. Texture is a critical factor when grilling produce, and many times the frozen stuff is soft and limp.

> ## Make Marinating a Snap
>
> A zip-top plastic bag is a fast and effective way to coat vegetable pieces. Pour your oil or marinade into the bag, add the veggies, seal, and shake.

4 hearts of romaine lettuce, cut in half lengthwise

¼ cup white balsamic vinegar

Extra-virgin olive oil for drizzling

Kosher salt and freshly ground black pepper

1 cup or more freshly shaved Parmesan cheese (use a vegetable peeler to do this)

Larry Janes's
grilled romaine

Larry Janes is from Detroit, Michigan, where he fascinates his neighbors and friends with this unusual take on salad. Occasionally he will add an anchovy or two to each serving and, for a change of pace, use *agrimato*, a lemon-infused olive oil, in place of the extra-virgin olive oil.

– ᜪᜧᜩᜪᜯ –

1. Light a charcoal fire or preheat your gas grill on high. Oil the grill's cooking surface. Let the coals burn down to a medium fire or adjust the gas grill burners to medium.

2. Douse the romaine with the vinegar over a bowl. Place the lettuce, cut side down, on the grill and cook for about 4 minutes, no more than 6 minutes. You want some char and a small amount of wilting.

3. Remove from the grill to individual salad plates. Drizzle liberally with olive oil. Season with salt and pepper and divide the cheese shavings among the servings. Serve immediately.

8 large beets, peeled and sliced into
¼-inch-thick rounds

4 large onions, sliced into ¼-inch-thick
rounds

Kosher salt and freshly ground black
pepper

Extra-virgin olive oil

Balsamic vinegar (optional)

1. Light a charcoal fire or preheat your gas
grill on high. Oil the grill's cooking surface.
Let the coals burn down to a medium fire or
adjust the gas grill burners to medium.

2. Meanwhile, place the beet and onion
slices on a baking sheet in one layer. You
may need two sheets. Generously salt and
pepper the slices on both sides, then drizzle
with olive oil.

3. Arrange the beets and onions on the
grill in a single layer. Cook, turning several
times, until the onions are soft and the beets
tender, about 15 minutes total. Adjust your
fire so as not to burn the vegetables, but
you do want some nice browning on both
the onions and the beets to bring out their
sweetness.

4. Remove the onions and beets from the
grill and put in a large bowl. Drizzle with
a little additional olive oil and toss. (While
Winnie does not do this, I've found that a
little balsamic vinegar is also good as they
are coming off the grill.) Serve as a side dish
or over lettuce as part of a salad.

Winnie Bolton's
grilled beets and onions

Winnie Bolton may be one of the most fun people I've ever met. She
was hosting a dinner for the United Arts Council for Wake County (North
Carolina), and the subject of grilling came up. "Oooh, Fred, you've got to
try my grilled beets," exclaimed Winnie and most of her neighbors agreed.
So she and her husband, Michael, planned another dinner party and we
had some outstanding fried catfish, as good as any I've had in Mississippi,
steamed oysters, and, the pièce de résistance, these grilled beets and
onions that are so simple but oh so good.

4 ears sweet corn in their husks

LOUISIANA BUTTER

1 teaspoon paprika

½ teaspoon onion powder

½ teaspoon kosher salt

¼ teaspoon dried thyme

¼ teaspoon dried oregano

⅛ teaspoon cayenne pepper

¼ cup (½ stick) unsalted butter, softened

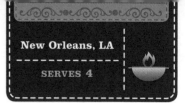

New Orleans, LA

SERVES 4

Pableaux's
cajun corn with louisiana butter

Pableaux Johnson is a true character and a true friend. A man for many seasons, he loves his New Orleans lifestyle and mourns for the changes Hurricane Katrina has caused. His recipe for corn on the cob will have you tearing up the farm stands, waiting for the first corn to come in.

– ⌖ –

1. Soak the ears of corn in cold water for at least 30 minutes, with a plate set over the top of them to keep the ears submerged. Drain.

2. In a small bowl, mix together the paprika, onion powder, salt, thyme, oregano, and cayenne. Add the butter and mash it with the back of a fork to blend the seasonings.

3. Pull back the husks on each ear of corn, leaving them attached at the stem. Remove and discard the corn silk. Spread about 1 tablespoon of the seasoned butter evenly over the kernels and use string or a thin strip of husk to tie them at the top.

4. Light a charcoal fire or preheat your gas grill on high. Oil the grill's cooking surface. Let the coals burn down to a medium fire or adjust the gas grill burners to medium.

5. Place the corn on the grill, close the lid, and cook until the kernels are tender, 25 to 30 minutes, turning 3 or 4 times. Don't worry if the husks brown or burn.

6. Remove from the grill, let cool slightly, and carefully pull the husks back. Serve as soon as possible.

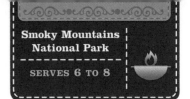
12 ears sweet corn, shucked and silked

¾ cup (1½ sticks) unsalted butter

Salt and freshly ground black pepper

1. Light a charcoal fire or preheat your gas grill on high. Oil the grill's cooking surface. Let the coals burn down to a low fire or adjust the gas grill burners to low.

2. Meanwhile, for each ear of corn, place 1 tablespoon of butter with the corn and roll it up tightly in a sheet of heavy-duty aluminum foil.

3. Place the wrapped-up ears on the grill and roast, turning occasionally, for about 1 hour. If cooking with charcoal, replenish the coals as needed.

4. Remove the ears from the grill and, when cool enough to handle, unwrap the corn, pouring the melted butter back over the corn. Season with salt and pepper and serve immediately.

Joe and company enjoy Labor Day camping.

Joe's
corn on the cob

I've done some crazy things to find great grillers for this book. One Labor Day weekend, I was near Knoxville, Tennessee, and decided to go to Elkmont Campground in the Smoky Mountains and literally nose around until something smelled fantastic. That's how I met Joe Creasman. He was cooking chicken breasts, but what caught my attention was his corn on the cob. He had wrapped it in foil and was slow roasting it for an hour. Surely it would be dry and hard, right? Absolutely not. It had more corn flavor than any I had ever tasted, with all the juiciness that you want in corn on the cob. Try this next corn season.

Grilled Garlic

Anytime you have you a grill set up for indirect heat, grill some garlic. It's simple, takes no concentration, and you can use it in endless ways, from enhancing mashed potatoes to adding depth to a sauce or dressing, or just simply to spread on a toasted baguette like butter—sweet and creamy.

Remove the loose, papery outer skin from a head of garlic, and cut off the head to expose the cloves. Drizzle a teaspoon of olive oil over the cloves, and place the garlic on a large square of aluminum foil. Fold up the sides to make a packet but not too tightly. Grill over indirect medium heat until the cloves are soft, 45 minutes to 1 hour. Remove the garlic from the grill and allow to cool, then unwrap the foil and squeeze out the cloves into a small bowl. Use immediately, or pour a thin coat of olive oil over, cover tightly, and store in the refrigerator, where it will keep for several weeks.

JALAPEÑO-CARAWAY DRESSING

1 jalapeño, seeded and chopped

2 tablespoons white wine vinegar

1 tablespoon Dijon mustard

2 teaspoons sugar

1 teaspoon kosher salt

¼ teaspoon Tabasco sauce

¼ cup olive oil

1 tablespoon caraway seeds, toasted lightly in a dry skillet over medium heat

2 teaspoons grated lime zest

---

3 leeks, trimmed to about 7 inches, split in half lengthwise, the roots trimmed, tough outer leaves discarded, and washed well

Lake Placid, NY

SERVES 6 TO 8

Friends Lake Inn

grilled leeks with jalapeño-caraway dressing

If your view of New York State is strictly the über-urbanization of New York City and the surrounding areas, you need to take a drive north past Saratoga Springs, up into the Adirondack Park. Here you'll find Lake Placid, the scene of that thrilling hockey victory in the 1980 Olympics and some of the most beautiful mountains and lake country on the continent. The area is littered with inns, bed and breakfasts, and really great small restaurants. This leek recipe from Friends Lake Inn takes what is typically a very haute French first course and spices it up. The Tabasco and jalapeño in the vinaigrette act as an excellent foil to the sweet smokiness of the grilled leeks. Don't hesitate to use these as a full-fledged vegetable beside grilled lamb, steak, or venison.

– ເຊຣຊ –

1. In a blender, process together the jalapeño, vinegar, mustard, sugar, salt, and Tabasco. With the motor running, add the oil in a slow stream and blend until smooth. Transfer the dressing to a large, shallow dish and stir in the caraway seeds and lime zest.

2. Bring a large pot of salted water to a boil, add the leeks, reduce the heat to a simmer, and cook until just tender, 7 to 10 minutes. Using tongs, transfer them to paper towels to drain. Brush the cut sides of the leeks lightly with some of the dressing.

3. Meanwhile, light a charcoal fire or preheat your gas grill on high. Oil the grill's cooking surface.

4. Place the leeks on the grill, cut side down, and cook until golden brown, 1 to 2 minutes per side. Transfer to the dish of dressing, turn to coat them, cover with plastic wrap, and let marinate in the refrigerator overnight. Bring them to room temperature before serving.

1 pound portobello mushrooms, stems removed and wiped clean

3 tablespoons olive oil

Kosher salt and freshly ground black pepper

2 tablespoons minced shallot

2 teaspoons minced garlic

½ teaspoon chopped fresh parsley

½ teaspoon chopped fresh sage

½ teaspoon chopped fresh rosemary

½ teaspoon chopped fresh thyme

1 tablespoon balsamic vinegar

2 teaspoons fresh lemon juice

Grilled
portobello hash

This mushroom concoction is based on a grilled shiitake relish that Tom Douglas serves occasionally with salmon at his restaurant Etta in Seattle, and developed by Belinda Ellis. For me, it's a little easier to grill portobellos than other mushrooms because they won't fall through the grill grates, plus they're a little less expensive than other brown mushrooms and always available. This hash is an ideal foil for grilled salmon or tuna and makes an excellent topping for a porterhouse steak.

– ◦◦◦◦◦ –

1. One by one, in a medium bowl, toss the mushroom caps with 2 tablespoons of the oil and a sprinkle of salt and pepper.

2. Light a charcoal fire or preheat your gas grill on high. Oil the grill's cooking surface. Let the coals burn down to a medium-hot fire or adjust the gas grill burners to medium-high.

3. Grill the mushrooms on both sides until cooked through, about 5 minutes total. Remove from the grill and thinly slice.

4. Heat the remaining 1 tablespoon oil in a small skillet over medium heat. Add the shallot and garlic and cook them until soft and aromatic, 2 to 3 minutes, but without color. Set aside to cool.

5. In the bowl you used to oil the mushrooms, combine them with the shallot-garlic mixture and the remaining ingredients, tossing gently to combine well. Season to taste with salt and pepper. Serve at room temperature. You can make this up to 1 day ahead, cover, and refrigerate. Bring to room temperature before serving.

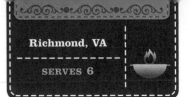

2 pounds potatoes, peeled and cut into large chunks

4 ounces feta or goat cheese, crumbled

4 scallions (white and green parts), thinly sliced

3 tablespoons chopped fresh dill or basil

1 tablespoon fresh lemon juice

1 large egg, beaten

Kosher salt and freshly ground black pepper

2 tablespoons olive oil

Grilled
potato and feta pancakes

Myra Daleng serves these wonderful "pancakes" with many grilled items, but they are especially good as a perky side for grilled white fish.

- ~ -

1. Place the potatoes in a large saucepan and cover generously with water. Salt the water and bring to a boil. Reduce the heat a little and let continue to boil until the potatoes are tender when poked with a knife.

2. Drain the potatoes, then mash them. Stir in the feta, then the scallions, dill, lemon juice, and egg until well combined. Season generously with salt and pepper. Cover with plastic wrap and chill until firm.

3. Light a charcoal fire or preheat your gas grill on high. Oil the grill's cooking surface. Let the coals burn down to a medium fire or adjust the gas grill burners to medium-high heat.

4. Meanwhile, shape the potato mixture into small balls and flatten them slightly. Brush lightly with the olive oil. Place them on a grill rack or non-stick aluminum foil on the grill and cook until browned on both sides, turning them once. Serve immediately.

2 large sweet potatoes

2 teaspoons canola oil

Kosher salt and freshly ground black pepper

FRESH ORANGE DRESSING

½ cup fresh orange juice

¼ cup rice vinegar

1 tablespoon maple syrup

¼ cup seeded and finely minced green bell pepper

¼ cup seeded and finely minced red bell pepper

1 jalapeño, seeded and finely chopped

2 scallions (white and green parts), thinly sliced

1 teaspoon peeled and finely chopped fresh ginger

¾ cup extra-virgin olive oil

Kosher salt and freshly ground black pepper

3 to 4 cups mixed salad greens

Grilled Sweet Potato Salad
with fresh orange dressing

Here is a surprising salad to serve alongside barbecue. Combine the health benefits of sweet potatoes and the fact that this potato salad is mayonnaise free and you've got a dish that is good for you as well as good tasting, especially with pork. The caramelization the potatoes get from the fire reinforces their sweet sumptuousness.

– ∽⊙⊙∾ –

1. Place the sweet potatoes in a large pot and cover with water. Bring to a simmer and cook until a knife can easily be inserted into about ¼ inch of the potato, but the center remains very firm, about 15 minutes. Drain the potatoes and let cool completely, then peel and cut into ¾-inch-thick slices. Brush with the canola oil and season well with salt and pepper.

2. Meanwhile, light a charcoal fire or preheat your gas grill on high. Oil the grill's cooking surface.

3. Place the sweet potato slices on the grill and cook for about 3 minutes, no longer than 5 minutes per side. They should still be firm but have softened. Remove from the grill to a plate.

4. In a medium bowl, whisk together the orange juice, vinegar, maple syrup, bell peppers, jalapeño, scallions, and ginger. Whisking, slowly drizzle in the olive oil. Taste for salt and black pepper.

5. Divide the greens among 6 plates. Arrange the sweet potato slices on top of the greens. Drizzle the vinaigrette over the sweet potatoes and salad and serve immediately.

1 red onion, cut into 8 wedges

5 cloves garlic, sliced

2 pounds ripe Roma tomatoes, cut in half

2 tablespoons fresh basil cut into thin ribbons

1 cup vegetable broth

1 cup heavy cream

Kosher salt and freshly ground black pepper

1 tablespoon dry sherry

Toasted croutons

Fresh basil leaves for garnish

Grilled-Roasted Tomato
basil bisque

Mississippi was once the tomato capital of the world. Donald Bender and Martha Foose offer a similar soup at their wonderful Mockingbird Bakery in Greenwood, Mississippi. Grilling tomatoes super-intensifies their flavor while adding a distinctive smoky caramelization. Add some garlic and onion to the grill and puree it all into a soup base and you have a first course that your friends and family will absolutely adore.

– ৵৯৶ –

1. Light a charcoal fire or preheat your gas grill on high. Oil the grill's cooking surface.

2. Place the onions on the grill. Equally divide the garlic slices among the tomatoes, pushing them into the flesh of the tomatoes. Place the tomatoes on the grill, cut side up. Grill the vegetables until they become soft and are beginning to char, about 10 minutes.

3. Transfer the grilled vegetables to a food processor. Add the basil ribbons, and pulse to create a smooth puree.

4. Transfer the puree to a large saucepan over medium heat, add the broth and cream, and bring to a simmer. Do not boil. Taste and season with salt and pepper. Stir in the sherry.

5. Divide the soup among 4 bowls. Top each with a crouton and basil leaf and serve immediately.

3 ribs celery, cut into 2-inch lengths

One 32-ounce bottle V-8® juice

One 16-ounce can tomato juice

3 tablespoons fresh lemon juice

1 tablespoon Worcestershire sauce

1 large clove garlic, peeled

2 teaspoons fresh thyme leaves, chopped

1 medium yellow summer squash, cut in half lengthwise

1 medium zucchini, cut in half lengthwise

1 red bell pepper, seeded and cut into 1-inch-wide strips

1 yellow bell pepper, seeded and cut into 1-inch-wide strips

2 to 3 tablespoons olive oil or as needed

1 teaspoon kosher salt or less to taste

½ teaspoon freshly ground black pepper

1 medium onion, cut into ½-inch-thick slices

2 ripe, meaty tomatoes, cut in half and seeded

Grilled Summer
vegetable soup

When you have a garden, invariably things start to pile up on you. While I like gazpacho, I can only deal with so much of it over the summer. When I had an abundance of yellow squash and peppers, I decided to try to make a grilled soup—something I could put together, stash in the refrigerator, and heat up for a quick lunch. I think you'll like the delicate smoky flavor that permeates this soup, and I know you'll enjoy the convenience of having it made ahead. If you wish, you could totally puree it for an excellent first course at your next dinner party.

– ᕲᔓᕬᑎ –

1. Combine the celery, V-8, tomato juice, lemon juice, Worcestershire, garlic, and thyme in a food processor and process until smooth. Pass the puree through a fine sieve to remove any fibers. Pour 1 cup of the tomato mixture into a bowl and set the remaining mixture aside.

2. Light a charcoal fire or preheat your gas grill on high. Oil the grill's cooking surface. Let the coals burn down to a medium-hot fire or adjust the gas grill burners to medium-high.

3. Toss the squash, zucchini, and peppers in the olive oil to coat. Remove and season with the salt and pepper. Place on the grill and cook until just charred and tender, 2 to 3 minutes per side. Place the onion slices on the grill and cook for about 4 minutes per side. Remove from the grill and set aside.

4. Take half the tomatoes, zucchini, squash, onions, and peppers and place in a food processor. Add the 1 cup of the tomato juice mixture and process until smooth. Transfer to a soup pot. Cut the remaining tomatoes and grilled vegetables into small dice and stir into the puree. Taste and season with salt and pepper, if desired. Bring to a slow boil over medium heat, then reduce the heat to low and simmer until heated through, about 5 minutes. Serve immediately or you can also serve at room temperature or chilled. This will keep refrigerated for several days or frozen for several months.

4 medium-large zucchini, ends trimmed and cut in half lengthwise

4 medium-large yellow crookneck squash, ends trimmed and cut in half lengthwise

5 tablespoons olive oil

Kosher salt and freshly ground black pepper

½ cup chopped fresh basil

⅓ cup freshly grated Parmesan cheese

2 tablespoons balsamic vinegar

1 tablespoon sesame seeds (optional), toasted in a dry skillet over medium heat until light brown

Grilled
zucchini and summer squash salad

This is my vegetarian friend Katrina Moore's favorite way with grilled squash. The balsamic vinegar, basil, and Parmesan make this a yummy dish. I sprinkled some toasted sesame seeds for a little texture.

– ᥫ᭡ –

1. Light a charcoal fire or preheat your gas grill on high. Oil the grill's cooking surface. Let the coals burn down to a medium fire or adjust the gas grill burners to medium.

2. Place the zucchini and squash on a large baking sheet and brush all over with 3 tablespoons of the oil. Sprinkle with salt and pepper.

3. Transfer the vegetables to the grill and cook until tender and brown, about 10 minutes total, turning them a few times. Transfer them back to the baking sheet and let cool.

4. Cut the zucchini and squash on the diagonal into 1-inch-wide pieces. Place in a large bowl. Add the basil, Parmesan, vinegar, and the remaining 2 tablespoons oil and toss to blend. Season to taste with salt and pepper, sprinkle with the toasted sesame seeds, if using, and serve immediately.

1 cup extra-virgin olive oil

¼ cup dry white wine

2 tablespoons finely minced garlic

1 cup chopped fresh basil

¼ cup chopped fresh rosemary

1 teaspoon kosher salt

1 teaspoon freshly ground black pepper

1 pound fresh asparagus, woody ends removed

4 medium zucchini, cut lengthwise into ¼-inch-thick slices

4 yellow squash, cut lengthwise into ¼-inch-thick slices

4 red bell peppers, cut in half, cored, and seeded

4 small eggplant, cut crosswise into ¼-inch-thick slices

Katrina's Mixed
vegetable grill

Vegetarian Katrina Moore gave me this recipe. She grills veggies all the time in Birmingham, Alabama, where she is a theater major at Samford University. Grilling vegetables adds an essence that makes even vegetable haters want seconds. If you end up with any leftovers, do like Katrina does and puree them, then add some vegetable stock and make a hearty soup with an incredible smoky essence—you can also add the puree to pasta sauces. Crumbled goat cheese sprinkled over the hot vegetables is a nice addition.

– ⁊◌◌◌⁊ –

1. Combine the oil, wine, garlic, basil, rosemary, salt, and pepper in a large bowl, cover, and let the flavors develop for 2 hours.

2. Add the vegetables and toss to coat. Let sit at room temperature for another hour.

3. Light a charcoal fire or preheat your gas grill on high. Oil the grill's cooking surface.

4. Remove the vegetables from the marinade and place on the grill in a single layer. Cook each until well marked and tender. The asparagus and squash will take about 5 minutes, and the peppers and eggplant about 10 minutes. When done, transfer to a platter and serve.

2 ripe nectarines

¼ cup good farmer's cheese

2 to 3 teaspoons white truffle honey

1. Halve the nectarines and remove the pits. Cut a small slice from the bottom of each half so it can sit flat.

2. Light a charcoal fire or preheat your gas grill on high. Oil the grill's cooking surface.

3. Place the nectarine halves on the grill, cut side down. Cook for 4 minutes, turn, and cook 3 minutes longer.

4. Transfer the fruit to dessert plates. Fill each empty pit with a tablespoon of the farmer's cheese. Drizzle with the truffle honey and serve immediately.

Jill's

grilled nectarines with truffle honey

From Sonoma, California, Jill Hunting writes about all things truffles. Not the chocolate variety, but those black and white fungi that are ridiculously expensive but oh so good. Jill also has an interest in wine and the foods of Northern California. This is a simple fruit dessert that you could also enjoy as an afternoon snack or, if you're really nuts about truffles, breakfast.

4 firm, ripe pears

3 tablespoons unsalted butter, melted

3 tablespoons ginger jam (look for this in specialty-food stores)

Vanilla ice cream for serving

Pound cake or corn bread (optional)

Grilled Pears
with ginger jam and ice cream à la jennifer

This delicious and easy dessert from Jennifer Linder McGlinn of Pennsylvania features the rich flavor of caramelized grilled pears and spicy ginger jam. It pairs beautifully with vanilla ice cream, but Jennifer said, "If you want to take the dessert a bit further, serve it with grilled thick slices of pound cake or sturdy corn bread." I had it with the corn bread and think that's the way to go. The sweet corn is a perfect foil for the other flavors.

– ⌒⌒⌒ –

1. Light a charcoal fire or preheat your gas grill on high. Oil the grill's cooking surface. Let the coals burn down to a medium-hot fire or adjust the gas grill burners to medium-high.

2. Slice the pears in half lengthwise. Core the pears, leaving the stems intact, and brush all over with the melted butter. Place the pears, cut side down, on the grill and cook until caramelized, 5 to 10 minutes. Remove from the grill and brush the cooked side with the ginger jam.

3. Set each pear half on a dessert plate and serve with ice cream and a slice of pound cake or corn bread if desired.

4 firm but ripe pears

Confectioners' sugar

Hot fudge sauce

Vanilla ice cream (optional)

Fred's
simple grilled pears with hot fudge sauce

Pears, along with pineapples, are my favorite fruits. I developed this dish as part of a complete meal from the grill. The sugar dusting caramelizes, and the pears become a fabulous base for ice cream and chocolate.

– ∾⦿⦿∾ –

1. Light a charcoal fire or preheat your gas grill on high. Oil the grill's cooking surface. Let the coals burn down to a medium fire or adjust the gas grill burners to medium.

2. Meanwhile, quarter the pears vertically and core them. Lightly dust the pears all over with the confectioners' sugar and tap off any excess.

3. Place the pears on the grill and cook until tender, 5 to 7 minutes, turning once. Remove the pears to serving dishes. Drizzle with the hot fudge sauce and top with a scoop of vanilla ice cream, if desired, and serve immediately.

GRILLED PINEAPPLE

1 fresh pineapple, peeled, cored, and cut into ½- to ¾-inch-thick slices

1/2 cup orange liqueur (I used Grand Marnier®)

½ cup water

½ teaspoon ground ginger

1 teaspoon ground cinnamon

1 cup firmly packed light brown sugar

PINEAPPLE POUND CAKE

One 16-ounce box pound cake mix

¾ cup pineapple juice

1 teaspoon vanilla extract

2 large eggs

Melted butter (optional)

Vanilla or coconut ice cream

2 tablespoons chopped fresh mint

Belinda's
grilled pineapple with pound cake

Belinda Ellis was as excited as I had ever seen her. "I've been working on a recipe and came up with this kicking grilled pineapple." She emailed me the recipe and I gave it a try. Now, I love pineapple, so this was going to have to be really good—it was. I threw in the pound cake to make a full-fledged dessert.

– ᘓᘐᘐᘑ –

1. Place the pineapple slices in a large zip-top plastic bag. In a medium bowl, whisk together the liqueur, water, ginger, cinnamon, and brown sugar. Pour into the bag, seal, turn upside down to coat the slices, and let marinate at room temperature for at least 30 minutes, but 2 hours is better.

2. Preheat your oven to 350°F. Lightly coat a 9x13-inch baking dish with nonstick cooking spray. In a large bowl, combine the pound cake ingredients and, using an electric mixer on low speed, mix for 30 seconds. Increase your speed to medium-high and mix for 3 minutes. Pour into the prepared pan and place in the oven. Bake for 16 to 20 minutes, until a toothpick inserted into the center comes out clean. Place on a cooling rack for 10 minutes, then turn the cake over onto the rack. Slice or use a 2½- to 3-inch biscuit cutter for a more interesting presentation.

3. Light a charcoal fire or preheat your gas grill on high. Oil the grill's cooking surface. Let the coals burn down to a medium-hot fire or adjust the gas grill burners to medium-high.

4. Just prior to grilling, drain the marinade into a saucepan. Bring to a boil. Reduce the heat and cook until the liquid has reduced, 4 to 5 minutes. Keep warm.

5. Place the pineapple slices on the grill. Be careful because the alcohol in the marinade may make the fire flare. Cook for about 4 minutes per side, until soft and nicely browned. Remove to a platter.

6. Toast the pound cake slices on the grill for a couple of minutes per side, brushing the cake first with melted butter. Place cakes on individual plates and divide pineapple slices over them. Drizzle with the reduced marinade. Top with ice cream and mint, and serve.

10 rub me, sauce me, throw me on the grill:

rubs, sauces and marinades

Rubs, sauces, and marinades change the merely good into the outstanding. ✑✑✑✑✑✑

These are your core seasonings, along with what the outdoor fire brings to the flavor of your food. They are also the way to **personalize your food** to the tastes and wants of your family and friends.

Rubs are seasoning blends that almost always include salt, sugar, some pepper, and additional spices. Everybody I met has a variation on a rub. Some have one for every type of grilling. I don't know how many "secret sauces" and marinades I tried to cajole from people. These are the very secrets that people want to keep to themselves and what makes this whole experience fun—even among the pros. Throughout this book you will find many rubs, sauces, and marinades that are embedded in a particular recipe. Many of these recipes were so good or versatile that I

thought they needed to be separated out for you to consider with grilling ideas that may be floating around in your culinary brain. You will also find styles from all over the country, those that have made a particular barbecue famous. Kansas City sweet to Eastern North Carolina vinegar to a salmon glaze from the North-west, you will have the tools to make your grilling experience great.

Rubs, sauces, and marinades also team up with **salsas, marmalades, and chutney-like side flavorings** that can be just as key to your final product as the initial seasoning. Be sure to check them out as well, for use with a recipe you might develop.

So go to your spice cabinet and pantry and blend up some greatness.

2½ tablespoons dark brown sugar

2 tablespoons paprika

2 teaspoons dry mustard

2 teaspoons onion powder

2 teaspoons garlic powder

1½ teaspoons dried basil

1 teaspoon ground bay leaf (about 1 leaf)

¾ teaspoon ground coriander

¾ teaspoon ground savory

¾ teaspoon dried thyme

¾ teaspoon freshly ground black pepper

¾ teaspoon freshly ground white pepper

⅛ teaspoon ground cumin

Kosher salt to taste

Combine all the ingredients in a small bowl. This will keep in an airtight container at room temperature for up to 4 months.

Goode's
bbq beef rub

MAKES ¾ CUP

Houston pitmaster Jim Goode shared this recipe for his barbecue beef rub. Now, whether it's exactly what he uses, I'm not willing to swear to. It doesn't really make much difference—this rub is great on any form of beef, lamb, or smoked turkey. If you're doing some long cooking, you might want to check out his mop recipe (see p. 301) as well.

---

5 tablespoons McCormick® Pork Rub

1 tablespoon Lawry's seasoned salt

1 tablespoon Emeril's® Essence

1 teaspoon garlic powder

Pinch of cayenne pepper or more to taste

Combine all the ingredients in a small bowl. This will keep in an airtight container at room temperature for up to 1 month.

Cam Campbell's
georgia dry rub

MAKES ½ CUP

This is the rub Cam and his brother-in-law Steve Lyons use on smoked pork. It also makes a good rub for ribs or chicken.

Making Your Own

If you want to play with making a rub, think in terms of some sort of salt, a sugar, pepper, a savory spice such as granulated garlic or onion, maybe something like cinnamon or nutmeg, and chili powder. Start from there and put something together that tastes good to you.

½ cup kosher salt

⅓ cup Chinese five-spice powder

¼ cup granulated sugar

¼ cup firmly packed light brown sugar

¼ cup freshly ground black pepper

½ teaspoon cayenne pepper

Combine all the ingredients in a small bowl until well combined. This will keep in an airtight container at room temperature for about 1 month.

Chinese
asian-style rub

MAKES ABOUT 1½ CUPS

Trying to duplicate the deep, sweet, and exotic notes that you find in true Chinese barbecue is difficult. This rub sets a flavor base that gets you on your way. Use it on ribs, chicken, pork loin and shoulder, and especially duck.

½ cup paprika

¼ cup kosher salt

¼ cup sugar

¼ cup chili powder

¼ cup ground cumin

¼ cup granulated garlic

2 tablespoons freshly ground black pepper

2 tablespoons dry mustard

Combine all the ingredients in a medium bowl. This will keep in an airtight container at room temperature indefinitely, Mike says.

Mike's
magic dust

MAKES 2½ CUPS

Mike Mills is a friend I don't get to see enough. Mike is from apple country in southern Illinois. He is a past Memphis in May champion, started the apple-wood smoking craze, and has security clearance for Air Force One—President Clinton insisted on having his ribs. I met Mike at the Big Apple Barbeque Block Party—a gathering of pitmasters showing New York City what good 'que is all about. I picked at Mike for two years to get this recipe. Check out Mike's own book on barbecue, *Peace, Love and Barbeque*.

¼ cup firmly packed light brown sugar

¼ cup paprika

1 tablespoon pure chile powder, like ancho or chipotle

1 teaspoon cayenne pepper

1 teaspoon kosher salt

Cracked black peppercorns to taste

Combine all the ingredients in a small bowl. This will keep in an airtight container in the refrigerator for several weeks.

My Quick, Simple, and Wonderful
all-purpose rub

MAKES ABOUT ½ CUP

Rubs don't have to be complicated to be good. Start with this one and you can build it out in any direction you choose, although most folks I've given this recipe use it just as I gave it to them. It pairs nicely with ribs, chicken, and turkey.

---

1 cup full-bodied dry red wine

1 cup fruity extra-virgin olive oil

3 cloves garlic, minced

1 bay leaf, crumbled

1 tablespoon minced fresh oregano or 1 teaspoon crumbled dried

Kosher salt and freshly ground black pepper to taste

Combine all the ingredients in a medium bowl, blending well.

Red Wine
marinade/sauce

MAKES 2 CUPS

I prefer making this marinade with merlot or zinfandel for lamb and cabernet sauvignon or pinot noir for beef, venison, or duck. After marinating and basting the meat, strain the remaining marinade into a saucepan and boil over high heat until reduced to a syrupy sauce, then spoon the sauce over the grilled meat. Four hours is perfect for most meats in this marinade, but overnight won't hurt anything.

3/4 cup fruity extra-virgin olive oil

1 1/2 tablespoons minced fresh thyme
or 1 1/2 teaspoons crumbled dried

4 bay leaves, crumbled

3 cups grated yellow onions (do this in a
food processor)

1 tablespoon minced garlic

1/2 cup fresh lemon juice

Kosher salt and freshly ground black
pepper to taste

Tabasco sauce to taste

Combine all the ingredients in a large bowl
and mix well.

Onion
marinade

MAKES ABOUT 4 1/4 CUPS

This quick marinade is good on just about any cut of beef or lamb. You'll taste
the onion flavor in just an hour, but an overnight bath in it is even better.

---

4 cups beef broth, preferably homemade

2 bay leaves

1 teaspoon dried oregano

2 tablespoons unsalted butter

1/4 cup chopped onions

1/4 cup chopped celery

1/4 cup seeded and chopped green
bell peppers

1/4 cup minced garlic

2 tablespoons Goode's BBQ Beef Rub
(p. 298)

1/2 teaspoon dry mustard

1/2 teaspoon kosher salt

1/2 teaspoon freshly ground white pepper

1/2 teaspoon freshly ground black pepper

1/4 teaspoon cayenne pepper

Finely grated zest of 2 lemons

Juice of 2 lemons

2 tablespoons soy sauce

2 tablespoons white wine vinegar

1 tablespoon olive oil

1 tablespoon toasted sesame oil

1 pound sliced bacon, finely chopped

Goode's Garlicky
bacon fat bbq mop

MAKES ABOUT 6 CUPS

Jim Goode liberally mops his beef briskets with this concoction as they cook,
which may be the secret of his successful barbecue joint in Houston. I like
mopping a whole turkey with it while I'm smoking it. And don't be bashful
about using it with any of the smoked beef rib recipes in this book.

– ꙮ –

1. Bring the broth to a boil in a medium saucepan. Reduce the heat to a
simmer and add the bay leaves and oregano.

2. Meanwhile, melt the butter in a large nonstick skillet over medium-
high heat. Add the onions, celery, bell peppers, garlic, beef rub, mustard,
salt, peppers, and cayenne, and cook, stirring, until the vegetables begin to
brown, 5 to 7 minutes. Then add this to the beef broth and stir to combine.
Stir in the lemon zest and juice, soy sauce, vinegar, olive oil, and sesame oil.

3. Cook the bacon in the same skillet until soft but not crisp, about 6 minutes. Add the bacon and any rendered fat to the broth mixture and continue
simmering until reduced by one-fourth, 45 minutes to 1 hour. Adjust the seasonings and baste away. Any unused sauce will keep in an airtight container
in the refrigerator for up to 3 days or it can be frozen indefinitely.

½ cup (1 stick) unsalted butter,
cut into pieces

1 cup Worcestershire sauce

Juice of 2 lemons

3 tablespoons ketchup

1 tablespoon prepared yellow mustard

Melt the butter in a small saucepan over medium heat. Add the remaining ingredients and stir until the butter completely melts and everything is well combined. Continue cooking for about 10 minutes. This will keep in an airtight container in the refrigerator for up to 1 week.

Dad's Special
barbecue sauce

MAKES ABOUT 2 CUPS

At my parents' house, my dad cooked a steak every Saturday night that I can possibly remember. Occasionally he would throw this sauce together and baste the steaks as he cooked them. It also got used on chicken from time to time. It's an old-fashioned sauce that still rings true today. It's mighty fine on hamburgers too.

---

2 cups cider vinegar

½ cup water

½ cup ketchup

2 tablespoons light brown sugar

1 tablespoon hot sauce

2 teaspoons red pepper flakes

2 teaspoons kosher salt

1 teaspoon freshly ground pepper

In a medium bowl, whisk all the ingredients together until the sugar and salt dissolve. Use immediately or store in an airtight container in the refrigerator for up to 4 weeks. Shake before using.

Lexington-Style
north carolina barbecue sauce

MAKES ABOUT 3 CUPS

In North Carolina, vinegar is the base of choice for barbecue sauces, but even then it gets a little complicated. There are two styles of 'que in the state—Eastern and Lexington (which starts in the Piedmont and stretches west)—and the favorite party game of the devotees of each is to slam the lack of good taste of the other. Here, sugar and ketchup (the hallmarks of Lexington-style sauce) make an appearance with the vinegar. In the areas where Lexington-style barbecue is king, this sauce is called a "dip." Use it to toss with pulled pork and as a table sauce.

2 quarts White House® cider vinegar

¼ cup kosher salt

2¼ cups sugar

1½ tablespoons red pepper flakes

1½ teaspoons cayenne pepper

1½ teaspoons freshly ground black pepper

One 24-ounce bottle Heinz® ketchup

Bourbon as necessary for the cook

1. Pour the vinegar in a large pot. Add the salt, sugar, red pepper, cayenne, black pepper, and ketchup. Take the ketchup bottle and fill it one-quarter of the way up with water. Swirl to rinse the remaining ketchup out of the bottle and pour it into the sauce. Stir the mixture very well. At this point, Frank suggests pouring your first glass of bourbon.

2. Place the pot over medium heat. Cooking the dip slowly is as important as the ingredients. Never let the dip come to a boil and stir often. After about 30 minutes, slowly increase the heat to medium-high. A red foam will begin building on the top. The dip is done when the foam completely covers the surface. Immediately remove from the heat. Let cool and pour into containers. This will keep in airtight containers in the refrigerator for up to 6 weeks.

Frank Bell's Original
lexington-style barbecue dip

MAKES ABOUT 2 QUARTS

I never had the good fortune of meeting Frank Bell. He died when he was 82 but from what I hear he was a proud old Southern boy, like most of the World War II generation. When he came back from the war with a Purple Heart, five Bronze Stars, and one Silver Star, he began working in the local barbecue restaurants around Lexington, North Carolina. Later in his career, he helped many folks open their own barbecue joints in and around Lexington. Frank became famous for his sauce, which really is the gold standard of Lexington dips. Most barbecue restaurants in that area water their sauce, but this is the way you want to make it for yourself when you're smoking pork shoulders, turkeys, and chickens. A "dip" is a table sauce as much as anything and lives strictly in the Piedmont of North Carolina. Like most North Carolina sauces, this one is thin. You would also toss this sauce with pulled pork or shredded chicken or turkey.

When Frank was dying of cancer, a close friend, Barry Ferguson, asked him for the recipe. When I got ahold of it, the instructions were a handful of this, a handful of that, shakes of this, and shakes of that. I think I've gotten it pretty close to Frank's original. Warning: This makes a lot of sauce, enough for the entire neighborhood.

What You Don't Know. . .

Frank occasionally deviated from this recipe. For instance, if people wanted the sauce a little hotter, he added more red pepper. And then he had the "church women's" version—Frank had little use for the church women because they thought he drank too much. But whatever they may have thought, they would always ask him to make his dip when they were having barbecue for their Wednesday night meetings. The secret ingredient in the church women's sauce? Half a cup of bourbon that he stirred in at the end. In 40 years of Wednesday night meetings, they never knew.

1 1/2 cups cider vinegar

1 1/2 cups distilled white vinegar

1 tablespoon sugar

1 tablespoon red pepper flakes

1 tablespoon freshly ground black pepper

1 tablespoon kosher salt

1 tablespoon hot sauce

Combine all the ingredients in a medium bowl. Use it immediately or store in an airtight container, where it will keep up to 2 months at room temperature.

Eastern North Carolina-Style
barbecue sauce

MAKES ABOUT 3 CUPS

This is the one that will pucker your taste buds and that most folks want to try when they come to North Carolina. You can toss this sauce with your pulled pork, serve it on the side, or use it as a "mop" or basting sauce while smoking a pork shoulder or whole hog.

---

1 1/2 cups yellow mustard, like French's®

1/2 cup firmly packed light brown sugar

1/2 cup tomato paste

5 tablespoons cider vinegar

1 tablespoon Worcestershire sauce

1/2 teaspoon cayenne pepper

1/2 teaspoon granulated garlic

1/2 teaspoon freshly ground black pepper

Combine all the ingredients in a medium, heavy saucepan over medium heat and cook, stirring, until the sugar dissolves. Remove from the heat and let cool. This will keep in an airtight container in the refrigerator for a couple of weeks.

South Carolina
mustard barbecue sauce

MAKES ABOUT 2 CUPS

Maurice Bessinger has made quite a name for himself, and some of it even involves barbecue. If you are ever near West Columbia, make sure you pay a visit to his Piggie Park. Bessinger is famous for the mustard sauce he uses for his pulled pork. Maurice wouldn't part with the recipe, but Charlestown barbecue expert Jimmy Hobgood gave me the guidelines.

1 cup ketchup

One 8-ounce can tomato sauce

1 cup firmly packed light brown sugar

1 cup cider vinegar

1 tablespoon Worcestershire sauce

1 tablespoon paprika

1½ teaspoons onion salt

1 teaspoon dry mustard

1 to 2 teaspoons hot sauce or to taste

Combine all the ingredients in a medium saucepan over low heat, stirring, until the sugar melts and everything is well blended. Let simmer about 10 minutes. This will keep in an airtight container in the refrigerator up to 2 weeks.

East Tennessee-Style
barbecue sauce

MAKES ABOUT 3½ CUPS

When East Tennessean Belinda Ellis challenged North Carolina barbecue at a Southern Foodways Alliance meeting, I decided to go and sample what she thought was great barbecue. What I found was barbecue that was similar to North Carolina's Lexington style, with two exceptions. First, they cut their meat in slightly larger chunks and second, ketchup has found its way into their sauce in a *big* way. That being said, East Tennessee barbecue sauce is darn good stuff. Thicker than North Carolina sauce, it still has that characteristic Carolina vinegar bite. Not only is this good for smoked pork shoulder, but it's also much better than any store-bought sauce for chicken and other pork cuts. You can use it as a basting sauce for chicken and ribs during the last 10 minutes or so of their cooking time, toss it with pulled pork barbecue, and use as a table sauce.

So What's the Deal with Cross-Contamination?

The last thing you want at a cookout is folks getting sick. Cross-contamination is a problem you want to avoid. We all know we shouldn't put a cooked protein on the same plate that the raw came to the grill on. But what about basting and such? A marinade that raw items have been sitting in can be used again if you bring it to a boil and cook it for a couple of minutes. But don't cross-contaminate by dipping your brush into that boiled sauce, then basting raw meat that you just put on the grill. Make sure you sear all the surfaces of the meat before you start basting or saucing. And stop basting a few minutes before the food is done, to give anything that might still be lurking in your basting sauce time to get cooked. Heat is always your best defense against food-borne illness.

2 cups ketchup

1/2 cup firmly packed dark brown sugar

1 tablespoon paprika

2 to 3 teaspoons hot sauce to your taste

1/2 cup (1 stick) unsalted butter

1/2 cup cider vinegar

1 clove garlic, mashed

1/4 cup prepared chili sauce

1 to 2 teaspoons kosher salt to taste

Combine all the ingredients in a medium, heavy saucepan over low heat. Stir and cook until the sugar and butter melt and the sauce is well blended. Simmer, stirring frequently to prevent sticking and burning, for about 20 minutes. Use warm or cold. This will keep in the refrigerator in an airtight container for up to 2 weeks.

Kansas City
sweet and hot barbecue sauce

MAKES ABOUT 3 1/2 CUPS

This is a thick, sweet sauce that is typical of those found in the Kansas City area, with the exception of Arthur Bryant's Barbeque Restaurant's famous (and secret) orange-colored sauce. It is what most Americans think of as a barbecue sauce. Make this once and I doubt you will buy store-bought sauces again. It's great on ribs, chicken, and turkey.

---

1 cup water

3/4 cup firmly packed light brown sugar

3/4 cup ketchup

1/2 cup distilled white vinegar

1/2 cup Worcestershire sauce

1/2 cup (1 stick) unsalted butter

1/4 cup fresh lemon juice

1 1/2 tablespoons dry mustard

1 1/2 tablespoons chili powder

1 1/2 tablespoons paprika

1 tablespoon kosher salt

2 teaspoons cayenne pepper

Combine all the ingredients in a large saucepan over medium heat, stirring, until the butter melts and the sugar dissolves, about 8 minutes. Use immediately or let cool and store in an airtight container in the refrigerator for up to 2 weeks.

Kansas City
spicy barbecue sauce

MAKES 4 CUPS

Use this sauce on ribs, pork chops, pork tenderloin, even grilled chicken. It doesn't pack a lot of heat, just a nice little kick. This isn't nearly as sweet as other Kansas City sauces, but it's still true to the thick and clingy traditions of the city.

¾ cup ketchup

¼ cup canola oil

1 small onion, chopped

2½ tablespoons sugar

2 tablespoons Worcestershire sauce

2 tablespoons cider vinegar

1½ tablespoons molasses

1½ teaspoons spicy brown mustard

1½ teaspoons Tabasco sauce

1 clove garlic, chopped

Kosher salt and freshly ground
black pepper

1. Combine all the ingredients in a blender and process until smooth.

2. Pour into a medium, heavy saucepan and bring to a boil over medium heat. Reduce the heat to low and simmer, stirring often, for 20 minutes, until slightly thickened. Use immediately, or this will keep in an airtight container in the refrigerator for a couple of weeks.

Mock Ridgewood
barbecue sauce

MAKES 2 CUPS

"This is what ketchup will taste like in heaven," stated University of North Carolina professor and sociologist John Shelton Reed. John is a scholar of Southern culture, but to me he's also a scholar of Southern barbecue. This recipe is based on the barbecue sauce served at The Ridgewood, a barbecue restaurant in Piney Flats, Tennessee. The recipe was a closely guarded secret, which really means that everybody in town has been trying to break the code. A bunch of women from nearby Kingsport, Tennessee, gathered to create their own Ridgewood-like barbecue sauce. This is the result, and I personally couldn't care less what the barbecue sauce tastes like at Ridgewood. This one is just too good. I hope John is right because this sauce will certainly make heaven a better place. While this sauce was originally used with pork, there's not much that it's not good with—try it on chicken, beef, even brushed on steaks.

¼ cup bourbon

¼ cup soy sauce

¼ cup Dijon mustard

¼ cup ketchup

¼ cup firmly packed light brown sugar

3 scallions (white and green parts), finely chopped

1 tablespoon minced fresh rosemary

Combine all the ingredients in a small bowl until well mixed. This will keep in an airtight container in the refrigerator for up to 2 weeks.

Bourbon
barbecue sauce

MAKES ABOUT 1¼ CUPS

Southern based with some international twists, this sauce is good with just about everything—game birds like quail and duck, beef, lamb, even burgers.

One 14-ounce bottle ketchup

One 14-ounce bottle distilled white vinegar

$\frac{1}{2}$ cup prepared yellow mustard

$\frac{1}{2}$ cup Worcestershire sauce

$\frac{1}{2}$ cup vegetable oil

$\frac{1}{4}$ cup Louisiana hot sauce

2 tablespoons plus 2 teaspoons sugar

2 tablespoons freshly ground black pepper

2 tablespoons kosher salt

5 dashes Tabasco sauce

Juice from $\frac{1}{4}$ lemon (pitch the rind into the sauce as well)

1 small onion, grated

Steve Marcember's 100-Year-Old
family-secret bbq sauce

MAKES ABOUT 4 CUPS

A 100-year-old secret comes to an end with this recipe. This is a great sauce in the style of southeast Georgia and northern Florida. Mustard is a key ingredient, but it does not dominate as in South Carolina's sauces. This sauce is fabulous with any smoked pork, longer-cooked chicken, and even as a mop sauce for ribs.

– මෙම –

Combine all the ingredients in a large saucepan over medium heat and simmer for 10 to 15 minutes. Remove the lemon rind. Serve hot or at room temperature. This will keep in an airtight container in the refrigerator for up to 2 weeks.

$\frac{1}{2}$ cup hoisin sauce

$\frac{1}{2}$ cup ketchup

$\frac{1}{4}$ cup store-bought barbecue sauce, such as Bull's Eye

$\frac{1}{4}$ cup sake or rice wine

$\frac{1}{4}$ cup dry sherry

1 tablespoon rice vinegar

1 tablespoon peeled and minced fresh ginger

2 large cloves garlic, minced

1 teaspoon Chinese Asian-Style Rub (p. 299) or Chinese five-spice powder

Combine all the ingredients in a medium, heavy saucepan. Place over medium heat and bring to a boil slowly. Reduce the heat to medium-low and simmer until the sauce thickens and the flavors have mingled, 5 to 10 minutes. Let the sauce cool and use immediately or pour into airtight containers and store in the refrigerator, where it will keep for several months.

East Meets West
barbecue sauce

MAKES ABOUT 2 CUPS

This recipe pulls from many Asian cultures, but the hoisin sauce is the key ingredient. Hoisin is made from soybean paste, garlic, sugar, and Asian spices and is easy to find in supermarkets today. It is the main ingredient in those wonderful lacquered meats we enjoy in Chinatown. Use it with Chinese Asian-Style Rub for a layered Asian flavor.

Tarting Up Store-Bought Sauce

Don't be afraid to doctor up a bottled sauce. First, cut it with some liquid—for more kick, add vinegar or maybe a Pepsi or 7-Up to give it some sweetness. You might want the depth that Worcestershire brings. Maybe a little chili powder or yellow mustard. Stay away from liquid smoke because it can be strong and salty.

1 cup chopped yellow onions

1 cup granulated sugar

1 cup ketchup

½ cup distilled white vinegar

¼ cup prepared yellow mustard

½ teaspoon freshly ground black pepper

½ cup homemade white sauce (recipe follows) or pepper gravy mix prepared as the package suggests

Combine all the ingredients in a medium saucepan over medium heat and slowly bring to a boil. Reduce the heat slightly and cook until thickened, about 10 minutes, stirring occasionally. Thin with a little water if it gets too thick. Serve on anything your heart desires. This will keep in an airtight container in the refrigerator for up to 3 weeks.

white sauce

1 tablespoon butter

1 tablespoon all-purpose flour

½ teaspoon salt

⅛ teaspoon black pepper

⅔ cup whole milk

Melt the butter in a small saucepan. Whisk in the flour, salt, and pepper. Slowly whisk in the milk. Bring almost to a boil and cook until thick, about 5 minutes.

Virginia Pruitt's Original Perfect Barbecue Sauce
with fred's tasty mistake

MAKES ABOUT 2 CUPS

When I first tested what is now called Virginia Pruitt's Original Perfect Barbecue Sauce, I made a mistake. The old handwritten recipe called for 4 tablespoons "W sauce" and down below there was a white sauce recipe. My conclusion was that W sauce was the white sauce. But no, W sauce was Worcestershire sauce, and it was pure happenstance that the white sauce recipe was even on that piece of paper. Well, the thing is that I like it both ways, so you can choose whichever one suits you.

I have tried this on ribs, brisket, smoked pork butt, and grilled chicken, all with fabulous results. I've also found that using a black pepper-based gravy mix instead of the white sauce shortcuts the process slightly, and I like the additional flavor it brings to the pot.

1 cup chopped yellow onions

1 cup sugar

1 cup ketchup

½ cup cider vinegar

¼ cup prepared yellow mustard

¼ cup Worcestershire sauce

½ teaspoon freshly ground black pepper

In a medium saucepan over medium-high heat, combine all of the ingredients. Bring to a boil, stirring, then reduce the heat to a simmer and cook until slightly thickened, about 10 minutes. Use immediately or let cool and refrigerate, where it will keep in an airtight container for up to 3 weeks.

Virginia Pruitt's Original Perfect
barbecue sauce

MAKES ABOUT 2 CUPS

Virginia Pruitt of Bonner Springs, Kansas, is way too modest to proclaim this sauce great or perfect; it's just good. This is a family recipe that has roots in several states, plus a little experimentation over its 50-year history. Ms. Pruitt got the recipe from her aunt-in-law, Ruth Reed, who lives in Denver. The original version came from Ruth's mother, who was brought up in Kentucky. The sauce is a great blend of sweet, tart, and tang—it can be used for basting during the last 10 minutes or so of cooking and is an outstanding table sauce. I have tried this on ribs, brisket, smoked pork butt, grilled chicken, and tossed with pulled pork, all with fabulous results.

2½ cups ketchup

1⅓ cups Worcestershire sauce

¾ cup cider vinegar

¾ cup fresh lemon juice

1½ cups firmly packed light brown sugar

¾ cup (1½ sticks) unsalted butter

¼ cup paprika

¼ cup kosher salt

1 tablespoon dry mustard

2 medium onions, chopped

4 cloves garlic, minced

Rachel's
barbecue sauce

MAKES 8 CUPS

My neighbor, Rachel Thomas, makes this marvelous sauce that she uses on chicken (see Robin and Rachel's Grilled Barbecued Chicken Breasts on p. 150). But don't stop there—try it on ribs and pork chops, even shrimp.

- ⋐⊚⥾ -

Combine all the ingredients in a large saucepan and bring to a simmer over medium heat, stirring until the brown sugar and salt dissolve. Reduce the heat to medium-low and simmer gently for 10 minutes. Use immediately or let cool, then store in the refrigerator in an airtight container, where it will keep for several months.

1 pound (2 sticks) plus 1 tablespoon unsalted butter

6 tablespoons finely minced shallots

Kosher salt and freshly ground black pepper

¼ cup Jack Daniel's sour mash whiskey

6 tablespoons sauce Robert

1. Melt 1 tablespoon of the butter in a non-stick sauté pan over medium heat. Add the shallots, lightly season with salt and pepper, and cook for about 1 minute. Off the flame, add the Jack Daniel's. Return to the heat and bring to a simmer. Reduce the heat to medium-low and let the liquid cook until the pan is almost dry, about 10 minutes. Remove from the heat and let cool.

2. Place the remaining 1 cup butter in a food processor. Add the cooled shallot mixture and the sauce Robert and process until smooth and well combined. Transfer to a stainless-steel bowl and cover with plastic wrap. Leave the sauce at room temperature if using the same day or refrigerate in an airtight container for up to 1 week, letting it come to room temperature before serving.

Almost the Trellis
steak sauce

MAKES ABOUT 2½ CUPS

The Trellis Restaurant has long been the keystone of fine dining in Williamsburg, Virginia. Their take on steak sauce is rich and bold and relatively easy to make. At the restaurant they actually baste their steaks as they cook them with this sauce, then also serve it on the side. Don't hesitate to use this sauce on any cut of beef—it's especially good on a classic hamburger.

Sauce Robert is available in 6-ounce bottles under the Escoffier™ brand in most gourmet and fancy food stores. If you have difficulty finding it, you can substitute 3 tablespoons tomato paste. The steak sauce won't be as deep in flavor, but it will still be very tasty. I wouldn't recommend making your own sauce Robert, unless, of course, you're knee deep in sous-chefs.

---

2 tablespoons water

2 tablespoons tamari or low-sodium soy sauce

2 tablespoons Worcestershire sauce

¼ cup pineapple juice

1 tablespoon dry sherry

Pinch of ground ginger

Garlic salt to taste

Homemade
teriyaki sauce

MAKES ABOUT ½ CUP

I don't use store-bought teriyaki sauce because I think it's too salty and invariably the whole dish gets oversalted. A food-styling associate from Japan, Motiko, shared this recipe for homemade teriyaki.

– ୭୭୭୭ –

Combine all the ingredients in a small saucepan over medium-high heat. Bring to a boil, reduce the heat to medium-low, and simmer for about 10 minutes, until just slightly thickened. This will keep in an airtight container in the refrigerator for about 1 week.

¼ cup Thousand Island dressing (I use the refrigerated type)

2 tablespoons French dressing

2 tablespoons good-quality mayonnaise

2 tablespoons sweet pickle relish, drained

1 tablespoon finely grated onion, rinsed with hot water to tame the flavor

1 teaspoon sugar

1 teaspoon distilled white vinegar

Kosher salt to taste

Combine all the ingredients and mix well. Refrigerate for at least 30 minutes to let the flavors develop. This will keep in an airtight container for about 2 weeks.

Your Own
special sauce

MAKES ABOUT ½ CUP

Most people think that McDonald's[SM] Big Mac® Special Sauce is Thousand Island dressing. I taste something a little more complex. This is my concoction, which I believe tastes closer to Mickey D's. Make it your special sauce. By the way, it's good on roast beef and deli sandwiches like pastrami and corned beef. Try this sauce on smoked brisket, too.

⅓ cup packed fresh mint leaves

¼ cup rice vinegar

3 tablespoons light corn syrup

2 cloves garlic, minced

2 tablespoons water

1 tablespoon soy sauce

1 tablespoon toasted sesame oil

Generous pinch of red pepper flakes

Combine all the ingredients in a blender and process until smooth. Transfer to a bowl and let stand 1 hour at room temperature for the flavors to develop. This can be made 1 day ahead and refrigerated in an airtight container. Bring to room temperature before serving.

Mint Chili
dipping sauce

MAKES ABOUT ⅔ CUP

Cooling mint and the bite of dried red peppers blend to make a wonderful dipping sauce for straight-up grilled shrimp and fish or instead of the usual peanut sauce with a chicken satay. This sauce was originally served to me as a dipping sauce for pot stickers in a Vietnamese restaurant in what has become New York's true Chinatown: Flushing, Queens. Great with the pot stickers, it's 10 times better with something grilled.

½ cup seasoned rice vinegar

½ cup tamari or low-sodium soy sauce

1 tablespoon sugar

3 tablespoons minced garlic

1 tablespoon red pepper flakes

¼ cup toasted sesame oil

2 tablespoons minced fresh cilantro

1 tablespoon chile oil

Whisk all the ingredients in a small bowl until the sugar melts. This will keep in an airtight container in the refrigerator for about 2 weeks.

Sweet and Sour
dipping sauce

MAKES 1½ CUPS

This smoky, spicy dipping sauce has layers upon layers of flavor. Use it with anything that has an Asian flare. It's especially good with South of the Border-Pacific Rim Chile-Marinated Chicken Breasts (p. 151), turkey, or pork.

¾ pound fresh poblano chiles or yellow bell peppers

2 teaspoons vegetable oil

2 cloves garlic, chopped

1 cup chopped onion

1 cup low-sodium chicken broth

Kosher salt

1. If you have a gas stove, roast the peppers over the open flame of one burner, holding them with tongs; with electric, stick them under a preheated broiler or roast them on a hot grill. You want the skins to be blistered and have brown patches. Transfer to a plastic bag, seal, and let sit about 20 minutes to loosen the skins. Peel the peppers, cut off the tops, discard the seeds, then chop them.

2. In a medium skillet, heat the oil over medium-low heat, add the garlic and onion, and cook, stirring, until softened, about 3 minutes. Stir in the broth and peppers and simmer 1 minute. Transfer to a blender and process until smooth. Season with salt. Keeps for about 1 week.

Poblano
chile sauce

MAKES ABOUT 2 CUPS

Carolyn Taylor, a photographer buddy from Port Chester, New York, has taught me volumes about how to effectively use chiles. She heads off to the mountains of New Mexico every chance she gets for a little mountain climbing and a lot of chile eating. Just five years ago, a poblano chile was hard to find outside of a specialty-food store. Now most grocery stores routinely carry them, which is great.

Poblanos are not about heat but flavor. They are earthy and rich. I like to make this sauce and keep it in a jar in the refrigerator, where it lasts for about 2 weeks. It adds an extra bonus brushed on to simply grilled chicken breasts, white fish, even pork.

2 pounds ripe plum tomatoes, cut in half and seeded

3 tablespoons canola oil

1 large onion, finely chopped

4 cloves garlic, minced

3 tablespoons cider vinegar

2 tablespoons firmly packed light brown sugar

½ teaspoon ground allspice

¼ teaspoon ground cumin

¼ teaspoon ground nutmeg

1. Set your grill for either direct or indirect heat. You will get more smoke flavor with indirect, but either way the result is delicious.

2. In a large bowl, toss the tomatoes with 1 tablespoon of the oil until well coated. Place them, cut side down, on the grill, and cook until they are wrinkled, have some black spots from the fire, and are soft, about 15 minutes over direct heat, 30 to 45 minutes over indirect heat.

3. Transfer the tomatoes to a food processor and pulse into small bits.

4. In a medium skillet over medium heat, heat the remaining 2 tablespoons oil. Add the tomato pulp and the remaining ingredients and cook, stirring occasionally, until thickened, 25 to 30 minutes.

5. Let cool, then chill before using. This will keep in an airtight container in the refrigerator for up to 2 weeks.

Smoked
ketchup

MAKES 1 CUP

You want superior ketchup? Then try this recipe. My James Beard Award-winning chef buddy, Ben Barker, regularly grills and smokes tomatoes to enrich their flavor at his restaurant Magnolia Grill, in Durham, North Carolina. I took a cue from him and a couple of ketchup recipes to bring you this great condiment. It is worth the effort. For even better flavor, make it with a mixture of heirloom tomatoes. Smoking the tomatoes in advance, when you've already got the grill going, is a good way to go.

Ben Barker and his wife, Karen.

¼ cup olive oil

3 cups chopped onions

6 cloves garlic, minced

2 tablespoons seeded and minced jalapeño

3½ pounds ripe tomatoes, seeded and chopped

6 tablespoons red wine vinegar

1½ tablespoons sugar

½ cup chopped fresh cilantro

Kosher salt and freshly ground black pepper

Verla's
spicy tomato jam

MAKES ABOUT 3 CUPS

My gourmet neighbor in Manhattan, Verla Gabriel, shared this recipe with me one spring weekend. She had made it as a change of pace from mint jelly for her Easter leg of lamb. I have found out that this stuff is good with grilled fish, pork, chicken, even beside a crab cake. Sometimes it's not the protein but what's served with it that makes a superior dish.

- ⌒⌒⌒⌒ -

1. Heat the oil in a large, heavy pot over medium heat. Add the onions and cook, stirring, until softened, about 8 minutes. Add the garlic and jalapeño and cook, stirring, for 4 minutes. Add the tomatoes, vinegar, and sugar, and cook until almost dry, stirring frequently, about 40 minutes.

2. Stir in the cilantro. Season to taste with salt and pepper. Let cool. This will keep in an airtight container in the refrigerator for up to 2 days.

---

2 cups whipping or heavy cream

2 large egg yolks

2½ tablespoons prepared mustard of your choice

2½ tablespoons all-purpose flour

½ cup (1 stick) unsalted butter, cut into pieces

½ cup chopped onions

Juice of 1 lemon

¼ teaspoon dried tarragon

½ teaspoon dried parsley flakes

Pour the cream into a medium, heavy saucepan. Add the remaining ingredients and whisk to combine. Place the saucepan over low heat and cook, stirring, until the mixture thickens, about 5 minutes. Serve warm.

Dodie's
salmon cream sauce

MAKES 2½ CUPS

Dodie Scott is a crew member on the fishing vessel *Sabrina*, which operates out of Noyo Harbor in Fort Bragg, California. This cream sauce is excellent over grilled or pan-seared salmon fillets or steaks.

1 ripe mango, peeled and cut off the seed into ½-inch dice

1 papaya, peeled, seeded, and cut into ½-inch dice

1 pint strawberries, hulled and quartered

2 tablespoons sugar

1 red Serrano chile or jalapeño, seeded and minced

2 tablespoons minced fresh mint

In a medium bowl, stir together the mango, papaya, strawberries, sugar, and chile. Let stand for 10 minutes, then stir in the mint and serve.

Fred's
spicy fruit salsa

MAKES ABOUT 2 CUPS

This interesting fruit salsa thrills my cooking classes no matter where I am. It's excellent with simply grilled chicken or fish, literally lighting up the dish. The mint, which you add at the last minute, adds a sweet fresh-ness. If you want, a tablespoon of chopped shallots can be added. If you can't find the papaya, stir in a cup of diced fresh pineapple. This salsa should make you right happy.

---

3 tablespoons olive oil

1¼ pounds red or yellow onions, finely chopped (about 4 cups)

2 jalapeños, seeded and minced

2 tablespoons honey or sugar

3 to 4 tablespoons red wine vinegar, to your taste

¼ cup water

Kosher salt and freshly ground black pepper

Jalapeño-Onion
marmalade

MAKES ABOUT 2 CUPS

Cooked onions will enhance almost any dish. I also threw in some jalapeño for a little kick and extra heat and to offset the sweetness of the sugar in the onions, but it's really the red wine vinegar that brings everything together. You can serve this with pork, fish, or veal that have been sea-soned either in an Asian manner or have more of a Southwest sensibility. Heck, you can eat this with a fork by itself.

– ⋙⋘ –

In a large, heavy skillet, heat the oil over medium heat, add the onions, and cook, stirring a few times, until softened, about 5 minutes. Add the jalapeños and cook, stirring, 1 minute. Add the honey and cook, stirring, 1 minute. Add the vinegar and simmer, stirring, until almost all the liquid is evaporated. Add the water and simmer, stirring, until the mixture is slightly thickened and the onions are very tender, about 10 minutes. Sea-son with salt and pepper to taste. This will keep in an airtight container in the refrigerator for up to 2 days. Reheat before serving.

3/4 pound tomatillos, husked and rinsed

1/4 cup packed fresh cilantro leaves

1 clove garlic, peeled

Kosher salt

3 ripe avocados

Juice of 1 lemon

1. Bring a medium saucepan full of salted water to a boil. Add the tomatillos, reduce the heat to medium, and let simmer until tender, 8 to 10 minutes. Transfer with a slotted spoon to a bowl and let cool.

2. In a food processor or blender, process the tomatillos with the cilantro, garlic, and salt to taste until smooth. Transfer the mixture to a medium bowl.

3. Halve and pit the avocados, then chop the flesh. Add it to the tomatillo mixture, and sprinkle it with the lemon juice. Taste and adjust the flavor with additional lemon juice and/or salt.

Sunspot-Inspired Tomatillo
guacamole salsa

MAKES ABOUT 2 CUPS

Up the hill from the old city in Knoxville, Tennessee, lies the University of Tennessee. There's always one unique restaurant around every college or university that serves classic fare updated. Sunspot is that restaurant in Knoxville. As soon as you're seated, they bring out a basket of warm tortilla chips and an absolutely awesome tomatillo salsa. I took my cue from that salsa, added in some mashed avocado, and came up with what most folks think is a fabulous topping for hamburgers, grilled skirt or hanger steak, or even fish that has a little Southwestern seasoning. Cool with a kick, it ain't bad with tortilla chips.

– ᥱᥕᗜᥫᥕ –

Smoky Tomatillo Guacamole Salsa: For a smoky change of pace, skip the boiling water step and slice the tomatillos in half. Put them on a hot grill, cut side down, cook for 3 minutes, turn, and cook another 3 minutes, until the tomatillos are soft but still hold their shape. Continue with the recipe. The charred skin of the tomatillos adds another dimension to an already great salsa.

---

1 pound ripe tomatoes, seeded and chopped

1/2 cup chopped red onions

1/4 cup packed chopped fresh cilantro

1/4 cup fresh lime juice

2 small cloves garlic, minced

1 1/4 tablespoons seeded and minced jalapeño or serrano chiles

Kosher salt

Combine the tomatoes, onions, cilantro, lime juice, garlic, and jalapeño in a medium bowl; toss to blend well. Season to taste with salt. Let stand at least 30 minutes at room temperature for the flavors to develop. This is best eaten fresh.

Meredith Deeds's
pico de gallo

MAKES ABOUT 2 CUPS

This is a required accompaniment with Meredith's fish tacos (p. 223), but don't limit its use to that. Any grilled item with a little south-of-the-border flair will welcome this on the side. Try grilling tuna with just salt and pepper, and then spoon some of this over.

11 sassy sides and winning endings

What's a glorious grilled or barbecued centerpiece without some equally great companions?

And some foods cry out for particular sides. Lexington-style barbecue requires red slaw. Memphis ribs want baked beans. I wouldn't think of serving Jean Lynn's Kansas City-style brisket without her potato salad. Don't even consider trying a Southern barbecue recipe without washing it down with sweet tea. And I don't know many of us who would pass on a sweet note to end a meal. Whatever your tastes, there's something in these pages to make it even better.

This chapter is full of nongrilled items, but don't overlook the possibilities that abound in the grilled vegetables and fruits chapter (p. 278).

6 regular-size tea bags

⅛ teaspoon baking soda (a good pinch)

2 cups boiling water

1½ to 2 cups sugar (if you are new to sweet tea, start with 1¼ cups)

6 cups cold water

Ice for serving

1. In a glass measuring cup or ceramic teapot large enough to accommodate the boiling water, place the tea bags and baking soda. Pour the boiling water over the tea. Cover and let steep for 15 minutes.

2. Remove the tea bags, being careful not to squeeze them (squeezing the bags adds bitterness).

3. Pour the concentrate into a 2-quart pitcher and add the sugar. Stir until almost dissolved. Stir in the cold water.

4. Let cool, then chill and serve over ice.

Fred's
sweet tea

MAKES 2 QUARTS

No self-respecting barbecue house would ever stop serving sweet tea. Most, for many years, gave no option, *but* sweet tea and the righteously committed still only serve the sugary brew. In Georgia, the state assembly considered a law that all restaurants in the state serve sweet tea. And sweet it is. A visitor to the South once commented "that it made his teeth hurt."

Why so sweet? I always thought it was to cut the vinegar-based barbecue sauce or round out the fried flavor of our favorite foods. Start with this mix if your sauce is vinegar based. Use less sugar as your sauce becomes sweeter and thicker.

3 cups fresh blackberries

7 cups cold water

1 cup sugar

1 cup fresh lime juice (from 6 to 8 limes)

Ice for serving

Blackberry
limeade

MAKES ABOUT 2 QUARTS

This is a good recipe to have during the summer. It's especially refreshing and special for people who tend not to drink alcohol at your cookout. It sips nicely and it goes with food well. But in case you want a little libation, 1/2 cup vodka doesn't hurt this recipe at all. Don't like or can't find blackberries? Raspberries work just as well.

– ⌁⌁ –

1. In a blender, puree the blackberries with 1 cup of the water. Strain through a fine sieve. Set aside.

2. Combine the sugar and 1 cup of the water in a small saucepan and bring to a boil. Reduce the heat to medium and simmer until reduced to 1 cup, about 15 minutes. Remove from the heat and let cool.

3. In a pitcher, combine the blackberry puree with the sugar syrup, lime juice, and the remaining 5 cups cold water, stirring until well combined. Refrigerate until chilled. Serve in tall glasses over ice.

3/4 cup orange-flavored vodka

2 cups Dole® Orange-Pineapple-Banana Juice

1/4 cup cranberry juice cocktail

Combine all the ingredients in a pitcher and pour over 4 ice-filled glasses.

Carolina's
the carolinian

SERVES 4

Carolina Spissu, who shared her Argentinean-style steak on p. 38, wants to make sure you have something refreshing to drink while the meal cooks.

Three 32-ounce cans pork and beans, drained

2 pounds country sausage, browned and crumbled

2 medium onions, cut in half and thinly sliced into half-moons

1 cup dark corn syrup

1 cup firmly packed light brown sugar

¼ cup prepared yellow mustard

2 teaspoons Worcestershire sauce

3 teaspoons dry mustard

1. Preheat your oven to 350°F.

2. Pour the pork and beans in a 9x13-inch baking dish. Add the sausage and onions and stir to mix. Pour in the corn syrup, brown sugar, prepared mustard, Worcestershire, and dry mustard. Stir to blend throughout the beans.

3. Bake for at least 1 hour; 1½ hours is better. Cooking the beans the day before and reheating for about 30 minutes is the best way to get great flavor.

Martha and Fred's
fabulous baked beans

SERVES 8 TO 10 OR MORE

My neighbors have been after this recipe for years and when I finally gave it up, it took on a life of its own. The recipe has been passed on to friends and relatives in North Carolina, South Carolina, Maryland, Tennessee, Indiana, and even to Texas—Houston to be exact. After I published it in my newspaper column, it became the second most requested recipe, after my ribs.

When I found out about Houston, I laughed. Here was a recipe that had come full circle—literally. I wish I could claim this recipe as my own creation, but alas, I can't. In my recipe files, it's called "Martha's Baked Beans," after Martha Sanderson. Martha's husband, David, and their family had moved to North Carolina from Houston. David and I were in the same Indian Princess tribe with our daughters many moons ago. During that first fall of tribal activity, the "Little Hummingbirds" tribe was off to its required overnight camping trip at Jordan Lake. Martha had sent these beans to have with our hamburgers and hot dogs. They were absolutely the best I'd ever eaten, and I begged for the recipe, which Martha generously supplied. She couldn't take credit for them either, as they came from a relative in Houston.

One warning about this recipe, or any you have that everybody loves—once you part with it, find something else to bring to the party 'cause the rest of the crowd will be calling dibs, especially on these beans.

One 1-pound package dried cannellini beans

3 cloves garlic, peeled

1 medium onion, quartered

2 bay leaves

1/3 cup olive oil

2 tablespoons fresh lemon juice

1/2 cup chopped fresh parsley

Kosher salt and freshly ground black pepper

Tuscan
white beans

SERVES 8

This is a straightforward Italian side dish. It's wonderful with the Sliced Steak with Radicchio and Parmesan on Arugula (p. 36) and any of the Mediterranean-based lamb dishes. Try this in place of a baked potato for your next rib-eye steak experience or grilled veal chop. The beans are also marvelous under simply grilled fish or those with a Mediterranean flair.

– ᘓᐧᐧᐧᐧᐧ –

1. Soak the beans overnight in cold water to cover.

2. Drain and place in a Dutch oven with the garlic, onion, bay leaves, and water to cover by 2 inches. Bring to a boil, reduce the heat to medium-low, and simmer, covered until tender, 30 to 45 minutes.

3. Drain and discard the garlic, onion, and bay leaves. Toss with the olive oil, lemon juice, and parsley, and season to taste with salt and pepper. Serve at room temperature.

1 pound dried pinquito, pinto, or small red beans

2 strips thick-cut apple wood-smoked bacon, chopped

½ cup chopped smoked ham

1 clove garlic, finely chopped

¾ cup canned tomato puree

¼ cup prepared chili sauce

1 tablespoon sugar

1 teaspoon dry mustard

1 teaspoon kosher salt

Skip Skipworth's
santa maria-style beans

SERVES 8 TO 10

If you're having Santa Maria barbecue, you got to have Santa Maria-style beans. To be authentic, the dish should be made with pinquito beans, which are unique to the Santa Maria Valley in California. Some gourmet stores carry them, but you can easily substitute pinto beans, even though they're almost twice the size of the pinquitos. Small red beans also work well. If you want a change of pace from baked beans or are looking for something interesting to serve with a brisket dinner, give this recipe a try.

– ℰℴℊℴ –

1. Rinse the beans and remove any foreign material. Place them in a large bowl and add enough water to cover by 2 inches. Soak overnight.

2. Drain the beans, place in a large saucepan or Dutch oven, and add enough fresh water to cover by 2 inches. Bring to a boil, then reduce the heat to a simmer, cover, and cook until tender, about 2 hours. The exact cooking time will depend on the age of the dried beans—the older the beans, the longer it takes.

3. While the beans cook, heat the bacon and ham in a small skillet over medium heat until both are browned, stirring a few times. Add the garlic and cook for 1 minute. Stir in the tomato puree, chili sauce, sugar, mustard, and salt. Remove from the heat.

4. Drain all but about 1 cup of the cooking liquid from the beans. Stir the sauce into the beans and place back over medium heat. Cook until heated through. Serve hot.

Two 15.5-ounce cans field peas or two 10-ounce packages frozen field peas, defrosted

3 large ripe tomatoes, sliced

3 medium green bell peppers, seeded and cut into ¼-inch-thick rings

3 large white onions, thinly sliced

½ cup freshly grated Parmesan cheese

6 bacon slices (I like thick-cut apple wood smoked)

Kosher salt

Cayenne pepper

Henry Mayer's
new orleans-style field pea casserole

SERVES ABOUT 8

Henry Mayer was a close friend of Marcelle Bienvenu. Henry and his wife and Marcelle and her husband, Rock, hung out in great bars and restaurants from Lafayette to New Orleans. His field pea casserole is great with almost any kind of barbecued meat or fish and especially good with Henry's Barbecue Crabs (p. 241).

– ఇౚౕఴ –

1. Preheat the oven to 400°F.

2. Pour a single layer of peas into a 9x13-inch baking dish, then make a layer of tomato slices, bell pepper rings, and onion slices. Repeat the layering until all the vegetables are used up.

3. Sprinkle the top evenly with the cheese, and arrange the bacon slices over all. Season with salt and cayenne. Cover with aluminum foil and bake for 1 hour.

4. Remove the foil. Turn the oven up to broil and place the casserole under the broiler until the bacon is crisp. Serve hot.

CORN BREAD

¼ cup (½ stick) unsalted butter, melted, plus extra for buttering the pan

1 cup all-purpose flour (White Lily preferred)

¾ cup medium-ground yellow cornmeal

½ cup finely shredded pepper jack cheese

1 teaspoon baking powder

1 teaspoon kosher salt

2 large eggs

1 cup milk

3 tablespoons honey

PUDDING

1 tablespoon unsalted butter, plus extra for buttering the pan

1 cup thinly sliced onions (about ½ large onion)

¾ cup grated dry jack or Parmesan cheese

2 teaspoons chopped fresh parsley

½ teaspoon chopped fresh rosemary

½ teaspoon chopped fresh thyme

2 cups heavy cream

4 large eggs

1 teaspoon kosher salt

½ teaspoon freshly ground black pepper

Belinda's
corn bread pudding

SERVES 6

I asked Belinda Ellis, who heads the test kitchen for White Lily® Flour Company, to develop a decadent "something" to go with barbecue and grilled foods. She took very much to heart the word decadent and came up with this corn bread pudding, which is rich in taste, wonderful in texture, and beautiful on a plate. There's no humbleness to this side dish, and you can serve it with anything from pulled pork to grilled lobster.

– ୧ଡ଼ଡ଼ –

1. Preheat the oven to 425°F. Butter an 8-inch square baking dish. Combine the flour, cornmeal, cheese, baking powder, and salt in a large bowl. In a medium bowl, whisk together the eggs, milk, and honey. Add the wet ingredients to the dry ingredients, stirring until just combined. Add the melted butter and stir into the mixture. Pour into the prepared pan and bake until a toothpick comes out clean, 15 to 20 minutes. When cool enough to handle, cut a chunk of it into 1-inch cubes; you only need 2⅔ cups for this recipe. Enjoy the rest of it warm.

2. To make the pudding, preheat the oven to 350°F. Put the corn bread cubes in a buttered 8-inch square baking dish. Set aside.

3. Heat the 1 tablespoon butter in a small skillet over low heat and cook the onions very slowly until soft and golden brown, at least 20 minutes, stirring occasionally. Remove from the heat. Scatter the onions, cheese, and herbs over the corn bread cubes. Whisk together the heavy cream and eggs with the salt and pepper in a medium bowl and pour over the cubes. Let sit for 10 minutes so the corn bread absorbs some of the custard. Bake until set and golden, about 40 minutes. Serve hot.

Make-Ahead Notes

The corn bread can be made and stored in the freezer, covered tightly, for a few weeks. The onions can be caramelized a day ahead and stored, covered, in the refrigerator. The corn bread pudding can be baked a day in advance and stored in the refrigerator, covered. Before serving, reheat it, covered with aluminum foil, in a preheated 375°F oven until warmed through, 35 to 40 minutes.

3 tablespoons olive oil

1 large onion, thinly sliced

¼ cup seeded and finely diced red bell pepper (optional)

5 medium squash, thinly sliced

Kosher salt and freshly ground black pepper

Tony Inscore's
old-fashioned panned squash

SERVES 6

If you've been looking through the pork chapter, you've already run across Tony's exceptional ribs. He always serves this squash with the ribs and they blend perfectly. It's really a forgotten method to many of us. Simply caramelize some onions and cook the squash along with them. This dish will complement most any kind of grilled pork and is wonderful with grilled fish and chicken as well.

– ༄༅ –

In a large skillet over medium-high heat, heat the oil, then add the onions, tossing to combine with the oil. Reduce the heat to medium and cook for about 15 minutes, stirring occasionally, until lightly golden. If desired, add the bell pepper and cook for 2 to 3 minutes longer, stirring a few times. Otherwise, add the squash and toss to combine with the onions. Cook for about 10 minutes, stirring a few times. Season with salt and pepper, and cook until the squash is flavorful and soft and is a little brown around the edges of the slices, about another 10 minutes. Serve immediately.

Tony Inscore and his wife, Marie. Try her burgers on p. 248.

2 pounds carrots, sliced into ¼-inch-thick rounds

One 10.75-ounce can condensed tomato soup

1 cup sugar

¾ cup red wine vinegar

½ cup vegetable oil

1 teaspoon kosher salt

1 teaspoon prepared yellow mustard

1 teaspoon Worcestershire sauce

¼ teaspoon freshly ground black pepper

½ medium green bell pepper, seeded and diced

2 medium onions, chopped

Robin Kline's
copper pennies

SERVES 6

I laughed until tears came into my eyes when Robin Kline from Des Moines, Iowa, sent me this recipe. It has been at least two decades since I last had Copper Pennies, but they truly are a perfect side dish for barbecue, grilled chicken, pork chops, or even grilled fish. It's easy to make, tastes wonderful, and keeps for a week. So laugh if you like, with its addition of canned soup, but I think, like me, you'll be pleased to reconnect with this recipe.

– ⌘ –

1. Place the carrot slices in a large saucepan and cover with water. Place over medium-high heat and bring to a boil. Reduce the heat to a simmer and cook for 10 to 15 minutes. The carrots should be soft but not mushy.

2. While the carrots cook, combine the remaining ingredients in a large bowl.

3. When the carrots are done, drain well. Let them cool for a couple of minutes, then add to the soup mixture. Toss to combine and coat well.

4. Cover with plastic wrap and refrigerate for at least 48 hours before serving. Use a slotted spoon to serve.

1 cup mayonnaise

¼ cup white wine vinegar

¼ cup sugar

1 bunch broccoli, cut into bite-size florets (discard the stems)

½ cup chopped red onions or scallions (white and green parts) or both

½ cup golden raisins

½ cup peanuts or sunflower seeds

8 slices bacon, cooked until crisp, drained, and crumbled

Fred's Sweet and Crunchy
broccoli salad

SERVES 6

In my part of the world, this broccoli salad recipe and its variations are highly guarded secrets. The heck with that. Here's the recipe, and it's a great side dish for most any grilled or barbecue meal. Plan to take some along on your next picnic.

– ∽◦◎◦∾ –

1. In a small bowl, combine the mayonnaise, vinegar, and sugar. Cover with plastic wrap and refrigerate several hours or overnight to let the flavors develop.

2. Combine the remaining ingredients in a large bowl. Pour the dressing over the salad and mix until well combined and well coated. This can be made several hours ahead and refrigerated, tightly covered, until ready to serve.

5 pounds russet potatoes, peeled and cut into large cubes

1 tablespoon kosher salt

5 large eggs, hard-boiled, peeled, and chopped into chunks

1 medium sweet onion, such as a Vidalia, chopped

One 24-ounce jar sweet gherkins, drained, juice reserved, and the pickles chopped

2 cups Miracle Whip salad dressing

½ cup sugar, plus maybe a little more

1 tablespoon distilled white vinegar

½ teaspoon prepared yellow mustard

Jean Lynn's
potato salad

SERVES 16, BUT THE LEFTOVERS WILL BE GOOD FOR A WEEK

Jean's potato salad is a thing of beauty to the taste buds, and I hesitate to divulge the recipe so publicly. It's my tragic flaw—I get ahold of a great neighborhood potluck dinner dish and I can't keep my mouth shut.

There are a few important keys to the success of this recipe. The potatoes and the rest of the ingredients must come together while the potatoes are still warm. Russet potatoes are the better choice, just as they are for really good mashed potatoes. Miracle Whip, no matter what your feelings on that subject, is essential. I've tried it with mayonnaise and it just doesn't work. You must chop whole sweet pickles, not use a pickle relish—if you use relish or salad cukes, the flavor will be dull and muted.

I've taken to pulsing the pickles in my food processor.

This potato salad is best served slightly warm, but dead cold it is still awesome. I have eaten it for a week with great pleasure, but I'll bet it won't last that long at your house.

Food is always from the heart, and Jean and her husband, Hugh, sum it up perfectly: "There is nothing better than friends and food; I don't know which is better," states Hugh. "Always friends," chimes in Jean.

– ⌇⌇⌇ –

1. Place the potatoes in a large Dutch oven or soup pot. Cover generously with water and add the salt. Place over low heat and bring to a slow boil. Cook, uncovered, until the potatoes are very soft when tested with a fork. Drain and mash the potatoes. Jean actually whips the potatoes with a hand mixer. Stir in the eggs, onions, and pickles.

2. In a large bowl, whisk together the Miracle Whip, sugar, vinegar, and mustard. Taste. You want a sweet-tart taste; additional sugar, some of the reserved pickle juice, or vinegar may be needed. Add the warm potato mixture to the dressing and stir to combine. Serve warm.

Jean, Hugh, their daughter Julia, and son Hugh IV with a feast.

¼ cup low-salt chicken broth

¼ cup dry white wine

¼ cup olive oil

4 scallions (white and green parts), chopped

2 tablespoons Dijon mustard

2 tablespoons white wine vinegar

2 tablespoons capers, drained and rinsed

Kosher salt and freshly ground black pepper

3¼ pounds small red-skinned potatoes

French
potato salad

SERVES 8

This Provence-inspired rustic side dish is perfect for picnicking or most any kind of grilled meal, especially during the summer. Not like your grandmother's potato salad, there's no mayonnaise here. The warm potatoes soak up the dressing and explode with flavor. Without the mayonnaise, the salad tastes fresh and bright. When the day is hot and you're concerned about a mayonnaise-based salad, pull this one out. I guarantee that it won't be the only excuse you'll make for throwing together this wonderful potato salad.

– ⊱⊶⊰ –

1. In a large bowl, whisk together the broth, wine, oil, scallions, mustard, vinegar, and capers. Season with salt and pepper to taste. The dressing can be prepared 1 day ahead and refrigerated, tightly covered. Bring to room temperature before continuing.

2. Place the potatoes in a large pot of water to cover by about 2 inches, salt generously, bring to a boil, reduce the heat to medium, and cook until just tender, about 35 minutes. Drain. Return the potatoes to the pot, and set over low heat until any remaining liquid evaporates, about 2 minutes.

3. Cut the warm potatoes into ⅓-inch-thick slices. Add to the dressing and toss gently to coat. Let stand at least 1 hour at room temperature, then toss again and serve. You could also refrigerate it, tightly covered, for up to 2 days, but bring it back to room temperature before serving.

1 medium green cabbage, cored and shredded

2 medium green bell peppers, seeded and chopped

1 pound ripe tomatoes, seeded and chopped

2 cups sweet pickle relish, drained and juice reserved

3/4 cup chopped onions

1/2 cup sugar

1/2 cup distilled white vinegar

1 teaspoon kosher salt

1/4 teaspoon freshly ground black pepper

1. In a large bowl, toss together the cabbage, bell peppers, tomatoes, relish, and onions until well combined.

2. In a small bowl, stir together the sugar, vinegar, salt, and pepper. Let the sugar somewhat dissolve in the vinegar. Pour this mixture over the vegetables, tossing to coat. Let sit for at least 30 minutes before serving. Use any reserved pickle juice or additional salt to adjust the seasoning to your taste. You can make this several hours in advance, maybe when you start smoking some ribs.

Hugh Lynn's
texas barbecue slaw

SERVES 10 TO 12

Hugh Lynn goes back to his Texas roots with this slaw, which is excellent with beef brisket and smoked sausages, even Memphis-style ribs. It's quick and colorful, and I also have a feeling that his buddy, Cotton, had a hand in this recipe.

Slaw Basics

- A medium head of cabbage, about 1 1/2 pounds, will yield about 6 cups of chopped cabbage. Be sure to remove the core before you start shredding.

- A food processor is a beautiful thing when it comes to chopping cabbage for slaw. Cut the cabbage head into 8 wedges, then cut each of those in half. Only half fill your processor bowl, and pulse until the cabbage is a size you like.

- If your cabbage wilts, put it in a bowl of ice water for 15 minutes, then drain and toss on paper towels to dry. Some folks do this routinely, claiming it yields a crisper slaw—the choice is yours.

- Slaw is always better when made at least a few hours ahead.

- If you like onion in your slaw, by all means add it. Try this trick to keep the onion flavor from getting too strong— place the chopped onion in a strainer and run cold water over it for 1 minute.

½ cup Miracle Whip salad dressing, or more to taste, if you like

¼ cup sweet pickle relish, with the juice

2 tablespoons prepared yellow mustard

1 tablespoon sugar

1 teaspoon kosher salt

¼ teaspoon celery seeds

Freshly ground black pepper to taste

6 cups finely chopped green cabbage

2 carrots, grated

In a large bowl, combine the Miracle Whip, pickle relish, mustard, sugar, salt, celery seeds, and pepper. Add the cabbage and carrots and fold to blend. You can prepare this several hours ahead and refrigerate, tightly covered, until ready to serve.

Eastern
north carolina-style barbecue slaw

SERVES 8

This slaw is loosely based on the slaw at Wilbur's Barbeque in Goldsboro, North Carolina, and Holt Lake BBQ in Smithfield, North Carolina, both of which serve up excellent examples of Eastern-style barbecue. It's the perfect pairing to vinegar-based barbecue, whether pork or chicken, as well as hot dogs and fried chicken. And make sure you use Miracle Whip—regular mayo doesn't cut it.

¼ cup prepared yellow mustard

¼ cup mayonnaise

¼ cup sugar

¼ cup distilled white vinegar

½ teaspoon kosher salt

¼ teaspoon celery seeds

Freshly ground black pepper to taste

6 cups thinly shredded cabbage

½ red bell pepper, seeded and cut into thin strips

Combine the mustard, mayonnaise, sugar, vinegar, salt, celery seeds, and pepper in a large bowl. Add the cabbage and bell pepper and toss together with the dressing until everything is well combined and well coated. This can be prepared several hours in advance and refrigerated, tightly covered, until ready to serve.

Memphis-Style
rib slaw

SERVES 8

Memphis and to some extent Kansas City like a sweet mustard-based slaw with their ribs. Barbecue champion Mike Mills talked me through this style. This slaw works beautifully with either smoked or grilled baby back ribs or spareribs. The red pepper is traditional, and some folks like to add a shredded carrot. You could chop the cabbage, but the long, thin shreds of cabbage just seem to eat better with the ribs. You can take a shortcut and buy the prepackaged angel hair cut cabbage. One caveat—this slaw really doesn't work with North Carolina-style barbecue.

½ cup cider vinegar

½ cup ketchup

¼ cup sugar

½ teaspoon kosher salt

5 to 6 cups finely chopped green cabbage (it should be chopped fine enough that the pieces are the size of BBs)

1 teaspoon freshly ground black pepper or more to taste

1 teaspoon Texas Pete hot sauce, if desired

In a large bowl, mix the vinegar, ketchup, sugar, and salt together until the sugar dissolves. Add the cabbage and toss with the dressing until well combined and well coated. Add the pepper and taste for spiciness. Add more pepper and/or the Texas Pete if you want a little more heat. This can be prepared up to 1 day in advance.

Lexington-Style
red slaw

SERVES 8

Nope, we're not using red cabbage. This is the slaw typically served with Lexington, North Carolina-style barbecue. It marries so well with the deep flavors of hickory- and oak-smoked pork shoulders. If you are using a ketchup-based sauce when you smoke a pork shoulder, give this slaw a try. Believe it or not, this is great on a hot dog and complements grilled smoked sausages.

1½ pounds ground round

1 medium onion, chopped

One 16-ounce can tomato paste

¾ can of water

1½ tablespoons red pepper flakes

1½ tablespoons sugar

1 tablespoon chili powder

½ teaspoon dried oregano

½ teaspoon kosher salt

1. Place a large skillet over medium-high heat. Add the ground beef and cook until browned and no pink remains, about 10 minutes, breaking up any clumps. Drain any fat.

2. Add the remaining ingredients, stir to combine, let come to a boil, reduce the heat to low, and let simmer for 1½ hours, stirring occasionally.

Dad's Hot Dog
chili sauce

Gene and Veronica Pawlak, of South Bend, Indiana, have been making this chili sauce for their family and friends for more than 50 years. Gene is retired from Notre Dame University, and they still live in the first house they bought. Their daughter, Linda, is my backdoor neighbor in North Carolina, and she was the one to introduce me to this exceptional chili. It is perfect spooned over hot dogs and hamburgers. You can adjust the heat by adding more or less of the chili powder and red pepper flakes.

8 slices bacon

Two 3-pound chickens, cut into serving pieces and patted dry with paper towels

1½ pounds boneless beef (round or chuck), trimmed of excess fat, cut into 1-inch pieces, and patted dry with paper towels

3 large onions, chopped

3 ribs celery, leaves included, chopped

1 large green bell pepper, seeded and chopped

Vegetable oil, if needed

1 large smoked ham hock, trimmed of skin

4 large ripe tomatoes, chopped and juices retained

3 sprigs fresh parsley, chopped

2 small red hot chiles, seeded and minced

1 teaspoon dried thyme, crumbled

1 teaspoon dried basil, crumbled

Kosher salt and freshly ground black pepper

6 cups low-sodium beef or chicken broth

10 cups water

2½ cups fresh or frozen corn kernels

2½ cups fresh or frozen lima beans

2 cups fresh or frozen sliced okra

2½ cups mashed boiled potatoes

Jim Villas's Georgia
brunswick stew

SERVES 8

Jim Villas has challenged the food world to keep both old customs alive and to introduce new trends. He's won multiple awards for his writing and is a Southerner right down to his toes. One of my favorite of his recipes is this Brunswick stew. No self-respecting barbecue joint would be without a kettle of this bubbling in the kitchen. The stew freezes well, so don't be concerned with the quantity that this recipe makes. Jim calls this stew the "unchallenged aristocrat of American stews." I think you'll agree.

- ᴄᴼᴼᴼᴼ -

1. In a large, heavy pot, fry the bacon over medium-high heat until crisp. Drain on paper towels, crumble, and set aside.

2. Add the chicken pieces to the pot in batches, and brown on all sides over medium-high heat. Transfer to a platter. Add the beef to the pot, brown on all sides, and transfer to the platter. Add the onions, celery, and bell pepper, and stir until softened, adding a little oil if there appears not to be enough fat in the pot.

3. Return the chicken and beef to the pot. Add the ham hock, tomatoes, parsley, chiles, thyme, basil, salt, pepper, broth, and water and stir well. Bring to a boil, reduce the heat to low, cover, and simmer until the chicken is tender, about 1 hour. Skim the surface from time to time of any foam.

4. Using a slotted spoon, transfer the chicken back to the platter and continue to simmer the stew 1½ hours longer, until the beef is so tender it shreds. When the chicken is cool enough to handle, remove and discard the skin and bones. Shred the meat and set aside.

5. Add the corn, lima beans, and okra to the pot, reduce the heat to low, and let simmer for 30 minutes.

6. Remove the ham hock with a slotted spoon, pick the meat from the bone, shred, and return to the pot. Add the bacon and chicken and mashed potatoes, stir well, and cook for another 15 minutes. Taste the stew for salt and pepper and serve.

One 8-ounce container sour cream

Two 3.4-ounce boxes instant vanilla pudding, prepared according to package instructions using whole milk

One 12-ounce box Nabisco® Nilla® wafers

7 to 8 medium ripe bananas, peeled and sliced

One 8-ounce container Cool Whip® non-dairy topping

Susan Boyer's
busy mom's banana pudding

SERVES 10 TO 12

A barbecue without banana pudding just isn't a barbecue. Here's one that is both good and fast, so it doesn't heat up the kitchen. Susan Boyer is originally from Ponca City, Oklahoma, and now lives with her husband, Dale Bartels, and daughter, Belinda, in Louisville, Kentucky. "I love banana pudding so much that one year I asked for it instead of a birthday cake!" says Susan. Susan is an engineer, who spends a lot of time running her daughter, a high school student, to band practice and swim meets.

– ✐✎ –

1. Stir the sour cream into the pudding mixture.

2. Layer the bottom of a 9x13-inch baking dish with vanilla wafers. Cover the wafers with half of the sliced bananas. Spread about half of the pudding mixture over the bananas. Spread about half of the Cool Whip over that. Repeat the layers.

3. Cover with plastic wrap and refrigerate overnight. Serve chilled.

CRUST

1⅓ cup all-purpose flour (White Lily preferred)

⅔ cup finely chopped pecans

3 tablespoons firmly packed light brown sugar

½ teaspoon kosher salt

5 tablespoons chilled unsalted butter, cut into ½-inch pieces

3 tablespoons chilled vegetable shortening, cut into ½-inch pieces

About 3 tablespoons ice water

FILLING AND TOPPING

1¾ cups plus ⅓ cup granulated sugar

⅓ cup cornstarch

1½ cups water

½ cup fresh lemon juice

5 large eggs, separated

2 tablespoons grated lemon rind

½ teaspoon cream of tartar

Lemon Meringue Pie
with pecan crust

SERVES 8

Most lemon meringue pies leave me wanting for a better-tasting crust. I complained about this recently to White Lily's recipe genius, Belinda Ellis. She came back with this crust, which has the added texture of chopped pecans and brown sugar.

– ෨෧෨ –

1. Combine the flour, pecans, brown sugar, and salt in a large bowl. Add the butter and shortening. Using an electric mixer, beat at low speed until the mixture resembles coarse meal. Add 2 tablespoons of the ice water and beat until the dough holds together, adding more water by ½ tablespoonfuls if dry. Gather into a ball and flatten into a disk. Wrap in waxed paper and chill until firm enough to roll, at least 1 hour

2. Roll out the dough between sheets of waxed paper to a 12-inch round. Peel off the top sheet of paper. Invert the dough into a 9-inch-diameter glass pie dish and peel off the paper. Press the dough gently into the dish. Trim the overhang to ¾ inch, turn it under, and crimp the edge decoratively. Freeze the crust until firm, about 30 minutes. Position the rack in the center of the oven and preheat to 375°F.

3. Line the crust with foil; fill it with dried beans. Bake until golden at the edge, about 15 minutes. Remove the foil and beans; bake until the crust is pale golden, piercing it with a fork if it bubbles, another 12 minutes. Let cool completely on a rack. Reduce the oven temperature to 325°F.

4. Prepare the filling. Whisk 1¾ cups of the sugar and the cornstarch together in a heavy saucepan. Gradually add the water and lemon juice, whisking until smooth and the cornstarch dissolves. Whisk in the egg yolks and lemon rind. Cook over medium-high heat, whisking until the filling thickens and boils, about 8 minutes. Pour into the crust.

5. With an electric mixer, in a large bowl beat the egg whites and cream of tartar until soft peaks form. Gradually add the remaining ⅓ cup sugar, beating until stiff and shiny. Mound the meringue on top of the filling, spreading it to seal to the crust at the edges. Be sure to get it on the filling while it's still hot; it can keep the meringue from getting weepy underneath. Bake until the meringue is golden, about 20 minutes. Let cool, refrigerate up to 6 hours, and serve cold.

FILLING

2 cups sugar

1 cup (2 sticks) unsalted butter, at room temperature

Grated zest of 1 lemon

8 large egg yolks

2/3 cup strongly brewed black tea (Martha uses orange pekoe)

1 tablespoon vanilla extract

1/2 teaspoon fresh lemon juice

1/2 teaspoon cider vinegar

2 tablespoons all-purpose flour

2 teaspoons cornmeal

Candied lemon peel and fresh mint leaves for garnish (optional)

1. Preheat your oven to 350°F.

2. In a large bowl with an electric mixer, cream the sugar, butter, and lemon zest together until light and yellow. Add the egg yolks one at a time, beating after each one. On low speed, add the tea, vanilla, lemon juice, and vinegar, and mix until combined. Mix in the flour and cornmeal, then pour into the crust, and bake until slightly bubbly and almost set, about 40 minutes.

3. Let cool at room temperature at least 2 hours. Refrigerate if you'll be serving later (up to 2 days), covered with plastic wrap. Garnish with candied lemon peel and mint leaves, if desired.

Martha Foose's
sweet tea pie

MAKES ONE 9-INCH PIE; SERVES 6

Two of the Mississippi Delta's secrets are a town called Greenwood and a baker named Martha Foose. Greenwood is a town built on King Cotton, but its revival has become the passion of a man named Fred Carl, inventor and owner of Viking® Range. Mr. Carl has revitalized several blocks in the town with a first-class hotel, a spa with a Southern twist, Viking's offices, and Mockingbird Bakery. Martha, who, with her husband, Donald Bender, owns Mockingbird Bakery, is crazy, funny, a great storyteller, and the ultimate Delta girl. She developed this pie as an ode to my book *Iced Tea*.

For the crust, egg-size pieces of dough are gathered together, then pressed and smeared. All the smears are then formed into a disk. This method, widely used in Europe, seems to create a flakier, more tender pie crust.

Martha also wants to warn you that the filling will look like a curdled mess, but never mind, that's just the way it looks before baking.

martha's pie crust

2 cups White Lily all-purpose flour (or 1 1/2 cups all-purpose flour and 1/2 cup cake flour if not using White Lily)

1 teaspoon kosher salt

1 teaspoon sugar

3/4 cup (1 1/2 sticks) cold butter, cut into pieces

1/4 cup cold vegetable shortening or lard, cut into pieces

Up to 1/4 cup ice-cold water

To make the crust, combine the flour, salt, and sugar in a food processor and pulse once or twice. Add the butter and pulse several times. Add the shortening and pulse until no piece is bigger than a black-eyed pea and the ingredients resemble a coarse meal (Martha calls this a "shaggy" dough). Pour out onto your work surface, take egg-size handfuls, and smear it on the surface with the palm of your hand. Continue with the remaining dough. Gather up all the smears and form into a disk. Cover in plastic, place in the freezer for 10 minutes, then roll it out between two pieces of plastic wrap until 1/8 to 1/4 inch thick. Fit it into a 9-inch pie pan. Trim off any excess dough. Keep cold while making the filling.

CRUST

1½ cups crushed graham cracker crumbs

¼ cup (½ stick) unsalted butter, melted

¼ cup pine nuts

2 tablespoons sugar

FILLING:

One 14–ounce can sweetened condensed milk

4 large egg yolks

½ cup fresh lime juice

¼ cup tequila

2 large egg whites

1 tablespoon sugar

Whipped cream, if desired

Fresh lime slices, if desired

Carolyn's
tequila lime tart

SERVES 6 TO 8

Photographer Carolyn Taylor gave me this recipe after a vacation she and her husband had in Santa Fe. We both are huge tequila fans, and the idea of having a key lime pie spiked with tequila was almost more than I could stand. I also think that you'll find the crust, with its addition of pine nuts, an added bonus. It's the perfect ending for any fish or shellfish meal, and it's especially good after you've gnawed your way through a rack of ribs.

- ᘓᘔᘓᘕ -

1. Combine the crust ingredients in a food processor and process until small clumps form. Press the mixture into the bottom and up the sides of a 9-inch-diameter tart pan with a removable bottom.

2. Preheat the oven to 325°F.

3. In a medium bowl, stir the condensed milk, egg yolks, lime juice, and tequila together to blend. Set aside.

4. Using an electric mixer, in a large bowl, beat the egg whites with the sugar until soft peaks form. Using a rubber spatula, gently fold 1½ cups of the condensed milk mixture into the whites. Fold the remaining milk mixture into the whites until just blended. Pour this into the prepared crust.

5. Bake until the filling puffs up slightly and a tester inserted into the center comes out with some moist filling attached, about 40 minutes. Let cool completely on a rack. Chill until cold, at least 2 hours and up to 8 hours. Remove from the tart pan, garnish with whipped cream and lime slices, and serve.

1 ½ cups whole milk

3 large egg yolks

1 ½ cups sugar

2 tablespoons unsweetened cocoa powder

5 tablespoons all-purpose flour

¼ cup (½ stick) unsalted butter, cut into small pieces

1 teaspoon vanilla extract

One 9-inch prebaked pie crust (store-bought is fine)

1. Combine the milk and egg yolks in a medium-size saucepan over low heat and whisk until the milk is just hot to the touch. Dip your finger in the milk and hold it to your lip. When it's warm to hot, you are ready to proceed. Whisk in the sugar, flour, butter, and vanilla and continue to whisk until thick.

2. Pour the filling into the pie crust and let cool at room temperature, then refrigerate for a couple of hours until firm before serving.

Mayor Dempsey's
chocolate pie

MAKES ONE 9-INCH PIE; SERVES 6 TO 8

The mayor of Byhalia, Mississippi, "Scooter" Dempsey, contributed this pie to the gathering I was invited to at Bobby and Susan Bonds' home, one of the best backyard events I've had the pleasure of attending. Charles and Alice Crain, Tommy and Susan Ray, Billy and Linda Sproles, Phil Marlowe, and Don and Becky Hollingsworth (try her crawfish dip on p. 17) combined for a great combination of old friends and golfing buddies, exactly what a cookout should be. Mayor Dempsey's pie was just the right ending to the meal—not too rich, but velvety and full-bodied.

5 ounces bittersweet (not unsweetened) or semisweet chocolate, chopped

¼ cup (½ stick) unsalted butter

1 tablespoon brandy

2 large eggs

2 large egg yolks

5 tablespoons sugar

1 teaspoon vanilla extract

1½ teaspoons instant espresso powder or instant coffee powder

Large pinch of kosher salt

1 tablespoon all-purpose flour

½ cup chilled whipping or heavy cream

Delores's
molten chocolate cakes

SERVES 4

It's a long way from her roots in Oregon, but Delores Custer has made Manhattan her own. One of the top food stylists in the world, Delores still enjoys cooking for friends and family. This molten cake is the perfect ending to an elaborate grilled meal—like a prime aged steak or grilled rack of lamb. It's just as decadent as the protein and a chocoholic's dream.

– ദ്ധൈ –

1. Preheat the oven to 400°F. Generously butter four ¾-cup soufflé dishes or custard cups. Arrange on a baking sheet.

2. Stir the chocolate and butter together in a small, heavy saucepan over low heat until melted and smooth. Remove from the heat and stir in the brandy. Let cool for 10 minutes, stirring occasionally.

3. Using an electric mixer, beat the whole eggs, the yolks, 4 tablespoons of the sugar, the vanilla, 1 teaspoon of the espresso powder, and the salt together in a medium bowl until a very thick ribbon falls when the beaters are lifted, about 6 minutes. Sift the flour over the batter and fold in the flour. Fold in the chocolate mixture until there are no streaks in the batter. Divide the batter among dishes, filling them completely.

4. Bake until the tops are puffed and dry and a tester inserted into the center comes out with moist batter still attached, about 15 minutes. Remove from the oven and let cool for 5 minutes.

5. In a small bowl, beat together the cream and the remaining 1 tablespoon sugar and ½ teaspoon espresso powder using an electric mixer until firm peaks form. Top the cakes with the whipped cream and serve warm.

One 15-ounce can sweetened condensed milk

½ cup plus 2 tablespoons fresh or bottled key lime juice (don't use regular lime juice)

1 cup heavy cream

2 large eggs

½ teaspoon vanilla extract

3 sheets graham crackers

Scenes from Peter McKee's Annual Jackson Fresh Air Cook-off and Feed.

McKee
lime pie ice cream

MAKES 1 QUART

The king of Seattle's backyard barbecues, Peter H. D. McKee (check out his rib recipe on p. 112) sent this inviting ice cream recipe, which is a perfect excuse to go out and buy an ice cream maker.

– ᥱᤥᤥᥲ –

1. In a large bowl, beat the condensed milk and lime juice together with an electric mixer on low speed until just combined. Add the cream and beat again just until combined. Add the eggs and vanilla and beat once again until well combined.

2. Stack the graham crackers on top of each other. Using a knife, chop into nickel-size chunks. Dump all the chunks and any crumbs into the ice cream mixture. Pour into your ice cream freezer and churn, following the manufacturer's instructions.

3. When done, repack into a container, place in your freezer, and freeze overnight. Let soften slightly before scooping.

index